HANDBOOK
OF
DENOMINATIONS
IN THE UNITED STATES

HANDBOOK

OF

DENOMINATIONS

IN THE UNITED STATES

13th EDITION

Craig D. Atwood

Frank S. Mead

Samuel S. Hill

Abingdon Press
NASHVILLE

THE HANDBOOK OF DENOMINATIONS IN THE UNITED STATES
Thirteenth Edition

Library of Congress Cataloging-in-Publication Data

Atwood, Craig D.
Handbook of denominations in the United States / Craig D. Atwood, Frank S. Mead, Samuel S. Hill. -- 13th ed.
p. cm.
"Rev. ed. of: Handbook of denominations in the United States / Frank S. Mead, Samuel S. Hill"--T.p. verso.
Includes bibliographical references and index.
ISBN 978-1-4267-0048-4 (casebound : alk. paper) 1. Sects--United States. 2. Christian sects--United States. 3. United States--Religion. I. Mead, Frank Spencer, 1898- II. Hill, Samuel S. III. Mead, Frank Spencer, 1898- Handbook of denominations in the United States. IV. Title.
BL2525.M425 2010
200.973--dc22

2010007092

Printed in the United States of America
10 11 12 13 — 5 4 3 2 1

In Memory of
Frank S. Mead (1898–1982)

CONTENTS

ALPHABETICAL TABLE OF CONTENTS
FOR RELIGIOUS GROUPS

1

PREFACE

For over half a century Frank Mead's *Handbook of Denomination in the United States* has been one of the most used reference books for the topic of religion in America. The *Handbook of Denominations* was written to help individuals navigate the confusing and shifting waters of American religion. I hope that readers will better understand not only American religion in all its diversity but also their neighbors who belong to a different faith community. It is important to remember that each of the religious organizations in this book is made up of flesh and blood individuals who voluntarily gather to sing, chant, pray, work, teach, and learn.

This is the thirteenth edition of the *Handbook,* and like its predecessors, it attempts to portray some of the depth and breadth of the major religious traditions in the United States. It is not a comprehensive guide to American religion, however. That would require several volumes. Neither is it merely a comparison of church statistics or listing of facts. Rather it is a narrative of American religious life that includes brief descriptions of over 250 bodies in the broad Abrahamic religious tradition in the United States. I hope that this volume excites the curiosity of readers. A list of suggested readings is provided to assist further investigation.

The most difficult editorial decision concerns the scope of this volume. The diversity and complexity of American religion is amazing and daunting. Rather than treat the many world religions in America superficially or drastically limit the space given to various denominations, the *Handbook* includes only those religions stemming from the Abrahamic-monotheistic tradition. All of the religious bodies presented here claim, in some way, allegiance to the God of Abraham. Therefore they share much in common, especially in ethics, worship, and sacred texts. Eastern religions and many newer religions, such as Scientology, are not included in the *Handbook* because they are not in the Abrahamic tradition.[1] With few exceptions, the religious organizations included here have at least five thousand active members. Some smaller bodies are included because of their historical or social importance.

---

[1]For more information on groups not included in this Handbook, see J. Gordon Melton, *Encyclopedia of American Religions.* 7th ed. 3 vols. (Detroit: Gale Research, 2003); The Religious Movements Homepage of the University of Virginia (www.religiousmovements.lib.virginia.edu).

This focus on Judaism, Christianity, Islam, and their branches is not meant to suggest that they alone are real or important religions; it is intended to provide conceptual coherence and definition for the book. The Abrahamic traditions continue to be by far the dominant forms of religious expression in America, but readers should be aware that the American religious experience is becoming increasingly global. The old Protestant hegemony that was present when Frank Mead wrote the first edition of the *Handbook* has disappeared. Every year the most religiously diverse country in history becomes even more diverse. The "Pluralism Project" at Harvard University is demonstrating that non-Western religions are daily becoming a more visible and vibrant part of American religion and culture.[2] America is now home to Sikhs, Jains, Hindus, Buddhists, Taoists, Confucianists, and a host of new religious movements. Americans spent millions of dollars each year on spellbooks, crystals, charms, and guides for meditation. Some follow ancient Eastern or neo-pagan religions strictly, while others combine Eastern ideas or practices with traditional Christian or Jewish theology and rituals.

The religious bodies described in this edition of the *Handbook* are grouped in family categories that help tell the story of American religion both historically and typologically. The large headings, such as "Judaism," "Christianity," and "Islam" are arranged chronologically. The family groupings within the major traditions (Orthodox, Catholic, Lutheran) are also arranged chronologically. This way the reader can gain a better sense of the development and changes within Western religion through the centuries. Within those family groupings, religious bodies are arranged alphabetically.

An alphabetical listing of the religious bodies is provided to make it easier to look up organizations by name rather than by category. A star (*) next to a term in one of the articles indicates that there is a separate entry for that religious organization in the *Handbook*. The family groupings are not intended to be prescriptive or normative. In many cases, one church could be placed in two or more categories, and I apologize to any who feel that they have been "misplaced." Some have been moved in this edition.

One of the additions to this edition of the *Handbook* is a section on interdenominational or parachurch organizations. Since the Great Awakening in the 1740s, Protestant churches have formed various interchurch organizations to enable more effective work in the world. Such voluntary associations in the nineteenth century helped bring about major changes in American society, such as prison reform and the abolition of slavery. In the twentieth century, this type of cooperate effort was expanded to include Catholic and Orthodox churches, and now even the White House promotes grass-roots interfaith social service. Jewish and Muslim agencies

---

[2]The Pluralism Project, Harvard University (www.pluralism.org); Diana Eck, *A New Religious America: How a "Christian Country" Has Become the World's Most Religiously Diverse Nation.* San Francisco: HarperSanFrancisco, 2001.

were formed in the twentieth century to address issues that specifically affect Jews and Muslims in America. This type of interdenominational and interfaith cooperation demonstrates that American religion is diverse but not necessarily divisive.

The title of this *Handbook* reflects a distinctly American (and modern) understanding of religion. The word denomination simply means "name." It is a way we identify things, such as the denomination of money. It is a neutral term that is applied to religious communities in order to identify them without passing judgment on their validity. Terms such as church, sect, and cult have an implied judgment. No one considers their own community of faith a "sect" or a "cult;" those terms are reserved for others. As used in this *Handbook,* a denomination is merely a self-conscious religious organization that includes but is greater than a local community of faith. Since the term was developed to describe different Christian bodies, it can only be used loosely for non-Christian religions. Properly speaking, the various branches of Judaism and Islam are not denominations.

When churches use the word "denomination" to describe themselves and others, there is an implicit acknowledgment or even acceptance of the legitimacy of other churches. Because of this implicit acceptance of pluralism, at least within the broad Christian tradition, many churches do not describe themselves as denominations. They view themselves as the one true church. Other Christian bodies do not use the term denomination because it is not a biblical term.

Many newer communities of faith (see NEW PARADIGM CHURCHES) avoid the word denomination because it is associated with national corporations. It is interesting that a term that once implied an acceptance of pluralism has come to mean administrative authority and control. The word denomination has become associated with so-called "mainline" or "oldline" Protestant churches, many of which have seen dramatic membership declines since 1980. As a result, some scholars claim that denominationalism is dead.

If denominationalism refers to bureaucratic national religious organizations, then it does appear that we have entered a "post-denominational" era of American history. Some of the fastest growing religious groups are entrepreneurial rather than bureaucratic; therefore they lack typical denominational structures. Many of these expanding groups have embraced the most recent communication technologies and focus on a younger demographic rather than traditional faith communities. Although these groups reject the label "denomination," they are also included in this *Handbook.*

Future editions of the *Handbook* may require a different title since most of the bodies included do not consider themselves denominations, but we have retained the familiar title to emphasize the continuity of this edition with its predecessors. Despite changes in the American religious landscape, the drive toward establishing national organizations remains strong, and millions of Americans are active members of the religious organizations included in this volume.

11

It is important to recognize that this *Handbook* is based on information provided by the religious organizations themselves, and it focuses on the doctrines, statistics, and histories of institutions. Such information is valuable and helpful in making sense of our culture and our neighbors, but much of the inner life and meaning of each denomination is omitted from such a presentation. Most of the statistics used in the *Handbook* are self-reported from the various religious organizations directly to the editor or appear in reference works such as the *Yearbook of American and Canadian Churches* or the Association of Religious Data Archives (ARDA).[3] Reports of religious adherence are not always reliable, especially for comparative purposes. Some denominations report all members whether or not they attend services; others report only those who have made an adult profession of faith. Newer churches tend to report average worship attendance. Many religious bodies do not keep membership records at all. All statistics in this *Handbook* are merely the best estimates currently available.

It is important to recognize that many, perhaps most, of the groups in this *Handbook* originated in the midst of conflict. A chart is provided in Appendix 1 to show the "family tree" of Christian churches. Most of the branches on that tree represent divisions and divorces. Religious schisms have many roots. Sometimes they are a result of reform efforts. For instance, some denominations broke with parent bodies over the issue of abolition or revival methods. Sometimes new denominations are formed because of disagreements over fundamental teachings or different interpretations of God's will. Devout people may disagree over dietary rules or observance of the Sabbath, for instance. The *Handbook* tries to let each denomination tell its own story rather than attempting to adjudicate claims to a particular tradition.

When reading about American religion, we should keep in mind that some religious divisions are the result of power struggles or cultural differences. One of the distinctive aspects of religion in America is the way in which race and ethnicity continue to divide churches and mosques. Many of the denominations in the *Handbook* provided havens for persecuted minorities. Thus we can speak of the "Black Church" in America, which includes a variety of African American Protestant denominations that share a common heritage and style of worship.

---

[3]Eileen W. Lindner, *Yearbook of American and Canadian Churches 2009* (New York: National Council of Churches of Christ; published by Abingdon Press, 2009). Also valuable is the demographic, geographical, and historical materials in Edwin Scott Gaustad and Philip L. Barlow, *New Historical Atlas of Religion in America* (New York: Oxford University Press, 2001); American Religion Date Archive (ARDA) of Pennsylvania State University (www.TheARDA .com). See also The Hartford Institute for Religion Research of Hartford Seminary (www .hirr.hartsem.edu); Institute for the Study of American Evangelicals (ISAE) at Wheaton College (www.wheaton.edu/isae); Institute for the Study of American Religion (www.american religion.org).

For much of the nineteenth and twentieth centuries, the Abrahamic religious bodies argued over the meaning of the Bible in a modern world. Many religious teachers and pastors wanted churches, synagogues, and mosques to use modern historical-critical methods of reading Scripture in an attempt to make the ancient text relevant to modern society. This attempt at modernization caused a great deal of controversy, and many institutions were formed to defend traditional doctrines and ways of reading the Bible. Thus, there are now Reformed and Orthodox Jewish seminaries and synagogues, as well as liberal and conservative churches. Since World War II, religious bodies have been caught up in the so-called "culture wars" in American society, especially over issues of gender and sexuality. Many of the new denominations that have already appeared in the twenty-first century are the result of schisms over the issue of homosexuality.

This is the thirteenth edition of the *Handbook,* and numerous individuals have generously contributed to its production through the years. It is unfortunate that they cannot all be named. Dr. Mead regularly updated the work several times during his long career, and after his death the task of revision fell to Samuel Hill, the leading scholar in the area of religion in the southern United States. Dr. Hill expanded the scope of the *Handbook* as well as updated it. Some of the work of professors Mead and Hill remains in this edition of the Handbook, as does the work of numerous anonymous writers who submitted information on their denominations through the years. One of my former students, Jerod Patterson, prepared the section on interdenominal agencies. Also worthy of gratitude are Andy Hogue, Roger Olson, Albert W. Wardin, Scott Thumma, Edwin Gaustad, and Julia Corbett. My work study student Chrissy Tatum helped with mailings, and my daughter, Sarah Atwood, helped verify websites. Most especially I wish to thank my wife, Julie, for her charm, wisdom, and patience, particularly when I was typing at 3:00 a.m. some nights.

—Craig Atwood, Wake Forest University, August 2010

RELIGION IN AMERICA

Craig D. Atwood

Religion is one of the most powerful human forces. Religion lifts the heart, challenges the mind, and inspires great achievements. A disproportionate number of Nobel Peace Prize winners have been people whose religious convictions led them to confront injustice and seek to reconcile warring enemies. Religion plays a role in much that is noble and good in the world. It is impossible to understand American (or world) history and culture without a knowledge of the religious fabric of our society.

In nearly every church, synagogue, and mosque in the United States similar things happen. Births are celebrated; children are taught to be virtuous and compassionate; adults learn to enjoy what is beautiful, good, and true; parents grow in wisdom and patience; the hungry are fed; the naked are clothed; and the lonely are redeemed from their isolation. Rabbis, imams, pastors, priests, and lay leaders bless marriages, bury the dead, comfort those who mourn, and challenge their flocks with a vision of a more peaceful and just society.

But there is a darker side to American religion. Some of the oldest houses of worship in the United States were built by Native Americans who had been subjugated by Europeans building global empires. No one knows how many tens of thousands of natives died during the conquest of the Americas, but we do know that in the 1690s some of the tribes in New Mexico revolted against their oppressors. They reclaimed their pueblos from the Spanish priests, and the only church they did not burn was that built by the Acoma people. It was spared, in part, because of respect for the dead who rested in the cemetery. Three centuries later, the violence of the Christian conquest and native revolt is a painful memory, and most of the Acoma people today are Catholics who live peacefully with relatives who prefer to worship in the traditional kivas. This is the history of American religion in a nutshell. Conflict and bitterness often yield to tolerance and mutual respect.

In an effort to avoid the religious violence that had plagued Europe for centuries, the authors of the United States Constitution guaranteed freedom of religion in the First Amendment. The great American experiment in religious freedom has always been a challenge, and the terrorist attacks on September 11, 2001, were a harsh reminder that Americans have not escaped religious violence in the modern age. The terrorist attacks and events that followed challenged many Americans' tolerance of other religions. Religious beliefs, no matter how noble, can be twisted into tools of hatred and murder. No religion is exempt from the type of fanaticism that inspired 9/11.

A disturbing trend in the twenty-first century has been the increasing number of murders in the sacred spaces of America. Some of the murders in churches and synagogues were related to domestic disputes, but others were the direct result of religious fanaticism. People of every faith face the choice once presented by the prophet Moses: "I have set before you life and death, blessings and curses. Choose life so that you and your descendants may live" (Deuteronomy 30:19, NRSV). The path of life includes the pursuit of knowledge and understanding of others.

Reports of religious violence are so shocking and tragic that it is easy to overlook the fact that millions of Americans drew upon their faith after the 9/11 attacks and found the courage to reach beyond the boundaries of their own religious communities and embrace their neighbors in love. Across the country there were reports of Jews, Christians, Muslims, and others joining hands to protect mosques and synagogues. People of all faith traditions performed unheralded and heroic acts of mercy and charity. Millions of ordinary Americans discovered that people with different religious beliefs also love their families, work hard, care for their neighbors, love their country, and can be good friends.

One of the most interesting statistics from a 2005 study of American congregations was the dramatic increase in interfaith worship and service projects since 2001.[1] More than twenty percent of American congregations participated in interfaith worship, and nearly forty percent joined in interfaith service projects in 2005, a dramatic increase from the year 2000. Countless numbers of ordinary people formed their own version of "The Faith Club," in which Muslims, Jews, and Christians get to know each other as people and as people of faith.[2] This *Handbook* is one of many tools to help people discover more about their friends, neighbors, and themselves.

Some people have responded to recent religious violence by rejecting religion itself. There has been an increase in unbelief and atheism in America in the twenty-first century. Almost every major religious body has reported a loss of members since 2000, and surveys indicate declining zeal among those who do attend worship. The trend away from organized religion is most pronounced among those

---

[1]David Roozen, *American Congregations 2005* (Hartford, CT: Hartford Institute for Religion Research, 2007), 20.
[2]Ranya Idliby, Suzanne Oliver, and Priscilla Warner, *The Faith Club: A Muslim, A Christian, and A Jew – Three Women Search for Understanding* (New York: Free Press, 2006).

under the age of forty, and there is a significant "graying" of American religion, especially among the clergy. About sixteen percent of Americans in 2009 reported that they have no religious affiliation, but nearly a quarter of those under thirty have no affiliation.[3] These are the highest numbers in many decades.

Americans remain more religious than people in Europe, but denominational loyalty continues to erode. Nearly half of Americans reported that they have changed their religious faith, either switching denominations or adopting a new religion.[4] This indicates both a significant level of religious interest and dissatisfaction with religious institutions. The religious groups that grew most in the past decade tended to be those that appealed to spiritual seekers.

Despite this apparent turning away from religion, the United States remains the most religious industrialized nation in the world, both in terms of personal profession of belief and the role that religion plays in public life. The 2008 presidential campaign featured much discussion of the faith of the candidates. For a brief time, a preacher named Jeremiah Wright was the focus of media scrutiny, and many white Americans discovered "Black Theology" for the first time through cable news networks. The Catholicism of Joseph Biden and the evangelicalism of Sarah Palin helped frame the vice-presidential debate.

America is not only the most religious industrialized nation; it has become the most religiously diverse nation in history. Not only has the First Amendment made room for a bewildering variety of Protestant groups, it has provided shelter for many world religions to take root. America has also been the birthplace of more religions than any country other than India.

What is it that makes American religion so diverse, adaptable, and confusing? Why was it in the United States that the idea of "denominations" emerged so that we can speak of different religious groups without using the often pejorative word *sects*? How does religion relate to social change and politics in America? In order to answer those questions, we need to take a step back in history and review some factors that are central to American religious experience.

First of all is the First Amendment. Until modern times—indeed, until the rise of the United States—it was assumed that civic harmony depended on religious conformity. There should be "one king, one faith, one law," in the famous phrase of Louis XIV, the king of France. Religion was seen as the warp of the social fabric, the glue that held different estates together and balanced conflicting interests. Religious diversity was equated with civic unrest and upheaval. The idea that a nation could tolerate not only different Christian churches but also radically different religions was considered lunacy until after the American Revolution. Modern Americans who have always lived under the Bill of Rights and its guarantee of

---

[3]*United States Religion Landscape Survey,* Pew Forum on Religion & Public Life (http://religions. pewforum.org/reports).
[4]*Ibid.*

freedom of worship have difficulty realizing what a truly radical experiment the First Amendment was when proposed by James Madison and Thomas Jefferson.

Once the Bill of Rights was ratified, the federal government was forbidden to intervene in matters of personal faith. There have been notable cases in which local and national authorities have impinged this civil right, but for the most part the spirit of freedom of religion has prevailed in the United States for over two centuries. This means that no force other than popular opinion could prevent the formation of new religious organizations, new churches, and even new religions. Anyone who could gain followers could be the founder of a new denomination. Sometimes these new religions have been ridiculed by the public and have been termed cults, but some of them have developed into very popular and dynamic faith traditions.

Rather than leading to the demise of religion as many detractors (and a few supporters) of the First Amendment expected, this freedom of religious expression led to a marked increase in religious belief and practice in the United States. In contrast to other industrialized nations, the United States continues to have high levels of personal belief, membership in religious organizations, and participation in religious activities. It may appear ironic that the world's first completely secular government has fostered one of the most religious societies, but the reason is rather simple. In the free-enterprise system of American religion, religious bodies have always had to compete for the hearts and minds of the masses. Denominations in the United States have to present their message in a way that appeals to current and potential members. Even those churches that stress hierarchical and traditional values have had to adopt the methods of conversion-oriented churches in order to retain members.

Free competition has made American religion unusually responsive to changes in society as religious organizations adapt popular culture, especially music, for the purpose of attracting members. Each generation has seen the creation of new religious bodies and the transformation of older bodies as religious leaders have tried to address the anxieties of their age and offer hope for the perceivable future. This process of adaptation and change has often led to splits within denominations with one party embracing new techniques, such as revival meetings, and the other party promoting traditional approaches, such as the use of ancient liturgical forms.

New denominations may be innovative or traditionalist, but even the traditionalists have to "sell" members and potential members on the virtues of tradition. The pages that follow trace the way new churches develop out of older churches. The free-enterprise approach to religion has also encouraged experimentation with worship forms, doctrines, and even scriptures. Many of American denominations emerged during the heady days of the Second Great Awakening (1800–30), in the days of the early Republic when it seemed that the common person could achieve any dream. If backwoodsmen could serve in Congress and farmers create a new government, why shouldn't an angel appear to an ordinary man and reveal a new scripture? Why couldn't a former housewife be the new incarnation of Christ?

Most of these new religious movements, like the Shakers and the Mormons, were radical variations on ancient Christian themes. Even among those that stayed closer to traditional Protestantism, there was a widespread sentiment that religious authorities could be ignored and that common people could recreate the church based on their own understanding of the Bible. Out of this conviction arose the denominations associated with Alexander Campbell and Barton Stone. Later Pentecostals, Adventists, and even the Jehovah's Witnesses would also draw upon this idea of remaking the church according to one's own understanding of Scripture. The old Reformation slogan of "Scripture alone" produced a cornucopia of denominations in the United States as ordinary individuals took up the challenge of interpreting the Bible and judging religious authorities.

A **second** major factor in the diversity of American religion is immigration. Many churches began as ethnic churches as each wave of immigration brought different national churches. In fact, by the time the Constitution was written there were so many denominations that it would have been difficult, if not impossible, to have created a state church. Among the English colonists there were Congregationalists in New England, Quakers in Pennsylvania, and Anglicans in New York. There were Scots Presbyterians in Virginia and the Carolinas, and Roman Catholics were tolerated in Maryland. In addition, there were Dutch, Swiss, and German Reformed churches in the Middle Colonies living alongside Swedish and German Lutherans. French Huguenots, Dutch Mennonites, German Brethren, and Sephardic Jews added spice to the religious stew of colonial America. After the Revolution, the variety increased as Irish, Italian, and Romanian Catholics came through Ellis Island with Jews from the Ukraine and Orthodox Christians from Greece and Russia.

Even within the same church, most noticeably the Roman Catholic and Lutheran churches, the United States has been home to an impressive array of ethnic communities that often posed a challenge to church hierarchies trying to maintain institutional unity. Italian and Irish Catholics shared a faith, but much of the day to day practice of religion was different in different ethnic parishes. Holy days, festivals, rituals, and especially language varied greatly within some churches. Hasidic Jews from eastern Europe were not always welcomed in established synagogues in American cities, so they formed their own communities. Religion has provided each immigrant group with an identity in a foreign land. Religion has provided a way of being grounded in the old culture while adjusting to a new and confusing society. Ethnic culture in the United States is inseparable from ethnic religious tradition.

Over the decades, though, these ethnic denominations tend to adapt to the American setting as they struggle to win the allegiance of children and

19

grandchildren who were born in the United States. The transition to English in worship is one benchmark of the Americanization process. Gradually immigrant churches grow to resemble their neighboring churches more than the national churches that gave them birth. Some denominations aggressively resist this process of assimilation, but in doing so they also adopt American techniques of marketing and organizational structure. Only in America do you see bumper stickers that say, "Orthodoxy: Proclaiming the truth since AD 33."

In the second half of the twentieth century, immigration from Asia, Africa, and the Caribbean basin brought the religions of the world, including folk religions such as Santeria, to American shores. This dramatic increase in religious diversity will be one of the major factors of religious life in the United States during the twenty-first century. No longer will the symphony of American religion be composed of variations on the Abrahamic theme. Currently many denominations are struggling and even dividing over the issue of how to deal with other religions. The question of whether there can be truth and salvation in other religions is profoundly affecting the American religious scene.

Globalization is profoundly affecting American religion in another way in the twenty-first century. During the nineteenth and twentieth centuries, American churches contributed vast resources to the evangelization of the world, especially in Africa and Asia. For many decades that mission effort was hampered by being associated with colonialism, but after World War II indigenous churches grew rapidly in the non-industrialized world. Many of these growing churches were Pentecostal churches that required very little superstructure. Long before "globalization" became a buzz word in American business, American religion was establishing extensive global networks. Increasingly, American denominations report that they have more members outside of the United States than inside. Many Americans are in contact with Africans and Asians through their faith communities, often establishing close friendships across national and linguistic barriers. A famous example of this globalization of religion was when Malcolm X made his pilgrimage to Mecca and discovered that Islam is a world religion encompassing many races and tongues. When he returned from Saudi Arabia he led many African Americans out of the Nation of Islam and into Sunni Islam.

What is new in American religion is that immigrants are now bringing with them the faith that their parents and grandparents learned from American missionaries. Two of the largest congregations in the United States are Korean Presbyterian churches. Most American denominations are struggling with issues of language, culture, worship, and theology as immigrants from former "mission fields" seek inclusion in American denominations. The Abrahamic tradition in America has become a global tradition.

A **third** distinctive feature of American religion has been interchurch cooperation in the midst of competition. Again, one can use an economic analogy and point to the American penchant for large corporations and mergers.

Interdenominational, para-church, and cooperative ministries have brought together believers from different backgrounds throughout American history. In times of disaster it is not at all surprising to see Catholics, Protestants, Jews, and Muslims working hand in hand. The individuals helping are motivated by their religious values, which have been nurtured in a particular faith tradition. But in working together, they learn to respect other faiths. A special section on interdenominational agencies has been added to this edition of the *Handbook*.

Sometimes these cooperative efforts have led to the creation of new denominations, such as the United Church of Christ and the United Methodist Church. Such ecumenical efforts have generally increased religious toleration on the local level. This is the essence of denominationalism: diverse religious traditions and organizations openly compete for adherents while respecting other religious organizations as valid. It is rare, for instance, to hear a Presbyterian in the United States declare that Methodists are not really Christian. Furthermore, as the presence of world religions increases in the United States, one sees this sense of toleration being extended beyond Christian boundaries. Of course, as with every movement, the ecumenical trend has also led to the creation of new denominations that reject this perspective and insist on doctrinal or ecclesiastical conformity and exclusiveness.

Sociologists have noticed the strength of this ecumenism in American religion and have concluded that we are now in a "post-denominational" period when religious identity has lost its importance in individuals' lives. It is relatively easy for an Episcopalian to join a Lutheran church, for instance. Even the conversion from Catholic to Protestant or vice versa no longer carries the weight it did fifty years ago. There has been a tendency toward homogenization of religion as churches learn from each other and adopt successful practices. Most Americans have an eclectic faith stitched together from many different threads of tradition and contemporary ideas and attitudes. Even so, denominations remain vibrant because they provide a form of religious identity amid the pluralism of belief. They also provide needed resources for local communities of faith, such as facilities for training ministers, for publishing curriculum resources, and for overseeing certification procedures. However, churches freely share resources, and many theological schools are functionally ecumenical.

It is noteworthy that as denominations unite, splinter groups always form, thus acknowledging the usefulness of denominational structures even while they are rejecting the authority of the parent organization. It is interesting as well that many non-denominational churches gradually evolve their own denominational structures. In this edition of the *Handbook,* there are entries on "mega-churches," which are congregations that function like small denominations. Many of them create their own national networks.

A **fourth** characteristic of American culture that affects religious institutions and belief is the close connection between politics, popular culture, public morality, and religion. The disestablishment clause of the Bill of Rights did not remove religion from the "public square." Throughout the past two and a quarter centuries people have been motivated by their faith to participate actively in the political process and in the social arena. This was most evident in the abolition movement, women's suffrage, and many campaigns for humane treatment of prisoners, human rights, voting rights, police reform, public education, and economic justice. The Prohibition movement in the early twentieth century was one of the most successful "crusades" politically and least effective socially.

Each of these campaigns was fought in the public square and in the pulpit. Each created new divisions in American religion and new alliances. Denominational identity became less important than political identity for many Christians, but by and large, the different denominations allowed for a diversity of political opinions among clergy and laity. It was rare for religious organizations to identify with a particular politician or political party. By the end of the twentieth century, there were signs that the old assumptions no longer held. Religious leaders established lobbying organizations, political action committees, and participated enthusiastically in campaigning for candidates who supported their positions on issues such as abortion, gay rights, and private schools.

Politics, they say, makes strange bedfellows, and that is particularly true when religious leaders enter the political fray. In the 1960s and 1970s radical Catholic priests shared jail cells with atheist political activists. In 2004, some Roman Catholic bishops urged Catholics to vote for a "born again" southern evangelical Republican rather than a Roman Catholic Democratic senator because he had opposed efforts to outlaw abortion. It is likely that in the future denominational affinity and political opinion will grow closer together.

A **fifth** major factor in American religion is media. American religious leaders have always been adept at exploiting new communication technologies. George Whitefield used the popular press to advertise his evangelistic rallies in the 1740s, and Billy Graham used television to become the most famous preacher in the world in the 1960s. Some of the denominations in this *Handbook* evolved out of the radio and television ministries of popular preachers.

The new media today is the Internet. Religion is one of the major topics discussed in chat rooms, Web sites, blogs, and tweets. The Internet has even allowed for the creation of new denominations that gather primarily in "cyberspace." The factors discussed above all figure in the Internet's influence on American religion. Denominations use it to compete for followers; individuals use it as a resource in building their personal belief system; and immigrant churches use it as a resource to keep scattered members of the flock connected with the ethnic tradition. The Internet has also accelerated the globalization of American religion as people discuss issues of faith and morality across continents.

American religion is complex, and will grow increasingly so. This *Handbook* merely presents some of the more objective aspects of religion, such as membership statistics, to assist the reader in making sense of our world. It is no substitute for the lived experience of the different communities of faith where people find joy, strength, and hope day after day. If this book helps readers to get to know their neighbors, join a worshiping community, and better appreciate the intricate social fabric of America, then it has fulfilled its purpose.

Suggestions for Further Reading

Ahlstrom, Sydney E. *A Religious History of the American People*. 2 vols. New Haven: Yale University Press, 1972.

Bowden, Henry W., ed. *Dictionary of American Religious Biography*. 2nd. ed. Westport, CT: Greenwood Press, 1993.

Corbett, Julia Mitchell. *Religion in America*. 3rd ed. Upper Saddle River, NJ: Prentice Hall, 1997.

Eck, Diana. *A New Religious America: How a "Christian Country" Has Become the World's Most Religiously Diverse Nation*. San Francisco: HarperSanFrancisco, 2001.

Gaustad, Edwin Scott and Philip L. Barlow. *New Historical Atlas of Religion in America*. New York: Oxford University Press, 2001.

Hatch, Nathan O. *The Democratization of American Christianity*. New Haven: Yale University Press, 1989.

Hill, Samuel S, ed. *The South and the North in American Religion*. Athens: University of Georgia Press, 1980.

James, Janet W., ed. *Women in American Religion*. Philadelphia: University of Pennsylvania Press, 1980.

Lincoln, C. Eric, and Lawrence H. Mamiya. *The Black Church in the African-American Experience*. Durham, NC: Duke University Press, 1990.

Lippy, Charles H., and Peter W. Williams, eds. *Encyclopedia of American Religious Experience: Studies of Traditions and Movements*. 3 vols. New York: Scribner, 1988.

Marty, Martin E. *Modern American Religion*. 2 vols. Chicago: University of Chicago Press, 1986.

Melton, J. Gordon. *Encyclopedia of American Religions*. 7th ed. 3 vols. Detroit: Gale Research, 2003.

Moore, R. Laurence. *Selling God: American Religion in the Marketplace of Culture*. New York: Oxford University Press, 1994.

Noll, Mark A. *A History of Christianity in the United States and Canada*. Grand Rapids: Eerdmans, 1992.

Noll, Mark A. *America's God: From Jonathan Edwards to Abraham Lincoln*. New York: Oxford University Press, 2002.

Porterfield, Amanda. *The Transformation of American Religion: The Story of a Late Twentieth-Century Awakening*. New York: Oxford Univ. Press, 2001.

Raboteau, Albert J. *Slave Religion: The "Invisible Institution" in the Antebellum South*. New York: Oxford University Press, 1978.

Roof, Wade Clark. *Spiritual Marketplace: Baby Boomers and the Remaking of American Religion*. Princeton: Princeton University Press, 1999.

Ruether, Rosemary Radford, and Rosemary Skinner Keller, eds. *Women and Religion in America*. 3 vols. San Francisco: Harper & Row, 1981.

Wuthnow, Robert. *The Restructuring of American Religion: Society and Faith Since World War II*. Princeton, NJ: Princeton University Press, 1988.

ABRAHAMIC TRADITIONS

According to ancient tradition, the story of Western monotheism began in Mesopotamia (modern-day Iraq) when a virtuous man named Abram answered a summons from the Creator. Abram and his wife Sarah left their home and journeyed westward to the land of Canaan, which today is known to millions as "the holy land." God, the Creator, sealed a covenant with Abram that was passed down through many generations. According to the covenant, Abram and his descendents would worship only the one God, study his teachings, and try to live according to his laws of justice and mercy. God, in turn, would bless those who worshiped and followed him. God changed Abram's name to Abraham, and he fathered two sons: Ishmael, son of Hagar, and Isaac, son of Sarah.

Judaism, Christianity, Islam, and their numerous branches all trace their ancestry to Abraham and his children. For Jews, Isaac and his son Jacob (also called Israel) were the heirs of the covenant. The ritual of circumcision marked the descendents of Jacob as a Chosen People, a priestly nation serving the one God.

Nearly two millennia later, the disciples of a rabbi named Jesus proclaimed that he was the promised Jewish messiah who had fulfilled the original covenant with Abraham and had given a new covenant sealed by his own death and resurrection. Gentiles (people who are not Jewish) could become children of Abraham through "adoption" because they had faith in the one God revealed in Jesus the Christ.

Six centuries after the time of Jesus, Muhammad proclaimed to the Arabs that they were also children of the covenant given to Abraham and his elder son, Ishmael. All who submit to the rules of righteousness given to Abraham were the true children of Abraham. The followers of Muhammad were to be Muslims, which means those who submit. They were to obey the one God just as Abraham had.

The history of Western civilization is bound up with this story of those who claim to be children of Abraham by birth, adoption, or obedience. There has been much conflict between and within the Western religions as each fought to promote and protect their understanding of the covenant with God. Some modern scholars argue that monotheism is intrinsically violent because of its exclusivism and drive to uniformity of belief and practice. There is truth in that observation, but that is not the whole story. As this book demonstrates, the Abrahamic tradition has itself produced great diversity of beliefs, practices, and communities of faith. Through the centuries the three great Abrahamic religions have learned much from each other despite frequent strife.

The Abrahamic religions share many features that have profoundly shaped Western society. For example, they teach that God is concerned about ethics and that the ethical life is a happy life. They are all religions "of the book," which means that their sacred writings provide the norms for doctrine, rituals, and daily living. To varying degrees, each encourages believers to devote themselves to study as well as work in the world. Each shares a basic conviction that the physical world is a product of God's good will and that nature works according to God's laws. Through reason, one can discern the presence of God in creation and understand God's instructions for right living. More profoundly, through faith, one can experience the presence of God in one's life and learn to love both God and one's neighbors. Each Abrahamic religion offers its followers hope for a better tomorrow, either in this world or the world to come.

The Abrahamic religions differ in many significant ways. Jews and Muslims proclaim the unity and oneness of God and resist all attempts to create images of God. Christian churches, with a few exceptions, proclaim that God is three as well as one and that Jesus the Christ was the incarnation of God the Son. Those called the Latter Day Saints believe that Jesus was God, but that the faithful can also become divine in the way Jesus is divine.

Jews and Muslims agree that living according to the laws of God are central to following and loving God, but they disagree over the details of those laws. They also agree that Abraham, Moses, and Isaiah were prophets, but they disagree over whether Jesus and Muhammad were prophets of God. Christians and Muslims believe that God has entrusted them with the sacred task of convincing all the people of the world that there is one God whom they should love and serve, but they disagree on the nature of God and what it means to serve God. Jews, for the most part, feel no need to bring outsiders into their covenantal relationship with God, but they do call for Gentiles to live justly as God demands.

The Abrahamic religions, therefore, share a common "worldview," but it is important to look at each religion and denomination in terms of its particularity or individuality. Each elaborates on the basic tradition in important ways that give meaning and guidance to its followers. In the pages that follow, we will look at each of the Abrahamic traditions according to when it appeared on the world scene.

Suggestions for Further Reading

Armstrong, Karen. *A History of God: The 4,000-year Quest of Judaism, Christianity, and Islam.* New York: Alfred A. Knopf, 1993.

Armstrong, Karen. *The Battle for God: A History of Fundamentalism.* New York: Ballatine Books, 2001.

Corrigan, John, Frederick M. Denny, Carolos M. N. Eire, and Martin S. Jaffee. *Jews, Christians, Muslims: A Comparative Introduction to Monotheistic Religions.* Upper Saddle River, NJ: Prentice Hall, 1998.

Eck, Diana. *Encountering God: A Spiritual Journey from Bozeman to Banares.* Boston: Beacon Press, 1993.

Feiler, Bruce. *Abraham: A Journey to the Heart of Three Faiths.* San Francisco: HarperCollins, 2002.

Kimball, Charles. *When Religion Becomes Evil.* San Francisco: HarperSanFrancisco, 2002.

Neusner, Jacob, ed. *World Religions in America: An Introduction.* Louisville: Westminster/John Knox Press, 1994.

Occhiogrosso, Peter. *The Joy of Sects: A Spirited Guide to the World's Religious Traditions.* New York: Image Books, 1996.

Oxtoby, Willard G., ed. *World Religions: Western Traditions.* New York: Oxford University Press, 1996.

Smith, Huston. *Why Religion Matters: The Fate of the Human Spirit in an Age of Unbelief.* San Francisco: HarperSanFrancisco, 2001.

Smith, William Cantwell. *Patterns of Faith Around the World.* Oxford: Oneworld, 1998.

Wuthnow, Robert. *Growing Up Religious: Christians and Jews and Their Journeys of Faith.* Boston: Beacon Press, 1999.

JUDAISM

Judaism is one of the oldest religions of the world. All Western religions trace their origins in some way to Judaism. Today there are about twelve million Jews in the world, half of whom live in the United States. Judaism can refer to both a religion and an ethnicity, and there are, of course, disagreements among Jews as to what truly makes a person Jewish—whether it is a matter of birth, cultural heritage, or religious observance.

Unlike Christianity, which is generally defined in terms of doctrines and beliefs, Judaism as a religion is defined primarily by rituals and ethics. Put briefly, Jews understand themselves as the people to whom God gave the commandments to observe as their obligation to God. By following God's instructions, the Chosen People in turn become a blessing to the entire world as they help to establish God's realm of justice and peace (*shalom*).

History. Jews trace their heritage back to the patriarch Abraham, who answered the call of God and left his home in Mesopotamia to seek a promised land beyond the Jordan River. According to tradition, Abraham's grandson was Jacob, whose name was changed to Israel after he wrestled with an angel. The twelve sons of Jacob/Israel became the fathers of the twelve tribes of ancient Israel.

The defining event for the Israelites and their descendents was the Exodus. After many years serving as slaves to Pharaoh in Egypt, a prophet named Moses was called by God to lead the people to freedom. Moses parted the waters of the Red Sea (or the Sea of Reeds) and led the people to Mt. Sinai. There he established a priesthood and gave instructions on how they should live. Israel's obligations to God became known as the Torah ("Law" or "Instruction"). Torah is the centerpiece of all forms of Judaism down to the present day.

Around 1000 BCE, the second king of Israel, David, established a strong and prosperous centralized government with a standing army and efficient bureaucracy. He captured the Canaanite city of Jerusalem and made it the capital of his realm. Despite his personal flaws and failings, David was heralded as the perfect king, God's own son. Prophets and priests alike proclaimed that God had made a special covenant with the house of David so that there would always be a son of David on the throne in Jerusalem. Jewish kings were known as the Lord's

Anointed, which in Hebrew is *Messiah*. David's son Solomon expanded the kingdom and built a large central temple in Jerusalem. Jerusalem was proclaimed to be the holy city, the dwelling place of God. Centuries after the destruction of the Temple, Jerusalem is still viewed as the holy city by most Jews, and the Temple Mount is the most holy land in the Holy Land.

After Solomon's death, there was a rebellion against the Davidic kings, and the kingdom divided into two unequal parts. The smaller southern kingdom of Judah consisted primarily of the tribe of Judah, and its capital city was Jerusalem, where the descendents of David ruled until the sixth century BCE. The words *Judaism* and *Jew* come from "Judah." The northern kingdom was known as Israel, and its capital was Samaria. In the early eighth century this kingdom was destroyed by the Assyrians. The people were dispersed, never to reunite. From that time on, the southern kingdom assumed the heritage of Israel. Around 587 BCE the kingdom of Judah was conquered by the Babylonians. The temple was destroyed and thousands of citizens were taken into captivity. During the forty years of exile, the prophets, priests, scribes, and scholars began the process of codifying the writings that became the sacred Scripture.

Eventually the Jews were allowed to return to the land of the patriarchs and they built a nation under Persian and later Greek control. There was no longer a king; instead the high priest served as the chief administrator of Judea. In the second century BCE their Hellenistic overlord, the Syrian Emperor Antiochus IV, tried to crush the Jews and their religion in order to make them more subservient to his rule. Copies of the Torah (the scrolls of the first five books of the Bible) were burned, Jews were forbidden to circumcise their boy babies (the physical sign that one is in the covenant), and the Temple was desecrated by the sacrifice of an unclean animal to a pagan deity. Rather than crush the spirit of the Jews, these measures led to open revolt. This revolt of the Maccabbees on behalf of the right of Jews to observe the commandments of God is commemorated each year at Hanukkah.

Within a hundred years of the revolt against foreign domination, though, Judea fell into Roman hands. At the time of Jesus, it was administered by a Roman governor. Rebellion again broke out in 66 CE, but this time, the Jews were defeated. Jerusalem and the Temple were destroyed in 70. By that time, there were Jewish communities throughout the Roman and Persian worlds, and they grew in importance when the heart of Judaism was destroyed. The Diaspora, or scattering, of the Jews was facilitated by the development of a mobile form of religion that was based in the family and small community. In diaspora Judaism, it takes only ten men to form an assembly and conduct worship. Even without a synagogue, Judaism can be observed in the home, in secret if need be.

As Christianity* emerged as the religion of the Roman Empire, anti-Semitism grew in the Empire. But with the rise of Islam,* which has many affinities to Judaism, Jews were met with a measure of toleration in the new Islamic Empire.

Jews often had positions of great power and influence, particularly in the learned professions, such as medicine. Jews in the Islamic world generally spoke Arabic or other local languages and even translated the Torah into Arabic. They assimilated outwardly while maintaining Jewish observance and theology. These Jews of the Mediterranean basin would eventually be called Sephardic, from the Hebrew word for "Spain." Spain had a thriving Jewish community until Isabella and Ferdinand consolidated their rule over the Iberian Peninsula. In 1492, the year Columbus sailed west, the Jews were forced to leave Spain or face the wrath of the Spanish Inquisition. Many Sephardic Jews made their way to the New World, settling in Brazil, New York, and Rhode Island.

Jews in the Christian kingdoms of the West had a more tenuous existence than did those in Islamic lands. During the struggle to define Christianity as separate from Judaism in the patristic period, much anti-Semitism found its way into Christian theology and practice. Throughout the Middle Ages, Jewish communities were subject to harassment by Christian mobs. In the thirteenth and fourteenth centuries, Jews were expelled from England and France. Many made their way eastward into the sparsely settled lands of Germany, Poland, Hungary, and Russia. There they established separate communities, often building entire farming villages, where they could observe the Torah in relative peace. These Jews became known as Ashkenazi, from the Hebrew word for "Germany," and they developed a unique German dialect known as Yiddish, which is written in Hebrew letters. The Ashkenazi were generally less sophisticated and secular than the Sephardim.

Persecution of the Ashkenazi Jews in Eastern Europe began in earnest in the nineteenth century, and thousands immigrated to the United States. Soon anti-Semitism increased in Germany and throughout Central Europe. Hatred of Jews reached a fever pitch in the first half of the twentieth century. When the National Socialist (Nazi) Party came to power in Germany through popular elections, violence against Jews increased. Adolf Hitler (1889–1945) and his aides put in place a series of anti-Jewish laws that stripped Jews of their civil rights. Soon, the Nazi regime began shipping Jews to concentration camps, where as many as six million Jews, along with millions of Gypsies, Slavs, and other hated groups, were brutally tortured and murdered. This Shoah, or Holocaust, marked a watershed in Jewish history that continues to affect Judaism in profound ways. Never before had the threatened destruction of the Jewish people been so close to fulfillment. Perhaps half of the world's Jewish population died during the Nazi era.

The founding of the State of Israel in 1948 was connected with the horrors of the Holocaust. Since the nineteenth century, when many peoples of Europe had agitated for their own nations, there had been calls for a Jewish nation. This Zionist, or Jewish nationalist, movement was led by Theodor Herzl (1860–1904), who laid the groundwork upon which the Jewish homeland would be erected. Initially a rather small movement among secularized Jews, many of whom had socialist convictions, Zionism grew in power as Jews learned the truth about the Holocaust. A Jewish state free from Gentile control seemed to be the best solution to Jewish survival. In the 1960s and 1970s, religious Jews became firm supporters of the Jewish state as well; and many people perceived a link between the future of Israel as a nation and the establishment of the long-hoped for messianic age. In the last quarter of the twentieth century there was a growing fundamentalist movement focused on Zionist goals.

Jews in the United States. Sephardic Jews arrived early in American history. During the colonial period synagogues were established in New Amsterdam (1654), Newport, Savannah, Charleston, and Philadelphia (1730s and 40s); however, the first official rabbi did not arrive until the middle of the nineteenth century.

President George Washington was able to assure a delegation of Jewish leaders that the new Constitution of the United States guaranteed freedom of worship and conscience to all people, not just Christians. Because of this guarantee of freedom from persecution, America gradually became a second "promised land" for world Jewry. In the nineteenth century, some Jews embraced American culture so completely that they redefined Judaism in terms familiar to liberal Protestants. Hebrew was dropped, except in special services, the rules of ritual observance were relaxed, and organs were added to synagogues. Some synagogues even began worshiping on Sunday rather than on the Sabbath. Other Jews rejected this assimilation to the Protestant American mainstream and retained traditional elements of worship and observance.

The massive influx of Eastern European Jews, the Ashkenazi, profoundly affected the American Jewish community. Millions of immigrants settled in the major northern cities, creating large Jewish neighborhoods where they could maintain much of their Old World identity in the midst of industrial America. There were about half a million Jews in the United States in 1900. By 1940 there were over four million, and they made a significant impact on American popular culture. The Ashkenazi tended to be more conservative than the Sephardic Jews who had lived in the United States for decades. Many of the most famous American entertainers came out of this Yiddish culture, with its distinctive foods and traditions. By the end of the twentieth century, Judaism was so well established in American society that an observant Jew, Joseph Lieberman, could be nominated for vice president in 2000.

While the local synagogue is very important to Jewish life in the United States, there are hundreds of Jewish organizations that help to define and defend Judaism. They range from those focused on Jewish rights to youth societies. There are some two hundred periodicals and newspapers and two news syndicates dedicated to Judaism. The American Jewish Committee is organized to protect the civil and religious rights of Jews around the world. It seeks equality in economic, social, and educational opportunities and gives aid and counsel in cases of intolerance and persecution.

Jewish institutions of higher learning, affiliated with the various movements, serve the community nationwide, not only by training rabbis, but also providing general Jewish learning for all interested people. The most important are (Orthodox) Rabbi Isaac Elchanan Theological Seminary of Yeshiva University in New York City; (Reform) Hebrew Union College—Jewish Institute of Religion in New York, Cincinnati, Los Angeles, and Jerusalem; (Conservative) Jewish Theological Seminary in New York City; and Reconstructionist Rabbinical College in Philadelphia. Yeshiva University in New York City is the only Jewish college that awards a B.A. degree; Brandeis University in Waltham, Massachusetts, is the only nonsectarian Jewish sponsored college or university in the United States.

Theology and Practice. Rabbinic Judaism was the only form of Judaism to survive ancient times and the destruction of the Temple. It actually developed at the same time that Christianity was being formed. In fact, in the first century, Christianity was simply one of many forms of non-rabbinic Judaism. By the sixth century, the two religions had developed the basic structures, theology, and practices that define each to the present.

Judaism as a religion is based on the Hebrew Scriptures (for Christians, the Old Testament), but it is distinct from the form of religion described in those texts. The ancient religion of the Israelites focused on cultic observances, particularly animal sacrifice, and revelation given by prophets. Priests were in charge of seeing that cultic rites were properly performed and that ritual purity was maintained. Prophets served social and religious functions as well. They were men (and occasionally women) through whom God spoke, especially in judgment. Prophets challenged the leaders of society, even the king, to live by the ethical demands of the covenant. Justice for the poor, the outcast, and the oppressed was a major theme of the prophetic judgment.

Over time, scribes codified the pronouncements of the prophets and the laws of the priesthood, producing an enormous body of legal and ethical material that has profoundly shaped Western society. However, many of the laws and instructions contained in the scriptures clearly reflect the world of an ancient agricultural people. First the priests and later the rabbis helped people understand and apply the Torah in radically different historical and social contexts.

Rabbinic Judaism grew out of the Pharisee movement. The Pharisees in the first century CE were a Jewish party that controlled most of the synagogues in and around Palestine. They differed from the priests and other Jews by their strict interpretation of the demands of the Torah: It should be observed as faithfully as humanly possible. To make observance of the Torah easier, the Pharisees taught, Jews should keep themselves separate from Gentiles, especially at meals, when it would be hard to observe dietary restrictions. Marriage to Gentiles was also forbidden. The Pharisees deemphasized Temple observances and the sacrifice of animals and focused on the demands of the Torah in day-to-day living. Justice, not sacrifice, was what God demands, the prophet Micah had said, and the Pharisees agreed. For the rabbis, prayer and study of Torah served the religious needs that the priests had once met.

One of the key concepts of rabbinic Judaism is that there are two Torahs. The written Torah was given to Moses and is contained in the scrolls of Moses (Genesis, Exodus, Leviticus, Numbers, and Deuteronomy). These writings were revealed by God through the prophetic lawgiver, but the written Torah can be very confusing and difficult to observe unless you live in a small agricultural society. Here is where the second Torah of the rabbis comes in. This is the oral Torah, which was also communicated to Moses by God on Mt. Sinai. The oral Torah is the key to understanding Scripture and to applying the teachings of Scripture to one's daily life. The written Torah says to observe the Sabbath and keep it holy. The oral Torah tells you how to do this. According to tradition, this oral Torah was passed down by a succession of prophets and scribes, such as Ezra.

After the destruction of the Temple, though, it became necessary to codify and clarify this oral tradition and preserve it in written form. This culminated in the production of the Talmud around 600 CE. The Talmud is one of the masterpieces of world literature and intellectual history. It contains the debates of the rabbis on questions of biblical interpretation and how to understand and apply the Torah. There are, in fact, two Talmuds, one produced in Babylon by the descendents of Jews who had not returned to Israel, and one produced in Palestine centuries after the destruction of the Temple.

The Talmud has two main parts, one of which, the *Haggadah,* deals with biblical interpretation, customs, legends, and edifying stories. The other part concerns *Halakah,* the rules of the covenant with God. *Halakah* involves the traditional 613 commandments that Jews are to obey and practice in their daily lives. This can be difficult as the world changes, so the Talmud also provides guidelines for interpreting *Halakah.* This process of interpretation, adaptation, and even disagreement over the meaning of Torah is the thread that runs through the history of Judaism.

There are some features of Jewish theology and observance that are common throughout the various branches of Judaism. The core of Jewish theology is the concept of the oneness of God. There is only one God, and God's will is known in the covenant. Every day the practicing Jew repeats the ancient verse that introduces the Ten Commandments in Deuteronomy: "Hear, O Israel! The Lord is our God, the Lord alone" (Deut 6:4 NJPS). There is but one Creator, who ultimately controls the destiny of humankind and the world.

Humankind, created by this one God, is inherently good. There is no idea of original sin in Judaism. Humans are made in God's image and are endowed with an intelligence that enables them to choose between good and evil. Torah assists in this process of choosing good over evil, but all people, Jews and Gentiles alike, will be judged. The righteous will be rewarded and the wicked punished. However, concern for life after death is an issue of minor significance for most Jews. More important is the way one lives in this life.

Judaism looks forward to the establishment of a divine kingdom of truth and righteousness on the earth. Orthodox Jews believe the time will come when God sends the Messiah, the descendent of David who will restore the kingdom. Other Jews speak of a messianic age. To work toward the divine kingdom, Jews have been established by God as "a kingdom of priests and a holy nation," the "servant of the Lord."

Judaism follows a liturgical calendar, dating from ancient times. It is based on the lunar year rather than the solar year, so the dates vary from year to year. The year begins in the autumn with Rosh Hashanah, a New Year festival that begins the High Holy Days. For ten days, Jews are encouraged to examine their lives and make reconciliation with those they have wronged, including God, in preparation for Yom Kippur, the Day of Atonement. On this day, God judges the sins of the people and provides for atonement.

Some weeks after Yom Kippur is Succoth, the Feast of Tabernacles or Booths, during which Jews relive the years of wandering in the wilderness. Hanukkah, in December, commemorates the purification of the Temple during the Maccabean revolt. This feast day has grown in importance in the United States because of the commercial power of Christmas. In the spring, Pesach, or Passover is a memorial of the liberation of Jews from Egypt. Shabuoth, also known as the Feast of Weeks or Pentecost, follows Passover in late May or early June. It was once a harvest festival but now commemorates Moses' receiving of the Torah.

Other observances follow the life cycle of the individual. These include the circumcision of male children on the eighth day after birth, the *bar mitzvah* (a rite of entry into adult accountability for the covenant), weddings, and funerals. Also important in Judaism is the observance of the Sabbath (sundown Friday until sundown Saturday) as a sacred day of rest and study of the Torah. Most synagogues have Sabbath services, although Sabbath observance is actually a home obligation.

Local congregations are independent and elect their own president and officers. There are no synods, assemblies, or hierarchies of leaders, but there are rabbinical councils and organizations that make rulings about the law and establish credentials for rabbis. Jewish worship varies according to theology and culture. Traditional Orthodox synagogues, for instance, have no instrumental music, the congregation worships with covered heads, and the men and women sit separately. In Reform, Conservative, and Reconstructionist houses of worship, sermons are in English and there is no segregation by sex.

At the head of the congregation stands the rabbi, trained in seminary and fully ordained. He (in some cases, she) officiates at marriages and grants divorce decrees in accordance with Jewish law after civil divorce has been granted by the state. Rabbis conduct funerals and generally supervise burial as Jewish law requires. Orthodox rabbis may supervise the slaughtering of animals and validate other aspects of dietary law. Many congregations engage readers, or cantors, who lead most of the service.

Suggestions for further reading:

Eisen, Arnold M. *The Chosen People in America: A Study in Jewish Religious Ideology.* Bloomington: Indiana University Press, 1983.

Handlin, Oscar. *Adventure in Freedom: Three Hundred Years of Jewish Life in America.* New York: McGraw-Hill, 1954.

Idel, Moshe. *Hasidism: Between Ecstasy and Magic.* Albany: State University of New York Press, 1995.

Meyer, Michael A. *Response to Modernity: A History of the Reform Movement in Judaism.* New York: Oxford University Press, 1989.

Neusner, Jacob. *An Introduction to Judaism: A Textbook and Reader.* Louisville: Westminster/John Knox Press, 1991.

Neusner, Jacob. *The Way of Torah: An Introduction to Judaism.* 4th ed. Belmont, CA: Wadsworth, 1988.

Rosenthal, Gilbert S. *The Many Faces of Judaism: Orthodox, Conservative, Reconstructionist, and Reform.* Edited by S. Rossel. New York: Behrman House, 1978.

Sklare, Marshall. *Conservative Judaism: An American Religious Movement.* New ed. New York: Schocken Books, 1972.

Steinberg, Milton. *Basic Judaism.* New York: Harcourt Brace, 1986.

ORTHODOX UNION

Founded: 1898
Membership: est. 600,000 in 1,500 synagogues (2000)

Roughly forty percent of the synagogues in the United States are identified as Orthodox, but only about ten percent of the Jews in America identify themselves as Orthodox. Orthodox Judaism was an attempt to maintain traditional European Judaism in opposition to the rise of what would be called Reform Judaism* in the nineteenth century. The Orthodox sought to preserve synagogues from what they viewed as theological corruption and to maintain traditional forms of worship and observance of *Halakah.* This often included preservation of Eastern European customs as well as a strict observance of dietary laws. For the Orthodox, the Torah is binding on all Jews and is not subject to interpretation or change.

The Orthodox Union in America was founded by Dr. Henry Pereira Mendes (1852–1937), a Sephardic leader in New York. He hoped that this union would unify traditionalists, promote the observance of the Torah, and halt Jewish assimilation. Initially the Union focused on protecting Jewish children and immigrants from Protestant missionaries and promoting the strict observance of the Sabbath. Another concern was the difficulty of maintaining the rules of *kashrut* (kosher laws) in the United States. In 1924, the Orthodox Union created the first non-profit kosher certification program, which now certifies over two hundred thousand products and supervises some two thousand corporations with four thousand certified plants in over fifty countries. The Orthodox Union also helps American soldiers to follow *kashrut,* even on the battlefield, and educates the public about Jewish dietary restrictions.

The Orthodox view intermarriage and assimilation as threats to the survival of Judaism. The National Conference of Synagogue Youth (NCSY), an outreach ministry for teenagers, stresses Jewish identity and the need to marry within the faith. The NCSY spurred the birth of the North American Teshuva movement as well. Following the social disruptions of the 1960s, there was a revival of interest in traditional Jewish faith and practice among American youth. Many Conservative synagogues moved more toward Orthodox observance. Orthodox Jews have been particularly active in working with Russian Jewry and have been strong supporters of the State of Israel.

For more information: www.ou.org
Headquarters: 11 Broadway, New York, NY 10004-1003

LUBAVITCHER COMMUNITY
(HASIDIC JUDAISM)

Founded: roots to the 1700s
Membership: est. 165,000

Hasidic Jews are often confused with the Orthodox; however, they represent one of the most distinctive types of Judaism. Like the Amish* among Christians, the Hasidim are so conservative that they generally wear the same style of clothing as their ancestors did in nineteenth century Europe. By choice they live in segregated communities and clearly define themselves against the dominant culture. They are similar to the Orthodox in their strict observance of *Halakah* and literal approach to the Torah, but theologically and liturgically they are often far removed from Orthodoxy.

Hasidic Judaism developed in Eastern Europe during the early 1700s when groups of pious laypersons began reading the *Kabala* (medieval Jewish mystical writings) and followed the Torah strictly. In doing so they developed a number of controversial practices, such as rocking back and forth during prayer, which set them off from others in the synagogue.

The key figure in early Hasidism was Israel b. Eliezar Ba'al Shem Tov (ca. 1700–60), known as the Besht, who would enter into an ecstatic state and be guided by the Spirit of God. The Besht was a charismatic figure who attracted a large following of disciples, for whom he served as an adviser and guide. His visions and revelations soon took on the force of truth among his followers. In 1780, Jacob

Joseph wrote *Toledot Ya'akov Yosef,* a memoir that included many sayings of the Besht. This was the first attempt at any kind of theoretical formulation of Hasidic beliefs. Among these beliefs are that the separation between the Creator and the creation is merely an illusion. God is hidden in the creation, but is present in this hiddenness. There is only one God, and God is all. God is completely in creation; therefore, all are one with and in God.

The key to the religious life and to understanding the Torah is to understand and experience the reality of union with God. This mystical idea undergirds all aspects of life for the Hasidim. Rituals are not meaningless if the mind and heart are properly prepared. The proper attitude for devotion and life is joy rather than melancholy. Melancholy and despair are the great enemies of faith because these emotions deny the reality of God's presence in the world. If God is all, then we must be joyful. Distinctive Hasidic practices, such as dancing in worship, flow from this burning desire for a joyful union with God through celebration of creation.

The key to the spread and development of Hasidism was the Zaddikim, the holy men, who continued to demonstrate the real presence of God in the world through their own experience and activities. These Zaddikim were seen as mediators between God and the community, offering people vicarious fulfillment through their spiritual accomplishments. Now known as Rebbes, these charismatic figures continue to shape Hasidism. The most influential Rebbe in the United States was Menachem Schneerson (1902–94), the Lubavitcher Rebbe in New York City. Before Schneerson's death in 1994, there had been a split among the Lubavitcher over whether he was the expected Messiah.

For more information: www.lubavitch.com

Headquarters: 770 Eastern Parkway, Brooklyn New York 11213

UNION FOR REFORM JUDAISM

Founded: 1873
Membership: est. 1,500,000 in approx. 890 synagogues

The earliest roots of Reform Judaism can be traced to the Hashalah movement in Europe during the Enlightenment. In the 1740s, Moses Mendelsohn (1729–86) urged his fellow Jews to learn from the secular world and speak the languages around them instead of Hebrew or Yiddish. He translated and published the Torah in German, and he encouraged others to translate the Talmud so that both Jews and Gentiles would be able to read and understand Jewish laws.

Those in the Hashalah movement advocated that Jews fully assimilate into their local culture: that they speak, dress, act, and even eat like those around them. This would be the path of emancipation from persecution; Jews would overcome cultural alienation and be able to participate fully in life around them. The more religious leaders in the movement wanted to reformulate Judaism from what they considered an archaic past, thus they are known as Reform Jews.

Rabbi Isaac Mayer Wise (1819–1900) brought the Hashalah movement to the United States when he immigrated in the 1840s. His American plan (*Minhag America*) included new liturgies for use in the congregations. The prayers dropped all mention of rebuilding the Temple in Jerusalem and focused on living righteously in the modern world. Wise attempted to unify Judaism in America by convoking a Cleveland Conference, where he called for an "American Judaism, free, progressive, enlightened, united, and respected." In 1873, Wise founded Hebrew Union College in Cincinnati, one of the most important Jewish schools, and for many years he was a leader in the Union of American Hebrew Congregations.

Since Wise's time, Reform Judaism has continued to interpret Judaism in terms of "ethical monotheism," in which the ethical demands of the Torah are vital rather than the ceremonial and dietary aspects. Reform Judaism promotes assimilation into American culture in part as a way to move this nation toward the pursuit of justice and peace.

For more information: www.urj.org

Headquarters: 633 Third Ave., New York, NY 10017-6778

UNITED SYNAGOGUE OF CONSERVATIVE JUDAISM

Founded: 1913
Membership: est. 1,500,000 in 800 synagogues

More religious Jews identify themselves as Conservative than anything else (nearly half), and the number of Conservative synagogues appears to be on the rise. The basic conviction of Conservative Judaism is that the whole Jewish community should be united in a type of Judaism that is adapted to modern living but is still devoted to the Torah and *Halakah*. In other words, Conservative Judaism is willing to make changes in Jewish custom, such as removing segregated seating for men and women, but it strives to observe the requirements of the Torah as closely as possible.

Solomon Schechter (1847–1915), head of the Jewish Theological Seminary in New York and founder of the United Synagogue of Conservative Judaism, provided the Conservative movement with its intellectual and organizational foundation. Education has been a major focus of the Conservative movement. The oldest department of Schechter's United Synagogue is the department of education, which produces and sets standards for textbooks and Jewish school curricula. The United Synagogue congregational religious school system has over 100,000 students, and there is also a Solomon Schechter Day School system. Youth programs are designed to help Jewish teens and young adults learn to live as Jews in a Gentile world.

Conservative Judaism emphasizes observance of the Sabbath, Jewish holy days, and *kashrut* ("rules of purity"). Synagogues are encouraged to have schools for children and follow the *Halakah*. Each congregation is free to accept changes in *Halakah* observance recommended by the Committee on Jewish Law and Standards if and when they so decide. Some Conservative rabbis find they have a great deal in common with the Orthodox, while others relate better to the Reformed.

For more information: www.uscj.org

Headquarters: 155 Fifth Ave., New York, NY 10010-6802

JEWISH RECONSTRUCTIONIST FEDERATION

Founded: 1954
Membership: est. 100,000 in approx. 100 synagogues

Originating in 1934 under the leadership of Mordecai M. Kaplan (1881–1983) of the Jewish Theological Seminary in New York City, Reconstructionism is a movement indigenous to the United States. Reconstructionism defines Judaism as an evolving religious civilization, and it attempts to assure the physical and spiritual survival of Judaism by demonstrating that a maximum Jewish life can be lived within the setting of a modern democratic state. Viewing Judaism as a civilization, Reconstructionists have strong commitments both to Jewish tradition and to the search for modern meaning.

Reconstructionists accept that Judaism has evolved over the centuries. Rabbinic Judaism is not identical to the Judaism of King David, for instance. However, they do not want to break with the historical process. Instead, "the past has a vote" in determining what the present and the future will be. The whole Jewish heritage, not just the Talmud, is embraced as a resource for building a Jewish civilization in the midst of modern culture. As such, the Zionist cause figures prominently in Reconstruction, but so too does an energetic program of scholarly endeavors to give laypersons resources for understanding the Jewish heritage.

Theologically, Reconstructionists believe it is the duty of all Jews to question and to study in order to find unique paths to the divine. They believe in a God who inhabits this world and especially the human heart. This God is the source of generosity, sensitivity, and concern for the world.

For more information: www.jrf.org

Headquarters: 101 Greenwood Ave. Suite 430, Jenkintown, PA 19046

JEWISH FUNDAMENTALISM

Founded: 1940s
Membership statistics unavailable

"Fundamentalism" is a term borrowed from Protestant Christianity to describe many conservative movements in religion. Unlike other Jewish movements that emphasize strict observance of the traditional Torah, such as Hasidism* and Orthodoxy,* Jewish fundamentalism is closely connected to the reclamation of the Land of Israel and the establishment of the messianic kingdom. As with other fundamentalist movements, Jewish fundamentalists established separate schools and printing presses to promote their vision.

One of the earliest theorists of Jewish fundamentalism was Rabbi Abraham Yitzak Kook (1865-1935), who immigrated to Palestine in 1904 as rabbi for a community of European settlers who were inspired by Theodore Herzl's vision of a Jewish state. Kook was influenced by Jewish Kabalah, and he longed for the completion of Jewish redemption in the messianic kingdom. He rejected the secularism of Zionism and offered instead a mystical/theological vision of Israel restored. The son of Rabbi Abraham Kook, Rabbi Zvi Yehuda Kook emerged as the leading voice of Jewish fundamentalism in the 1960s and 70s. Unlike his father, Zvi Kook justified violence against the perceived enemies of the Jews, and he welcomed the Six Days War as a significant event in the expected redemption of Israel.

The failure of the State of Israel to use its military might to reclaim all of the land promised to Abraham led the Kookists to become more extreme. In 1974 the most militant formed the "Bloc of the Faithful," or Gush Emunim, which quickly became one of the most strident fundamentalist organizations. It began to attract support in the United States where similar separatist movements were established.

The most visible voice for Jewish fundamentalism in America was Rabbi Meir Kahane, who had established the Jewish Defense League in response to racial tension between Jews and blacks in New York City. In 1974 Kahane immigrated to Israel where he became the spokesman for a militant fundamentalism that denied that the "enemies of the Torah" had human rights. The Dome of the Rock was to be destroyed and the Temple rebuilt. Until that happens, the messiah can not return. When Prime Minister Yitzhak Rabin attempted to make peace with the Palestinians, he was assassinated by a former soldier inspired by the teaching of Gush rabbis.

For more information: www.kahane.org

MESSIANIC JEWISH ALLIANCE OF AMERICA

Founded: 1915
Membership: est. 100,000 in over 200 synagogues

The MJAA is the largest organization for Jews who believe that Yeshua (Jesus of Nazareth) is the messiah and savior of the world. It is primarily a network of synagogues that proclaims faith in Yeshua while maintaining their Jewish identity. Such synagogues are not recognized as Jewish by the main Jewish bodies. The MJAA was founded for three primary purposes: to provide visible testimony to the growing numbers of Jewish people who believe in Yeshua as the messiah and savior; to provide an organization for Jewish and Gentile Christians to work together for Jewish revival; and to introduce the Jewish people to Yeshua.

In addition to the Tanach (The Torah, Prophets, and Writings) of the Old Covenant, the MJAA teaches that the B'rit Chadasha, or the New Covenant Scriptures, is the inspired and authoritative Word of God. In other words, they accept both the Old and New Testaments as revealed Scripture. Messianic Jews believe in one God as declared in the Sh'ma (Deuteronomy 6:4), but they teach that God is Echad (a compound unity) and eternally existent in three forms: Father, Son, and Holy Spirit. They accept the basic teachings of the Apostles' Creed about Jesus, but they also believe in God's eternal covenant with Abraham, Isaac, and Jacob. Therefore they continue to follow the traditional Jewish calendar and religious observances, as did Yeshua himself.

For more information: www.mjaa.org
Headquarters: P.O. Box 274, Springfield, PA 19064

CHRISTIANITY

Christianity is the largest religion in the world today, but it began as a small sect of Judaism two thousand years ago. Around 26 CE, a Galilean Jew named Jesus of Nazareth was baptized by John the Baptist and began a ministry of healing and teaching. Many of those who followed him believed that he was the long-awaited Jewish Messiah, but he did not reestablish the kingdom of David. Instead he was crucified by the Roman governor of Judea. Three days after his death, he appeared to some of his followers who proclaimed that he was not just a prophet or messiah. They went out into the world with the message that Jesus was the Son of God who had overcome death and had ascended into heaven. Those who had faith in him and followed his way of truth and life would also pass from death into eternal life.

Under the guidance of an early teacher and missionary named Paul of Tarsus, Christians welcomed Gentiles into their fellowship, and slowly a new religion was born. Christians continued to use the Jewish Scriptures, but they added a New Testament that focused on the life, teachings, death, and resurrection of Christ, and what Christ means for the church and the world. The Old and New Testaments together are called the Bible.

As Christians moved from the synagogue to the church, they adapted many Jewish practices to reflect their new understanding of salvation. Passover became the Eucharist or Holy Communion, which was celebrated each Sunday rather than once a year. In most churches the Eucharist retains its connection to the story of the Exodus from Egypt, but it is primarily a remembrance of the sacrifice of Jesus on the cross. His body and blood provided a new Exodus from sin and death to life with God.

The annual Passover celebration was transformed into a remembrance of the crucifixion on Good Friday and a celebration of the resurrection of Jesus on Easter morning. Baptism replaced circumcision as the sign that one had entered the new covenant, having died to one's old life and risen to a new life in Christ. Gradually, Sunday rather than the Sabbath became the Christian holy day in honor of the resurrection of Christ, but the church followed the basic outline of worship in the synagogue: prayers, psalms, Scripture reading, and a sermon.

Early Christian theologians believed that all truth comes from God; therefore they used the insights of pagan philosophers like Plato to formulate Christian theology. As it spread around the world, Christianity was remarkably adept in incorporating beliefs and practices from the traditional ("pagan") religions of the people who converted. Missionaries and bishops often transformed traditional shrines into Christian churches or shrines. Local religious calendars were adapted to promote belief in Jesus. For instance, the old Roman Saturnalia festival in December was transformed into a celebration of Christ's birth, and the Celtic Samhain became a time to remember all the saints who had given their lives in devotion to Christ.

Within a century of Jesus' death, a basic structure of leadership emerged in the church. Some men and women took ascetic vows and lived lives of perpetual prayer and service. They are called monks and nuns. Other men, called priests, were set aside to be pastors of local congregations. They administered the sacraments and proclaimed the gospel. Deacons assisted priests in acts of service and mercy in the congregation. Bishops were overseers of all of the congregations in a region and were responsible for establishing doctrine and discipline. Bishops of major urban centers, such as Alexandria, Antioch, Constantinople, and Rome were called archbishops or patriarchs.

As the church spread geographically and developed theologically, conflicts and divisions arose. Councils of bishops decided that some theological movements within early Christianity, such as Gnosticism, Montanism, and Arianism, were heretical and forbidden. Modern scholarship is recovering the actual teachings and practices of some of the excluded groups, and some churches view these "heretics" as witnesses to the truth.

Some of the most significant divisions of the early church were primarily the result of growing divisions between different language groups: the Latin-speaking West, the Greek-speaking East, Coptic-speaking Egypt, and Syriac-speaking Asia Minor. The first official separation of the church took place in the middle of the fifth century after the Council of Chalcedon, when the Coptic* Orthodox and Syrian* Orthodox churches separated from the Greek Orthodox. The separation between the Greek Orthodox and the Roman Catholic Church developed slowly. In addition to differences in language and liturgy, the churches disagreed over who should be the temporal head of the church. The final break between the Catholic* and Orthodox* churches was formalized in 1054.

The Roman Catholic* Church became the dominant social institution in Western Europe. During the Middle Ages, many zealous reformers established religious orders, such as the Franciscans, that attempted to institutionalize the reformer's vision for the church and world. Some of those who attempted to reform church and society, though, were deemed heretical. Such was the case of the Cathars, Waldensians*, and Hussites (see Unitas Fratrum).

In the sixteenth century, several vigorous reformers, such as Martin Luther and Ulrich Zwingli, called for a radical reform of the church's doctrine and structure based on Scripture rather than tradition. As a result, Christianity in Western Europe was divided between Roman Catholicism and Protestantism. The Protestants, in turn, were divided into four major camps: Lutherans,* Reformed*, Anglicans,* and radicals (see Mennonite and Anabaptist Churches*).

The common ideas shared by the Protestants were: a rejection of the papacy, the priority of Scripture over tradition, a greater role for laity in the church, and the use of national languages rather than Latin in worship. Otherwise there was almost as much conflict among the Protestant groups as between Catholics and Protestants. Some of the most horrifying European wars were fought in the name of religion following the Reformation. The Peace of Westphalia (1648) brought an end to major military conflict over religion in Europe and established permanent Protestant and Catholic territories. The development of Christianity in different regions of America depended in part on the nationality of the settlers.

Christianity came to America around the same time that the Protestant Reformation was taking place. When Columbus sailed West in 1492, he saw himself as an agent of God destined to bring Christianity to the Indies. Of course, the "Indies" he discovered were a New World rather than Asia. Undeterred, he and his successors established Catholicism in the Spanish and Portuguese colonies. British, Dutch, Swedish, and German settlers in the British colonies established their Protestant churches. Radical Protestant groups, like the Society of Friends, also came to the colonies. Russian Orthodox priests served in California in the 1700s. Each wave of European immigration brought other types of Christian churches. As Christianity adapted to American culture, new forms of Christianity were created.

When one considers the diversity of Christian churches, each with their own forms of worship and doctrinal traditions, it is hard to imagine that they are part of a single religion. How could the sensually rich liturgy of the Orthodox Church be related to the silence of a Friends* meeting? How could the Catholic Stations of the Cross be related to a Pentecostal* healing service? Yet, in the midst of diversity, confusion, and conflict, the various Christian churches see the Old and New Testaments as authoritative Scripture and proclaim Jesus Christ as Lord. This proclamation of faith in Christ was the basis for the ecumenical movement of the twentieth century and continues to fuel mission efforts in the twenty-first century.

Suggestions for further reading:

Atwood, Craig D. *Always Reforming: A History of Christianity Since 1300*. Macon, GA: Mercer University Press, 2001.

Cameron, Euan. *The European Reformation*. Oxford: Clarendon, 1991.

Gonzalez, Justo L. *The Story of Christianity*, 2 vols. San Francisco: HarperSanFrancisco, 1984.

Hatch, Nathan O. *The Democratization of American Christianity*. New Haven: Yale University Press, 1989.

Irvin, Dale T. and Scott W. Sunquist, *History of the World Christian Movement.* Vol. 1: *Earliest Christianity to 1453.* Maryknoll, NY: Orbis, 2001.

MacHaffie, Barbara J. *Her Story: Women in Christian Tradition.* Philadelphia: Fortress Press, 1986.

Malone, Mary T. *Women and Christianity,* 2 vols. Maryknoll, NY: Orbis, 2001.

Marty, Martin E. *Protestantism in the United States: Righteous Empire.* 2nd ed. New York: Scribner; London: Collier Macmillan, 1986.

Noll, Mark A. *A History of Christianity in the United States and Canada.* Grand Rapids: Eerdmans, 1992.

Pelikan, Jaroslav. *Credo: Historical and Theological Guide to Creeds and Confessions of Faith in the Christian Tradition.* New Haven, Conn.: Yale University Press, 2003.

Walker, Williston, et al. *A History of the Christian Church.* 4th ed. New York: Scribner, 1985.

Orthodox and Oriental Orthodox Churches

With more than two hundred million members around the world, the Orthodox churches represent one of the three major branches of Christianity (the others being Roman Catholic and Protestant). Though there are over four million Orthodox in the United States, their churches remain mysterious to most Americans.

Unlike the Roman Catholic Church*, the Orthodox churches (also known as the Eastern churches) do not have a single hierarchical institution. Instead there are dozens of national bodies, each of which worships in its native language with its own independent (autocephalous) hierarchy. Each Orthodox church thus reflects its own national heritage and ethnic customs in its liturgy. Unlike the Protestant churches, which also demonstrate a wide variety of institutions and forms, most of the Orthodox churches are in communion with one another and hold to the same basic theology based on the ancient creeds of Christianity. A few Orthodox bodies are in communion with the Roman Catholic Church and are known as Uniate* churches.

A few of the main Eastern bodies, however, reject the statements of the Council of Chalcedon (451 CE), in particular the phrase relating to Jesus Christ being one person in two natures: divine and human. These are known as non-Chalcedonian or Oriental Orthodox Churches. Included among these bodies are the Armenian Church, the Coptic Church, the Ethiopian Church, the Eritrean Church, the Syrian Church of Antioch, and the Syrian Indian Church of South India.

Orthodox church services are elaborate, ritualistic, and beautiful. Virtually every architectural feature of the sanctuary, every movement of the priest's body, and every word spoken by the worshipers has symbolic value. The liturgy is an ancient drama that celebrates Christ's incarnation, crucifixion, and resurrection. Lighting, clerical vestments, altar adornments, icons, music, and consecrated bread and wine bring the kingdom of God into the present.

The word "orthodox" means "true glory" as well as "straight teaching." The keynote of this tradition is "Giving glory to God is the purpose of life." Praising God, giving God thanks, and receiving God's presence in the sanctified gifts capture the heart of worship. Through worship, and in God-informed relationships and responsibilities, these Christians mean to move toward sanctification. The Christian goal is *theosis*, "perfection" or "deification," living in genuine unity with God in the here and now and for eternity.

History. Western history books will often state that the Orthodox churches of the East separated from the Catholic Church* of the West, but that is not an accurate presentation. The Eastern Orthodox tradition claims direct descent from Christ and the apostles. For centuries, Christianity was primarily Eastern in orientation, with most of the episcopal sees of the early church being in Greece, Turkey, Egypt, and Syria. Greek, not Latin, was the language of the New Testament, early Christian liturgy, and early theology. The ecumenical councils that continue to define the beliefs of most of the world's Christians were held in the East and were attended primarily by Eastern bishops and theologians.

Of the five ancient patriarchal Sees (Rome, Alexandria, Antioch, Constantinople, and Jerusalem), only Rome was in the West. For centuries these five patriarchs, guided by councils of bishops, governed the world-wide Christian church. It is still the practice in the Orthodox churches that no one patriarch is responsible to any other patriarch. The bishops of the two capitals of the Roman Empire after 330, Constantinople and Rome, had the greatest authority, but in 1054, the bishops of Constantinople and Rome mutually excommunicated each other along with their followers, creating a formal breach in Christianity that has only recently begun to heal.

Long before the official schism between East and West, the two churches had already developed certain basic differences. The East was primarily Greek in speech and attitude, while the West was Latin and Roman. The transference of the imperial capital from Rome to Constantinople in the East meant a shifting of the center of political, social, and intellectual influences. As the Roman Empire decayed in the West and the Germanic tribes began pouring into Italy and Gaul, the bishop of Rome became a symbol of unity and stability for Westerners. When the pope crowned Charlemagne as Holy Roman Emperor in 800, it marked a clear break with the Roman Empire in the East (commonly called the Byzantine Empire). Conflict deepened between the pope at Rome and the patriarch at Constantinople. One major point of controversy was the addition of the words "and the son" (*filioque*) to the Nicene Creed in referring to the procession of the Holy Spirit.

The church in the East was integrally related to the Byzantine Empire, and the great cathedral of Hagia Sophia ("Holy Wisdom") in Constantinople was the center of both the church and the empire until it fell to the Turks in 1453. A number of the schisms in the East were both political and theological in nature, the most important of which involved the understanding of the person of Christ. In Syria, some churches embraced the views of Nestorius (ca 351-451), who held that there were two separate persons in the incarnate Christ, one divine and one human. In Egypt and Armenia other churches accepted the teaching of Cyril of Alexandria (d. 444) as expressed in the phrase "one Incarnate nature of the Word." Most of the Eastern churches, though, remained in communion with the patriarch of Constantinople.

As the Byzantine Empire expanded to the west and north, Orthodox missionaries, such as the celebrated brothers Cyril (826–869) and Methodius (ca. 815–885), converted the Slavic peoples of Bulgaria, Serbia, and Russia to Christianity. The Divine Liturgy and holy books were translated into Slavic tongues, and monasteries and schools were established throughout Eastern Europe. As these peoples gained political independence, national Orthodox churches were gradually established, the first being the Bulgarian Orthodox Church.

The Orthodox churches were profoundly affected by the dramatic rise and spread of Islam in the seventh century. Three of the ancient patriarchal sees (Antioch, Alexandria, and Jerusalem) quickly came under Muslim control and were effectively separated from Constantinople. Christianity in Muslim countries continued to exist as a minority faith living under severe restrictions. As a result, those churches were unable to grow numerically or exert influence on the surrounding culture. Relations with the Catholic Church in the West were nearly destroyed by the sack of Constantinople in 1204 by Latin crusaders in the Fourth Crusade.

The harshest blow to Orthodoxy came when the Turks captured Constantinople in 1453 and put an end to the Byzantine Empire. Hagia Sophia was converted into a mosque, and the Ecumenical Patriarch was forced to give allegiance to the Muslim rulers. For centuries the Orthodox churches in the Balkans struggled for existence under Turkish rule. During this time, the Russian Orthodox Church rose in power and prestige. Some considered Moscow to be "the third Rome." As the Ottoman Empire declined in the nineteenth century, other Slavic churches asserted their independence from Greek and Russian rule while still remaining in communion with the Ecumenical Patriarch.

The Russian Revolution of 1917 and the spread of Communism to Eastern Europe following the Second World War led the Eastern Orthodox churches in Poland, Finland, Estonia, and Latvia to assert their independence. The Orthodox Church managed to survive Communist rule despite persecution. After World War II, Estonia and Latvia were reintegrated into the Russian Orthodox Church.

Nearly all European and Asiatic bodies of this ancient church have established dioceses in the United States; some are governed by one of the five patriarchates, while others have declared themselves independent and self-governing (autocephalous). In the United States today, Albanian, Bulgarian, Greek, Romanian, Russian, Serbian, Ukrainian, Carpatho-Russian, and Syrian churches are under the supervision of bishops of their respective nationalities and usually are related to their respective mother churches in tradition and spirit, if not in administration. The patriarch of Moscow and of Alexandria each has jurisdiction over a few parishes. In recent years a number of churches of Protestant origin moved into the Orthodox orbit.

Beliefs and Practices. The Nicene Creed in its original form is central to the Orthodox faith in all its branches. It is recited whenever the Divine Liturgy is celebrated and is the heart of Orthodox theology and mysticism. For the Eastern churches faith is expressed more fully in liturgy than in a doctrinal statement.

It is the long tradition of the church, not the pronouncements of individual theologians or canon law, that defines Orthodoxy. This tradition includes the decisions of the seven Ecumenical Councils as well as the tradition of the Divine Liturgy itself. Many of the doctrines and practices of the Roman Catholic and Protestant churches are rejected as inappropriate innovations. For instance, the dogma of the pope as the sole "vicar of Christ on earth" is rejected, together with that of papal infallibility. Members of Orthodox churches honor the Virgin Mary as *theotokos* ("the bearer of God") but do not subscribe to the dogmas of the Immaculate Conception and the assumption. They show reverence to the cross, the saints, and nine orders of angels but reject the teaching of the treasury of merits of the saints and the doctrine of indulgences. Purgatory is denied, but prayers are offered for the dead. It is believed that the dead can and do pray for those on earth. Both faith and works are considered necessary for salvation.

Icons (consecrated pictures) of revered persons and events are central to Orthodox devotion. Orthodox Christians hold that since God became incarnate in Christ, God's human nature may be depicted in a sacred image. Refusal to venerate an icon is seen as denying the concrete reality of the Incarnation; however, the Orthodox reject three-dimensional statues as being too close to "graven images" forbidden in Scripture.

The mysteries, which are called sacraments in the Western church, are central in Orthodox life. These are physical items or actions that communicate spiritual reality. The seven that are definitive in the Roman Catholic Church (baptism, confirmation, the Eucharist, penance, extreme unction, holy orders, and matrimony) are important in the Orthodox tradition as well, but there is little disposition to restrict the number of mysteries formally to seven. Other rites have a sacramental character. In fact, for the Orthodox, worship itself is a mystery or sacrament. For some Orthodox theologians and mystics, even creation is a sacrament since creation communicates the presence of God to all people.

The Holy Eucharist, or Communion, is the "mystery of mysteries." It is the chief service on all Sundays and holy days, and it is treated with great reverence. All Orthodox churches teach that the bread and wine are the body and blood of

Christ, but this is not described as transubstantiation. Mysteries cannot be defined by human intellect.

Polity. The government of all Orthodox churches is episcopal and hierarchical to a degree. There is usually a synod of bishops over which an elected archbishop, metropolitan, or patriarch presides. In America each jurisdiction is incorporated, with a church assembly of bishops, clergy, and laity. The three orders of ministry are deacons (who assist in parish work and in administering the sacraments), priests, and bishops. Deacons and priests may be either secular or monastic. Candidates for the diaconate and priesthood may marry before ordination but are forbidden to marry thereafter. Bishops are chosen from members of the monastic communities and, therefore, are under lifelong vows of poverty, chastity, and obedience.

The history of the Orthodox in North America is primarily the story of immigration and ethnic identity. The church has been a way for immigrants to keep a connection with their homeland, their language, and their customs. Membership statistics are confusing and often unreliable, since membership is based on baptismal records rather than communicant status, but there are at least three and a half million Orthodox in the United States, and the number is probably growing.

After a century or so of "creeping disunity" within Orthodoxy, during the period of heavy immigration and the formation of various Orthodox communities of faith, there have been movements toward closer cooperation. One such movement was the organization in 1960 of the Standing Conference of Canonical Orthodox Bishops in the Americas, which is composed of nine jurisdictions that represent the majority of the Orthodox in North America. Another was the formation of two pan-Orthodox seminaries.

There are a number of so-called Orthodox churches in the United States that are not recognized as canonically "Orthodox." These irregular Eastern churches might be called autogenic, or self-starting, but they are not in canonical relationship with the Patriarch of Constantinople and with one another. These autogenic churches are to be distinguished from the ancient non-Chalcedonian Orthodox Churches, such as the Coptic Church.

Suggestions for further reading:

Constantelos, Demetrios J. *Understanding the Greek Orthodox Church: Its Faith, History, and Life.* Brookline, Mass.: Hellenic College Press, 1998.

Erickson, John H. *Orthodox Christians in America.* New York: Oxford University Press, 1999.

Fitzgerald, Thomas E. *The Orthodox Church.* Westport, Conn.: Greenwood Press, 1999.

Meyendorff, John. *The Orthodox Church.* Crestwood, New York: St. Vladimir's Seminary Press, 1981.

Ware, Kallistos T. *The Orthodox Way.* Crestwood, New York: St. Vladimir's Seminary Press, 1995.

AFRICAN ORTHODOX CHURCH

Founded: 1921
Membership: est. 5,000 (1999)

This body is not in communion with Orthodox churches generally, but it claims to be in apostolic succession through the West Syrian Church of Antioch. It was established in 1921 by George Alexander McGuire (1866–1934), who was an immigrant to the United States from Antigua. McGuire had served as a priest in the Protestant Episcopal Church but left that body because of racial prejudice. This quest for equality led him to Marcus Garvey's (1887–1940) Universal Negro Improvement Association. Once McGuire founded the African Orthodox Church, Garvey used his periodical, entitled *The Negro World*, to disseminate news about the denomination throughout Africa. The periodical also carried the story of McGuire's consecration by a white bishop named Joseph Rene Vilatte (1854–1929). In 1924, the church was established in South Africa, where it became a potent force among the black population.

The church puts strong emphasis on the apostolic succession and historic sacraments and rituals; it celebrates the seven sacraments of baptism, confirmation, Eucharist, penance, extreme unction, holy orders, and matrimony. Its worship is a blend of Western and Eastern liturgy, creeds, and symbols, though the liturgy is usually Western with a mingling of Anglican,* Greek, and Roman patterns. The common creeds, Athanasian, Nicene, and Apostles', are used. Bishops are in charge of dioceses, or jurisdictions, and groups of dioceses form a province, each led by an archbishop and a primate. The primate, in turn, presides over the provincial synod. At the head stands a primate archbishop metropolitan, a general overseer of all the work of the church, which now extends over the United States into Canada, Latin America, and South Africa.

For more information: netministries.org/see/churches.exe/ch26904
Headquarters: 122 West 129th Street, New York City, New York 1002

ALBANIAN ORTHODOX ARCHDIOCESE IN AMERICA

Founded: 1919
Membership: est. 40,000

The Albanian Orthodox Archdiocese in America has been part of the Orthodox Church of America* since 1971, but its bishops and clergy continue to minister to the special needs of the Albanian community. The history of the church in Albania is complex, filled with a series of persecutions and changes in the religious and political struggles of the Balkans. Christianized by both Latin and

Greek missionaries, Albania, as part of Illyricum, had both Latin- and Greek-rite Christians and was at various times under the authority of the patriarch of Constantinople and the pope. When the Turks conquered Albania in 1478–79, half of its people became Muslim. The Christian minority remained divided between Latin-rite Christians in the North and Greek-rite Christians in the South.

When Albania became an independent nation in the twentieth century, its people demanded a liturgy in their language rather than in Greek. They turned to the Russian Orthodox Church for assistance, and in 1908 the Russian Orthodox Church in America set up an Albanian diocese under an Albanian archimandrite-administrator, Father Theophan S. Noli (1880–1965), who translated the liturgy into Albanian.

With the outbreak of the Russian revolution, the ties with the Russian Church were severed, and Noli was consecrated the bishop in 1923 at the Korche Cathedral in Albania as the Archbishop and Metropolitan of Durres. In doing so, he became the first bishop of a completely independent Albanian Archdiocese, a "mother church" that, strangely enough, spread its influence back into Albania. Noli returned home to establish a metropolitan throne with its See in Boston. Because of the official closing of all religious institutions in Albania in 1967, communication between the American church and the Albanian church was not possible until the collapse of communism. Another body, the Albanian Orthodox Diocese of America, was established in 1950 under the authority of the Ecumenical Patriarchate of Constantinople. It has two parishes with about 2,510 members.

For more information: www.orthodoxalbania.org

Archdiocese Office, 523 East Broadway, South Boston, MA 02127

AMERICAN CARPATHO-RUSSIAN ORTHODOX CHURCH

Founded: 1938
Membership: 12,840 in 80 parishes (2008)

The Carpatho-Russian people derive their name from the Carpathian mountain region of eastern Europe, where they have resided for centuries. For many years the mother church endured strife between Orthodoxy and Roman Catholicism. Under political pressure in the seventeenth century, it became a Uniate* church, with Eastern rites and customs, but recognized the supremacy of the Roman Catholic pope.

The struggle to separate from Rome and become completely Eastern was transferred to North America when large numbers of members immigrated to the United States, especially to the coal-mining and industrial areas of the northeast. In 1891, Alexis Toth, a Carpatho-Russian Uniate priest, led his Minneapolis parish back to the Orthodox Church. Along with several other pastors and parishes they were absorbed into the Russian Orthodox Church in the United States

In 1938, a new American Carpatho-Russian Orthodox Greek Catholic diocese was established and canonized by Benjamin I, the ecumenical patriarch of Constantinople. Orestes P. Chornock (1883–1977) became its first bishop. Both the diocesan headquarters (Christ the Saviour Cathedral) and Christ the Saviour Seminary are located in Johnstown, Pennsylvania. The diocese maintains a youth camp, a retreat, and a conference center in Mercer, Pennsylvania.

For more information: www.acrod.org

Headquarters: 312 Garfield St., Johnstown, PA 15906

ANTIOCHIAN ORTHODOX CHRISTIAN ARCHDIOCESE OF NORTH AMERICA

Founded: 1975, with roots to 1895
Membership: est. 430,000 in 256 parishes (2007)

Antioch, in Syria, was one of the first cities to be evangelized by the apostles and its church was one of the most important ancient patriarchal Sees. The faithful managed to maintain the existence of the church through centuries of Muslim rule, even adopting Arabic as a liturgical language, but as the Ottomon Empire collapsed in the late nineteenth century, thousands of Antiochene Christians immigrated to North America. Their spiritual needs were first met through the Syro-Arabian Mission of the Russian Orthodox Church (now called the Orthodox Church in America*). In 1895, a Syrian Orthodox Benevolent Society was organized by Antiochian immigrants in New York City, with Dr. Ibrahim Arbeely, a prominent Damascene physician, serving as its first president.

Arbeely convinced Raphael Hawaweeny, a young Damascene clergyman serving as Professor of the Arabic Language at the Orthodox Theological Academy in Kazan, Russia, to come to New York to organize and pastor the first Arabic-speaking parish on the continent. Hawaweeny was consecrated as a bishop in New York in 1904, making him the first Orthodox bishop of any nationality to be consecrated in North America. He crisscrossed the United States and Canada, gathering the scattered immigrants into parish communities. He founded *al-Kalimat* (*The Word*) magazine in 1905, and published many liturgical books in Arabic for use in his parishes, in the Middle East, and in immigrant communities around the world.

The mission suffered because of the early death of Hawaweeny in 1915, the disruptions of the First World War, and the Russian Revolution. The Syro-Arabian Mission fell into divisiveness until 1975, when jurisdictional and administrative unity were restored with the merger of the Antiochian Orthodox Christian

Archdiocese of New York and the Antiochian Archdiocese of Toledo. The resulting Archdiocese is divided into four chancellories located in New Jersey, Ohio, Kansas, and California. The General Assembly, the largest legislative body of the Archdiocese, consists of all the pastors and representatives of every parish and mission. It meets in convention every other summer.

There are nearly four hundred priests and deacons who minister at the local level. Candidates for ordination complete an undergraduate program and then receive their theological education at either St. Vladimir's Orthodox Theological Seminary in New York or St. John of Damascus Orthodox Theological Academy near Tripoli, Lebanon. Their program is augmented by specialized courses offered annually by the Antiochian House of Studies, held for two weeks at the Heritage and Learning Center in Ligonier, Pennsylvania. Twenty-four established departments and commissions deal with specific needs of the Archdiocese, such as communications, translations, clergy education, and parish development.

A pioneer in the use of the English language in the Orthodox churches since the 1930s, the church has translated and published liturgical and devotional works into English. The Antiochian Village, a 280-acre property located in southwestern Pennsylvania, serves as a retreat center and popular summer camp that attracts children and young adults from throughout North America. The St. John of Damascus Sacred Art Academy is also headquartered at the Village.

For more information: www.antiochian.org

Headquarters: P.O. Box 5238, Englewood, NJ 07631

APOSTOLIC CATHOLIC ASSYRIAN CHURCH OF THE EAST, NORTH AMERICAN DIOCESE

Founded: ca. 35 CE
Membership: 35,118, 19 parishes (2000)

This church claims that it was founded by the Apostle Thomas shortly after the resurrection of Jesus, and it claims a close connection to the apostles Thaddaeus and Bartholomew, as well. Saints Mari and Addai were key figures in the founding and spreading of this church in the Persian Empire, and one of its great scholars was Theodore of Mopsuestia, who was head of the school of Antioch in the fourth century. The church sent the first Christian missionaries to India, and it has a long relationship to the Syrian Orthodox community in India. This was the first church to establish Christianity in China, during the Tang dynasty (seventh and eighth century), especially in the city of Xian, but the Mongol invasions of the thirteenth century decimated the church. The Nicene Creed is central to this church's liturgy and theology.

Erroneously called the Nestorian Church, the Assyrian Church of the East rejected the Council of Ephesus and the monophysite theology of Cyril of Alexandria. The church insists that Christ had two natures (human and divine) in one person. It rejects the phrase *Theotokos* or "Mother of God" for the Virgin Mary. Instead, they pray to the "Ever Virgin Blessed Mary Mother of Christ" or *Christotokos*. During the Nestorian controversy, the Persian emperor gave refuge to Nestorius and others condemned by the Patriarch of Constantinople. The school of Edessa was moved to Nisibis in Persia.

In the nineteenth and twentieth centuries the church suffered a schism between patriarchs and was persecuted for supporting the British during the two world wars. The current Catholicos Patriarch, Mar Dinkha IV, resides in Baghdad, Iraq. The church has three dioceses in the United States: Eastern, Western, and California. With the invasion of Iraq, thousands of Iraqi Christians have sought refuge in the United States, many of them members of this church.

The church's worship is similar to other Eastern churches, but the liturgy is based on the ancient Liturgy of Saints Mari and Addai. The cross is particularly important to the Assyrian Church, and making the sign of the cross is seen as a sacrament.

For more information: www.cired.org

Media Contact: 7201 N. Ashland, Chicago, IL 60626

APOSTOLIC EPISCOPAL CHURCH

Founded: 1980s
Membership: est. 12,000 in 200 parishes (2006)

The Apostolic Episcopal Church is one of the many bodies that separated from the Episcopal Church* because of changes in the 1928 *Book of Common Prayer* and the admission of women to the ordained ministry. Like many of the Continuing Churches,* the Apostolic Episcopal Church moved more toward Eastern Orthodoxy than toward Roman Catholicism because of the Orthodox Church's policy of autocephalous national bodies. In 2000 the AEC signed concordats with several Orthodox bodies in the United States and became a Western Rite Orthodox Church under terms first established by the Holy Synod of St. Petersburg in 1905.

For more information: http://bertilpersson.com/

Headquarters: 8046 234 St., Queens, NY 11427-2116

ARMENIAN APOSTOLIC CHURCH OF AMERICA
ARMENIAN APOSTOLIC, DIOCESE OF AMERICA

Founded: 301; came to the United States in 1887
Membership: est. 1,010,000 in 108 parishes (2007)

Armenia is generally recognized as the first nation to become Christian when Christianity became the state religion in 301. Tradition holds that the apostles Thaddeus and Bartholomew first brought the message of Christ to Armenia. Saint Gregory the Illuminator became the first head of the national church in 314 and was given the title Patriarch Catholicos of All Armenians. A translation of the scriptures by St. Sahag and St. Mesrob and their students in the early part of the fifth century is accepted as the authoritative Armenian version of the Bible. The translators created an Armenian alphabet in order to give the Armenians the scriptures in their own language.

The Armenian Church administers seven sacraments: baptism, confirmation or chrismation, Eucharist, penance, matrimony, ordination, and extreme unction or order of the sick. Baptism, ordinarily of infants, is administered by immersion. Chrismation (anointing with oil) and communion follow immediately after baptism. The Eucharist is offered on Sundays and on special feast days of the church. At the conclusion of the Eucharist, fragments of thin unleavened bread, simply blessed, are distributed to those not receiving Communion.

The hierarchical organization of the Armenian Church consists of the Catholicos, the supreme head of the church, who resides in the ancient city of Etchmiadzin, Armenia, and the Catholicate of Cilicia, located in Antelias, Lebanon. The two patriarchates are Jerusalem and Constantinople. There are three major orders of clergy, according to the tradition of all ancient churches: deacon, priest, and bishop. Parish priests are ordinarily chosen from among married men, but bishops are chosen from among the celibate clergy. Widowed priests may be promoted to the episcopate. Clergy are trained in seminaries attached to Etchmiadzin, Jerusalem, and Antelias.

One of the most important aspects of the Armenian Church administration is its conciliar system. The administrative, doctrinal, liturgical, and canonical norms are set and approved by a council through a participatory decision-making process. The Council of Bishops (or the Synod) is the highest religious authority in the church.

The Armenian Church has sustained its people throughout a history marked by tragedy. It suffered in the conflict between the Byzantine Empire and Persia and sustained persecutions by the Turks, culminating in the genocide of 1915. Thousands of Armenians escaped to North America before World War I, but the bulk of emigration occurred after the war. The first Armenian Church in the United States was established in Worchester, Massachusetts, in 1891. The Armenian

56

Diocese of America was organized in 1898, headed by a primate appointed by the Mother See of Holy Etchmiadzin in Armenia, under whose jurisdiction the diocese functioned.

In 1933 a dispute over matters related to the church in Soviet Armenia led to a split in the church in the United States. One group of churches, the Armenian Apostolic Church of America, chose to remain independent until 1957, when these churches placed themselves under the jurisdiction of the Holy See of Cilicia in Antelias. The other group, the Armenian Church of America, remained within the jurisdiction of the Mother See of Etchmiadzin. Dogma and liturgy were not affected by the division. Deacons, priests, bishops, and archbishops are ordained and elevated by the hierarchical authorities of the respective jurisdictions. The Armenian Church of America has seventy-two churches; the separated Apostolic Church has thirty-six.

The Armenian Church is in communion with the Oriental Orthodox Churches. Also known as Monophysites ("one nature of Christ"), these are churches that did not ascribe to the doctrinal statements adopted at the Council of Chalcedon in 451 CE. It should be noted that the Armenian Church accepts the decisions of the first three ecumenical councils. It affirms the Christological formula of St. Cyril of Alexandria (d. 444), which asserts that divine and human were united in one incarnate nature in Christ. In 1990, the theologians and official representatives of both Eastern and Oriental Orthodox churches agreed in a formal statement that their theological understanding, especially their Christology, is "orthodox." The statement called for unity and communion among the Eastern and Oriental Orthodox churches.

For more information: www.armenianprelacy.org

Headquarters: 138 E. 39th Street, New York, NY 10016-4885

BULGARIAN EASTERN ORTHODOX CHURCH

Founded: 1938
Membership: est. 70,000 in 23 parishes (1990)

Christianity was introduced to the Bulgar peoples in the ninth century during the reign of Tsar Boris. The church is similar to other Orthodox churches in theology and worship. For centuries, the church struggled for independence from Constantinople, an independence won for brief periods. There was a schism between the Bulgarians and the Ecumenical Patriarch until the end of World War II. After the war, Bishop Boris was assassinated by the Communists and other church leaders were imprisoned. Eventually the church came to an accord with the government and was allowed to function. With the collapse of Communism in 1989, the church has been free to operate in Bulgaria.

Before the outbreak of the Macedonian revolution in 1903, very few Bulgarians emigrated to the United States. In 1940 there were still only about sixty thousand residents. They brought with them memories of the church's long struggle for independence from Constantinople. The first Bulgarian Orthodox Church in the United States was built in Madison, Illinois, in 1907. In 1922 the Bulgarian Orthodox Mission of the Holy Synod of Bulgaria began attempts to organize the Bulgars. It established a bishopric in 1938.

Attached directly to the Holy Synod of Bulgaria, the membership of this church is made up of descendants of immigrants from Bulgaria, Macedonia, Thrace, Dobruja, and other parts of the Balkan Peninsula. Services are in the Bulgarian and English languages, and doctrine is in accord with that of other Eastern Orthodox churches. The American church is part of a larger diocese that includes Canada and Australia.

For more information: www.bulgariandiocese.org/

Headquarters: Diocese of the USA, Canada and Australia, 550-A West 50th Street, New York, NY 10019

COPTIC ORTHODOX CHURCH

Founded: 60 CE, first American diocese founded in 1993
Membership: est. 300,000 in 100 parishes (2002)

The Coptic Church is one of the oldest Christian churches in the world, tracing its origins to the time of the apostle Mark. The word Coptic refers to both the native people and the language of Egypt before the Arab conquest in the seventh century. Alexandria in Egypt was one of the original patriarchal sees, and it produced some of the most significant theologians and bishops of early Christianity. Centuries later the works of Origen, Clement, Athanasius, and Cyril are still studied by Orthodox, Catholic, and Protestant theologians. Egyptian or Alexandrian theology was instrumental in the formation of the Nicene Creed recited weekly throughout the Christian world.

The hierarchy of the Egyptian church in Alexandria was primarily Greek, but by the year 500 Christianity had spread to the native peoples up the Nile. Coptic missionaries brought Christianity to Nubia and the Sudan over a thousand years before the great period of Protestant missions to the tribes of Africa. The story of Mary and Joseph's flight into Egypt to escape Pharaoh captured the popular imagination, and an elaborate pilgrimage route developed so worshipers could honor Jesus and the Blessed Virgin. Pagan shrines were converted to Christian worship, and the Copts developed a distinctive liturgical calendar based on the ancient Egyptian calendar.

The greatest contribution of the Egyptian church to Christianity came out of the desert. Two hundred years after Christianity was brought to Egypt, there were a few devout souls who felt that the urban churches were too comfortable with the sensuous culture of the pagan world. One of these was a wealthy man named Anthony who heard Jesus' call to "sell your possessions and give to the poor" (Matthew 19:21). He did so and retreated in the desert to the mountains where he lived alone in a cave. Anthony is reputed to be the first such monk (from the Greek word for solitary), and his story inspired hundreds of men and women to do likewise. Monasticism and its spirituality gradually spread to the whole Christian world and was the mainstay of Christianity until the Protestant Reformation. The desert monasteries provided much of the stories of saints and miracles that nourish the Coptic faithful today.

The Coptic Church was caught up in the political struggles of the Byzantine Empire in the fifth century, and many of the bishops believed that the Council of Chalcedon was more about imperial politics than theology. The iconography, liturgy, veneration of relics, and theology of the Coptic Church is very similar to other Orthodox churches, but the Coptic Church emphasizes the unity of Jesus Christ as God and human.

The Egyptian church split between the Greek hierarchy in Alexandria (Greek Orthodox) and the Coptic-speaking church of the people who were persecuted by the Empire, despite their similarities. The monastic caves became the centers of the opposition movement. The oppression of the native population was so severe that many people actually supported the Arabic conquerors in the seventh century since they broke the yoke of Constantinople. Initially the Muslim rulers were tolerant of Coptic Christianity, but the church faced many obstacles, including the prohibition of converting Muslims. At times, though, persecution could be severe; the age of martyrs in Coptic Christianity lasted longer than in other churches.

Coptic Christianity came to America with Egyptian immigration in the twentieth century. The American Coptic Church is part of the world-wide network of Copts who continue to worship in the language of their ancestors and honor their saints and martyrs. Like most immigrant churches, the Coptic Church enjoys the freedom of worship and evangelism America offers while it tries to help its people negotiate the permissiveness of American culture. The church in America is closely connected to the world-wide Coptic Church led by Pope Shenouda III, the 117th Pope of Alexandria and the See of St. Mark. Dialogue with other Catholic and Orthodox churches has helped heal the old theological division over the nature of Christ.

For more information: www.coptic.net

Headquarters: P.O. Box 384, Cedar Grove, NJ 07009

GREEK ORTHODOX ARCHDIOCESE OF AMERICA

Founded: 1922
Membership: 1,500,000 in 560 parishes (2006)

The Greek Orthodox Church is one of the largest Orthodox bodies in the United States due to the massive immigration of Greeks to the United States between 1890 and 1929. Greece was one of the earliest and most vital centers of Christianity, but the capture of Constantinople by the Turks and the subjugation of the patriarch to Muslim rule was a severe blow to the Greek Orthodox Church. In the nineteenth century, the church in Greece established a Holy Synod independent from (but in communion with) the Ecumenical Patriarch. Orthodox priests were sent to the United States either by the Holy Synod of Greece or by the Ecumenical Patriarchate of Constantinople.

In 1864, the first Greek Orthodox Church in the United States was founded in New Orleans, Louisiana. By 1910 there were approximately thirty-five congregations in various parts of the country. A period of confusion existed from 1908 to 1922, during which time the jurisdiction of American churches shifted from the Ecumenical Patriarchate of Constantinople to the Holy Synod of Greece and back again. This was finally resolved with the Founding Tome of 1922, which established the Greek Orthodox Archdiocese of North and South America.

Archbishop Athenagoras Spyrou of Corfu was appointed to head the Greek Church in America in 1931, and under his leadership the church increased to 286 parishes. In 1948, Athenagoras was elected Patriarch of Constantinople and was succeeded by Archbishop Michael Constantinides of Corinth, who was enthroned in the New York Cathedral of the Holy Trinity. Since 1996, Archbishop Spyridon, appointed by Constantinople's Ecumenical Patriarch, has led the Greek Orthodox Archdiocese of North America. He oversees work in nine dioceses, each headed by a bishop. Worship, doctrine, and polity follow historical Orthodox patterns, with the service of worship being the center of congregational life. In the 1980s and 1990s the church began attracting Protestants and Catholics, some of whom felt their churches were too accommodating to modern culture, others who were attracted to the artistry and depth of Orthodox worship.

The church supports eighteen parochial schools; nine summer camps; a school for orphans and children from broken homes; Hellenic College and Holy Cross Greek Orthodox School of Theology, both in Brookline, Massachusetts; three homes for teenage boys; and a home for the aged. Other sources list the membership at around five hundred thousand.

For more information: www.goarch.org

Headquarters: 8-10 East 79th St., New York, NY 10021

HOLY EASTERN ORTHODOX CATHOLIC AND APOSTOLIC CHURCH IN NORTH AMERICA

Founded: 1927
Membership: statistics not available

The Holy Eastern Orthodox Catholic and Apostolic Church in North America is one of the bodies to come out of the Russian Orthodox Church (see "Orthodox Church in America"). It has six bishops and claims to be the first Orthodox church established in North America specifically to serve English-speaking worshipers. The church is not in communion with other Orthodox bodies, but it identifies itself as Orthodox. The church relies on the Holy Scriptures, the Orthodox Canons and Traditions, and traditional Orthodox and Catholic liturgies. The church has adopted more of the Western (Catholic) rite, and has permission to serve Holy Communion to Catholic worshipers. Present in twelve states, the church has one religious order, the Society of Clerks Secular of Saint Basil, which was founded by Archbishop Ofiesh and Bishop Ignatius. In 2003 Archbishop Nikon became the first Patriarch of the church.

For more information: www.theocacna.org

Contact: Abp. Leland, Vicar of the Eastern United States, 722 Cedar Point Blvd. #1, Cedar Point, N.C. 28584

MALANKARA ORTHODOX SYRIAN CHURCH AND MAR THOMA ORTHODOX SYRIAN CHURCH (INDIAN ORTHODOX)

Founded: 52 in India; in the United States 1978 (Malankara); 1988 (Mar Thoma)
Membership: est. 70,000 in 154 parishes (2006)

These are the two major bodies of independent Indian Christian churches in the United States. Both bodies claim descent from Thomas the apostle, who legend says went to India as an evangelist after the resurrection of Christ. The Malankara church was named for a town where Thomas is believed to have arrived in India in 52 CE. It uses the liturgy, calendar, language, and traditions of the Syrian Orthodox Church.

The church in India is indeed ancient and historically had close ties to the Syriac church in Persia (See "Apostolic Catholic Assyrian Church of the East"), which was rooted in the theological tradition of Antioch and rejected the agreement of Chalcedon. The Persian/Syrian church is often called "Nestorian" because of its adherence to the doctrine attributed to the fifth century theologian Nestorius of

Antioch that a distinction should be made between the divinity and humanity of Christ. This idea contrasted strongly with the Alexandrian theology (see "Coptic Orthodox") that Christ is a single person with a single nature ("monophysites"). Symbolic of the difference between this view and that of the Orthodox churches is that the Syrians and Indians never refer to Mary as "the mother of God." Instead, they call her "mother of Christ" (Christotokos). Missionaries from Persia established the church in India, and the ancient Indian churches used Syriac rather than one of the Indian languages in worship.

In 1599, under the influence of Portuguese missionaries, most Malankara Christians, who lived in southwest India, rejected Nestorianism. Many united with Rome as a Uniate* church. Others, however, turned to the Syrian Orthodox Church for guidance. The Mar Thoma Church was established to preserve the native Indian church from forced Latinization by the Portuguese colonizers of the Malankara region. It is in communion with the Syrian Orthodox Church of Antioch and uses the Orthodox liturgy and calendar. In the nineteenth century, Christianity in India experienced further fracture during the period of British rule as Anglican and Protestant missionaries poured into India.

The American Diocese of the Malankara Syrian Orthodox Church was established in 1978 to serve Indian immigrants to the United States and their children. It includes about thirty thousand members in eighty parishes. The Mar Thoma Church is independent and is in communion with the Anglican Church. The American diocese was organized in 1988 to serve members in the immigrant community. It has about twenty-five thousand members in seventy parishes.

For more information: http://malankaraorthodoxchurch.in; http://marthomachurch.org/

Headquarters: Malankara Diocesan Center, 80-34 Commonwealth Boulevard, Bellerose, NY 11426; Sinai Mar Thoma Center, 2320 S. Merrick Ave., Merrick, NY 11566

ORTHODOX CHURCH IN AMERICA
(RUSSIAN ORTHODOX)

Founded: 1970, with roots to 1794
Membership: est. 900,000 in 725 parishes (2002)

The Orthodox faith came to the New World shortly after the American Revolution by way of Alaska rather than from the East. This was because Alaska was part of Russia until 1867. Eight Russian Orthodox monks entered Alaska in 1794 and established headquarters at Kodiak. Orthodox monks and bishops created an alphabet and printed a grammar in the Aleutian language; translated portions of the Bible; and built a cathedral at Sitka.

Russia itself joined the Orthodox fold with the baptism of Grand Prince Vladimir of Kiev in 988 CE. The church was ruled at first by metropolitans appointed or approved by the Patriarch of Constantinople, but eventually an independent patriarchate was established in Moscow, which came to be regarded by Slavs as the "Third Rome." Russian Orthodoxy was modeled on the church in Constantinople, but over the centuries it developed distinctive qualities. Russian iconography is greatly valued by art collectors, but it is valued even higher by the faithful for whom the saints provide a connection to God and history. As with many churches, Russian Orthodoxy is closely connected with Russian patriotism, and many saints are national heroes. For centuries the Russian Church was governed by a Holy Synod rather than a patriarch.

Early in the nineteenth century, a chapel was built at a Russian trading post near present-day San Francisco. The Episcopal See was transferred to that city in 1872, but moved to New York City in 1905 as waves of immigration brought thousands of Slavs to the eastern states. For many years, the Russian hierarchy in the United States cared for immigrants from other Orthodox countries, such as Serbia, Syria, and Bulgaria. Many Eastern-rite Catholics from the old Austro-Hungarian Empire also transferred to the jurisdiction of the Russian Orthodox Church rather than accept the administration of Irish and Italian Catholic bishops.

Bishop Tikhon, who later became Patriarch of the Russian Church, founded the first Russian Orthodox Theological Seminary in Minneapolis, Minnesota, in 1905. Bishop Tikhon also transferred the Episcopal See and its Ecclesiastical Consistory from San Francisco to New York City, where the Russian Orthodox headquarters for this hemisphere are still located. Under Tikhon, St. Nicholas Cathedral in New York was built in 1901. In 1919 the Russian Church in America held its first Sobor, or general council, at Pittsburgh.

The history of the church in the United States has been tied to political events in Russia. In 1917 the Bolsheviks took over the government of Russia and instituted restrictive religious policies. The patriarch and the Holy Synod resisted, but the government found some priests and bishops ready to support the new regime. These officials held an assembly that deposed the patriarch, endorsed communism, and declared itself the governing body of the Russian church.

Calling itself the Renovated, or Living, Church, this group changed the ancient disciplinary rules and instituted liturgical reforms. With the support of Soviet authorities, who hoped thus to divide and weaken the church, that body held control for several years but was never recognized by the great majority of clergy or people. The government considered opposition to the Living Church a civil offense and, on this basis, banished thousands of bishops, clergy, monks, and laypersons to labor camps.

The Living Church faction in Russia, supported by the communist government, sent an emissary to secure control of Russian Orthodox Church property in the United States; through action in the civil courts, it gained possession of the cathedral in New York City. In 1924, an assembly of the Diocese of North America, in an attempt to prevent further seizures, declared that, on a temporary basis, it was administratively, legislatively, and jurisdictionally independent of the church in Russia. But this independence was not recognized by the Patriarchate of Moscow or by the Russian Orthodox Church Outside Russia, headquartered at that time in the former Yugoslavia.

In 1927 the Soviet government prevailed upon Metropolitan Sergius, the *locum tenens* (that is, temporary substitute) of the then-vacant patriarchal See, to submit the policy of the church totally to the Soviet regime. Stalin engineered the meeting of a small group of bishops to elect Metropolitan Sergius as Patriarch of Moscow and All Russia. Sergius called upon his people to support the government in the defense of their country during World War II, and this marked a turning point in the Soviet policy toward the church. The Living Church was discarded, and the patriarch's authority was recognized by the state. Many surviving clergy and bishops who had been banished were permitted to return, and gradually the patriarchal administration became again the sole authority in the Orthodox Church of Russia.

Under the authority of the Ecumenical Patriarch, a body of Russian émigrés formed the Russian Orthodox Church Outside Russia in 1920. They hold that the Moscow Patriarchate forfeited its right to be considered a true Orthodox church because it adopted a position of submission to the atheistic Soviet regime, not only in regard to politics and external matters but also with respect to its internal policies and affairs. In 1950 this church came to the United States. It has about 175 parishes dedicated to the traditions of the pre-Soviet Russian church.

Despite the conflicts in the church in Russia, the main body of believers in the United States maintained their institutional life and worked to bring other Slavic peoples together into a vibrant Orthodox Church. On May 18, 1970, a delegation of hierarchs, clergy, and laity of the Russian Orthodox Metropolia in America, headed by Bishop Theodosius, went to Moscow to receive the Thomos of Authocephaly—the document of independence—from the head of the Russian Orthodox Church. Since that time, the Orthodox Church in America has been independent.

Relations between the Orthodox in the United States and Russia have improved greatly since the collapse of the Soviet Union and restoration of the authority of the church in Russia to govern its own affairs and doctrine. In recognition of this, one of the most venerated Russian icons, which had been smuggled to the United States for safe-keeping during the Soviet era, was returned to St. Petersburg in 2004. Throngs of the faithful greeted the icon as it made its procession through Russia before being enthroned in the cathedral.

From administrative offices in New York City, the primate of the Orthodox Church in America oversees the work of eleven dioceses, which are in turn headed by bishops. The primate and bishops make up the Holy Synod of Bishops, which is the highest decision making body in the church. Church ministry units include education and community life ministries, mission and stewardship ministries, pastoral life ministries, witness and communication ministries, and church order ministries. The church administers three theological seminaries: St. Tikhon's in Pennsylvania, St. Vladimir's in New York, and St. Herman's in Alaska. The church also operates several monasteries throughout the United States.

For more information: www.oca.org

Headquarters: P.O. Box 675, Syosset, NY 11701-0675

ROMANIAN ORTHODOX EPISCOPATE OF AMERICA

Founded: 1929
Membership: 10,635 in 64 parishes (2006)

Christianity came to Romania in the fourth century. Originally Western and Latin in orientation, the church there gradually came under the authority of Constantinople and adopted Greek liturgical practices and customs. In 1859, the church declared itself independent of Constantinople as a national church, a move that was officially acknowledged twenty-five years later. The church in the United States was organized at a congress convened in Detroit, Michigan, by clergy and lay representatives of Romanian Orthodox parishes in the United States and Canada. It remained under the canonical jurisdiction of the Romanian Orthodox Patriarchate in Bucharest until political conditions forced its separation. It is now a diocese under the autocephalous Orthodox Church in America.* The archbishop is a member of the Holy Synod of the Orthodox Church in America, and the diocese is recognized as an administratively self-governing body.

For more information: www.roea.org

Headquarters: 2535 Grey Tower Road, Jackson, MI 49201-9120

SERBIAN ORTHODOX CHURCH

Founded: 1921
Membership: 67,000 in 68 parishes (2005)

Saints Cyril (826–869) and Methodius (815–885) were sent by the Patriarch in Constantinople to strengthen and spread Christianity among the Slavic peoples. One of their great achievements was creating the first Slavic alphabet, which they used to translate the Orthodox liturgy and the Gospels into the old Slavonic language. Most famous for their work in Moravia (the Czech Republic) and Kiev, they were also instrumental in establishing Christianity among the Serbian people.

From the seventh century until the thirteenth, the church in Serbia was under the jurisdiction of the Patriarchate of Constantinople. It became the independent National Serbian Church in 1219 during the Western occupation of Constantinople. The church made notable contributions to art and architecture during the glory days of the medieval Serbian empire until the defeat by the Turks at Kosovo in 1389. The Ottoman Turks governed their Christian subjects in part through church officials, most notably the Ecumenical Patriarch in Constantinople (now Istanbul); therefore the Serbian Church, like other Orthodox churches, became a symbol of national identity as well as religious faith. It played an important part in the Serbian struggle for independence, which was won in the nineteenth century. In 1879 the church also achieved independence from the Patriarch of Constantinople following the freedom of the nation from Turkish control.

Through the close of World War I, the ecclesiastical and political situation in the Balkans was turbulent and complicated. Attempts were made to unite several Orthodox groups into one church. The fruit of the effort came in 1920 when the union of five autonomous bodies was proclaimed. Metropolitan Dimitriji of Belgrade was appointed patriarch, uniting in himself the historic titles of Archbishop of Ipek, Metropolitan of Belgrade and Karlovci, and Patriarch of Serbs.

Serbian immigrants came to the United States more for political than economic reasons and began arriving in large numbers around 1890. They worshiped at first in Russian churches, accepting the ministrations of Russian priests and the supervision of Russian bishops. The Serbian Patriarchate of Yugoslavia approved the organization of the Diocese of the United States and Canada in 1921. In 1926, with thirty-five Serbian churches making up the American Diocese, Archimandrite Mardary Uskokovich was consecrated by Patriarch Dimitriji of Serbia as the first bishop of the Serbian Orthodox Church of America.

Today the Serbian Eastern Orthodox Church has two dioceses in North America: the New Gracanica Metropolinate Diocese of America and Canada, based in Libertyville, Illinois; and the Diocese of Western America, based in Alhambra, California. The cathedral of the Serbian Church, built and opened in 1945, is located in New York City. The extended conflict in the Balkans during the 1990s brought great distress to Serbs living in North America. The Serbian Eastern Orthodox Church played an important role in conveying information to Serbs in the United States and Canada and in offering them spiritual and psychological support. It also sought to present a comprehensive picture of Serbian life and culture to the American public.

For more information: www.serbianorthodoxchurch.org

Office of External Affairs: 2311 M St, NW (Suite 402) Washington, DC 20037

SYRIAN ORTHODOX CHURCH OF ANTIOCH
ARCHDIOCESE OF THE EASTERN UNITED STATES

Founded: 50, American Archdiocese est. 1957
Membership: est. 32,500 in 37 parishes (2008)

The Syrian Orthodox Church dates back to the apostolic age. It was in Antioch that the followers of Jesus were first called Christian, and tradition holds that Peter established the first patriarchate in Antioch. The Syrian Orthodox use the ancient liturgy of St. James of Jerusalem in worship. The Syriac Scripture is one of the oldest translations of the Bible and continues to be vital for Syrian Christianity. The Syrian Orthodox Church continues to have its patriarchal See in Damascus. The Syrian Orthodox use a number of ancient liturgies in worship, the principal being that of St. James. The official liturgical language remains classical Syriac.

Syriac Christianity was divided during the Nestorian controversy. The followers of Nestorius, who taught that there were two separate persons in the incarnate Christ, one divine and one human, were persecuted in Syria and found refuge in Persia. The Syrian Orthodox Church has always held to the one-nature position of St. Cyril of Alexandria and professes the faith of the first three ecumenical councils. When the Council of Chalcedon adopted a formula that seemed to endorse Nestorius's ideas, the Syrian Orthodox refused to comply with the Patriarch of Constantinople. The Syrian Orthodox experienced persecution under the Byzantine Empire, but found a degree of toleration under Muslim rule until the Mongol invasions in the thirteenth century.

Syrians were few in number in the United States until the turn of the twentieth century. Syrian Orthodox silk weavers from Diyarbakir, Turkey, settled in New Jersey, a major area of the silk industry. Families from Harput, Turkey, were drawn to Massachusetts. The first priest, the Very Rev. Hanna Koorie, arrived in 1907; their first patriarchal vicar, Archbishop Mar Athanasius Y. Samuel, was appointed on May 13, 1952. On November 15, 1957, Patriarch Ignatius Yacoub III set his seal upon the document officially establishing the Archdiocese of the Syrian Orthodox Church in the United States and Canada. The next year, a cathedral in the name of St. Mark was consecrated in Hackensack, New Jersey. It was relocated in 1994 to a new complex in Teaneck, New Jersey.

From the 1960s through the 1980s, new Syrian Orthodox parishes were established throughout North America. Following the death of Archbishop Samuel in 1995, the Holy Synod of the Syrian Orthodox Church of Antioch divided the North American Archdiocese into three separate Patriarchal Vicariates: the Syrian Orthodox Archdiocese for the Eastern United States under His Eminence Mor Cyril Aphrem Karim; the Syrian Orthodox Archdiocese of Los Angeles and Environs under His Eminence Mor Clemis Eugene Kaplan; and the Syrian Orthodox

Archdiocese of Canada under His Eminence Mor Timotheos Aphrem Aboodi, who was succeeded by His Eminence Mor Athanasius Elia Bahi.

For more information: www.syrianorthodoxchurch.org

Headquarters: Archdiocese for Eastern USA, 260 Elm Ave., Teaneck, NJ 07666

UKRAINIAN ORTHODOX CHURCH OF THE U.S.A.

Founded: 1924
Membership: 50,000 in 118 parishes (2006)

Around the year 862, the first Orthodox Christian community was founded on the outskirts of Kyyiv (Kiev), during the reign of two princes, Askold and Dyr. Disciples of Saints Cyril and Methodius brought Slavonic liturgies and Scriptures to Kiev, bringing both a new faith and a written language to the Slavic people there. Instrumental in making Orthodox Christianity known in Rus-Ukraine was the Kyyivian Princess Olha, who was baptized in 975 and is the grandmother of St. Volodymyr (Vladimir) the Great. After considerable reflection and investigation, Volodymyr (whose baptismal name is Basil) proclaimed Orthodox Christianity the official faith of his kingdom of Rus-Ukraine in 988. Thus the introduction of Christianity to Russia came through the Ukraine.

In 1686 the Ukrainian church was forced to submit to the Patriarchate of Moscow, but after the 1917 Bolshevik revolution, the Ukrainian Orthodox Church sundered jurisdictional ties with Moscow and declared independence in 1921. The June 5, 1990, Sobor (council) of the Ukrainian Autocephalous Orthodox Church in newly independent Ukraine established its own patriarchate and elected as its first patriarch Metropolitan Mstyslav, at that time primate of the Ukrainian Orthodox Church of the U.S.A.

The Ukrainian Orthodox Church of the U.S.A. was established in 1924, when its first bishop, Metropolitan Ioan (John) Teodorovych, arrived from the Ukraine. He served as leader of the church until his death in 1971. Mstyslav followed him as Metropolitan and served from 1971 until his death in 1993, at age 95. In 1996 the church united with the former Ukrainian Orthodox Church of America.

The church has congregations in twenty-five states; the heaviest concentration of congregations is in the New York-New Jersey-Pennsylvania area. The church maintains St. Andrew Center, a Ukrainian cultural center, in South Bound Brook, New Jersey. The center is home to St. Andrew Memorial Church, a monument to Ukrainian Cossak Baroque architecture, and to St. Sophia Seminary.

For more information: www.uocofusa.org

Headquarters: 135 Davidson Ave., Somerset, NJ 08873

Catholic Churches

Christians in many different churches profess their faith in "the one, holy, catholic church" using the words of the Apostles' Creed. "Catholic" in this sense does not necessarily refer to a particular religious institution but to the idea of the universality of the church. The Catholic Church is the church that exists around the world and through the ages. Obviously, though, religious institutions will have differing understandings about the institutional expression of that catholicity. Those bodies that hold most dearly to a view of the church that is universal in time and space are included in this section. Although for most of its cultural and political history the United States has been dominated by Protestants, it is important to remember that Roman Catholicism came to the New World with Christopher Columbus. Today, the Roman Catholic Church is by far the largest religious organization in America. Though there are thousands of Protestant denominations, it is important to remember that most of the world's Christians are in the Roman Catholic Church.

Catholic churches see themselves in unbroken continuity with the institutional expression of Christian faith in the West since the days of the apostles. They differ markedly from Restorationist bodies (see CHRISTIAN and RESTORATIONIST CHURCHES), for example, which view most of Western history as a decline and fall of the church and thus sought to restore the New Testament church. For Catholics, the Holy Spirit continued to work through historical development in order to bring the faith to its richest and fullest expression. In particular, the writings of the Church Fathers (e.g., Jerome [c. 345–c. 420] and Augustine [354–430]) instruct the faithful in how to understand the Scripture and live a Christian life. It was during the Patristic Age (from the death of the Apostles to the close of the eighth century) that much Catholic doctrine, polity, and devotion were established.

Catholic History. The history of the Catholic Church for a thousand years is basically the history of Christianity. There is not enough space in this volume to give a full account of that history, but it should be noted that during the first five centuries of Christianity there were numerous struggles over the nature of Christian doctrine and ecclesiastical authority. Gradually the lines of orthodoxy were established through the authority of creeds, especially the Nicene Creed, and the episcopacy (bishops, archbishops, and patriarchs). During this process of development there were no fundamental divisions between Eastern and Western Christianity.

The East and the West did develop some distinctive liturgical and administrative practices, due in part to the greater sophistication of Byzantine (Eastern) culture. Most important, the Eastern bishops and theologians tended to define the church in terms of orthodox belief and practice (see ORTHODOX AND

ORIENTAL ORTHODOX CHURCHES), while in the West institutional allegiance became paramount, particularly during the rising social chaos of the early Middle Ages.

The church in the West gained secular authority and power when it emerged as the only body strong enough to provide stable government as Germanic ("barbarian") tribes migrated in large numbers into France and Italy. One of the most significant events in this period was the sack of Rome by the Vandals in 410 CE. Ravaged first by Goths, Vandals, and Franks then by Saxons, Danes, Alemanni, Lombards, and Burgundians, Western Europe found its only steadying hand in the Roman church. The church in the West was seen as a unifying force in the chaos of society, and thus the word *catholic* ("universal") was increasingly applied to those who were loyal to the bishop of Rome.

The first mention of the term *catholic* was made by Ignatius of Antioch in about 110–115 CE, but it was the theologian Augustine in the fifth century who provided the theological and philosophical structure that gave the papacy its justification and defense. In the early church the bishop of Rome was one of five patriarchs, and he had supreme authority over the church in the West. The general consensus in Western Christianity was that there should be a single ecclesiastical institution with a single head who served as Christ's representative in the church. The bishop of Rome was seen as the Vicar of Christ. To be catholic, in this sense, was to be under the authority of the Vicar of Christ who governed in Rome.

Until 1054 the bishop of Rome and the bishop of Constantinople served as the heads of the Western and Eastern churches, respectively, without one asserting absolute authority over the other, but in that year each bishop formally excommunicated the other. Relations between East and West were strained further when the Fourth Crusade conquered Constantinople instead of Jerusalem in 1204. The Crusaders of Western Europe looted the city and forced the patriarch to submit to the pope. Eventually, the emperor and patriarch regained control, but the break between East and West was complete.

The Roman Catholic Church was the most significant institution in Western society for most of the Middle Ages. It preserved and spread Christianity during the days of barbarian invasion; preserved and spread classical education through monasteries, convents, cathedral schools, and universities; stabilized feudal society; promoted architectural and artistic achievements; and established the basis for the Western legal system. The great cathedrals of Europe are an enduring testimony to the beauty and grandeur of medieval Catholicism.

For more than three hundred years, the church launched military campaigns, or crusades, against Muslims in the Middle East. Schisms, heresies, and divisions began appearing in the late Middle Ages (see AMERICAN WALDENSIAN SOCIETY), and the church established Inquisitions to enforce orthodox teaching and church authority. New religious orders, most notably the Dominicans,

Franciscans, and Templars, were established to deal with heresy and the perceived threat of Islam. In 1415 the Council of Constance executed the theologian John Hus, igniting the Hussite revolution in Central Europe (see MORAVIAN CHURCH (UNITAS FRATRUM)).

It was the Protestant Reformation, ignited by Martin Luther (1483–1546), that permanently splintered Western Christianity. Roman Catholic scholars acknowledge that there were corrupt individuals within the church and that reform was necessary. Indeed, reform was underway even before the Reformation. Erasmus (1469–1536), Thomas More (d. 1535), Savonarola (1452–98), and others wrote and preached against the corruption and worldliness of leaders and laypeople, but they tried to stay in the church.

Although the Catholic Church rejected most of the proposals of the Protestant reformers, the Reformation encouraged the Roman Church to reform and reorganize itself. Indeed, some historians, Catholic and Protestant alike, would date the founding of the modern Roman Catholic Church as a self-conscious and distinctive religious body to the great Council of Trent (1545–1563), where many Catholic doctrines were officially defined for the first time and where the current ecclesiastical structure was codified. The Tridentine (or post-Council of Trent) church was in many ways a stronger and more effective institution than the Renaissance church. The newly established Society of Jesus (Jesuits) led the way in winning back areas lost to Protestantism and, along with the Franciscans, in courageously bringing Christianity to the recently discovered lands east and west of Europe. Thanks, in part, to the success of European colonialism, by 1700 the Catholic Church was established across the globe. For a brief time, it appeared that even China might become Christian.

Having reformed the papacy of many of the abuses that had fueled the Reformation, the Tridentine church increasingly looked to the papacy as the guarantor of Catholic unity and continuity. As the Enlightenment took hold in Europe in the eighteenth century and revolutions convulsed the European kingdoms in the nineteenth, Catholic bishops and theologians held up the Roman pontiff as the symbol of stability, authority, and order in church and society.

This led to the declaration of papal infallibility by the First Vatican Council in 1870, a move that inspired a number of Catholics, calling themselves Old Catholics,* to separate from the Roman Catholic Church. These churches, which seek to be true to the historic Catholic Church without endorsing papacy supremacy, are discussed in this section of the *Handbook*. Also, within the nineteenth-century Anglican* church, the Oxford Movement stressed the idea that the Church of England was part of the Catholic rather than the Protestant tradition. This lead to the creation of a variety of small Anglo-Catholic bodies. Ecumenical dialogue between Anglicans and Catholics in the twentieth century brought the two bodies very close to reunion, but Catholics rejected the ordination of women and homosexuals in the Episcopal Church*.

Beliefs and Practices. The faith and doctrine of the Roman Catholic Church are founded upon what the First Vatican Council referred to as a "deposit of faith" given to it by Christ through the apostles and preserved by tradition. Thus, like other Catholic and Orthodox bodies, the church accepts the decisions of the first seven ecumenical councils; however, Roman Catholics view the later councils of the Western church, such as the Fourth Lateran Council (1215) and the Council of Trent as equally authoritative. According to Catholic teaching, these councils, down to the Second Vatican Council (1962-1965), clarify and enrich without changing the "deposit of faith," and they become part of the apostolic tradition. The church also accepts the Apostles' Creed, the Nicene-Constantinople Creed, the Athanasian Creed, and the Creed of Pius IV, also called the Creedal Statement of the Council of Trent. These creeds set forth many doctrines common to most Christian bodies, such as the Trinity and the full humanity and divinity of Christ.

Like the Orthodox, Roman Catholics stress the sacraments more than Protestants. The sacraments are a visible means of receiving God's grace and are thus holy. For Catholics there are seven sacraments:

(1) Baptism, necessary for membership in the church, is administered to infants born to Catholic parents or to adult converts. Anointing with oil (the holy chrism) in the form of a cross follows baptism.

(2) Confirmation, which is an adult profession of faith, is done with laying on of hands, ordinarily by a bishop, as a sign of the gift of the Holy Spirit. Today priests may confirm if necessary.

(3) The Eucharist, or Holy Communion, is the central act of Catholic devotion. The laity may receive the Eucharist in the forms of bread and wine. This is not a mere sign or ritual for believers. The body and blood of Christ are believed to be actually present in the eucharistic elements so that the worshiper communes spiritually and physically with the Savior. Since the bread (or Host) is the Body of Christ, it may be placed in a sacred vessel on the altar for veneration by the faithful.

(4) Through the sacrament of reconciliation (formerly called penance), post-baptismal sins are forgiven.

(5) Anointing of the sick is for the seriously ill, the injured, or the aged. It is particularly important for Catholics to receive penance and anointing at time of death, which is popularly called the Last Rites.

(6) The sacrament of holy orders is for the ordination of deacons, priests, and bishops. Ordination grants a man the authority and power to perform the sacraments. Women cannot be ordained to holy orders, but they may take vows and enter a religious order.

(7) Marriage is a sacrament that cannot be dissolved by any human authority which rules out remarriage after divorce. However, improper marriages may be annulled under certain circumstances.

Members are required to attend Mass on Sundays and on obligatory holy days. They should also fast and abstain on certain appointed days, confess at least once a year, and receive the Holy Eucharist during the Easter season. In addition, laity are expected to contribute to the support of the church and to strictly observe the marriage regulations of the church, which includes the prohibition of birth control.

The Roman Catholic liturgical calendar is more elaborate than that of Protestant churches, with days to remember and venerate hundreds of heroes of the faith, known as saints. Of particular importance in Roman Catholic devotion in the United States and around the world is Mary, the mother of Christ, who serves as an intercessor for the faithful. The importance of Mary in Catholic devotion increased over the centuries, and in 1954 the idea that she was conceived without Original Sin (the Immaculate Conception) was declared official Catholic dogma. Since then, some theologians have referred to her as a "Co-redemptrix" with Christ.

The central act of Catholic worship is the Mass. Its two principal parts are the liturgy of the Word and the liturgy of the Eucharist. Until 1963 Latin was the only appropriate liturgical language, but now the entire Mass is recited in the vernacular by both priest and people. Many Catholics also participate in devotions such as benediction, the rosary (a cycle of prayers usually counted on a string of beads), stations of the cross (prayers occasioned by depictions of Christ's journey from Pilate's house to the tomb), and novenas (a period of nine days of public or private devotion). Pilgrimages to holy sites, especially places where people had visions of the Virgin Mary, remain an important part of Catholic devotion.

Religious Orders. At least since the fourth century, religious orders have been an integral part of Catholicism. *The Official Catholic Directory* lists over 130 religious orders for men and nearly 450 for women. These orders differ widely in their work. Some are contemplative, which means that the members remain in monasteries or cloistered convents and focus on prayer and study. Most monks and nuns live in active or mixed religious orders that engage in teaching, caring for the sick, missionary work, writing, or social work. Brothers and sisters are required to take vows of poverty, chastity, and obedience, but are not ordained. Ordination is a separate step, and many priests are also members of a religious order. Parishes in the United States are typically under the charge of a particular order, such as the Franciscans.

Originally monks or nuns were individuals who embraced an ascetic lifestyle of poverty and celibacy as a way to share in the witness of the martyrs who died for the faith. Voluntary asceticism was viewed as a way to "take up the cross" and follow Christ. Over time more organization and discipline were provided for those who chose to serve Christ instead of pursuing family or personal ambitions. In the sixth century, Benedict of Nursia established a monastery on his estate of Monte Cassino in Italy. His rule for the men there became the basis for all Western monasticism, male and female. Among the key features of his rule were the vow of obedience to the abbot (head of the monastery) in addition to vows of poverty and chastity; moderation of ascetic excess; and participation in physical labor in addition to prayer.

Through the centuries other religious orders were established, some in an attempt to reform perceived abuses in an older order, some in order to respond to some unmet need in the church and society. Among the most important of these orders were the Cistercians and the Carthusians, established in the twelfth century in protest against the luxury and laxity of many Benedictine houses. These orders stress austerity and generally impose silence on the monks.

With the rapid urbanization of Europe in the late Middle Ages, new orders were established to reach out to secular society. The Franciscans embraced a radical devotion to poverty and initially lived by begging. The Dominicans also stressed poverty, but they focused their efforts on preaching, especially in areas where heresy was strong. Known as friars (brothers), rather than monks, members of these orders quickly established a strong presence in the burgeoning universities of the Middle Ages. The Franciscans have an order for women (the Poor Claires) and what is called a tertiary order for lay persons who continue to live in secular society. Altogether, the Franciscans are the largest Catholic order. The followers of Francis have been particularly active in service to the poor and outcast.

Numerous orders were established during the Reformation in order to reform the Roman Catholic Church internally and to respond to the Protestant challenge externally. Chief among them was the Society of Jesus (Jesuits), founded by Ignatius Loyola (1491-1556). Worldwide, there are over eighteen thousand Jesuits. The Jesuits were pioneers in missions, especially in Asia, but their involvement in European politics led to their suppression in the late eighteenth century. The order was reorganized and reestablished in 1814, and it played a strong role in the promotion of Catholic education and theology. There are now 235 Catholic colleges and universities in the United States, including Notre Dame, Fordham, Georgetown, Boston College, St. Louis University, Marquette, Loyola, and Villanova, most of them closely connected with various religious orders.

Religious orders have provided an important focus of ministry for women in the Roman Catholic Church since the early days of the church. Some of the male orders have branches for women, but in general women have established their own institutions. There are the Carmelites who produced the great mystic Teresa of Avila (1515-82); the Ursulines, who embraced a mission of educating young women; and the Sisters of Mercy, founded by Mother Teresa of Calcutta (1910-97). In the United States, religious women have been the backbone of the extensive Roman Catholic parochial school system. In the 1990s there were some seven thousand parochial and private schools in this country with about two million students, including over 1,300 Roman Catholic high schools.

Religious women have also been vital in staffing Catholic hospitals and establishing countless charitable institutions. It is indicative of the work of Roman Catholic women that the first American officially to be declared a saint of the church was Elizabeth Seton (1774–1821), noted for her sacrificial role in alleviating social misery. The National Conference on Catholic Charities helps to coordinate charity and welfare work on state and national levels; work is also conducted by several religious orders whose members devote full time to the relief of the poor in homes or institutions, and many dioceses have bureaus of charity.

The Society of St. Vincent de Paul is perhaps the largest and most effective charitable organization. But there are many others (particularly women's orders, such as Little Sisters of the Poor, Sisters of Charity, Daughters of Charity of the Society of St. Vincent de Paul, and Sisters of Mercy) that are active among the poor in Catholic hospitals, orphanages, and homes for the aged. The church operates over fourteen hundred homes for the aged and about 150 orphanages. More than seventy-five million patients are treated annually in Catholic hospitals and healthcare centers. One of every three beds in the nation's private hospitals is provided by the Catholic hospital system.

Besides religious orders and congregations, Catholics may join secular institutions whose members also observe poverty, chastity, and obedience but do not wear distinctive garb or live together in a community. Before receiving approval as secular institutes engaged in apostolic work, these groups may operate as approved "pious unions." Some of the prominent leaders of the American labor movement and other advocates for social justice were Catholic. Among them were Dorothy Day, Thomas Merton, and Daniel Berrigan. Catholic bishops have issued a number of important statements calling for great attention to social justice in America.

Catholicism in America. Missionaries came with Coronado and other early Spanish explorers to the southern and western regions of what would become the United States. The first permanent Catholic parish was established at St. Augustine, Florida, in 1565, half a century before the first Protestant baptism in the Americas. Intrepid French explorers, voyageurs, and colonizers such as Cartier, Jolliet, and Marquette, who now live in North American lore, were Roman Catholics. They were generally accompanied by missionaries or were missionaries themselves. New France became a vicariate apostolic in 1658, with Bishop Laval at its head. The See of Quebec (1675) had spiritual jurisdiction over the vast French provinces in North America, reaching down the valley of the Mississippi to Louisiana.

In 1634, Roman Catholics from England founded Maryland in part as a refuge for Catholics during the turmoil of the English Civil War and Puritan Commonwealth. Until after the American Revolution, though, Catholic activity in the English colonies was restricted by law, even in Maryland. In 1763, there were fewer than twenty-five thousand Roman Catholics in a colonial population of two million, and they were under the jurisdiction of the vicar apostolic of London. Even so, the Articles of Confederation, the Declaration of Independence, and the Constitution include signatures of three Catholics: Thomas Fitzsimmons (1741–1811), Charles Carroll (1737–1832), and Daniel Carroll (1730–96). Religious equality became law with the adoption of the Constitution in 1787.

The status of the Roman Catholic Church in the new nation was unclear until the Reverend John Carroll (1735–1815) of Baltimore, elder brother of Daniel Carroll, was named Superior, or prefect apostolic, of the church in the new United States. In 1800, he was the head of some one hundred and fifty thousand Roman Catholics. By 1890 that number had grown to over six million, primarily due to the flood of emigration from the Catholic countries of Europe.

Catholics faced a number of unique problems in the United States. There is only one Roman Catholic Church worldwide, with a single head, unlike most Protestant churches, which have separate national organizations. For example, while there is an Anglican communion worldwide, it is made up of largely independent Anglican churches in the various former British colonies. Episcopalians* in the United States are not under the direct authority of the Archbishop of Canterbury the way Roman Catholic bishops are under the authority of the pope. Thus, there has been tension in the Roman Catholic Church over the issue of Americanization: how much independence could the American bishops exert while still remaining obedient to Rome?

This was a particularly touchy problem following the First Vatican Council (1869–70), when the European bishops rejected a number of ideas, such as democratic government, that were at the core of American values. James Gibbons (1834–1921), the archbishop of Baltimore and primate of the Catholic Church in America, guided the church through these difficult issues and gained permission for Catholics in the United States to participate fully in American political and social life while remaining loyal to the Roman church. Ultimately, the Second Vatican Council (1962–65) approved of many proposals long advocated by American bishops.

Vatican II and Beyond. John XXIII (pope 1958-1963) summoned all the bishops of the church to the twenty-first ecumenical council, which met at the Vatican in Rome. Following John's death, Pope Paul VI reconvened the council, which made the most radical changes to Catholic life in centuries. Vatican II and the papacy approved the use of the vernacular in the Mass, encouraged modern methods of biblical study and interpretation, promoted more active involvement of the laity in the life of the parish, placed the church on the side of the poor in Catholic countries, and allowed Roman Catholics to participate in ecumenical and interfaith dialogue. Such changes alienated some conservative Catholics, however, leading to the formation of organizations dedicated to preserving pre-Vatican II Catholicism, especially the Latin Mass (see "Society of Saint Pius X").

Before Vatican II, Catholics had been forbidden to attend meetings of the World Council of Churches; now Catholic observers attend council sessions, and bishops of the church have entered into theological dialogue with several larger Protestant denominations. Since then, the church has been rebuilding bridges to the Orthodox* churches and has even exonerated Martin Luther (see LUTHER-AN CHURCHES) of heresy. John Paul II (pope 1979- 2005) even made dramatic steps toward greater friendship with Judaism and Islam, praying in synagogues and mosques. John Paul II was the first pope from Poland, and he was fluent in several languages. He was one of the most widely-traveled world leaders, having made official visits to 129 countries, often at great personal risk.

The current pope, Benedict XVI (2005-present), taught theology for many years in Germany before being named a cardinal. In 1981 he was named prefect of the Congregation for the Doctrine of the Faith (formerly called the Roman Inquisition). In that office he was responsible for insuring that Catholic professors taught official Catholic dogma. As pope, he has pulled back from the ecumenism of his predecessor and has taken a firm stance against women's ordination and birth control. Like John Paul II, Benedict has spoken against the materialism of Western society and urged governments to give greater attention to the steward-ship of God's creation.

In 1968, Pope Paul VI reaffirmed the official church position against any form of artificial birth control in the encyclical *Humanae Vitae*. Many theologians, priests, and laity protested this strict interpretation of sexuality, but the bishops of many industrialized nations such as France, Canada, Belgium, Holland, Swit-zerland, Austria, and West Germany interpreted the papal position in the light of freedom of the individual conscience.

Dissension has been a common feature in contemporary Catholic life in the United States, and many Catholics make their own judgments on birth control, abortion, the role of women in the church, and the official positions of the church on political and economic matters. The evidence of ecclesiastical misconduct on the part of bishops has encouraged further dissent in the church and has con-tributed to a decline in membership in the American church. Most of the newer Catholic denominations (see REFORMED CATHOLIC CHURCH) were formed in response to the growing conservatism of the Roman Catholic Church in the late twentieth century. Most of these new churches reject papal teaching on birth control, abortion, women's ordination, and homosexuality.

Another issue facing the Church worldwide, including in the United States, is the effect of Protestant movements on Catholicism. The Charismatic movement began making inroads in Catholic parishes in the 1970s, and now the number of "Spirit-filled" Catholics—that is, those who believe in and claim charismatic gifts, such as speaking in tongues, healing, interpretation, and prophecy—is well over three hundred thousand. It is not clear how these "born again" Catholics, politically conservative but liturgically innovative, will fit into the emerging Church. Worldwide the Catholic Church has lost many members to Pentecostal churches, especially in Latin America.

Suggestions for further reading:

Bokenkotter, Thomas S. *Concise History of the Catholic Church*. Rev. ed. New York: Image Books, 1990.

Chinnici, Joseph. *Living Stones: The History and Structure of Catholic Spiritual Life in the United States*. New York: MacMillan, 1989.

Dolan, Jay P. *In Search of an American Catholicism: A History of Religion and Culture in Tension*. New York: Oxford University Press, 2002.

Greeley, Andrew M. *The Catholic myth: The Behavior and Beliefs of American Catholics*. New York: Charles Scribners' Sons, 1990.

Johnson, Kevin Orlin. *Why Do Catholics Do That? A Guide to the Teachings and Practices of the Catholic Church*. New York: Ballantine, 1995.

Mann, Arthur. *The One and the Many: Reflections on the American Identity*. Chicago: University of Chicago Press, 1979.

Orsi, Robert A. *The Madonna of 115th Street: Faith and Community in Italian Harlem, 1880-1950*. New Haven: Yale University Press, 1985.

Pruter, Karl. *A History of the Old Catholic Church*. Scottsdale, AZ: St. Willibrord's Press, 1973.

AMERICAN CATHOLIC CHURCH IN THE UNITED STATES

Founded: 1999
Membership: fewer than 5,000 in 13 parishes (2009)

The ACCUS was founded in response to the growing conservatism in the Roman Catholic Church. It seeks to continue the reforms of the Second Vatican Council, and it welcomes those who have felt alienated in other churches. It does not exclude people from the sacraments because of marital status or sexual orientation. The church defines its ministry in terms of compassion rather than doctrine, and it offers support for persons facing difficult medical decisions. Priests are expected to have outside employment and receive no salary for administering the sacraments. There is also a zero tolerance policy for sexual abuse by clergy. The ACCUS has connections to the Old Catholic Churches* and claims to be in Apostolic Succession. The liturgy is Catholic and the seven traditional sacraments are the basis of devotion. The founding bishop was Lawrence J. Harms.

For more information: www.accus.us

Headquarters: 5595 Rivendell Place, Frederick, MD 21703-8673.

APOSTOLIC CATHOLIC ORTHODOX CHURCH

Founded: 1916
Membership: est. 8,500 in 10 parishes (2006)

The ACOC is one of the larger Old Catholic Churches*. It was established when Bishop DeLandes Berghes of the See of Utrecht consecrated Carmel Henry Carfora and William Francis Brothers. True to Old Catholic standards, the Eucharist is the central rite of the church, and it is not denied to anyone because of race, gender, or marital status. The church uses the traditional seven sacraments, and its priests are ordained by bishops in Apostolic Succession. The priesthood is open to both married and celibate men and women. The church affirms the ancient ecumenical councils and creeds. There are three orders of ministry, and the church emphasizes the importance of a loving local community that addresses spiritual and social needs of the world around.

For more information: www.apostoliccatholic.org

Headquarters: 1900 St. James Place, Suite 880, Houston, TX 77056-4129

EASTERN RITE CATHOLIC / UNIATE CHURCHES

Founded: various dates
Membership: est. 500,000 (2000)

The Eastern Rite churches, also known as Uniate churches, hold a special position within the Roman Catholic Church*. Historically and liturgically they are closely related to the Eastern Orthodox* churches, but each has chosen to come under the jurisdiction of the Roman Catholic Church* while preserving its own distinctive language, rites, and canon law. Most of these churches, for instance, are permitted to have married clergy and have always served both the bread and the wine of the Eucharist to the laity.

There are five major families of Uniate churches: Alexandrian (Copts and Ethiopians), Antiochene (Maronites, Syrians, Malankarese), Armenian, Chaldean (Chaldean and Malabarese), and Byzantine (Hungarian, Yugoslav, Melkites, Ukrainian). The largest Eastern Rite church is the Ukrainian Catholic Church, which was formed when Ukrainian subjects of the king of Poland were united with Rome in 1596. This church was outlawed by the Soviet Union following World War II, but has resumed open activity since the collapse of the USSR. The Maronites of Lebanon established ties with Rome during the Crusades.

Each of the Eastern Rite churches is headed by its own Patriarch who has jurisdiction over the bishops, the clergy, and the people of that rite. All of the patriarchs are members of the Congregation for the Oriental Churches, which governs the relations of the Vatican with the Eastern Rite Churches.

For more information: www.vatican.va/roman_curia/congregations/orient church/index.htm

ECUMENICAL CATHOLIC CHURCH + U.S.A

Founded: 2003
Membership: est. 5000 members in 14 churches

The Ecumenical Catholic Church is part of the Old Catholic* movement that was founded in direct response to the increasingly conservative direction of the Roman Catholic Church in the 1990s. The ECC defines itself as Catholic in doctrine and liturgy, and it considers its bishops to be in apostolic succession from Peter. Specifically, the ECC+USA promotes the ordination of women and allows divorced persons to remarry. The church also leaves the question of birth control up to the conscience of married couples. It also gives the laity a greater say in the life of the parish than is common in the Roman Catholic Church. About eighty-five percent of the current members were formerly Roman Catholic.

For more information: www.ecc-usa.org

Contact: Vilatte Institute, 1100 Whispering Pines Dr., Dardenne Prairie, MO 63368-6958

ECUMENICAL CATHOLIC COMMUNION

Founded: 2003
Membership: statistics unavailable

The Ecumenical Catholic Communion sees its mission as "a response to the messianic call of the Spirit to preach the Gospel of liberation and justice; to offer a refuge in Christ for those who suffer prejudice; to stand open to dialogue with others so called and, to conform our lives to the life and teachings of the Lord Jesus Christ." (see website) The ECC is made up primarily of former Roman Catholic parishes that wanted to further the reforms of the Second Vatican Council. In particular, the ECC promotes ecumenism and the ordination of women. It is tolerant of divorce and does not require its priests to be celibate. The ECC is now one of the Old Catholic Churches*, and it remains committed to a sacramental ministry with bishops in apostolic succession.

For more information: www.ecumenical-catholic-communion.org

Headquarters: 16738 E. Iliff Ave., Aurora, CO 80013

MARIAVITE OLD CATHOLIC CHURCH, PROVINCE OF NORTH AMERICA

Founded: 1906; US diocese founded in 1972
Membership: statistics not available

Mariavites are a unique type of Old Catholic Church*. They derive their name from the Latin phrase *Mariae vitae imitantur*, which means "to imitate the life of Mary," the mother of Christ. This ideal originated in late nineteenth-century Poland, a heavily Roman Catholic country. The Mariavite Order of priests and sisters was founded on August 2, 1893, by Maria Felicia Kozlowska (1862–1921), a Third Order Franciscan, and Jan Kowalski (1871–1942), a diocesan priest. Kozlowska had earlier formed a community of sisters in response to visionary experiences and Kowalski took up the movement about five years later, adding a community of secular priests. The motto of the order was, "Everything for the greater glory of God and the honor of the Most Blessed Virgin Mary." From the beginning, its members endeavored to practice an ascetic/mystical religious life, in accordance with the primitive Rule of St. Francis of Assisi. Their goal was to maintain a deep inner spiritual life among themselves and their faithful by being pastors and servants, not through cloistered or contemplative communities. Candidacy requirements were firm and sacrificial, with a tendency toward the ascetic.

Ecclesiastic and civil opposition marked the early decades of the Mariavites in Poland. The Roman Catholic Church* was skeptical of their mystical claims and denied their application for recognition as a religious order. In 1906 the group formed a church independent of Rome, and in 1909 it became part of the Old Catholic Church* at Utrecht, Holland. That church had been independent of Rome since 1871. At the time of Kozlowska's death in 1921, the Mariavite movement had some 50,000 adherents. However, the group went into decline, and the Old Catholics severed communion with the Mariavites in 1924. The latter were perceived as growing more fanatical, evidenced by Kowalski's ordination of women to the priesthood. Kowalski was eventually imprisoned by the Nazis and died in a concentration camp.

Mariavites first came to the United States around 1930. During World War II it was impossible for the churches to maintain close contact with Europe, and by 1972 the United States church had become autonomous and self-reliant. Archbishop Robert Zaborowski has led the church since 1974; its headquarters are in Wyandotte, Michigan. According to its own reports, this church has grown rapidly since 1972; some reports claim as many three hundred thousand members. However, information is difficult to obtain from church officials and actual membership is uncertain. Worship is celebrated according to the Tridentine Rite of 1570 in Latin, English, and Polish in the United States. The principal purpose of the Mariavite Church, which came to be known as the Work of Great Mercy, is

81

"the propagation of devotion to the Most Blessed Sacrament and the invocation of the Perpetual Help of Mary as a means of final salvation for a world perishing in its sins." (website)

For more information: www.mariavite.org

Contact: 2803 10th St, Wyandotte, MI 48192-4907

OLD CATHOLIC CHURCHES

Founded: 1871; came to the United States in 1914
Membership: statistics not available

Old Catholic churches in the United States are an outgrowth of the Old Catholic movement, centered in the See of Utrecht in the Netherlands. Conflicts between Dutch Catholics and the papacy date to the Jansenist controversy over grace and determinism in the eighteenth century, which resulted in a schism in the Roman Catholic Church* in Holland. The schismatic Dutch body continued its existence into the next century, attracting new followers when Pope Pius IX (1846–78) affirmed the First Vatican Council's statement on papal infallibility in 1870 (see CATHOLIC CHURCHES).

A significant number of Swiss, German, and Austrian Roman Catholic priests also refused to accept the doctrine of papal infallibility and were excommunicated in 1871. Ignatz von Döllinger (1799–1890) presided over a number of conferences attended by Catholics who could not accept the new dogma on papal authority and representatives of the Anglican and Lutheran churches in the mid-1870s. Old Catholic bishops were ordained by the bishops of Utrecht and were eventually welcomed into communion with the Anglican Church* and several Orthodox* bodies.

In 1889 the Declaration of Utrecht was issued as the doctrinal statement of Old Catholics. The declaration affirms the main lines of the Catholic tradition up to about the year 1000. Especially important for the Old Catholics are the first seven ecumenical councils (before the division between East and West) and most of the medieval liturgy. However, the declaration rejected more recent doctrines of the Roman Catholic Church*, especially papal infallibility, the immaculate conception of Mary, and compulsory celibacy of the priesthood. The church maintains that the five patriarchal Sees of the ancient church remain the equal heads of the church. The Slavic branch of the Old Catholic Church has a separate history (see POLISH NATIONAL CHURCH OF AMERICA).

The Old Catholic movement in the United States first emerged with the work of Père Joseph René Vilatte (1854–1929) in Wisconsin near Green Bay, where several parishes were organized. A group of English-speaking Old Catholics were also gathered together by a former Roman Catholic monk, Augustine de Angelis

(William Harding), who had organized a community of men devoted to the Religious Rule of St. Benedict at Waukegan, Illinois, around the turn of the century. The Old Catholic episcopacy in the United States was established in 1914 when the English Archbishop Arnold Harris Matthew (1852–1919) consecrated Bishop de Landas Berghes et de Rache (1873–1920), a prince of the house of Lorraine-Brapan. He was succeeded by Father Carmel Henry Carfora (1878–1958), an Italian Franciscan friar, who led the church until his death in 1958.

At that time, the North American Old Catholics split into several ecclesial bodies, not all recognized by Old Catholics in Europe. Perhaps as many as seventeen bodies have claimed to be Old Catholic in the United States, but the major bodies originating in the Utrecht movement are the Old Catholic Church of America, the Old Roman Catholic Church of North America, the North American Old Catholic Church, the North American Old Roman Catholic Church (Archdiocese of New York), and the Old Roman Catholic Church (English Rite). Most of the Old Catholic churches have fewer than ten parishes in the United States.

In the United States, the Old Catholics often represent a conservative form of Catholicism despite their early identification as "liberal." The sweeping liturgical and devotional changes of the Second Vatican Council led some conservative priests to join the Old Catholics in order to preserve the old traditions, such as prayers for the dead. Several conservative churches in the Anglican* tradition may be classified with the Old Catholic churches as well. Most of these bodies use the 1928 edition of *The Book of Common Prayer*, reject the ordination of women, and emphasize catholic ritual in worship. Most of these bodies would agree with the statement of purpose for the Holy Catholic Church (Anglican Rite): "to perpetuate the Faith, Order, Worship and Witness of Western Catholicism as it existed in the Church of England from around 200 A.D., to the time of the Great Schism, and set forth by the 'ancient catholic bishops and doctors,' and especially as defined by the Seven Ecumenical Councils of the undivided Church." (http://www.holycatholicanglican.org/about_us.php)

For more information: www.oldcatholic.org

Contact: 409 N. Lexington Parkway, DeForest, WI Wisconsin 53532

POLISH NATIONAL CATHOLIC CHURCH OF AMERICA

Founded: 1897
Membership: est. 60,000 in 126 parishes (2004)

The Polish National Catholic Church, along with a few smaller Slavic national churches in the United States, represented a different type of the Old Catholic* movement as Eastern European immigrants sought to have parishes in their native tongue. The Polish body was formally organized at Scranton, Pennsylvania, on March 14, 1897, in protest over the lack of a Polish bishop and a desire to have more control over parish affairs. Some 250 families then began work on a new church, St. Stanislaus, and called a native Pole, Francis Hodur (1866–1953), to be their priest. A constitution for the new church was adopted by the Scranton parish in 1897, claiming the right to control all churches built and maintained by Poles and to administer such property through a committee chosen by each parish. This action was not accepted by authorities in Rome, and Hodur was subsequently excommunicated.

Other Polish parishes followed the Scranton example and began referring to themselves as "National Churches." Joining together, they held their first synod at Scranton in 1904, with almost 150 clerical and lay delegates representing parishes in Pennsylvania, Maryland, Massachusetts, and New Jersey. Hodur was consecrated as bishop in 1907 at Utrecht, Holland, by three bishops of the Old Catholic Church*. Following the first synod, the vernacular—first Polish and then English—gradually replaced Latin as the liturgical language. In 1909, a second synod at Scranton officially adopted the church's present name. In 1914, at a general synod in Chicago, the Polish National Catholic Church adopted the "Confession of Faith" written by Bishop Hodur,.

There are five dioceses in the Polish National Catholic Church: Buffalo-Pittsburgh, Canadian, Central, Eastern, and Western. Polish and English are used in worship and in the educational programs of parish schools taught largely by pastors. Clergy have been allowed to marry since 1921, but only with the knowledge and permission of the bishops. Because of its opposition to the ordination of women, ties between the PNCC and the Old Catholic Church in Utrecht have been severed.

For more information: www.pncc.org

Headquarters: 1006 Pittston Ave., Scranton, PA 18505

REFORMED CATHOLIC CHURCH

Founded: 1988
Membership: est. 57,000 in 100 parishes (2006)

The RCC is one of several bodies that separated from the Roman Catholic Church* in the 1980s in order to promote greater openness to the modern world without denying traditional Catholic worship, spirituality, and sacramental theology. The church seeks to continue the reforming work of Pope John XXIII, whom it regards as a saint. Its constitution, ratified in 2006, describes the RCC as "an affiliation of autonomous member churches whose traditions and sacramental form of worship are Catholic, but who function fully independent of Rome." (Constitution of the Reformed Catholic Church, www.reformedcatholicchurch.org)The

church practices open communion for all Christians regardless of marital status or sexual orientation. It allows the ordination of women and homosexuals, and it leaves medical decisions up to individual conscience. Its liturgy is Catholic, but is influenced by Orthodoxy. The church is governed by a presiding archbishop who is elected by a college of bishops, and there are eight dioceses in the United States. The current presiding archbishop, Phillip Zimmerman, was consecrated in 2004. The church has close connections to the Old Catholic Churches*, but most of the clergy and members came from the Roman Catholic Church*.

For more information: www.reformedcatholicchurch.org

Headquarters: P.O. Box 28710, Columbus OH 43228

ROMAN CATHOLIC CHURCH

Founded: ca. 60 CE; came to the United States in the sixteenth century
Membership: 63.4 million in 19,081 parishes (2004)

The Roman Catholic Church is the largest single religious body in the United States and has the oldest continuous institutional existence. Nearly one in four Americans is a member of the Catholic Church, but over thirty percent of Americans were raised Catholic. Catholicism offers one of the most comprehensive and sophisticated theological systems of any religion. Moreover, the Catholic Church in the United States has played a very prominent role in the promotion of social justice, peace, religious toleration, and economic improvement. The church has had a profound impact on American society through its numerous educational and medical facilities. Many of the nation's most respected political figures were nurtured in the Catholic faith.

Officially, the Roman Catholic Church traces its beginning from the moment of Christ's selection of the apostle Peter as guardian of the keys of heaven and earth and chief of the apostles (Matthew 16:18-19). Although the basic liturgy, doctrine, and organization of the Catholic Church are standard throughout the United States, there is a great deal of diversity on the local level. Much popular Catholic devotion focuses on the praying of the rosary and veneration of Mary, the mother of Jesus. Parishes offer a variety of groups for fostering greater devotion and personal piety.

Structure. The government of the Roman Catholic Church is hierarchical, but Vatican II encouraged more lay participation in parishes. At the head of the structure stands the pope, who is also Bishop of Rome and Vicar of Christ on earth and the visible head of the Church. His authority is supreme in all matters of faith and discipline. Next is the College of Cardinals. Although laypeople once were appointed as cardinals, the office has been limited to priests since 1918. Many cardinals live in Rome, acting as advisers to the pope or as heads or members of the various congregations or councils that supervise the administration of the church. When a pope dies, cardinals elect the successor and hold authority in the interim. The Roman Curia is the official body of administrative offices through which the pope governs the church. It is composed of Roman congregations, tribunals, and pontifical councils and acts with the delegated authority of the pope.

In the United States there are eleven active cardinals, forty-five archbishops (seven of whom are cardinals), over three hundred bishops, and more than forty thousand priests. There are thirty-four archdioceses and over 150 dioceses. An archbishop is in charge of an archdiocese and has precedence in that province. Bishops are appointed by Rome, usually upon suggestions from the United States hierarchy. They are the ruling authorities in the dioceses, but appeals from their decisions may be taken to the apostolic delegate at Washington, D.C.

The parish priest, responsible to the bishop, is assigned by the bishop or archbishop and holds authority to celebrate Mass and administer the sacraments with the help of such other priests as the parish may need. Priests are educated in theological seminaries, typically connected to Roman Catholic colleges and universities. The usual course of study covers a period of eight years—four years of philosophy and four years of theology. Those in religious orders also spend one or two years in a novitiate.

The clergy of the church also includes deacons. Since the restoration of the Permanent Diaconate in 1967, more than eleven thousand people have completed the training course and been ordained deacons. Most of these deacons are married and over the age of thirty-five. They are empowered to preach, baptize, distribute Holy Communion, and officiate at weddings. Deacons typically support themselves in secular jobs and exercise their ministry during weekends and evenings.

Three ecclesiastical councils form an important part of the Roman Catholic system: (1) The general, or ecumenical, council is called by the pope or with his consent. It is composed of all the bishops, and its actions on matters of doctrine and discipline must be approved by the pope. (2) The plenary, or national, council is made up of the bishops of a given country; its acts, too, must be submitted to the Holy See. (3) Provincial and diocesan councils make further promulgation and application of the decrees passed by the other councils and approved by the pope.

With the most centralized government in Christendom, the Holy See at Rome has representatives in many countries of the world. Roman Catholic churches have been established in over 230 countries, with a total membership of more than one billion. The majority of Italians, Spanish, Irish, Austrians, Poles, Latin Americans, Belgians, Hungarians, southern Germans, Portuguese, French, and Filipinos are baptized Roman Catholics. The Society for the Propagation of the Faith is the overall representative missionary body.

Almost every diocese publishes a weekly newspaper; more than four hundred Catholic newspapers and magazines are published in the United States and Canada. Some of the largest and most influential periodicals are *The National Catholic*

Reporter, Commonweal, America, Columbia, United States Catholic, St. Anthony Messenger, Catholic Digest, Catholic World, Ligourian, Catholic Twin Circle, and *The National Catholic Register.*

Ethnic Parishes. One of the major issues that has faced the Roman Catholic Church in the United States is immigration. Catholics in Europe were united in their obedience to Rome, but they were organized on national lines. Spaniards had Spanish priests, Spanish bishops, and venerated Spanish saints. Likewise, the Catholic churches of Ireland, Germany, France, Poland, and elsewhere had their own national character. There was often great tension between ethic groups, and there was a correspondingly strong impulse for these ethnic identities to determine the structure of the Catholic Church in America. In other words, there were those who wanted to recreate the old national churches on American soil with separate hierarchies for each major ethnic group. There would have been many Catholic churches loyal to Rome, but separated from each other in the United States. This would have been similar to the Lutheran* pattern in America. In the late nineteenth century, James Cardinal Gibbons (1834-1921) charted the course that led to a parochial system in which local parishes could be organized on ethnic lines, but the national church would be a single American church. Thus diversity and unity were preserved.

There is much that Catholics share in common; however, it is important to note the rich diversity of traditions within Catholicism in the United States, even in a single metropolitan area. When immigrants arrive in this country, they tend to group in neighborhoods in major cities and recreate some familiar features of the Old World. Thus, although the basic elements of the Mass are the same in every Roman Catholic parish and the same high holy days are observed, at the local level there are many variations liturgically and in popular devotion. A sampling of a few of the major Catholic ethnic groups within the United States includes:

Irish. It is estimated that more than four million people fled Ireland for the United States during the nineteenth century, joining at least one hundred thousand more who arrived before the American Revolution. Irish emigration was connected with the subjugation of Ireland to the British crown. Once Protestantism was firmly established in England, Catholicism became a mark of national resistance for the native Irish who clung tenaciously to their faith.

In the New World, Catholicism continued to be a bond among the immigrants and to their homeland. Countless Irish benevolent and mutual aid societies were established in the United States, often with a close connection to the church. St. Patrick's Day became a major holiday in many northern cities and an expression of Irish pride. From the time of the first American bishop, John Carroll, to the present, more dioceses and archdioceses have had prelates of Irish descent than of any other nationality. In many ways, the Irish have largely defined American Catholicism, and it was a bishop of Irish descent, James Gibbons, who established the pattern for Catholicism in America.

Italians. By 1908 more than two and half million persons had immigrated from Italy to the United States, settling mainly in the major cities of the Northeast, particularly in New York City and the upper Midwest. The Franciscans provided most of the pastoral leadership for Italian immigrants. Notable among them were Father Pamfilo da Magliano, founder of St. Bonaventure's College at Allegany, New York (1858), and Father Leo Paccillio, pastor of the first Italian parish in New York, St. Anthony's. The Franciscans were followed by the Jesuits, the Scalabrini Fathers, the Salesians, the Passionists, and the Augustinians. In some cases priests of other nationalities learned Italian in order to minister to the needs of the Italians in areas where no Italian priest was available. Italian Catholics continued to honor the patron saints of their native Italian towns, naming benevolent societies after them and holding parish festivals on the saints' days. Particularly important in this regard have been St. Anthony and St. Joseph.

Poles. Poland gradually disappeared as a political entity during the eighteenth century as Russia, Prussia, and Austria divided the territory among them. Partition, however, did not destroy Polish identity or patriotism. Particularly in western Poland, German efforts to assimilate the Poles into German Protestant culture served to heighten devotion to the Roman Catholic Church. There were Poles in the United States during colonial days, and some served prominently in the American Revolution; but the immigration of the Polish masses began in the 1850s. In 1851, Father Leopold Moczygemba (1824–91), a Franciscan, came to the United States and soon after induced nearly one hundred families from Upper Silesia to come to Panna Maria, Texas, where they built the first Polish church in the United States in 1855. Immigration, particularly from Polish Prussia, increased rapidly, primarily to Illinois, Michigan, and Pennsylvania. By 1890 there were some 130 Polish churches. Most of the schools were conducted by the Felician Sisters and the School Sisters of Notre Dame. The election of the first Polish pope, John Paul II, in 1978, was a great boon to Polish Catholics in the United States

Hispanic. Catholicism came to the New World primarily by way of Spain, whose monarchs were strong supporters of the Counter Reformation. The first universities in the Americas were founded in the Spanish colonies, and indigenous cultures blended with the religious practices of the conquering Spaniards to create a great variety of vibrant subcultures of the faith. Missionaries to the American Southwest made some progress in converting native peoples, and by 1800 beautiful adobe missions dotted the West.

For most of United States history, Mexicans have been the dominant Hispanic group, and in some cities it is common to see devotion to the Virgin of Guadalupe and the spectacular Day of the Dead festival, which is celebrated around the time of Halloween. Since World War II, immigration has increased from other Latin American countries, making the Hispanic population the fastest growing portion of the Roman Catholic Church in the United States

By 1970, a quarter of Catholics in the United States spoke Spanish, and in that year the first Mexican-American Catholic bishop, Patricio F. Flores, was consecrated in San Antonio. During the 1970s, an organization of Hispanic priests called PADRES (Priests for Religious, Educational, and Social Rights) worked effectively to focus the church's attention to the special needs of the often neglected but rapidly growing Spanish-speaking population. In large part due to a shortage of priests and economic distress, there has not been as great a tendency among Hispanic Catholics toward the creation of parishes along national lines as there was among Europeans in the nineteenth century. Some parishes do primarily use Spanish, and many parochial schools teach in Spanish. But in general there has been a greater blending of immigrants from different Latin American countries and cultures than was the case with European immigrants in the nineteenth century.

Catholicism Today. The Roman Catholic Church remains a strong, vibrant, and growing religious body in the United States, but it also reflects the diversity and divisions in American society generally. By the end of the twentieth century, conservative Catholics often found they had more in common with conservative Evangelicals, despite their differing theologies, than with more liberal Catholics. Catholics and evangelicals often joined forces to oppose abortion and gay rights. Mel Gibson's highly successful movie, *The Passion of the Christ*, which reflects much Catholic devotion, found its largest audiences among Protestant Evangelicals.

In the 2004 presidential campaign, Senator John Kerry of Massachusetts was opposed by some of the bishops in his own church because he had not voted to restrict access to abortion, although he was endorsed by other Catholic leaders for his commitment to workers' rights and care for the poor. A similar situation occurred when Joseph Biden ran for vice president. The Catholic Church remains one of the dominant religious institutions in America, especially in the northern states. When John F. Kennedy ran for president in 1960, many wondered whether a Roman Catholic could be elected president. Fifty years later, two-thirds of the Supreme Court is Roman Catholic.

For more information: www.vatican.va;

Headquarters: 3211 Fourth Street, Washington, DC 20017

SOCIETY OF SAINT PIUS X

Founded: 1969
Membership: est. 20,000 in 103 chapels

The Society of Pius X views itself as a society of priests within the Roman Catholic Church rather than a separate denomination, but that claim is not recognized by the Vatican. It was founded by Archbishop Marcel Lefebvre, a priest of the Holy Ghost Order who had been bishop of Dakar before returning to his native France in 1962 as bishop of Tulle. He was a vocal opponent of the modernization of the church that took effect at the Second Vatican Council, and in he 1968 resigned as head of the Holy Ghost Order rather than implement the changes required by the Council. The following year he established a conservative seminary called the Society of Pius X, named for the first pope of the twentieth century to be canonized. Pius X was a key figure in resisting secularization and liberalism in France. Although initially supported by Vatican officials, the Society was officially suppressed in 1975. Lefebvre's defiant ordination of twelve traditionalist priests in the following year furthered the separation of the Society from the Vatican.

The major focus of the Society's work is promotion of the traditional Latin mass and the decrees of the First Vatican Council through an aggressive grassroots campaign. It may seem ironic that a society that proclaims the doctrine of papal infallibility could rebel against the Vatican and criticize the pope's words and actions, but in their view, the Second Vatican Council and its decrees corrupted the church and the papacy. Priests in the Society attempt (and sometimes succeed) in "liberating" parishes from the modern mass and restoring the pre-Vatican II liturgy. The Society has also founded many chapels around the country. Though stronger in France, Argentina, and Africa, the number of priests and seminarians is growing in the United States. There are no membership statistics for the laity since the Society does not view itself as a separate church. The Society operates twenty-three primary schools, one college, four retreat centers, and a seminary. Its publishing house is Angelus Press. In 2008 Pope Benedict XVI welcomed four of the schematic bishops back into the Catholic fold and gave priests permission to celebrate the Mass in Latin.

For more information: www.sspx.org

Headquarters: Regina Coeli House, 11485 N. Farley Road, Platte City, MO 64079

Episcopal and Anglican Churches

The Episcopal Church has been one of the most influential churches in American history and has provided many national leaders including presidents, Supreme Court justices, and generals. Episcopalians built numerous educational institutions, hospitals, homes for the elderly, and many of the most beautiful houses of worship in the country. The Episcopal Church and its offshoots trace their origins to the Church of England (the Anglican Church), which severed allegiance to the papacy during the Protestant Reformation. In doing so, however, the Church of

England sought to maintain an unbroken historical continuity to the Christian church in England from the early fourth century.

The Anglican Church has often been viewed as a "middle way" between Roman Catholicism and Protestantism. Through the years, there has been tension in Anglican churches between those who favor a more Catholic stance and those who adopt more Protestant principles. The historical succession of bishops, or the episcopacy, is the visible sign of this long tradition of English Christianity. Bishops are recognized as important symbols of unity in the church. The other two orders of ministry are priests and deacons.

Though King Henry VIII first rejected papal supremacy in the 1530s, it was his successors, Edward VI and Elizabeth I, who made the Anglican Church clearly Protestant with the adoption of the *Book of Common Prayer* and the Thirty-nine Articles of Religion. In the 1600s, Puritans agitated for a more Reformed* style of Christianity, but the episcopacy and the prayer book were firmly established in the Anglican Church with the restoration of the monarchy after the English Civil War.

The Anglican theologian Richard Hooker (ca. 1554–1600) helped shape the Anglican approach to worship and theology. The church's sources of belief and practice are the Bible, the tradition of the church, and reason. Aesthetic in orientation, Anglicanism incorporates theology into liturgy and makes use of the senses of sight and taste as well as those of hearing and speaking. This church is distinctive in leaving undefined the exact nature of the presence of Christ in the Eucharist, regarding it as a spiritual mystery.

The Anglican Church came to America along with English colonization. Francis Fletcher planted a cross and read a prayer when Sir Francis Drake landed on the western coast of North America in 1578, and the first Anglican baptisms were conducted in Sir Walter Raleigh's colony on the Outer Banks of North Carolina. In several colonies, especially in the South, the Church of England was the established church, but many colonists were suspicious of the state church. The Society for the Propagation of the Gospel was established in England in 1701 to help support the poorly paid American clergy and spread the work of the church westward. With this increased support, the church grew in the colonial period. The College of William and Mary in Virginia was established in 1693.

The American Revolution almost destroyed the colonial Church of England since clergy had to choose whether to flee to England or Canada, remain as Loyalists in the face of persecution, or break their vows of allegiance. Many leaders of the American cause, including George Washington and Patrick Henry, were Anglicans, but in the popular mind, episcopacy was associated with the British crown rather than with independence. At war's end the church in America had no bishop, no association of the churches, and not even the semblance of an establishment, but the clergy who remained in the new nation reorganized the church.

In 1783 a conference of the Anglican churches met at Annapolis, Maryland, and they formally adopted the name "Protestant Episcopal Church." Also in 1783, the clergy in Connecticut elected Samuel Seabury (1729–96) as their prospective bishop. He went to England to be consecrated but was denied by the English bishops. He then went to Scotland and obtained consecration there in 1784. Two other bishops-elect (from New York and Pennsylvania) were consecrated by the Archbishop of Canterbury in 1787 in recognition of the legitimacy of the American church. In 1789, the church constitution was adopted and the *Book of Common Prayer* was revised for American use, removing prayers for the British monarch.

The Anglican church spread to all parts of the British empire in the eighteenth and nineteenth centuries thanks to a vigorous mission program. There are about eighty million members of the Anglican Communion worldwide and forty-four national or regional churches. The episcopacy remained the glue that held this diverse and active church together. The Archbishop of Canterbury remains the titular head of the Anglican Communion, and the primates (highest ranking bishop of a national or regional church) meet regularly to discuss common mission and doctrine. After World War II, immigrants from former British colonies began moving to England and America in large numbers, bringing their form of Anglicanism with them.

The *Book of Common Prayer* has been one of the glues uniting the Episcopal Church in the United States. Two sacraments, baptism and the Eucharist, are recognized by Anglican churches as signs of grace. Baptism by any church in the name of the Trinity is recognized as valid. Without defining the holy mystery, the Episcopal Church believes in the real presence of Christ in the elements of the Eucharist. The church also recognizes a sacramental character in confirmation, penance, orders, matrimony, and the anointing of the sick.

So-called Anglo-Catholics in the church emphasize the church's roots in the Roman Catholic Church* and promote unity with the Catholic and Orthodox churches. They are sometimes referred to as "high church" because of their use of incense and other liturgical features associated with the High Mass. The "low church" perspective emphasizes the Anglican Church's roots in the Protestant Reformation. In the late nineteenth century, there was a desire for a greater sense of catholicity in the Episcopal Church. At the Lambeth Conference in Chicago in 1886, the bishops developed the Quadrilateral, which governs Anglican ecumenical discussion. The four key points of ecclesiology are: the Bible, the ancient ecumenical creeds, the sacraments of baptism and Eucharist, and the historic episcopacy.

Suggestions for further reading:

Albright, Raymond W. *A History of the Protestant Episcopal Church.* New York: MacMillan, 1964.

Butler, Diana Hochstedt. *Standing against the Whirlwind: Evangelical Episcopalians in Nineteenth-Century America.* New York: Oxford University Press, 1995.

Caldwell, Sandra M, & Caldwell, Ronald J. *The History of the Episcopal Church in America, 1607-1991: A Bibliography*. New York: Garland Publishing, 1993.

Konolige, Kit. *The Power of their Glory: America's Ruling Class, the Episcopalians*. New York: Wyden Books, 1978.

Prelinger, Catherine M. *Episcopal Women: Gender, Spirituality, and Commitment in an American Mainline Denomination*. New York: Oxford University Press, 1995.

Prichard, Robert W. *A History of the Episcopal Church*. Harrisburg, PA: Morehouse, 1991.

Woolverton, John Frederick. *Colonial Anglicanism in North America*. Detroit: Wayne State University Press, 1984.

ANGLICAN COMMUNION IN NORTH AMERICA

Founded: 2009
Membership: est. 100,000 in 735 churches (2009)

The Anglican Communion in North America was officially formed in 2009, in the wake of the controversy surrounding the consecration of the Rt. Rev. Gene Robinson as bishop of the New Hampshire diocese of the Episcopal Church* in 2003.The ACNA objected to the consecration of an openly homosexual man to the episcopacy, especially when this was done against the wishes of the majority of primates in the Anglican Communion. The ACNA was a merger of many organizations that came out of that controversy, including the Anglican Mission in the Americans, the Convocation of Anglicans in North America, the American Anglican Council, and the Anglican Network in Canada. The Reformed Episcopal Church* is also included as a founding member. Unlike the various Continuing Anglican Churches*, the Anglican Communion is committed to remaining in the worldwide Anglican Communion, and some of the primates in the Anglican Communion, including a former Archbishop of Canterbury, have supported the efforts of parishes and even dioceses to break with the Episcopal Church. There have been a number of court cases throughout the United States as parishes have attempted to leave the Episcopal Church while retaining possession of their buildings and other property. For the most part, the courts have recognized the legal claims of the Episcopal Church. In 2009 the Church of Nigeria became the first church in the Anglican Communion to formally recognize the ACNA and enter into full communion with the church. More important, the Church of Nigeria recognized the ACNA as its partner in North America rather than the Episcopal Church. The ACNA has also been recognized by the Church of Uganda, the Anglican Province of the Southern Cone, and the Church of the Province of Southeast Asia.

According to the church's mission statement, it exists "to bring the good news of Jesus Christ, as expressed in the Anglican tradition, both to those who have never heard it, and to those in our Church who have been given a 'different gospel.' We are committed to missionary work and church planting in North America and throughout the world. We especially seek to support the spiritually vibrant but materially poor ministries of our fellow Anglicans in the Global South." (Mission statement found on church's website: www.theacnea.org) Ordained persons can affiliate directly with the ACNA, but laity may do so only through parishes or dioceses. The church is seeking to be recognized as the thirty-ninth Province of the Anglican Communion. Robert Duncan was installed as the first Archbishop and Primate of the ACNA in June 2009. The church has parishes all over the United States and Canada, with large concentrations in Pennsylvania, Virginia, Texas, and Southern California.

For more information: www.theacna.org

Headquarters: 1001 Merchant Street, Ambridge, PA 15003

CONTINUING ANGLICAN CHURCHES

Founded: 1977
Membership: statistics not available, but est. over 75,000 in 300 parishes

In 1977 an international Congress of Concerned Churchmen comprised of nearly 2,000 Anglican bishops, clergy, and laypeople met in St. Louis to voice their opposition to changes in the Episcopal Church*, particularly the ordination of women and revisions to the prayer book. The Affirmation of St. Louis, which affirms traditional teachings as unalterable, serves as a primary doctrinal statement for several small bodies that were formed in the wake of the St. Louis meeting. They call themselves "continuing" Episcopal churches in opposition to the Episcopal Church, which they declared out of continuity with traditional Anglican teaching. The traditionalist churches promote the canon of Scripture; the creeds and statements of the seven ecumenical councils of the early church; the *Book of Common Prayer* (1928); the writings of the Church Fathers; and the historic succession of male bishops, priests, and deacons.

These churches generally see themselves as being in communion with the Eastern Orthodox* and Roman Catholic* churches because of their common affirmation of the decrees of the ecumenical councils before the division of 1054. Despite their common affirmation of the historical episcopacy, the continuing churches have had difficulty remaining in communion with one another.

In 1968 the American Episcopal Church was founded in Mobile, Alabama, by several traditionalist clergy and laity who wished to preserve the 1928 *Book of Common Prayer*. It developed into the Anglican Province of America, and currently it is in the process of uniting or at least having full communion with the Anglican Rite Synod of the Americas, the Episcopal Orthodox Church, the United Episcopal Church, and the Reformed Episcopal Church. It has also absorbed congregations from other traditionalist churches, such as the Southern Episcopal Church.

The Anglican Catholic Church was a direct result of the 1977 St. Louis meeting. Its constitution was adopted in 1978. The Province of Christ the King separated in 1979 and has about fifty parishes nationwide. The United Episcopal Church separated in 1980 and has about 20 parishes. The Anglican Rite Jurisdiction of the Americas was established in 1991 through a merger of the American Episcopal Church and a sizable portion of the Anglican Catholic Church. Also notable is the Evangelical Anglican Church of America, based in California, which draws upon the heritage of the eighteenth century evangelists John Wesley and George Whitefield to promote both personal conversion and traditional Anglican ritual.

Many traditionalist Anglican bodies adopt much of the practice of Eastern Orthodoxy* or identify themselves as part of the Old Catholic* movement. When the Rev. James Parker Dees resigned from the priesthood of the Protestant Episcopal Church in 1963 to protest its emphasis on the social gospel, he founded the Anglican Orthodox Church. Dees was consecrated bishop by Bishop Wasyl Sawyna of the Holy Ukrainian Autocephalic Orthodox Church and Bishop Orlando J. Woodward of the Old Catholic succession. The church is headquartered in North Carolina, but is in communion with bodies in Africa and Asia. It emphasizes the doctrines of the virgin birth, the atoning sacrifice of the cross, the Trinity, the bodily resurrection of Jesus, the Second Coming, salvation by faith alone, and the divinity of Christ. A split led to the formation of the Episcopal Orthodox Christian Archdiocese of America, which came under the jurisdiction of the Anglican Rite Synod in the Americas in 1999. That body, in turn, is under the jurisdiction of the Philippine Independent Catholic Church. Along with other traditionalist groups around the world, they are part of the Orthodox Anglican Communion.

Likewise, the Anglican Rite Archdiocese of the Americas is a traditional Anglican body that uses the 1928 *Book of Common Prayer* and the Anglican Missal. It is in alliance with the Orthodox Church of Canada. The church holds to the seven sacraments and the teachings of early Christianity and believes that other churches "diminish" the true faith through "social teachings" and political correctness. The church also identifies itself as "a safe harbor" from political and theological battles in other churches.

For more information: www.anglicansonline.org; www.anglicancatholic.org; www.anglicanprovince.org; www.eoc.orthodoxanglican.net.; www.celtchristian .net; www.anglicanpck.org; www.fidelium.org

EPISCOPAL CHURCH

Founded: 1789
Membership: 2,154,572 in 7,095 parishes (2006)

The largest body to come out of the Church of England in the United States has been known as the Episcopal Church since 1967. Members of the Episcopal Church profess two of the ancient Christian creeds: the Apostles' Creed and the Nicene Creed. Thirty-five articles derived from the Church of England's thirty-nine are accepted as a general statement of doctrine, but adherence to them as a creed is not required.

At their ordination, clergy profess their belief in the Scriptures and their willingness to conform to "the doctrine, discipline, and worship of the Episcopal Church." ("The Ordination of a Priest," *Book of Common Prayer,* pg. 526) The church also expects its members to be loyal to the doctrine, discipline and worship of the church in all the essentials, but permits great liberty in nonessentials. It allows for variation, individuality, independent thinking, and religious liberty. Some Episcopal churches are "high," with elaborate ritual and ceremony; others are described as "low," with less stylized ceremony and more of an evangelistic emphasis. Liberals, conservatives, modernists and evangelicals find common ground for worship in the prayer book. Stained-glass windows, gleaming altars, vested choirs, and a glorious ritual give the worshiper a deep sense of the continuity of the Christian spirit and tradition.

The local congregation, or parish, elects its own minister (rector or priest), who is vested with pastoral oversight of the congregation by the bishop. Lay officers administer the temporal affairs and the property of the parish along with the priest or rector. Each parish, mission, and chapel is represented in the annual diocesan convention by its clergy and elected lay delegates. Each diocese is in turn represented in the triennial General Convention of the church by its bishop (or bishops), clergy, and lay deputies. Between sessions of the General Convention, the work of the church is carried on by the presiding bishop and an executive council. The church maintains national headquarters in New York City.

All of the United States dioceses are self-supporting with the exception of the Church in Navajoland. The church participates actively with mission work in the Caribbean, South America, and Southeast Asia. The domestic missionary program has traditionally emphasized grants and ministry for urban missions and ministry to African American, Hispanic, Native American, and Asian American congregations and organizations. In recent years, attention and funding have turned to evangelism and the incorporation of youth in planning and decision making.

The church sponsors eleven accredited seminaries. There are eight Episcopal colleges and one university in the United States and two colleges overseas. Over a thousand Episcopal schools and early childhood education programs are in operation. Each diocese sponsors social service and health organizations including homes for seniors, youth care, hospitals and hospice centers, and centers for the homeless and destitute. Sixteen religious orders are scattered across the United States; the Church also recognizes eleven Christian communities.

When Presiding Bishop John Hines called a Special General Convention in 1969 to address the problems of racial segregation and urban decay, the Church entered upon a path of engagement with modernity and American culture. Since then, the Church has discussed and debated issues of liturgical reform, equal access to ordination, sexuality, and ecclesiastical authority. Black Episcopalians continue to lead the Church in addressing institutional racism and its complicity in the larger problem of racism in America. Women, who had so long provided the energy in labor and fundraising for the Church's missionary work, adjured their "auxiliary" status. This process opened the door to a series of profound changes in the understanding of authority, the stewardship of resources, and the full participation of the faithful in the life of the Church.

After much trial and debate, the General Convention adopted a new standard of the *Book of Common Prayer* in 1979. This was the first revision of the American Prayer Book since 1928, and it provides alternate rites that use more contemporary usage and idiom. A new hymnal, the first since 1940, was approved in 1982. Liturgical reform led directly to a participatory theology that was finally encoded in 1988 into the Church's canons emphasizing "the development and affirmation of the ministry of all baptized persons in the Church and in the world" and the full and equal ministry of all the faithful. (Canons of the Episcopal Church, pg. 63; http://www.episcopalarchives.org/e-archives/canons/Cand C_FINAL_11.29.2006.pdf)

Liturgical reform coincided with a vigorous pursuit of women's ordination. Ordination of women to the priesthood finally passed the General Convention in 1976, and in 1989 the Reverend Barbara C. Harris was ordained the Suffragan Bishop of Massachusetts and the first woman bishop in the historic succession. The inclusion of formerly marginalized groups into the circles of governance and program and ordinary parish life, begun in 1969, continues today. In 2003 the church chose to ordain an openly gay bishop, V. Gene Robinson, of the Diocese of New Hampshire. The ordination of homosexuals and the blessing of same sex unions promise to be difficult tests for the cohesion of the Episcopal Church, if not its essential unity. In 2009 six bishops requested permission to adapt the wedding ceremony in the *Book of Common Prayer* for use for gay couples getting married in states where that is legal.

Through all of the controversy, members have remained focused primarily on the work of ministry in parish communities. In 2000 the General Convention approved full formal communion with the Evangelical Lutheran Church in America*, and in 2009 full communion with the Moravian Church* was approved. Currently there is greater emphasis on domestic evangelism than in the past. In 2006 the church adopted the United Nations Millennium Development Goals as mission goals for the denomination. Church members are also becoming more aware and sensitive to the American church's place in the 73 million-member Anglican Communion, the majority of whom live on the African continent. In 2006 Dr. Katharine Jefferts Schori was elected Presiding Bishop of the Episcopal Church. She was an oceanographer before being ordained a priest in 1994. One of the challenges facing Bishop Schori is the continuing decline in membership in the Episcopal Church.

For more information: www.episcopalchurch.org

Headquarters: 815 Second Ave., New York, NY 10017

EVANGELICAL ANGLICAN CHURCH IN AMERICA

Founded: 1986
Membership: statistics not available, but less than 5,000

Most of the Anglican denominations separated from the Episcopal Church in order to preserve the tradition, especially the 1928 Prayer Book. A few new bodies have formed within the Anglican tradition in order to promote a more liberal perspective than found in the Episcopal Church* while maintaining the traditional ritual. The bodies are new and small, but merit mentioning because of their distinctiveness on the American scene. One example is the Universal Episcopal Church, which combines theosophical and Anglican traditions. More traditional is the Evangelical Anglican Church in America, which should not be confused with the traditionalist Evangelical Anglican Church of America. This church offers the seven sacraments "to all of the People of God with respect to the diversity of creation as the cornerstone of God's lavish love and welcome for creation." The church bases its practice and doctrine on the idea of the original blessing in creation and the call to bring the message of salvation to all people.

For more information: www.eaca.org

Headquarters: 1805 Las Lomas NE, Albuquerque, NM 87106

INTERNATIONAL COMMUNION OF THE CHARISMATIC EPISCOPAL CHURCH

Founded: 1992
Membership: 117 parishes (2009)

Founded by Randolph Adler, this communion seeks to combine Pentecostal*/charismatic experience with liturgical worship. Worship is liturgical, but it includes expressions of charismatic gifts, such as speaking in tongues and healing.

It is a fellowship of charismatic churches that maintain their identification with traditional Anglicanism. The church is not part of the Anglican communion, although it has an episcopal structure and many parishes use the 1928 *Book of Common Prayer*. Tracing its origins to an expressed desire among various evangelicals in the 1970s for connection with "historical Christianity," the church endeavors to bring the rich sacramental and liturgical life of the early church to searching evangelicals and charismatics. It is part of the Convergence Movement (see COMMUNION OF CONVERGENCE CHURCHES USA) inspired by the writings of Lesslie Newbigin and Robert Webber.

The governance of the church is in the hands of bishops who are understood to be pastors of the church and who must be rectors in their own parishes. In 1996, the church named its first patriarch, Randolph Adler, who had been consecrated a bishop four years earlier. In 1997 all of the clergy of the denomination were ordained by bishops in the Brazilian Catholic Apostolic Church, which was established by Rt. Rev. Carlos Duarte in 1945. Bishop Duarte broke with the Roman Catholic Church because the Vatican had given passports to Nazi war criminals fleeing to Brazil.

The Charismatic Episcopal Church's doctrine was given explicit formulation in the San Clemente Declaration of 1999. Church teaching gives priority to worship and liturgical practice in community life. The church explicitly affirms the authority of the Bible, the first seven ecumenical councils, and the historic episcopacy. It administers the seven traditional sacraments of the Catholic Church. Stressing that it is not a splinter group but an intentional religious community drawing on a rich theological and liturgical heritage, the Communion intends to "provide a home for all Christians who seek a liturgical-sacramental, evangelical, charismatic church and a foundation for their lives and gifts of ministry." (www.iccec.org) The Communion is an international body with more than 1,700 parishes worldwide. Its growth has been most dramatic in Africa and South America.

The church in the United States suffered a crisis in 2006 that led to the departure of seven bishops and nearly one third of the congregants. The church's presiding officers addressed several concerns raised about the denomination, and in 2008 Craig W. Bates was chosen to succeed Adler as the patriarch.

For more information: www.iccec.org

Headquarters: 122 Broadway, Malverne, NY 11565

REFORMED EPISCOPAL CHURCH

Founded: 1873
Membership: est. 10,000 in 152 parishes (2009)

The Reformed Episcopal Church was organized in New York City by Bishop George D. Cummins (1822-76), eight clergy, and twenty laypersons who had been members of the Protestant Episcopal Church. This body emerged during the long Tractarian controversy in England and the United States, in which the issues of church ritual and ecclesiastical authority became prominent. Cummins was a leader of the low-church, evangelical party within the Protestant Episcopal Church. He protested what he perceived to be intolerance of other Protestant churches among those influenced by the Oxford Movement, the movement within the church of England that sought to restore pre-Reformation ideas and practices of the church.

In October 1873, Cummins participated in an ecumenical, evangelical communion service held in Fifth Avenue Presbyterian Church in New York. In the face of public criticism from other bishops, and in the conviction that the ecumenical nature and mission of the Protestant Episcopal Church were being lost, Cummins withdrew to found the new denomination. In 1873 he drew up the Declaration of Principles, which are understood to be the evangelical response to the issues of the nineteenth century controversies.

Doctrine and organization are similar to those of the parent church, with some notable exceptions. Clergy are required to subscribe to the Church of England's Thirty-nine Articles of Religion, as revised by the Protestant Episcopal Church in 1801. The *Book of Common Prayer* (BCP) has been revised in accordance with the English prayer book tradition, bringing it into conformity with the English 1662 *BCP* and the American 1928 *BCP*.

Parish and diocesan units prevail in the administration of the church. The triennial General Council is like the General Convention of the Episcopal Church; however, its bishops do not constitute a separate house. The church has seven dioceses in North America (four in the United States) and carries out oversees work in India, France, Brazil, Liberia and Germany. There are seminaries in Blue Bell, Pennsylvania; Summerville, South Carolina; and Houston, Texas. The denomination is one of the founding jurisdictions of the Anglican Church in North America. The Presiding Bishop is the Most Rev. Leonard W. Riches.

For more information: www.rechurch.org

Headquarters: 826 Second Ave., Blue Bell, PA 19422

Lutheran Churches

In the early sixteenth century, a German theologian named Martin Luther (1483–1546) set out to reform the Roman Catholic Church* of his day. Although he did not intend to create a new church, his followers were nicknamed "Lutherans." These Protestants, as they were called after a famous protest at the Diet of Speyer in 1529, affirmed the message of the Bible as the sole authority for church life and Christian belief and practice without rejecting the historical church. To this day, Lutheranism retains much of the tradition of the ancient and medieval church, including a sense of participation in the historic people of God and in the traditional liturgy, revised to accord with Protestant biblicism. Lutherans are devoted to sound doctrine, systematically developed and expressed in thoughtful preaching. Luther's teaching on justification by faith and on the universal priesthood of believers might be called the cornerstone of Protestantism.

History. The story of Luther's rebellion against the Roman Catholic Church* is well known. His position, briefly, was that the papacy had no divine right in things spiritual. Scripture, not the priest or the church, has final authority over conscience. Luther believed that the Bible is the clear, perfect, inspired, and authoritative Word of God and guide for humankind. He also believed that the individual conscience is responsible to God alone; therefore all Christians should have access to God's word in the Bible. Luther's translation of the Bible in German remains a hallmark of German literature.

Luther argued that people are forgiven and absolved of their sins not by good works or by a church rite but by turning from sin directly to God, with the help of the Holy Spirit. Drawing on the writings of the Apostle Paul, Luther declared that justification is attained through faith alone, not through ceremonies such as penance. Faith, for Lutherans, is not subscription to the dictates of the church, but trust in Christ. Luther called this theology "evangelical" because it was rooted in the gospel (in Greek *evangelion*) message of justification by faith through grace alone.

In 1529 Luther wrote both his *Large Catechism* and his *Small Catechism*. A year later, Philip Melanchthon (1497–1560) authored the statement of faith known as the Augsburg Confession. The year 1537 brought the Schmalkald Articles of Faith, written by Luther, Melanchthon, and other German Reformers; in 1577, the Formula of Concord was drawn up. These documents, which offer an explanation of Luther's ideology and theology, form the doctrinal basis of Lutheranism.

Most prominent in Germany, Lutheranism spread to Poland, Russia, Lithuania, Bohemia, Austria, Hungary, France, and Holland. It became the state church of Denmark, Norway, Sweden, Finland, Iceland, Estonia, and Latvia. Each national church developed its own governing structure and style of worship, but most Lutheran churches ascribe to the *Book of Concord*.

Lutherans in the United States. The first Lutheran worship service in America was a Christmas service held at Hudson Bay in 1619. The first European Lutherans to remain permanently in this country arrived at Manhattan Island from Holland in 1623. The first independent colony of Lutherans, New Sweden, was established at Fort Christiana along the Delaware River in 1638, at present day Wilmington, Delaware. The great influx of Lutheran immigrants, however, went to Pennsylvania, where by the middle of the eighteenth century Lutherans numbered about thirty thousand. Four-fifths of this group were German, the remainder Swedish.

The first churches were small and poor, often without pastors. The situation was relieved with the coming of Henry Melchior Muhlenberg (1711–1787) from the University of Halle, the headquarters of the Pietist movement (see BRETHREN AND PIETIST CHURCHES). In 1748 he united the pastors and congregations in Pennsylvania, New Jersey, New York, and Maryland into what came to be called the Ministerium of Pennsylvania. Muhlenberg recognized the need for American Lutherans to govern themselves years before the American Revolution. Synods were formed in New York in 1786, North Carolina in 1803, Maryland in 1820, and Ohio in 1836.

Each synod adjusted itself to its peculiar conditions of language, natural background, previous ecclesiastical relationship with Lutheran authorities abroad, and geographical location. The need for even further organization was evident from the ever-increasing flood of Lutherans from Europe, resulting in the formation of the General Synod in 1820. The General Synod extended its efforts to the west, and the Missouri Synod* was formed in 1847. From 1850 until 1860, one million Germans arrived in the United States, the majority of whom were Lutheran. By 1870, Lutherans were the fourth largest Protestant group in the country, with approximately four hundred thousand members.

The Civil War brought the first serious break in Lutheran ranks, with the organization of the United Synod of the South in 1863. Three years later a number of other synods, led by the Ministerium of Pennsylvania, withdrew from the General Synod to form the General Council. To increase the complexity, Lutheran immigrants continued to arrive in larger and larger numbers. These immigrants spoke different languages and came from nations where the church was organized in different ways. From 1870 until 1910, approximately one million seventy-five thousand Scandanavians arrived, bringing a slightly different form of Lutheranism than the older, now established German congregations. Numerous small synods were organized.

At one time there were about 150 Lutheran bodies in the United States. Consolidation, unification, and federation in the twentieth century reduced that number to fewer than a dozen. In 1988 the American Lutheran Church merged with the Lutheran Church in America and the Association of Evangelical Lutheran Churches to form the Evangelical Lutheran Church in America. With each major merger, new separate churches were also formed in protest.

Groups of lay and ministerial delegates from major Lutheran churches in twenty-two countries formed a Lutheran World Federation in 1947 for the purpose of relief and rehabilitation on a global scale among Lutherans. Perhaps the most cooperative effort in the history of American Lutheranism is found in Lutheran World Relief, through which more than $300 million in cash and food (including United States government-donated commodities) has been distributed throughout the world.

Belief and Practices. In spite of their divisions, there has been real unity among Lutherans, based more on faith than on organization. All the churches represent a single type of Protestant Christianity, built on Luther's principle of justification by faith alone. Lutherans maintain that the Bible is the inspired Word of God and the rule and standard of faith and practice. They confess their faith through the three general creeds of Christendom (Apostles, Nicene, and Athanasian), which they believe to be in accordance with the scriptures. They also believe that the Augsburg Confession is a correct exposition of the faith and doctrine of evangelical Lutheranism, although there is disagreement over which version is preferred. The large and small catechisms of Luther, the Schmalkaldic Articles, and the Formula of Concord, are all considered faithful interpretations of Lutheranism.

Baptism and the Lord's Supper are not merely signs or memorials, but are believed to be channels through which God bestows forgiving and empowering grace upon humankind. The real body and blood of Christ are believed to be present "in, with, and under" the bread and wine of the Lord's Supper and are received by the faithful sacramentally and supernaturally. Pastors baptize infant children of members, and baptized persons are believed to receive the gift of regeneration from the Holy Spirit.

Polity. The local congregation is usually administered between its annual meetings by a church council consisting of the pastor and a number of elected lay officers. Pastors are called by the voting members of the congregation. Congregations are united in synods composed of pastors and lay representatives elected by the congregations and have authority as granted by the synod constitution.

Synods (conferences or districts) are united in a general body that may be national or even international and are called variously "church," "synod," or "conference." Some of these general bodies are legislative in nature, some consultative; they supervise the work in worship, education, publication, charity, and mission. Congregations have business meetings at least annually; synods, districts, and conferences hold yearly conventions; the general bodies meet annually or biennially.

Suggestions for further reading:

Cimino, Richard. *American Lutherans Today.* Grand Rapids, MI: Wm. B. Eerdmans, 2003.

Gritsch, Eric W. *Fortress Introduction to Lutheranism.* Minneapolis: Augsburg-Fortress Press, 1994.

Groh, John E. and Robert H. Smith, eds. *The Lutheran Church in North America.* St. Louis: Concordia Press, 1979.

Huber, Donald L. *World Lutheranism: A Select Bibliography for English Readers.* Lanham, MD: Scarecrow Press, 2000.

Knudsen, Johannes. *The Formation of the Lutheran Church in America.* Philadelphia: Fortress Press, 1958.

Neve, H. T. and B. A. Anderson, eds. *The Maturing of American Lutheranism.* Minneapolis: Augsburg Press, 1968.

Schlink, Edmund. *Theology of the Lutheran Confessions.* Trans. Paul F. Keohneke and Herbert J. A. Bouman. Philadelphia: Muhlenberg Press, 1961.

AMERICAN ASSOCIATION OF LUTHERAN CHURCHES

Founded: 1987
Membership: est. 16,000 in 70 congregations (2007)

The AALC was formed by laity and pastors of the former American Lutheran Church in America who did not wish to participate in that church's 1988 merger with the Lutheran Church in America and the Association of Evangelical Lutheran Churches (see EVANGELICAL LUTHERAN CHURCH IN AMERICA). The AALC holds to a high view of the divinely inspired, revealed and inerrant Word of God, joyfully submitting to this as the only infallible authority in all matters of faith and life. The emphasis has been on the primacy of reaching people through the ministries of evangelism and world missions through the local congregations.

The congregations of the AALC are divided into ten regions, mainly in the northern states. The primary decision-making body is the annual General Convention, to which each congregation has proportionate representation. The Joint Council, with three representatives from each Region, governs the church body the rest of the time. The elected Presiding Pastor, along with the Executive Committee, leads from the National Office in Bloomington, Minnesota. The American Lutheran Theological Seminary is located in Edina, Minnesota.

For more information: www.taalc.org

Contact: The *Evangeli*, 801 West 106th Street, Suite 203, Minneapolis, MN 55420-5603

APOSTOLIC LUTHERAN CHURCH OF AMERICA

Founded: 1872, 1928
Membership: est. 9,000 in 60 churches (2004)

Sometimes called the Laestadians for Lars Levi Laestadius (1800–61), a naturalist, a revivalist, and a minister of the state church of Sweden, this church originated with Finnish immigrants in and around Calumet, Michigan, in the middle years of the nineteenth century. The church was first incorporated in Michigan under the name "Finnish Apostolic Lutheran Church of America" in 1928.

Conservative in theology, this church stresses the infallibility of Scripture and the importance of an experience of justification by faith. Such an experience is required for voting membership in spiritual matters; supporting members may vote on temporal matters only. The church accepts the ecumenical creeds and puts strong emphasis on the confession of sins, absolution, and regeneration. Confession may be made to another Christian, but for some publicly known sins, a person should confess before the congregation in order to receive absolution. Local congregations are quite free to govern themselves. The annual church convention elects an executive board which elects officers for the denomination.

For more information: www.apostoliclutheran.org

Headquarters: 124 Binney Hill Road, New Ipswich, NH 03071

ASSOCIATION OF FREE LUTHERAN CONGREGATIONS

Founded: 1962
Membership: 44,000 in 276 churches (2008)

This association was formed by congregations of the Lutheran Free Church, which rejected merging with the newly formed American Lutheran Church in 1962 (now part of the Evangelical Lutheran Church in America*). It has its roots in a revival movement that swept through Scandinavian Lutheran churches in the late nineteenth century. It is conservative theologically and maintains that the local congregation is subject to no authority but the Word and Spirit of God. Doctrinal emphases include the inerrancy and supreme authority of the Bible as the Word of God, congregational polity, the spiritual unity of all true believers, evangelical outreach for the purpose of leading persons to an experience with and devotion to Christ, the Lordship of Christ in one's personal life, and conservatism on social issues.

The association elects a president and a coordinating committee that maintains a clergy roster and fosters cooperation between churches in ministry to youth, evangelism, parish education, and other matters. Association members also sponsor a theological seminary and a Bible school in Minneapolis, Minnesota.

For more information: www.aflc.org

Headquarters: 3110 E. Medicine Lake Blvd., Minneapolis, MN 55441

CHURCH OF THE LUTHERAN BRETHREN OF AMERICA

Founded: 1900
Membership: 14,427 in 110 churches (2006)

This is an independent Lutheran body made up of autonomous congregations scattered across the United States and Canada. The synod was organized in 1900 to assist in Christian education and in home and world missions. The church maintains a firm commitment to the supreme authority of the scriptures. It accepts the basic Lutheran teachings and emphasizes the need for a personal faith in the Lord Jesus Christ that demonstrates itself in daily life. Membership in the local congregation is based on an individual's personal profession of faith. Worship services use traditional and contemporary music, lay participation, and biblical teaching and preaching that is evangelistic and personal in application. The congregations support a seminary, a Bible school, and a four-year secondary academy. These institutions as well as the headquarters are located in Fergus Falls, Minnesota. Mission projects are carried on in Chad, Cameroon, Japan, and Taiwan.

For more information: www.clba.org

Headquarters: P.O. Box 655, Fergus Falls, MN 56538

CHURCH OF THE LUTHERAN CONFESSION

Founded: 1960
Membership: 8,390 in 87 churches (2006)

This confessional church was organized by clergy and laypeople who had withdrawn from several synods of the Synodical Conference of North America over the issue of uniting with other synods. The CLC holds firmly to the doctrine of verbal inspiration and inerrancy of the Bible, and it maintains that there can be no church union (even with other Lutherans) unless there is full agreement in doctrine. It holds without reservation to all the historic confessions of the Lutheran faith. Membership is concentrated in South Dakota, Minnesota, and Wisconsin. It also engages in mission work in India and Nigeria. A high school, a college, and a seminary in Eau Claire, Wisconsin, are supported by the church.

For more information: www.clclutheran.org

Headquarters: 501 Grover Rd., Eau Claire, WI 54701

EVANGELICAL LUTHERAN CHURCH IN AMERICA

Founded: 1988
Membership: 4,709,956 in 10,448 churches (2007)

The Evangelical Lutheran Church in America (ELCA) is the youngest of the large United States Lutheran church bodies, but it is also the oldest since it is a continuation of the first Lutheran body. The ELCA was constituted in 1987 and began operation in 1988 as a result of the union of the American Lutheran Church (ALC), Lutheran Church in America (LCA), and Association of Evangelical Lutheran Churches (AELC), but it traces its history through predecessor church bodies to the formation in 1748 of the first synod in North America, the

Ministerium of Pennsylvania. The ELCA represents historical continuity for Lutherans from colonial days as well as the weaving together into one body all of the threads of Lutheran history in North America.

Two of the uniting churches that formed the ELCA were the result of mergers. The American Lutheran Church was formed in 1960, bringing together four churches of German, Norwegian, and Danish heritage. Subsequently, in 1962 the Lutheran Church in America was established in a four-way merger of German, Danish, Finnish, and Swedish heritage churches. Those mergers of the early 1960s marked a movement away from ethnic identity for American Lutheran church bodies. The American Evangelical Lutheran Church, in contrast, resulted from a break in 1976 from the Lutheran Church–Missouri Synod in a dispute over the authority and interpretation of Scripture.

Efforts to form the ELCA formally began in 1982 when the three uniting churches elected a seventy-member commission to draft the constitution and other agreements. In August 1986, the conventions of the three churches approved the merger, and the ELCA's constituting assembly was held in May 1987. The Rev. Herbert W. Chilstrom was elected the first presiding bishop and the Rev. Lowell G. Almen the first secretary. The ELCA's main office is in Chicago. Its congregations are grouped into sixty-five synods throughout the United States and the Caribbean region. Each synod is led by a bishop elected by voting members at a Synod Assembly to six-year, renewable terms.

The highest governing authority in the ELCA is the Churchwide Assembly, which includes six hundred lay voting members, equally divided by gender, and about four hundred clergy voting members. A thirty-seven-member Church Council, elected by the Assembly, serves as the board of directors and interim legislative authority between assemblies. The presiding bishop is the ELCA's chief pastor and the executive officer of the churchwide organization. Both the presiding bishop and secretary are elected by the Churchwide Assembly. Their terms of office are six years and incumbents are eligible for reelection. The treasurer is elected by the Church Council to six-year renewable terms. A lay vice president, who is elected to the volunteer position by the Churchwide Assembly, chairs the Church Council.

Units within the churchwide organization include: congregational ministries, rostered ministries, outreach, higher education and schools, church in society, and global mission. Ecumenical relations are coordinated through the presiding bishop's office and include ecumenical, inter-Lutheran, and inter-religious activities as well as administration of relationships with the Lutheran World Federation, World Council of Churches, and National Council of the Churches of Christ in the USA. The publishing unit, located in Minneapolis, is known as Augsburg Fortress Publishers. The pension board is also based in Minneapolis and provides pension and other benefit programs for clergy, other church workers, and congregations. The main periodical of the ELCA is *The Lutheran*, published monthly.

A formal relationship of full communion was established in 1997 between the ELCA and the Presbyterian Church (USA)*, Reformed Church in America*, and the United Church of Christ*. In 1999, relationships of full communion were formed with The Episcopal Church* and with the Moravian Church*. As a member of the Lutheran World Federation, the ELCA affirmed in 1999 the Joint Declaration on the Doctrine of Justification with the Roman Catholic Church*.

The ELCA promotes the Lutheran theological and liturgical tradition while allowing greater freedom for laity and clergy to address contemporary social and intellectual concerns than most of the other Lutheran denominations. It also engages in extensive ministries to promote both greater social justice and mercy in the world.

For more information: www.elca.org

Headquarters: 8765 West Higgins Rd., Chicago, IL 60631

EVANGELICAL LUTHERAN SYNOD

Founded: 1918
Membership: 19,945 in 131 churches (2007)

This synod traces its roots to the formation of a synod for Norwegian immigration in the middle of the nineteenth century. The ELS was organized in 1918 by a minority group that declined to join the other Norwegian groups when they united in the Norwegian Lutheran Church (later, the Evangelical Lutheran Church) in 1917. The jurisdiction of the synod is entirely advisory. The officers and boards of the synod, however, direct work of common interest insofar as they do not interfere with congregational rights or prerogatives. The ELS is in fellowship with the Wisconsin Synod* and maintains Bethany Lutheran College and Bethany Theological Seminary at Mankato, Minnesotta.

For more information: www.evangelicallutheransynod.org; www.evluthsyn.org

Headquarters: 6 Browns Court, Mankato, MN 56001

LATVIAN EVANGELICAL LUTHERAN CHURCH IN AMERICA

Founded: 1975
Membership: 12,010 in 60 churches (2005)

This body grew out of the Federation of Latvian Evangelical Lutheran Churches and is part of the international network of Latvian Lutherans around the world as well as a member of the Lutheran World Federation. It holds to the traditional doctrinal statements of Western Christianity (the Apostles, Nicene, and Athanasian

Creeds) and the statements of traditional Lutheranism (the unaltered Augsburg Confession, the *Small Catechism*, the *Large Catechism*, and the *Book of Concord*). In addition to promoting Lutheran worship, spirituality, and theology, the LELCA has preserved the customs and traditions of Latvian Protestantism. It is a member of the World Council of Churches and the Lutheran World Federation.

For more information: www.dcdraudze.org

Headquarters: 7225 Oak Highlands Dr., Kalamazoo, MI 49009

LUTHERAN CHURCH—MISSOURI SYNOD

Founded: 1847
Membership: 2,383,084 in 6,075 churches (2007)

This second-largest Lutheran denomination in the United States was founded in Missouri by German immigrants who left their homes in 1839. Many of these immigrants had rejected the planned merger of the Lutheran and Reformed churches in Prussia. They were led by a pastor named C.F.W. Walther, who served as the first president of the synod. From the beginning the synod has included churches outside of Missouri, but it remained heavily German until the twentieth century. World War I accelerated the process of adopted English as the language of worship. The church has always been devoted to the maintenance of confessional Lutheranism, coupled with a strong sense of mission outreach. It stresses the authority of the classic Lutheran confessional statements and the inerrancy of Scripture. The church insists on the "three *solas*": salvation by *grace alone* through *faith alone* based on *Scripture alone*. The LCMS was the first Christian denomination to urge its members to donate body organs, and it has called for a constitutional amendment to ban abortions. The church views homosexual behavior as sinful and does not endorse gay marriage.

The LCMS stresses Christian education for members of all ages, and the synod operates ten universities and colleges as well as two theological seminaries in North America. In addition, its elementary and secondary school system is the largest of any Protestant denomination in the United States with over 1,300 preschools, one thousand elementary schools, and one hundred high schools. The synod has long been considered a leader in the field of communications. It operates the world's oldest religious radio station, KFUO, in St. Louis, Missouri. Since 1930 it has produced the "Lutheran Hour," heard in more than forty different languages and forty countries. It also operates Concordia Publishing House, one of the largest religious publishers in the United States. Its *LifeLight* curriculum has been enormously popular. In addition, for many decades the church has given great attention to ministry to deaf and blind persons. Each month, volunteers in sixty work centers distribute some two thousand Braille magazines, 6,500 large print publications, and 1,200 cassettes of devotional and educational material.

Because of differences in doctrine and practice, the Missouri Synod was not a part of the 1988 merger that united three other Lutheran denominations. However, it continues to cooperate with those churches in a variety of ministries, particularly in areas of social work, such as world hunger relief and the resettlement of refugees. The church has over nine thousand pastors and thirty thousand educators, and it began sending out foreign missionaries in the 1890s. It now has active work in eighty-five countries on every inhabited continent. In the early 1990s the church declared the United States to be a "world mission field" and it conducts intentional mission work among Latinos, African and Asian immigrants, Native Americans, Jews, and Arabic-speaking groups.

The church's headquarters are in the International Center in suburban St. Louis. Directors for the church body are set by a triennial convention of pastors and laypeople, whose members represent the congregations of the synod. The church is divided into thirty-five administrative districts, which in turn are organized into six hundred circuits containing eight to twenty congregations. National assemblies take place every third year. Though the denomination participates in many ecumenical dialogues, it does not share in communion with churches unless there is agreement in the confession of the Gospel in all articles.

For more information: www.lcms.org

Headquarters: 1333 S. Kirkwood Road, St. Louis, MO 63122-7295

WISCONSIN EVANGELICAL LUTHERAN SYNOD

Founded: 1850
Membership: 394,241 in 1,276 congregations (2007)

Organized in Milwaukee as the German Evangelical Lutheran Synod of Wisconsin, this church merged with the Minnesota and Michigan synods in 1917 to become the Evangelical Lutheran Joint Synod of Wisconsin and Other States. Today it is known as the Wisconsin Evangelical Lutheran Synod, or WELS. This synod subscribes to confessional Lutheranism and is committed without reservation to the inspiration and infallibility of Holy Scripture. It seeks fellowship with those who believe that full agreement in doctrine and practice is necessary for biblical fellowship.

Divided into twelve districts, the synod maintains its national headquarters in Milwaukee. Mission churches are supported in Malawi, Zambia, Cameroon, Nigeria, Albania, Bulgaria, Japan, Russia, Sweden, Norway, Finland, Hong Kong, Indonesia, Taiwan, Thailand, India, Brazil, Colombia, the Dominican Republic, Mexico, and Puerto Rico. There are also 190 locations in the West Indies and in

North America, including Arizona. WELS has one of the largest Christian prison ministries in the United States, distributing hundreds of thousands of Bibles to inmates and offering Bible correspondence courses to inmates.

For the education of its pastors, teachers, and staff ministers, WELS maintains a college in New Ulm, Minnesota, a seminary at Mequon, Wisconsin, and two preparatory schools in Watertown, Wisconsin, and Saginaw, Minnesota. The church has one of the larger parochial school systems in the country. Congregations in the synod operate 339 Lutheran elementary schools, 405 early childhood ministries, and twenty-four high schools. WELS is a member of the Confessional Evangelical Lutheran Conference, which includes twenty confessional church bodies throughout the world.

For more information: www.wels.net

Headquarters: 2929 North Mayfair Road, Milwaukee, Wisconsin 53222

Reformed, Congregationalist, and Presbyterian Churches

The year 2009 marked the five hundredth anniversary of the birth of John Calvin (1509-1564), the most influential theologian in the Reformed tradition of Protestantism. The anniversary year provided an opportunity for all branches of the Reformed faith to celebrate their rich heritage. To mark the occasion, the World Alliance of Reformed Churches and the Reformed Ecumenical Council united to form the World Communion of Reformed Churches, a body which represents more than seventy-five million Christians in over two hundred countries.

The Reformed family of churches originated in the Swiss Reformation, especially in Zurich and Geneva, where Calvin served as a pastor and teacher. Reformed churches are often called "Calvinist" because of Calvin's influence, but Reformed churches have often disagreed on how to apply his theology. Calvin viewed himself primarily as an interpreter of Scripture, and he bequeathed a strong biblicism to the Reformed tradition. Basic to Calvin's thought was God's sovereignty over the world and people's lives; humans are completely dependent upon God for their lives and salvation. The most controversial Calvinist proposition was "double predestination," which means that eternal salvation and damnation are predetermined by God. Calvin also taught that both the natural world and human history work according to God's rational law and providential will.

Doctrine in Reformed Churches is based primarily on the Belgic Confession (1561), the Heidelberg Catechism (1563), and the Canons of the Synod of Dort (1618). Presbyterian churches also use the Westminster Confession of Faith (1648). These confessions emphasize salvation through Christ and the primacy of God's power in human life. More cerebral and verbal than emotional and aesthetic, Reformed theology places particular value on understanding, learning, and doctrinal unity than most branches of Christianity. Reformed worship also tends to focus on biblical exposition and preaching rather than music and the sacraments.

The Reformed churches in Europe developed along national lines. Particularly strong were the Reformed churches in the Netherlands (Holland), Germany, England, Scotland, Hungary, Bohemia, and Poland. Presbyterian Churches are in the Reformed tradition, but the Scottish reformer John Knox (ca. 1513–1572) played as great a role in their formation as John Calvin. Though they were often tolerated or even supported by local governments, the Reformed churches were officially outlawed throughout Europe until the Peace of Westphalia in 1648. Their theology and church structure were thus formed in the midst of persecution and a struggle for religious and political independence. It was the Reformed churches that rejected the idea of "divine right" for monarchs.

In England, the Reformed tradition was represented by the Puritans who sought to reform the Church of England (see EPISCOPAL AND ANGLICAN CHURCHES) along Calvinist lines. During the English Civil War, the Westminster Assembly (1643–1648) met in an effort to resolve the struggle over the compulsory use of the Anglican *Book of Common Prayer* in all English parishes. That assembly produced a Larger and a Shorter Catechism; a directory for the public worship of God; a form of government; and the Westminster Confession of Faith, which became the doctrinal standard of Scottish, British, and American Presbyterianism.

The Reformed tradition was the most influential religious tradition in colonial America, and it has had a profound impact on American religion and culture. The Puritans (Congregationalists) in New England were representatives of the Reformed tradition, as were the Scots-Irish Presbyterians who immigrated to the middle colonies and southward. Many of the institutions of higher education in colonial America were founded by Reformed churches (Harvard, Yale, Princeton, Dartmouth), and those schools produced some of America's best theologians, such as Jonathan Edwards (1703–1758). Reformed thought and practice influenced American literature, law, education, and government during the formative period of the country.

Types of Reformed Churches. Many of the divisions among Reformed churches can be traced to different interpretations of Calvin's teaching and the authority of the basic confessions. Over time, many pastors and congregations in the Reformed tradition turned away from Calvin's strict teaching on predestination and adopted a more covenantal understanding of God's relationship to the world and to believers.

Because of their deep commitment to local authority, whether through congregations or presbyteries, Reformed churches developed along ethnic lines.

Language, culture, and national heritage were closely connected to theological and liturgical concerns. Several Reformed denominations in the United States continue to reflect their European national origins.

Other divisions within the Reformed family of churches involve church order. All of the Reformed churches rejected episcopacy (rule by bishops) and attempted to follow the structure of the New Testament church, but there were disagreements over the details of that structure. Calvin promoted a presbyterial system in which a council of clergy (presbyters) exercised authority within a geographical region. Reformed and Presbyterian churches follow Calvin's approach. The governing body in the local church is called a consistory, session, or council depending on the denomination. Typically, it is made up of elders, deacons, and ministers who undertake the administrative duties common to congregational life. Churches in a geographical area are then organized into a presbytery or classis that supervises congregations and clergy within its bounds. This body is generally comprised of elder delegates from each congregation and the ministers in the area. The presbytery or classis is in turn under the authority of regional synods that supervise planning and programming. The highest legislative and judicial body of most Reformed and Presbyterian churches is a representative body called General Synod or General Assembly, which meets once a year,

In Congregationalism, the assembled body of believers on the local level has final authority. Local and national assemblies may provide programming and assist in cooperative ministries, but they have little direct power over congregations and pastors. Many other denominations influenced by the Reformed tradition, such as the Baptists* and churches in the Stone-Campbellite tradition (see CHRISTIAN AND RESTORATIONIST CHURCHES) also hold to congregational polity. The Puritans in colonial New England were generally Congregationalists.

Congregationalists in America. In 1609, John Robinson (1575–1625) fled persecution in England and settled at Leiden in the Netherlands. There he met William Ames (1576–1633), Congregationalism's first theologian, who was also a fugitive from the ecclesiastical courts of England. Robinson and his congregation enjoyed peace and freedom under the Dutch but wanted to remain English. A large company sailed for the American colonies in 1620 aboard the historic *Mayflower,* earning the name "Pilgrims." Between 1630 and 1640, twenty thousand more Puritans, mostly Congregationalists, arrived at Massachusetts Bay. There they established a "theocratic" government based on Biblical law and Calvin's theology. Contrary to popular belief, it was not a stern and rigid regime of the saints, but rather strict and intolerant of religious dissent. When four Quakers (see FRIENDS), including a woman, were hanged on Boston Common in the 1660s, there was a public outcry in England. New England was forced to accept the Act of Toleration in 1689.

Congregationalists in New England were leaders in the American Revolution, in part because they rejected the "divine right of kings" and argued that the people can determine their own government under God's laws. During the next century Congregationalism played a major role in developing American institutional and religious life. In the field of education, Congregationalists founded Harvard in 1636, Yale in 1707, and Dartmouth in 1769. Dartmouth developed from Eleazer Wheelock's (1711–1779) school for Native Americans.

The American Board of Commissioners for Foreign Missions, organized in 1810, was concerned at first with both home and foreign missionary work. It included representatives from Congregationalist, Presbyterian, Dutch Reformed, and Associate Reformed churches. Missionaries were sent to more than thirty foreign countries and American territories. In 1826, the American Home Missionary Society was founded, and in 1846 the American Missionary Association, which was active in the South before the Civil War, was founded.

Meanwhile, differences of opinion between theological liberals and conservatives developed during the nineteenth century. A famous sermon by the Unitarian* William Ellery Channing (1780–1842) at Baltimore in 1819 made a division inevitable. In spite of the Unitarian separation, Congregationalism continued to grow until a national supervisory body became necessary. A council held at Boston in 1865 proved so effective that a regular system of councils was established.

Unity and cooperation across denominational lines have been outstanding characteristics of Congregationalism. Christian Endeavor, at one time the largest young people's organization in Protestantism, was founded in 1881 by a Congregationalist, Francis E. Clark (1851–1921). By 1885 it had become interdenominational.

Dutch and German Reformed Churches in America. The Reformed Church came to America along with the first Dutch colonists. As early as 1614, there was informal Reformed worship along the upper reaches of the Hudson River near modern Albany, New York. The Reformed were numerous enough to require the services of lay ministers, two of whom came from Holland in 1623 as "comforters of the sick." By 1628 the Dutch in New Amsterdam had a pastor of their own, Jonas Michaelius (b. 1577), who organized the first church in the middle colonies.

When the English took possession of New Amsterdam in 1664, perhaps eight thousand Dutch church people were holding services in their own language. It was difficult and expensive to send native-born ministerial candidates to Holland for education and ordination, so a college and seminary were established at New Brunswick, New Jersey. This institution later became New Brunswick Theological Seminary and Rutgers University. Michael Schlatter (1718–1790) was sent to the middle colonies by the Reformed Synod of South and North Holland. He worked tirelessly to bring organization to the Reformed churches and improve the quality of the ministry.

A large majority of the clergy and laypeople of the Reformed Church supported the American Revolution. As the Dutch became Americanized, the English language gradually became accepted in churches, but not without a struggle.

114

A second emigration from the Netherlands began in the middle of the nineteenth century, bringing entire congregations with their pastors. One group, led by Albertus van Raalte (1811–1876), established a community called Holland in western Michigan. Van Raalte and his group became part of the Reformed Church in America in 1850.

German Reformed churches in America originated in the flood tide of German immigrants to Pennsylvania in the eighteenth century. More than half the Germans there in 1730 were Reformed, but the congregations often lacked ministers and employed school teachers to lead the services. Johann Philip Boehm (1683–1749), a schoolmaster, led worship services and in 1725 he assumed the pastoral office for German Reformed settlers in southeastern Pennsylvania. He worked closely with the Dutch Reformed minister Michael Schlatter in expanding and organizing Reformed congregations. Nikolaus von Zinzendorf tried to unite all German Protestants (Lutherans, Reformed, and sectarians) into a Church of God in the Spirit in the 1740s, but the effort failed.

The American synod declared its independence in 1793, taking the name German Reformed Church. In that year it reported 178 congregations and fifteen thousand communicants. The word *German* was dropped from the name in 1869, and thereafter the denomination was called the Reformed Church in the United States. Difficulties arose in the early years of the nineteenth century. Older Germans preferred the use of the German language, but members raised in the United States demanded English. Some churches withdrew to form a separate synod, but returned in 1837 when compromises were made. District synods of both German-speaking and English-speaking congregations were created, and two Hungarian classes from the Old Hungarian Reformed Church were added in 1924.

The Evangelical and Reformed Church was the product of a union of the Evangelical Synod of North America and the Reformed Church in the United States in 1934. Few difficulties were encountered in reconciling the doctrines of the two bodies. Both churches were German in ethnicity and Calvinistic in doctrine.

Presbyterians in America. After Oliver Cromwell's death in 1658 and the ending of Puritan rule in England, British Presbyterians fled to North America with the Congregationalists. When the British crown attempted to establish episcopacy in Scotland in the 1660s, many Presbyterians left Scotland and settled in Northern Ireland. Economic difficulties and religious inequalities in Ireland drove many of these Scots-Irish to immigrate to the United States. From 1710 until 1750, between three and six thousand Scottish immigrants arrived annually, settling primarily in Pennsylvania and Virginia, from whence they migrated to the West and South.

The first American presbytery or association of local churches was founded in Philadelphia in 1706. In 1729 Presbyterians adopted the Westminster Confession of Faith, together with the Larger and the Shorter Catechism. The same synod denied civil magistrates any power over the church and banned the persecution of anyone for religious faith.

In the 1720s, William Tennent, Sr. (1673–1746), organized a "log college" in a cabin at Neshaminy, Pennsylvania to train Presbyterian ministers and evangelists. Eventually it became the College of New Jersey (later Princeton University), and it produced a stream of revivalistic Presbyterian preachers who played leading roles in the Great Awakening of the 1740s. Such preachers, especially Gilbert Tennent (1703–1764), promoted an emotional "new birth" revivalism, which conflicted with the old creedal Calvinism.

The camp-meeting revival, which had its roots in Scotland, grew out of that Great Awakening enthusiasm; however, it split the denomination. Preachers on the "old side" opposed revivalism, while those of the "new side" endorsed it, claiming that less attention should be paid to college training of ministers and more to recruiting regenerated common men. The two sides quarreled until they reunited in 1757.

The next year, in the first united synod, there were ninety-four ministers in the colonial Presbyterian Church, with two hundred congregations and about ten thousand members. One of the ablest of the new-side preachers was John Witherspoon (1723–1794), president of Princeton, who was the only ordained person to sign the Declaration of Independence. The Scots-Irish accepted the Revolution with relish; their persecution in England and Northern Ireland had made them solid anti-British dissenters. Their old cry, "No bishop and no king," was heard back in England.

After the Revolution, Presbyterian and Congregational preachers and laypeople moving into the new western territory worked together. Ministers of the two groups preached in one another's pulpits, and members held the right of representation in both the congregational association and the presbytery. The plan worked well on the whole, absorbing the fruits of the national revivals and giving real impetus to missionary work at home and abroad. This cooperation with the Congregations, though, contributed to the split between "Old School" and "New School" Presbyterians over matters of discipline and the expenditure of missionary money. The General Assembly of 1837 expelled four New School synods, which promptly met in their own convention to form a new General Assembly.

More tragic was the division between the Southern and Northern Presbyterians over the issue of slavery. In 1846, the Old School assembly regarded slavery as no bar to Christian communion, but in that same year, the New School condemned the practice strongly. By 1857, several Southern New School synods had withdrawn to form the United Synod of the Presbyterian Church. The greater schism came in 1861, following the outbreak of the Civil War, when forty-seven Southern presbyteries of the Old School formed the Presbyterian Church in the Confederate States of America. In 1867, following the war, they merged to form the Presbyterian Church in the United States (PCUS).

The Old School and New School bodies of the Northern Presbyterian Church were united in 1870 on the basis of the Westminster Confession. Most of the Cumberland Presbyterian churches joined them in 1907; the Welsh Calvinist

116

Methodists joined in 1920. In the decades from 1920 until 1950, an emphasis on theology was evident in a liberal/conservative struggle.

Suggestions for further reading:

Bercovitch, Sacvan. *The Puritan Origins of the American Self.* New Haven: Yale University Press, 1975.

Bozeman, Dwight. *To Live Ancient Lives: The Primitivisit Dimension in Puritanism.* Chapel Hill, NC: Univ. of North Carolina Press, 1988.

Bratt, James D. *Dutch Calvinism in Modern America.* Grand Rapids: Eerdmans, 1984.

Dunn, David, et. al. *A History of the Evangelical & Reformed Church.* Philadelphia: Westminster, 1961.

Gunnemann, Louis H. *The Shaping of the United Church of Christ.* New York: United Church Press, 1977.

Hart, D. G., and Mark A. Noll, eds. *Dictionary of the Presbyterian and Reformed Tradition in America.* Downers Grove, IL: InterVarsity Press, 1999.

Horton, Douglas. *The United Church of Christ. Its Origins, Organization, and Role in the World Today.* New York: Thomas Nelson, 1962.

Hutchinson, William R. *Between the Times: The Travail of the Protestant Establishment in America, 1900-1960.* New York: Cambridge University Press, 1989.

Miller, Perry. *The New England Mind,* 2 vols. Boston: Beacon Press, 1961.

Porterfield, Amanda. *Female Piety in Puritan New England: The Emergence of Religious Humanism.* New York: Oxford University Press, 1992.

Smylie, James H. *A Brief History of the Presbyterians.* Louisville: Geneva Press, 1996.

Thompson, Ernest T. *Presbyterians in the South,* 3 vols. Richmond, Va.: John Knox Press, 1963-73.

VandenBerge, Peter M., ed. *Historical Directory of the Reformed Church in America: 1628–1978.* Grand Rapids: Eerdmans, 1978.

AMERICAN WALDENSIAN SOCIETY

Founded: 1906, with roots to the twelfth century
Membership: under 5,000

Although the Waldensian Church is now part of the United Presbyterian Church, the Waldensians deserve special mention in the *Handbook* because of their importance in the history of Western Christianity. During the Middle Ages, the Waldensians were more of a movement than an institutional church, but they may legitimately claim to be the first Protestants. The Waldensians attempted to reform the Catholic Church in the twelfth century under the leadership of

Valdes (also known as Peter Waldo), a wealthy merchant who decided to give his wealth away to the poor. Valdes adopted "apostolic poverty" and began preaching reform in the area around Lyons, in southern France. He was a harsh critic of the wealth and corruption of the Catholic Church* of his day, and he gained a large following among the people.

Much like Saint Francis in the following century, Valdes used the Sermon on the Mount as a guide to reform. Unlike Francis, Valdes and his followers were repeatedly condemned as heretical by bishops and popes. In response to the violence of the Inquisition, the Waldensians sought refuge in the Italian Alps, where they established a permanent presence. They spoke a French dialect that can still be heard in the so-called Waldensian Valleys near Turin. The Waldensians translated the New Testament and portions of the Old Testament into their vernacular so that the laity could have access to Scripture. Throughout the later Middle Ages, Waldensians' ideas spread throughout Central Europe. The Waldensians played a role in the Czech Reformation of the fifteenth century (see Moravian Church).

During the Swiss Reformation, Waldensians sought refuge in Geneva and there adopted Calvinist doctrine and practice. Many of these Reformed Waldensians returned to the valleys and after years of conflict the Waldensians were granted toleration by the Italian government on February 17, 1848. The Waldensians became essentially the Reformed Church of Italy, and their seminary in Rome is the primary theological institution for Italian Protestants. There were significant numbers of Waldensians among the millions of Italians who immigrated to the United States in the late nineteenth and early twentieth centuries. Since the Waldensian Church was recognized as a Reformed Church, most of the Waldensian immigrants joined Presbyterian or Reformed churches. A group of Waldensians came to the mountains of North Carolina to work in the textile mills, and they founded the town of Valdese. There is a Waldensian Heritage Museum in Valdes and a "Trail of Faith" that tells the story of the church. The American Waldensian Society was founded in New York in 1906 specifically to help support impoverished Waldnesians in Italy. It now promotes the mission of the Waldensians worldwide, especially in the areas of religious freedom and social justice.

For more information: www.waldensian.org

Headquarters: P.O. Box 398, Valdese, North Carolina 28690

ASSOCIATE REFORMED PRESBYTERIAN CHURCH

Founded: 1782
Membership: 35,206 in 270 congregations (2006)

The Associate Reformed Presbyterian Church traces its origin to controversies in the national Presbyterian Church in Scotland in the eighteenth century, when a group of presbyters seceded from the national church in protest over a number of issues of polity and worship. The controversy over the "Seceders" and "Covenanters" was carried to Northern Ireland with the Scottish migration there. The Scots-Irish immigrants to North America established congregations along the lines followed in the British Isles, but in 1782 two of the seceding branches united to form the Associate Reformed Synod in Philadelphia.

Eight years later, the Associate Reformed Presbytery of the Carolinas and Georgia was formed in Abbeville County, South Carolina, followed in 1803 by the division of the entire church into four Synods and one General Synod. In 1822 the Synod of the South was granted separate status, and by the end of the nineteenth century was the sole remaining body of the Associate Reformed Presbyterian Church, as several mergers over the years had absorbed the rest of the denomination into the old United Presbyterian Church. There are now nine presbyteries in North America, primarily in the East.

The doctrinal standards of the Apostles' Creed and the Westminster Confession are followed. For some years the only music in this church was the singing of psalms. This was modified in 1946 to permit the use of hymns.

The General Synod of the church meets annually to elect officers and conduct business. The chief officers are the Moderator (one-year term), who presides over the General Synod and is the spokesperson for the church during the year, and the Principal Clerk (four-year term), who establishes and maintains the official records for the General Synod. These and other officers serve as the Executive Board of the General Synod.

Associate Reformed Presbyterian Church foreign mission fields are located in Germany, Mexico, Pakistan, Turkey, Spain, the Ukraine, Wales, and Scotland. *The Associate Reformed Presbyterian* is published monthly at Greenville, South Carolina; Erskine College and Erskine Theological Seminary are in Due West, South Carolina. The church supports an assembly ground, Bonclarken, at Flat Rock, North Carolina, and three retirement centers.

For more information: www.arpsynod.org

Headquarters: One Cleveland St. Suite 110, Greenville, S.C. 29601

CHRISTIAN REFORMED CHURCH IN NORTH AMERICA

Founded: 1857
Membership: 185,665 in 781 congregations (2008)

This Reformed group originated with Dutch immigrants in Michigan in 1847 during the great wave of Dutch immigration to the Midwest in the mid-nineteenth century. It was affiliated with the Reformed Church in America from 1850 until 1857, when it found itself in disagreement on matters of doctrine and discipline. A conference held at Holland, Michigan, effected the separation of the True Holland Reformed Church, which, after a series of name changes, became the present Christian Reformed Church in North America. Emigration from Holland brought several other groups into the new organization, rapidly increasing its membership.

The Christian Reformed Church (CRC) today is largely English speaking, although the Dutch, Spanish, French, Navajo, Zuni, Korean, Chinese, and Vietnamese languages are used in some of the churches. Conservative theologically, the CRC holds to the three historic Reformed statements as the basis of union: the Belgic Confession (1561), the Canons of Dort (1618), and the Heidelberg Catechism (1563). Organization bears the usual Reformed characteristics. There are forty-seven classes (thirty-five in the United States, twelve in Canada) that meet every four months (in some cases every six months) but there are no intermediate or regional synods between the classes.

A general synod made up of two clergy and two elders from each classis meet annually. The general synod makes decisions regarding theological, liturgical, and ethical matters. It also oversees the ministries shared by CRC churches generally. To this end, the synod has created eight boards and agencies to oversee its ministries, including general church administration, radio and TV ministry, Calvin Theological Seminary, Calvin College, home missions, world relief, publications, and world missions. The seminary recently adopted a new M.Div. curriculum that includes emphases upon preaching, spiritual formation, contextualized ministry, and congregational leadership.

Christian Reformed Home Missions provides guidance and financial assistance to some two hundred new and established churches that maintain ministries in many North American communities, including Navajos, Zunis, African Americans, Asian Americans, Hispanic Americans, and on many university campuses. Almost three hundred foreign missionaries are stationed in Latin America, the Caribbean, Africa, Eastern Europe, and Asia. The Christian Reformed World Relief Committee carries on a relief program serving in twenty-seven countries.

The "Back to God Hour" radio program, broadcast from a chain of stations in the United States and abroad, reaches Europe, Africa, and Asia as well as South America; a television ministry also broadcasts in the United States and Canada. The church sponsors a publishing house in Grand Rapids that provides literature for the church and its agencies, as well as educational material for many other churches.

For more information: www.crcna.org

Headquarters: 2850 Kalamazoo Ave. SE, Grand Rapids, MI 49560

CONSERVATIVE CONGREGATIONAL CHRISTIAN CONFERENCE

Founded: 1948
Membership: 41,772 in 284 churches (2007)

The origins of this group go back to 1935 and the work of H. B. Sandine, a pastor in Hancock, Minnesota. He was convinced that the Congregational Christian churches (see UNITED CHURCH OF CHRIST) had departed from the beliefs, policy, and practices of historic Congregationalism. He carried on an educational effort through mimeographed documents until 1939, when his efforts were consummated in a monthly publication. A Conservative Congregational Christian Fellowship was organized at Chicago in 1945. The ongoing process of merger among Congregational bodies precipitated the Fellowship's reorganization into the Conservative Congregational Christian Conference in 1948.

The Conference's statement of faith is conservative and evangelical. It includes belief in: the infallibility and authority of the scriptures; the Trinity; the deity, virgin birth, sinlessness, atoning death, resurrection, ascension, and promised return of Jesus Christ; regeneration by the Holy Spirit; the resurrection of both the saved and the lost; and the spiritual unity of all believers in Christ. Local churches are completely autonomous. An annual meeting of clergy and lay representatives from member churches elects a board of directors and a set of officers for the Conference. Work is largely in the areas of missions, church planting, and Christian education, carried on through recognized evangelical home and foreign mission agencies, Bible institutions, colleges, seminaries, and Sunday school publishing houses. The conference is especially active in the fields of church extension, pastoral placement, and regional activities.

For more information: www.ccccusa.org

Headquarters: 8941 Highway 5, Lake Elmo, MN 55042

CUMBERLAND PRESBYTERIAN CHURCH

Founded: 1810
Membership: 78,451 in 730 congregations (2007)

This church was a product of the great revival known as the Second Great Awakening that swept across the new nation around 1800. On February 4, 1810, in Dickson County, Tennessee, three Presbyterian ministers, Finis Ewing (1773–1841), Samuel King (1775–1842), and Samuel McAdow (1760–1844), constituted a new presbytery. They objected to the doctrine of predestination in the Westminster Confession of Faith and insisted that educational standards for ordination of the clergy be more flexible in view of the extraordinary circumstances that then existed on the American frontier. The General Assembly of the church was organized in 1829.

A confession of faith was formulated in 1814, drawing on the Westminster Confession, but affirming key points made by the founders of the church: (1) There are no eternal reprobates; (2) Christ died for all humankind, not for the elect alone; (3) there is no infant damnation; and (4) the Spirit of God operates in the world coextensively with Christ's atonement. This confession was revised in 1883 and again in 1984. The 1984 document expresses a clear recognition of God's action in the salvation of human beings, noting that repentance is a necessary condition of salvation but not a sufficient one, as God's grace is the fundamental element.

An attempted union with the Presbyterian Church (U.S.A.) in 1906 was only partially successful. A considerable segment of the Cumberland Presbyterian membership, to whom the terms of merger were unsatisfactory, perpetuated the church as a separate denomination. Congregations are located for the most part in Southern and border states. The church sponsors missionaries in Colombia, Japan, Hong Kong, and Liberia in West Africa. It supports Bethel College in McKenzie, Tennessee; Memphis Theological Seminary; and a children's home in Denton, Texas.

For more information: www.cumberland.org

Headquarters: 1978 Union Ave., Memphis, TN 38104

CUMBERLAND PRESBYTERIAN CHURCH IN AMERICA

Founded: 1874
Membership: 15,142 in 152 congregations (1996)

This church developed after the Civil War, when African American pastors and lay members of the Cumberland Presbyterian Church* sought to establish their own organization. It has been estimated that some twenty thousand African Americans were associated with the parent church at the time. Led by Moses T. Weir, a former slave, black ministers formed the Synod of Colored Cumberland Presbyterians in 1869. In 1874 the first General Assembly of the Colored Cumberland Presbyterian Church was held. The parent church offered some financial support in the early years of the denomination and has continued to work with the African American body on various issues, including theological formulations.

The Colored Cumberland Presbyterian Church eventually became known as the Second Cumberland Presbyterian Church and, late in the twentieth century, as the Cumberland Presbyterian Church in America. The church's doctrinal position is similar to that of the Cumberland Presbyterian Church. Members of the two bodies worked together on the 1984 Confession of Faith. This document gives contemporary expression to the historic Presbyterian witness, with particular emphasis on God's saving grace.

The Cumberland Presbyterian Church in America now has four synods, primarily in the Midwest and the South. The church's ministers are trained at the Cumberland Presbyterian Church College in McKenzie, Tennessee, and at its seminary in Memphis. Serious conversation continues concerning unification with the Cumberland Presbyterian Church.

For more information: www.cumberland.org/cpca

Headquarters: 226 Church St., Huntsville, AL 35801

EVANGELICAL ASSOCIATION OF REFORMED AND CONGREGATIONAL CHURCHES

Founded: 1998
Membership: statistics unavailable; about 75 churches

The Evangelical Association is made up primarily of congregations that left the United Church of Christ* because of disagreements over social issues. The church grew rapidly after 2005 when the UCC allowed same-gender marriage ceremonies and gay ordination. The Evangelical Association holds to basic Calvinist teachings and explicitly rejects abortion, extra-marital sexual relations, and same-gender sexual relations. The denomination is Congregationalist in ecclesiology, and member churches are permitted to be in more than one association. The national organization is minimal, operating with a budget of under a hundred thousand dollars. The denomination was founded in New Braunfels, Texas, but is strongest in North Carolina.

For more information: www.evangelicalassociation.org

Headquarters: P.O. Box 307, Lacey Spring, VA 22833

EVANGELICAL PRESBYTERIAN CHURCH

Founded: 1981
Membership: 89,190 in 207 congregations (2007)

The Evangelical Presbyterian Church (EPC) grew out of a series of meetings of conservative Presbyterian pastors and church elders held in St. Louis, Missouri, in 1980–1981. They wished to form a church informed by Scripture and the historic confessions of the Christian faith and committed to evangelism. The EPC is a conservative denomination composed of eight presbyteries in the United States, with churches in twenty-nine states. It identifies itself as "Reformed in doctrine, presbyterian in polity, and evangelical in spirit." (www.epc.org) The EPC places high priority on church planting in the United States and world missions. About eighty world outreach missionaries serve the church's mission at home and abroad. High priority is also placed on developing its women's ministries and youth ministries.

The Westminster Confession and its catechisms are the church's doctrinal standards. Unlike other conservative Presbyterian bodies, it includes chapter thirty-four, "Of the Holy Spirit," and chapter thirty-five, "Of the Love of God and Missions," in the Confession. The historic motto "In essentials, unity; in nonessentials, liberty; in all things, charity" expresses the irenic spirit of the EPC. To the broader world, the General Assembly bears witness on particular issues through position papers.

For more information: www.epc.org

Headquarters: 17197 N. Laurel Park Drive, Suite 567, Livonia, MI 48152-7912

KOREAN PRESBYTERIAN CHURCH IN AMERICA

Founded: 1976
Membership: 55,100 in about 300 churches (2003)

The Korean-American Presbyterian Church (KAPC) was established to serve Korean immigrants in North America. It is affiliated with the Presbyterian Church of Korea, one of the largest Christian churches in Korea. The first Korean Presbyterian pastor was Sun Sang-Ryun, who founded a congregation in 1884. An American physician named Horace Newton Allen (1858–1932) was sent to East Asia by the Presbyterian Board of Foreign Missions in 1883 and the next year arrived in Korea as part of the American Legation. In addition to founding medical centers, Allen helped change Korean policy toward Christian missions. By the end of the century, he was serving as the United States counsel in Seoul. Presbyterian missionary John Ross completed his translation of the Bible into Korean in 1887. Several Korean Presbyterian leaders participated in the March First Movement, which declared independence from Japanese control in 1919. The movement failed, and the church suffered persecution. Korean theologians used native Korean concepts, such as *han* (unjust suffering) to interpret Christian doctrine. Theologians like Kim Young-Sam created *Minjung* theology, which focuses on the image of God in all, people, especially the poor and oppressed. Until 1950, most Protestants in Korea lived in the North, but the Korean War and subsequent division of the country caused many to flee to the South. The South Korean government promoted Christianity as part of its anti-communist, pro-American policy, but some Christian leaders used *Minjung* theology to protest the militarism of the government. During the 1980s millions of Koreans converted to Christianity, in part because of the church's support of democracy and human rights.

During that same period, many Koreans immigrated to the United States, and the KAPC was formed to minister to them. The church is theologically conservative. In addition to the Westminster Confession and the Larger and Shorter Catechisms, pastors ascribe to a creed that emphasizes biblical inerrancy, the absoluteness of God, the sin of Adam and Eve, and the necessity of faith. Works and obedience to the law of God result from saving faith. The Presbyterian Church (U.S.A.) and the KPCA have spent years working toward a covenantal relationship that is set to be ratified in 2010. Two congregations, the Young Nak church in California and the Open Door church in Virginia have over six thousand members each.

For more information: www.kapc.org

Headquarters: 125 S. Vermont Ave., Los Angeles, CA 90004

NATIONAL ASSOCIATION OF CONGREGATIONAL CHRISTIAN CHURCHES

Founded: 1955
Membership: est. 70,000 in 432 churches (2004)

This association was organized in order to "preserve historical Congregational forms of freedom and fellowship (the Congregational Way)." (www.naccc.org) It is the largest of Congregational bodies that did not participate when the General Council of Congregational Churches and the Evangelical and Reformed Church merged to form the United Church of Christ* in 1957. The National Association brings local churches together for counsel, inspiration, and fellowship, but preserves the independence and autonomy of the local churches. It describes its mission as encouraging and assisting local churches "in their development of vibrant and effective witnesses to Christ in congregational ways." (www.naccc.org)

There is no binding ecclesiastical authority and no required creed or program. Members are "bound together not by uniformity of belief but by the acceptance of a covenant purpose to be 'the people of God.'" (www.naccc.org) The association leaves to each church any decision to participate in social and political questions and action. A moderator presides over an annual meeting of representatives of all the member churches; an executive committee of twelve acts for the association between meetings. There is widespread missionary work in the United States and around the world: in the Philippines, Mexico, Bulgaria, Kenya, Nigeria and Ghana, India, and Honduras.

For more information: www.naccc.org

Headquarters: P.O. Box 1620, Oak Creek, WI 53154

NETHERLANDS REFORMED CONGREGATIONS IN NORTH AMERICA

Founded: 1907
Membership: about 5,000 in 17 congregations (2007)

The Netherlands Reformed Congregations in North America broke away from the Christian Reformed Church* over doctrinal differences. This body stresses the classic doctrines of the Reformed tradition as expressed in the Belgic Confession of Faith (1561), the Heidelberg Catechism (1563), and the Canons of Dort (1618). The church stresses "experiential Calvinism," which means that feelings are as important as intellectual assent in matters of faith. It also stresses the need for regeneration or rebirth. The church has a formal liturgy based on Dutch models, and it remains closely connected to the church in the Netherlands. It supports several home and foreign missions and eleven schools. A seminary was established in Grand Rapids, Michigan, in 1996.

For more information: www.nrcrws.org

Contact: Netherlands Reformed Book and Publishing, 1233 Leffingwell NE, Grand Rapids, MI 49505

ORTHODOX PRESBYTERIAN CHURCH

Founded: 1936
Membership: 28,780 in 320 congregations (2008)

This church originated in protest against what were believed to be modernistic practices by the Presbyterian Church in the USA. The dissenters, led by Princeton professor J. Gresham Machen (1881–1937), were suspended from the Presbyterian Church in the U.S.A. and organized the Presbyterian Church of America. However, an injunction was brought against the use of that name by the parent body, and in 1938 the name was changed to Orthodox Presbyterian Church.

Orthodox Presbyterians lay strong emphasis on the infallibility and inerrancy of the Bible. They believe that the writers of the books of the Bible were "so guided by [God] that their original manuscripts were without error in fact or doctrine." (www.opc.org) Fundamental doctrines include original sin; the virgin birth, the deity, and substitutionary atonement of Christ; his resurrection and ascension; his role as judge at the end of the world and the consummation of the kingdom; the sovereignty of God; and salvation through the sacrifice and power of Christ for those "the Father purposes to save." (www.opc.org) Salvation is "not because of good works [but] in order to do good works." (www.opc.org) The Westminster

Confession and the Larger and the Shorter Catechisms are accepted as subordinate doctrinal standards or creedal statements.

The Orthodox Presbyterian Church has published *Trinity Hymnal,* probably the only hymnal designed as a worship supplement to the Westminster Confession of Faith. The denomination has churches in almost every state.

For more information: www.opc.org

Headquarters: 607 North Easton Road, Bldg. E, Box P, Willow Grove, PA 19090-0920

PRESBYTERIAN CHURCH IN AMERICA

Founded: 1973, with roots in the colonial period
Membership: 340,736 in 1,645 congregations (2007)

This denomination was formed in 1973 when delegates from 260 conservative congregations that had withdrawn from the southern Presbyterian Church, U.S. (PCUS), convened a general assembly. These congregations opposed the PCUS's ecumenical involvements in the National Council of the Churches of Christ, the World Council of Churches, and the Consultation on Church Union. They also opposed the impending merger with the more liberal United Presbyterian Church in the U.S.A. The Presbyterian Church in America (PCA) also rejected the ordination of women. At first known as the National Presbyterian Church, the present name was adopted in 1974.

The Westminster Confession of Faith is the Presbyterian Church in America's primary doctrinal standard. The church teaches that the Holy Spirit guided the writers of the scriptures so that the writings are free of error of fact, doctrine, and judgment. They also emphasize the doctrines' human depravity, salvation by grace, Christ's death for the elect only, and the perseverance of the saints. This is commonly called "five points Calvinism." The church takes a conservative stance on many social issues, especially related to homosexuality and abortion, and it sponsors dozens of military chaplains.

The PCA maintains the historic polity of Presbyterian governance: rule by presbyters (or elders) and the graded courts, the session governing the local church; the presbytery for regional matters; and the general assembly at the national level. It makes a distinction between the two classes of elders: teaching elders (ministers) and ruling elders (laymen).

In 1982, the Reformed Presbyterian Church, Evangelical Synod (RPCES), joined the PCA, bringing with it Covenant College on Lookout Mountain, Georgia, and Covenant Theological Seminary in St. Louis, Missouri. The PCA headquarters is in Atlanta, where work by three program committees is coordinated: Mission to the World, Mission to North America, and Christian Education and Publications.

The denomination has congregations in nearly every state and has grown rapidly in recent years. It also has an extensive mission to the world, with over five hundred full-time missionaries and thousands of short-term missionaries.

For more information: www.pcanet.org

Headquarters: 1700 North Brown Road, Suite 105, Lawrenceville, GA 30043

PRESBYTERIAN CHURCH (U.S.A.)

Founded: 1983, with roots in the colonial period
Membership: 2,941,412 in 10,820 congregations (2007)

Following formal separation that began during the Civil War and lasted for 122 years, the two largest American Presbyterian churches (PCUS and UPCUSA) were reunited on June 10, 1983. Over the next fifteen years, great effort was expended to work out the administrative details of combining the two denominations and their numerous presbyteries and ministry groups.

The Southern denomination had been established as the PCUS at the time of the Civil War, and its church government developed parallel to that of the Northern churches. Offices were gradually centralized in Atlanta under the General Assembly Mission Board; mission work was always undertaken on a worldwide scale, a special source of pride to Southern Presbyterians.

The Northern body (PCUSA) merged with the United Presbyterian Church of North America (UPCNA) in 1958. The UPCNA had been formed exactly a century earlier by a merger of the Associate Presbyterian Church with the Associate Reformed Presbyterian Church. Their doctrines, traditions, and institutions were preserved in the new church's presbyterial style of government by local sessions, presbyteries, synods, and general assembly.

The Westminster Confession (1647) had been the basic doctrinal statement of American Presbyterians since colonial times, but when the UPCUSA was formed in 1958 it was noted that the Westminster Confession was more than three hundred years old. In 1967, the first new major Presbyterian doctrinal statement since 1647 was ratified by the General Assembly. The confession is Christ-centered and avoids what many saw as the confusing terminology of the Westminster Confession. Instead it stressed the concepts of love, sin, eternal life, and the work of reconciliation in God, Christ, and the church.

Some felt that the new document watered down the Westminster Confession, but most United Presbyterians accepted the document as reflecting true Presbyterianism and as offering a wide theological basis on which all Presbyterians could stand together. With the acceptance of the new creed, the PCUSA has a *Book of Confessions* with nine creeds: the Nicene Creed, the Apostles Creed, the Scots Confession of 1560, the Heidelberg Confession of 1563, the Westminster

Confession of 1647, the Larger Catechism of 1647, the Shorter Catechism of 1647, the 1934 Theological Declaration of Barmen, and the Confession of 1967. This *Book of Confessions* was adopted by the Presbyterian Church (U.S.A.) with the reunification of 1983.

The PCUSA follows typical Presbyterian polity. The yearly General Assembly is the final authority, but it cannot amend the church's constitution without ratification from the presbyteries. There are two officers of the General Assembly: a stated clerk (the chief executive officer of the church) is elected for a four-year term and may be reelected; a moderator is chosen each year to preside over the meetings and often speaks for the church during the year.

In 1988 the national headquarters of the new denomination was dedicated in Louisville, Kentucky. The national organization was restructured in the 1990s, and the church struggles with declining membership. The church has operated two publishing companies, now united in Louisville as Westminster John Knox Press. The church has a long and rich history of education and theological inquiry. There are sixty-eight Presbyterian-related colleges, eleven seminaries, and six secondary schools in the United States. The PCUSA has a strong history of social justice ministries and advocacy for disadvantaged groups. In recent years, the denomination has experienced conflict over the issue of ordination of homosexuals and gay marriage.

For more information: www.pcusa.org

Headquarters: 100 Witherspoon Street, Louisville, KY 40202-1396

PROTESTANT REFORMED CHURCHES IN AMERICA

Founded: 1926
Membership: 7,630 in 29 congregations (2007)

In 1924, three consistories and the pastors of the Classes Grand Rapids East and Grand Rapids West of the Christian Reformed Church in North America* were deposed from that denomination as the result of a disagreement over the doctrine of common grace. This doctrine states that grace is extended in some measure to those who are not part of God's elect. Herman Hoeksema (1886–1965) was foremost among those who taught that grace for the elect alone is an essential aspect of Reformed faith. Those who objected to the doctrine and were forced out of the church formally organized as the Protestant Reformed Churches in America in 1926.

The PRC holds to the three basic Reformed confessions (the Heidelberg Catechism of 1563, the Belgic Confession of 1561, and the Canons of Dort of 1618) as the basis of their belief in the infallible Word of God. In government they are Presbyterian. There are two classes, organized geographically, and a general synod meets annually in June. Membership is found mainly in the upper Midwest. The church maintains a theological seminary in Grand Rapids, Michigan.

For more information: www.prca.org

Headquarters: 4949 Ivanrest Ave., Grandville, MI 49418

REFORMED CHURCH IN AMERICA

Founded: 1792
Membership: 264,863 in 891 congregations (2007)

The Reformed Church in America was established in North America in 1628, when the Dutch Reformed Church established its first congregation in New Amsterdam. By the time the English took possession in 1664, Dutch Reformed congregations had been organized in several boroughs. Gradually the churches became Americanized, severing ties with the Netherlands and adopting the English language. In order to provide an educated pastorate, the church established Queen's College (now Rutgers University) and New Brunswick Theological Seminary in New Jersey.

The Reformed Church remained largely an Eastern church until the mid-1800s, when a second wave of Dutch immigrants came to the new world. One group, led by Albertus van Raalte, established a community called Holland in western Michigan. Another was established in Iowa. Beginning in the 1920s the church spread westward. A substantial number of Reformed churches organized or revitalized in recent decades have been African American, Asian American, and Hispanic. The Reformed Church has been a mission-minded denomination from the beginning. RCA personnel were among the first Christian missionaries in Arabia, China, Japan, and India. The church continues to support more than one hundred missionaries on five continents.

The church holds to the traditional Reformed doctrinal statements, especially the Belgic Confession (1561), the Heidelberg Catechism (1563), and the Canons of Dort (1618), but it interprets them more flexibly than do many Reformed groups. The church also affirms the Apostles' Creed, the Athanasian Creed, and the Nicene Creed. A contemporary statement of faith, "Our Song of Hope," was approved in 1978. The church emphasizes the need to be obedient to the will of God, which includes active engagement in social justice.

The church follows typical Reformed polity. The highest representative body is the General Synod, which meets once a year. The services and ministries of the denomination are overseen by a representative body called the General Council. Today the greatest numerical strength is in New York, Michigan, New Jersey, Iowa, Illinois, and California. Its best known congregation is the Crystal Cathedral in Garden Grove, California, pastored by Robert H. Schuller. In 1998, the church entered into full communion with Evangelical Lutheran Church in America*, the Presbyterian Church (U.S.A.)*, and the United Church of Christ*. In 2007 it established full communion with the Christian Reformed Church in North America as well.

For more information: www.rca.org

Headquarters: 475 Riverside Dr., 18th Floor, New York, NY 10115

REFORMED PRESBYTERIAN CHURCH OF NORTH AMERICA

Founded: 1809
Membership: 6,347 in 80 congregations (2004)

This church traces its roots to the Covenanter Presbyterians of Scotland in the eighteenth century who resisted the king's attempts to impose religious beliefs and practices on them. A synod was constituted at Philadelphia in 1809, only to split into Old Light and New Light groups in 1833. This dispute concerned citizenship and the right of members to vote or participate in public affairs. However, restriction was finally removed in 1964, and members are free to participate in civil government and to vote on issues and for political candidates committed to Christian principles of civil government. The church places special emphasis on the inerrancy of Scripture, the sovereignty of God, and the Lordship of Christ over every area of human life. Church government is thoroughly Presbyterian, except that there is no general assembly. Members use only the Psalms in their worship services; no instrumental music is permitted. Members cannot join secret societies. Home missionaries work in seven states; foreign missionaries are stationed in Japan, Cyprus, and Taiwan. Geneva College is located at Beaver Falls, Pennsylvania, and the Reformed Presbyterian Theological Seminary is at Pittsburgh.

For more information: www.reformedpresbyterian.org

Headquarters: 7408 Penn Ave., Pittsburg, PA 15208

UNITED CHURCH OF CHRIST

Founded: 1957, with roots to the colonial period
Membership: 1,145,281 in 5,377 congregations (2007)

The UCC traces its origins to the Congregationalists of New England but it also represents one of the most significant products of the ecumenical movement. In 1957 four major American denominations united to constitute the United Church of Christ: the Congregational churches, the Christian Church, the Evangelical Synod, and the Reformed Church in the U.S. The first two bodies had merged in 1931 to become Congregational Christian Churches. The Evangelical Synod of North America and the Reformed Church in the United States united in 1934. Within the new denomination, local congregations for the most part continued to observe the liturgy and theological positions they had before the merger. In essence, the UCC remains a federation of four denominations with related but distinct identities.

On July 8, 1959, at Oberlin, Ohio, representatives of the Congregational Christian Churches and the Evangelical and Reformed Church, upon merging into the United Church of Christ, adopted a statement, understood as a "testimony rather than a test of faith." It affirms belief in God the creator who "in Jesus Christ, the man of Nazareth, our crucified and risen Lord, . . . has come to us and shared our common lot, conquering sin and death and reconciling the world to himself." (www.ucc.org/beliefs/statement-of-faith.html) The statement also identifies the church as a "covenant faithful people of all ages, tongues, and races," which is call to "the service of men." (www.ucc.org/beliefs/statement-of-faith.html) Although this statement was not intended to set forth doctrinal positions or to stand as a substitute for the historic creeds, confessions, and covenants of the churches involved, it served as a witness to the faith, charity, and understanding of the merging groups.

The United Church of Christ represents a union of congregationalism and presbyterianism. The church establishes congregationalism as the rule for the local congregation and presbyterianism as the basis of organization of the member churches' connectional life. The constitution is explicit: "The autonomy of the local church is inherent and modifiable only by its own action. Nothing . . . shall destroy or limit the right of each local church to continue to operate in the way customary to it." (www.ucc.org/beliefs/statement-of-faith.html)

Local churches in a geographical area are grouped into an association, which assists needy churches; receives new churches into the United Church of Christ; licenses, ordains, and installs clergy; adopts its own constitution, bylaws, and rules of procedure; and is made up of the ordained ministers and elected lay delegates of the area. Associations are grouped into conferences, again by geographical area, with the exception of the Calvin Synod, which consists of churches from the Hungarian Reformed tradition. A conference acts on requests and references from the local churches, associations, general synod, and other bodies. Its main function is to coordinate the work and witness of its local churches and associations, to render counsel and advisory service, and to establish conference offices, centers, institutions, and other agencies.

The General Synod is the highest representative body. It meets biennially and is composed of conference delegates and voting members of boards of directors of the Covenanted Ministries of the church. An Executive Council is elected by the General Synod to act for the synod between its meetings. It recommends salaries for officers of the church as part of a national budget, has responsibility for the church's publications, and appoints committees not otherwise provided. It also submits to the General Synod "any recommendation it may deem useful" for the work of the church. General church offices are located in Cleveland, Ohio, as is the church's publishing arm, Pilgrim Press.

Since 1985, the United Church of Christ has enjoyed an ecumenical partnership with the Christian Church (Disciples of Christ)*. Both denominations are active in the Consultation on Church Union, and they join in common witness through Global Ministries, which operates teaching and service ministries throughout the world. Twenty-nine colleges and universities are related to the UCC, six of which are historically African American. The UCC makes social justice a high priority in its Christian witness.

For more information: www.ucc.org

Headquarters: 700 Prospect Ave., Cleveland, OH 44115

Mennonite and Anabaptist Churches

Dating from the 1520s in Central Europe, these Protestants take their name from Menno Simons (ca. 1496–1561), an early Dutch leader of the "Radical Reformation." These reformers rejected the "magisterial Reformation" of Martin Luther (see LUTHERAN CHURCHES) and John Calvin (see REFORMED AND PRESBYTERIAN CHURCHES), whom they believed compromised Jesus' teachings. The first Anabaptist congregation of historical record was organized at Zurich, Switzerland, in 1525 by those who disagreed with Ulrich Zwingli (1484–1531) in his readiness to forge a union of church and state. They also denied the scriptural validity of infant baptism and hence were labeled Anabaptist, or Rebaptizers. On January 21, 1525 Conrad Grebel (1496-1526) baptized George Blaurock (1491-1529), who then baptized others. In 1527 a group of radical reformers in Germany signed the Schleitham Articles, which called for separation of church and state and restoration of the simplicity of the New Testament church.

There were many kinds of religious radicals during the Reformation who were treated as outsiders, heretics, and outlaws by Catholics and Protestants alike. Many of the early Anabaptist leaders were executed, often in gruesome fashion. Their primary concerns were not with proper theology, the sacraments, or liturgy. Rather, they believed themselves called to exemplify godly living based on the Sermon on the Mount (Matthew 5:1–7:29). Until recently, most of those quietly dedicated Christians frowned on involvement in secular activity, refusing to take oaths, bear arms, vote, or hold public office. They are a called-out (from the state, from conventional society) fellowship of believers. Always emphasizing the local congregation, some groups insist on living in "intentional communities."

Menno Simons, a former Roman Catholic priest who was baptized by an Anabaptist preacher in Holland, organized so many congregations that his name became identified with the movement. Simons was a strict pacifist, and his writings continue to influence the Mennonites. Mennonite beliefs are based on a confession of faith signed at Dordrecht, Holland, in 1632. In eighteen articles, the following doctrines were laid down: faith in God as Creator; humanity's fall and restoration at the coming of Christ; Christ as the Son of God, who redeemed humankind on the cross; obedience to Christ's law in the gospel; the necessity of repentance and conversion for salvation; baptism as a public testimony of faith; the Lord's Supper as an expression of common union and fellowship; matrimony only among the "spiritually kindred"; obedience to and respect for civil government, except in the use of armed force; exclusion from the church and social ostracism of those who sin willfully; and future reward for the faithful and punishment for the wicked.

Their pacifism and rejection of the state religion brought severe persecution, and the number of martyrs might have been much greater had it not been for the haven offered by William Penn (1644–1718) in the American colonies. Several families settled in Germantown near Philadelphia in 1683, and eventually a Mennonite congregation was established there. Mennonite immigrants from Germany and Switzerland spread over Pennsylvania, Ohio, Virginia, Indiana, Illinois, and into the far western United States and Canada; these were later joined by others from Russia, Prussia, and Poland.

The Lord's Supper is served twice a year in almost all Mennonite congregations; in most, baptism is by pouring. Most also observe foot-washing as an ordinance in connection with the Lord's Supper, after which they salute one another with the "kiss of peace." The sexes are separated in the last two ceremonies. Mennonites baptize only on confession of faith, refuse to take oaths before magistrates, oppose secret societies, and strictly follow the teachings of the New Testament. They have a strong intra-church program of mutual aid and provide worldwide relief through the Mennonite Central Committee.

The local congregation is more or less autonomous and authoritative, although in some instances appeals are taken to district or state conferences. The officers of the church are bishops (often called elders), ministers, and deacons (almoners). Many ministers are self-supporting, working in secular employment when not occupied with the work of the church. Other officers are appointed for Sunday school, young people's work, and other duties.

The Amish are the most conservative branch of the Mennonite movement. Jacob Amman (ca. 1656–c. 1730), a Swiss Mennonite bishop, insisted on strict adherence to the confession of faith, especially in the matter of shunning excommunicated members. This literalism brought about a separation in Switzerland in 1693. Early Amish immigrants to the United States concentrated in Pennsylvania and spread into Ohio, Indiana, Illinois, Nebraska, and other western states and into Canada.

Many Amish, distinguished by their severely plain clothing, are found in the Conservative Amish Mennonite Church and Old Order Amish Mennonite Church. They are still the literalists of the movement, clinging tenaciously to the Pennsylvania Dutch language and seventeenth-century culture of their Swiss-German forebears. Most Amish oppose the use of automobiles, telephones, and higher education and are recognized as extremely efficient farmers.

The Young Center for Anabaptist and Pietist Studies is part of Elizabethtown College, a Church of the Brethren institution in Pennsylvania. It provides wonderful resources for the study of Anabaptist culture, religion, and history.

Suggestions for further reading:

Dyck, Cornelius J. *An Introduction to Mennonite History.* Scottdale, PA.: Herald Pres, 1993.

Hostetler, Beulah Stauffer. *American Mennonites and Protestant Movements: A Community Paradigm.* Scottdale, PA.: Herald Press, 1987.

Hostetler, John A. *Hutterite Society.* Baltimore: Johns Hopkins University Press, 1974.

Hostetler, John A. *Amish Society,* 4th ed. Baltimore: Johns Hopkins University Press, 1993.

Kraybill, Donald B. and Mark A. Olshan. *The Amish Struggle with Modernity.* Hanover, NH: University Press of New England, 1994.

MacMaster, Richard K. *Land, Piety, Peoplehood: The Establishment of Mennonite Communities in America 1683-1790.* Scottdale, PA.: Herald Press, 1990.

Williams, George Huntston. *The Radical Reformation.* Philadelphia: Westminster, 1962.

BEACHY AMISH MENNONITE CHURCHES

Founded: 1927
Membership: est. 10,000 in 144 churches (2009)

These churches are made up mostly of Amish Mennonites who separated from the more conservative Old Order Amish* over a period of years, beginning in 1927. They were led by Bishop Moses M. Beachy, and they are now found principally in Pennsylvania and Ohio. They believe in the Trinity and that the Bible is the infallible Word by which all people will be judged. To some degree, they resemble the Old Order Amish in garb and general attitude, but their discipline is somewhat milder. Individuals confess their sins to elders before taking communion, and they practice footwashing. The focus is on humility and service rather than individual achievement. These Mennonites worship in church buildings, have Sunday schools, and are active in supporting missionary work. The Beachy Amish are not opposed to automobiles, electricity, or other modern conveniences, but television and movies are forbidden. Nearly all of the churches sponsor Christian day schools. The church does not have a national headquarters, but it does have a publishing arm and runs educational ministries. The Mission Interests Committee sponsors homes for the aged and handicapped as well as missions in the United States and Europe.

For more information: www.beachyam.org

Contact: 3015 Partridge Rd., P.O. Box 73, Partridge, KS 67566

CHURCH COMMUNITIES INTERNATIONAL

Founded: 1920; came to United States in 1954
Membership: est. 2,000 worldwide (2004)

Though small in terms of actual membership, the Church Communities International represent one of the newer manifestations of the Anabaptist communal witness. Originally called the Bruderhof, the movement began in Germany following the economic and social devastation of the First World War. Founded by Eberhard Arnold (1883–1935), a theologian and writer, the movement spread to England in the 1930s. As World War II heated up, the British government was suspicious of a community with German nationals in it, and in 1941 the Bruderhof chose to relocate to the jungles of Paraguay. In the 1960s, the group moved to the United States and gained national attention in North America during the 1960s. There are several communities in the United States, Australia, England, and Germany where men, women, and children live in common. They share their property, work and worship together, and in all things seek unity. Several thousand people are associated with the movement without being members.

Theologically the Church Communities International affirm the Apostles' Creed but place their emphasis on the expectation of God's kingdom coming to this earth. They hold that followers of Jesus are empowered by the Spirit to live now in accordance with God's rule and reign as expressed in the Sermon on the Mount (Matthew 5:1–7:29). The mission of the Church Communities International is to witness to the good news that in Christ it is possible to live a new life and to share this life together with others in brotherhood, community, and justice. "We acknowledge God's working in all who strive for justice and peace, no matter their religion or creed. All the same, we take Christ's commands seriously." (www.Churchcommunities.org)

Because of Jesus' teachings, the Church Communities International affirm the sanctity of every life; thus they oppose every form of violence and killing,

136

including abortion, capital punishment, war, and physician-assisted suicide. They also believe in the sanctity of marriage (between one man and one woman) and the sanctity of sex (sexual intimacy within marriage only). They do not proselytize but instead seek to work together with others, whatever their belief and wherever possible, in the spirit of Christian unity and common concern. In 2007 the Bruderhof Foundation was established to promote charitable work and the name of the church was changed to Church Communities International.

For more information: www.Churchcommunities.org

Contact: Woodcrest, 2032 Rte 213, Rifton, NY 12471

CHURCH OF GOD IN CHRIST, MENNONITE

Founded: 1859
Membership: 14,262 in 141 churches (2007)

This church grew out of the preaching and labors of John Holdeman (1832–1900), a member of the Mennonite church in Ohio, who became convinced that the church had moved from the doctrines and practices of its forebears. He preached ardently on the necessity of the new birth, Holy Ghost baptism, more adequate training of children in the fundamentals of the faith, disciplining of unfaithful members, avoidance of apostates, and condemnation of worldly minded churches. He separated from the Mennonite Church and in 1859 began to hold meetings with a small group of followers.

The church holds that the same confession of faith must be believed and practiced by all churches, "from the time of the apostles to the end of the world," (www .cogicm.org) and that the Bible, as the inspired, infallible Word of God, must govern all doctrine and teaching. It accepts the Eighteen Articles of Faith drawn up at Dordrecht, Holland, in 1632. Women are required to cover their heads and men to wear beards. Non-involvement in the military and in secular government is enforced. The church teaches nonconformity to the world in dress, bodily adornment, sports, and amusements.

Most congregations in the church maintain a Christian school for the education of their children. Around the world members are found in Belize, Brazil, Burkina Faso, Canada, Dominican Republic, Ethiopia, Ghana, Guatemala, Haiti, India, Jamaica, Kenya, Latvia, Malawi, Mexico, Mozambique, Nicaragua, Nigeria, the Philippines, Romania, Uganda, Ukraine, and Zimbabwe. In the United States, Kansas is the state of heaviest concentration.

For more information: churchofgodinchristmennonite.net

Contact: Information and Gospel Publishers, CGIC, Mennonite, P.O. Box 230, Moundridge, KS 67107

CONSERVATIVE MENNONITE CONFERENCE

Founded: 1910
Membership: 11,557 in 110 churches (2008)

The Conservative Mennonite Conference (CMC) is an autonomous affiliation of congregations within the Mennonite church that was formed in 1910 in a meeting of concerned Amish Mennonite church leaders who were reluctant to adopt the Old Order Amish Mennonite conservatism toward cultural expressions but who were also more conservative than the prevailing Mennonite approach of that time. The present name of the association was adopted in 1954.

The CMC subscribes to the Conservative Mennonite Statement of Practice (2007), the Conservative Mennonite Statement of Theology (1991). These documents affirm the full humanity and full divinity of Jesus Christ, the full inspiration and autographical inerrancy of the scriptures, believers' baptism, and nonviolence. Members are expected to refrain from gambling, alcohol, tobacco, immodest attire, swearing oaths, and premarital and extra-marital sexual activity.

The highest decision-making body is the semi-annual Minister's Business Meeting, which elects an executive board and a general secretary to oversee the day to day operations of the conference. Internationally affiliated church bodies are found in Costa Rica, Nicaragua, Ecuador, Haiti, India, Germany, and Kenya. Rosedale Bible College in Irwin, Ohio, offers an associate's degree in various Christian studies.

For more information: www.cmcrossdale.org

Headquarters: 9910 Rosedale-Milford Center Rd., Irwin, OH 43029

FELLOWSHIP OF EVANGELICAL CHURCHES

Founded: 1865
Attendance: 6,621 in 42 churches (2007)

Formerly the Defenseless Mennonite Church and Evangelical Mennonite Church*, this body was founded as a result of a spiritual awakening among the Amish in Indiana under the leadership of Henry Egly, who stressed the need for repentance and regeneration before baptism. Egly's practice of rebaptizing Amish who experienced conversion led to conflict within the Amish community, leading to the formation of the evangelical church. It continues to emphasize regeneration, separation, nonconformity, and nonresistance to the world.

The Fellowship of Evangelical Churches' program today is largely one of missions and church-extension evangelism. A children's home in Flanagan, Illinois, and a camp near Kalamazoo, Michigan, are maintained. Although the name Evangelical Mennonite Church was adopted in 1949, representatives voted on August 2, 2003, to change the name to the Fellowship of Evangelical Churches because of the changing constituency of the church. In so doing, the Fellowship of Evangelical Churches (FEC) affirmed its core values anchored in Evangelical theology and Anabaptist identity, and its mission to help the local church accomplish the Great Commandment and the Great Commission.

For more information: www.fecministries.org

Headquarters: 1420 Kerrway Court, Fort Wayne, IN 46805

HUTTERIAN BRETHREN

Founded: ca. 1530; came to the United States in the 1870s
Membership: est. 43,000 in 444 colonies in the United States and Canada (2000)

This is one of the few American bodies to stem directly from the Anabaptist movement without being connected to the Mennonites. Like others in the Radical Reformation, the Hutterian Brethren reject infant baptism and insist on separation of church and state. The New Testament, particularly the Sermon on the Mount (Matthew 5:1–7:29), is taken as the literal authority for true Christians; therefore, they embraced nonviolence. They got their name from their founder Jacob Hutter, a sixteenth-century Tyrolean Anabaptist who advocated communal ownership of property. The community thrived in the under-populated areas of Central Europe, particularly Moravia, but always lived under the threat of persecution. Hutter himself was martyred in Austria in 1536. Over time, they migrated to Russia, where the need for hard-working and peaceful farmers was evident. As persecution there increased in the nineteenth century, many Hutterites left Russia for Canada and the United States.

Most Hutterites are of German ancestry and use that language in their homes and churches. Aside from the idea of common property, they are quite similar to the Old Order Amish. They seek to express their Bible-centered faith in brotherly love and aim at the recovery of New Testament spirit and fellowship. They feel this requires non-conformity to the world; accordingly, they practice nonresistance, refuse to participate in local politics, and dress in traditional attire. Choral singing plays a major role in Hutterite worship and daily life. They maintain their own schools, in which the Bible is paramount. There are different branches of Hutterites in America, including the Schmiedeleut, Lehrerleut, and Dariusleu. Hutterites are not opposed to modern technologies that contribute to the welfare of the entire colony, such as farm equipment and computers.

For more information: www.hutterites.org

Contact: Crystal Spring Colony, Box 10, Ste Agathe, MB ROG 170 Canada

MENNONITE CHURCH U.S.A

Founded: 1525; organized in the United States in 1725
Membership: 109,174 in 935 churches (2006)

This is the major Mennonite body and was brought to Germantown, Pennsylvania, in 1683 by Dutch and German immigrants. In 2001 this church merged with the General Conference Mennonite Church (founded in 1860). In 1995, General Conference Mennonites and members of the Mennonite Church adopted a new "Confession of Faith in a Mennonite Perspective." The confession is the most recent in a series of historical Anabaptist faith statements, beginning with the Schleitheim Articles, written in 1527. The new confession of faith includes twenty-four articles that interpret Mennonite beliefs about God, Jesus Christ, the Holy Spirit, Scripture, creation, sin, salvation, the church, Christian life and mission, peace and justice, and the reign of God.

It is similar to the older confession adopted in 1963 which sought to set forth the major doctrines of Scripture as understood in the Anabaptist-Mennonite tradition. The confession stresses faith in Christ, the saved status of children, the importance of proclaiming God's Word and "making disciples," baptism of believers, absolute love, nonresistance rather than retaliation as one's personal response to injustice and maltreatment, and the church as a non-hierarchical community. Because of their insistence on freedom from the traditional Mennonite regulations on attire, this group has been regarded as "liberal in conduct" by some other Mennonites, but it still represents the Radical Reformation.

The General Assembly meets every two years. It brings together representatives from all area conferences and from many congregations throughout North America. Discussion is open to all; however, only elected delegates (women and men, ordained and lay) may vote. Church-wide program boards are in charge of mission, congregational ministries, education, publishing, and mutual aid work; all are under the supervision of the church's general board. Home missions stress evangelism, and missions are found in Asia, Africa, Europe, and Central and South America. The church sponsors hospitals, retirement homes, and child-welfare services. Membership is strongest in Pennsylvania and the Midwest states. Associated Mennonite Biblical Seminary in Elkhart, Indiana, trains General Conference and Mennonite Church pastors, missionaries, pastoral counselors, peace workers, and lay leaders.

For more information: www.mennonites.org
Headquarters: 421 South Second St., Suite 600, Elkhart, IN 46516

MISSIONARY CHURCH

Founded: 1969
Membership: 43,026 in 423 churches (2007)

The Missionary Church is made up of two groups that merged in 1969, the Missionary Church Association and the United Missionary Church. Both former denominations had a Mennonite heritage and came into existence through the holiness revivals of the late 1800s. The Missionary Church is conservative and evangelical in theology and practice. Local churches are free to manage their own affairs, but recognize and adhere to the authority of a general conference made up of clergy, missionaries, and laity, held biennially.

Working under the general conference is a general board that oversees a variety of agencies and mission activities. The president, vice president, and secretary are elected for terms of four years. The international ministry of the Missionary Church is done under the name of World Partners USA. Primary activities include evangelism, discipleship, church planting, Bible translation, theological education, leadership development, and community development. The denomination is currently in a process of restructuring, with a focus on church planting and making disciples. The church is affiliated with one educational institution in the United States: Bethel College in Mishawaka, Indiana.

For more information: www.mcusa.org

Headquarters: P.O. Box 9127, Fort Wayne, IN 46899

OLD ORDER AMISH CHURCHES

Founded: 1720s
Membership: est. over 100,000 in about 900 districts (2000)

The Old Order (*Ordnung*) Amish hold to the old traditions of the Amish movement more strictly than do the so-called Church Amish. For example, their "plain dress" requires the use of hooks and eyes instead of buttons or zippers, and members do not own automobiles. They are strict pacifists and seek to remain separate from all secular governments and the influence of secular culture.

It is impossible to give precise membership statistics since the Old Order is not a denomination in the usual sense of the word. There are no church buildings because believers worship in private homes. Moreover, there are no conferences. Members do not believe in missions or benevolent institutions or centralized schools; some, however, do contribute to the missions and charities of the Mennonite Church. There are nearly nine hundred Old Order Amish districts, each averaging about one hundred members, with approximately half that number baptized. The church continues to grow rapidly due to a higher than average birth rate in Amish families.

For more information: www.mhsc.ca

OLD ORDER (WISLER) MENNONITE CHURCH

Founded: 1872
Membership: 7,100 adults in 47 churches (2004)

This church was named for Jacob Wisler, the first Mennonite* bishop in Indiana, who led a separation from that church in 1872 to protest the use of English in the services and the introduction of Sunday schools. Similar to Old Order (*Ordnung*) Amish, these Mennonites maintain the old style of clothing, make only limited use of modern technology, and keep separate from the world. Joined in 1886, 1893, and 1901 by groups with similar ideas from Canada, Pennsylvania, and Virginia, the church is still maintained on the basis of those protests. Each section of the church has its own district conference, and there are conferences twice each year in each community. All churches take part in relief work, especially for the needy at home and in foreign lands, and some contribute to the work of the Mennonite Church.

For more information: www.mhsc.ca

Headquarters: 376 N. Muddy Creek Rd., Denver, PA 17517

U.S. MENNONITE BRETHREN CHURCHES

Founded: 1860
Membership: est. 30,000 members in 201 churches (2009)

Mennonites in Prussia in the eighteenth century found it difficult to avoid compulsory military service during the reign of Frederick the Great. Many of them accepted the offer of Czarina Catherine the Great to migrate to Russia where they established their own rural colonies in the Ukraine. These were agricultural communities where Mennonites could live as the "quiet of the land." In the mid-nineteenth century, a Lutheran* Pietist* preacher named Eduard Wuest was the catalyst for a major revival among the German-speaking Mennonites in Russia. There was conflict between the more traditional Mennonites and those who sought greater attention to prayer and Bible study. These Pietist Mennonites retained many features common to Anabaptists, but they wanted a more emotional form of spirituality and greater attention to church discipline. Eventually, the Mennonites in the Ukraine split over the issues of revivalism and home communion, and in 1860 eighteen people signed a "letter of separation" that became the charter for the Mennonite Brethren. The charter emphasized the need for experiential religion and personal holiness. A few years later, the Russian government began to insist that Mennonites enlist in the military. Thousands of Mennonites immigrated to North America, including hundreds of Mennonite Brethren. The first organizational meeting of the Brethren in the United States was held in 1878 in Nebraska. It was called for the purpose of supporting missions.

A General Conference of Mennonite Brethren Churches was formed in 1954, uniting Canadian and American Mennonite Brethren. The Krimmer Mennonite Brethren merged with this church in 1960, and the General Conference Mennonites continued to work closely with other Mennonites in mission. A 1982 study of members indicated a waning in the peace witness of the Mennonite Brethren, but a strong commitment to evangelism. In recent years the church has become more ethnically diverse and has a special district focused on Latino congregations in the Southwest. In 2000 the General Conference was disbanded and separate United States and Canadian conferences were organized. The church has five regional districts and is strongest in the Western states, but has a presence in North Carolina and Texas, as well. The church operates a theological seminary with campuses in Fresno, California; Langley, British Columbia, and Winnipeg, Manitoba. The seminary offers several masters degrees. The church also operates two colleges, one in Kansas and the other in Fresno. The denomination has a national office, but congregations retain a great deal of autonomy.

For more information: www.usmb.org

Headquarters: 315 South Lincoln P.O. Box 220, Hillsboro, KS 67063-0220

Friends (Quaker)

Dating from the 1650s in England, the Society of Friends is an unconventional but esteemed Protestant body. They believe in an "Inner Light," which is the spiritual nerve center that God has placed in every person. Since Friends believe that all people have the Inner Light, they typically deny the validity of clergy, liturgy, and sacraments. Friends believe that the practice of inward listening and obedience to God results in lives that begin to reflect the character of Jesus. From this arise the Friends' testimonies to peace, simplicity, equality, moral purity, and integrity. The fact that every person has this inward spiritual endowment has prompted Friends to stand for the equality of all people and thus to oppose slavery and to be exceptionally service minded.

Despite their small numbers, Friends have had a deep and lasting influence on Western society. Contributions in both religious and humanitarian spheres have won them universal respect and admiration, and their loyalty to their quiet faith offers a challenge and inspiration to all churches. Friends take seriously the prophetic vision of the world at peace, and cooperate with the historic peace churches in the context of the wider ecumenical movement. In the United States, seven colleges and three seminaries reflect Friends' long-standing emphasis on the importance of education.

History. The Society of Friends began with the vision of George Fox (1624–91), a seeker after spiritual truth and peace during the turmoil of the English Civil War and its aftermath. After failing to find satisfactory truth or peace in the churches of his time, Fox discovered what he sought in a direct personal relationship with Christ: "When all my hopes in [churches] were gone . . . I heard a voice which said, 'That is the Inner Voice, or Inner Light, based upon the description of John 1:9: *the true Light, which lighteth every man that cometh into the world.* (KJV)'" This voice, Fox maintained, is available to all and has nothing to do with the ceremonies, rituals, or creeds over which Christians have fought. Every heart is God's altar and shrine.

Fox and his early followers not only refused to attend the state church, they also insisted on freedom of speech, assembly, and worship. They would not take oaths in court and would not go to war. They condemned slavery and abuse of prisoners and the mentally ill. The names they adopted—Children of Truth, Children of Light, and Friends of Truth—aroused ridicule and fierce opposition. When Fox was hauled into court, the judge called him "a quaker," thus coining a term that became a name for the movement. Fox spent six years in jail. From 1650 until 1689, more than three thousand people suffered for conscience's sake, and three hundred to four hundred died in prison. In spite of persecution, the group grew, and the Religious Society of Friends was founded in 1652. When Fox died in 1691, Quakers numbered fifty thousand.

Friends soon brought their message to the American colonies. Ann Austin (d. 1665) and Mary Fisher (ca. 1623–98) arrived in Massachusetts from Barbados in 1656. They were promptly accused of being witches and were deported. Eventually, four Friends were hanged in Boston, but the passage of the Act of Toleration of 1689 ended most persecution. William Penn (1644–1718) was granted the colony of Pennsylvania by the British Crown and made it a refuge for his fellow Quakers. Penn's "Holy Experiment" allowed complete religious toleration in the colony of Pennsylvania, removing the government from the business of religion. This was a milestone on the path to full religious freedom in the American Constitution.

As persecution waned and Friends settled down to business and farming in the eighteenth century, many grew prosperous. Meetings and community life became well organized, and it was a time of creativity and mystical inwardness, and closely knit family life was emphasized. Quaker philanthropy increased and became widely admired. Their ideas on prison reform began to take effect, and their schools increased in number and attendance. The Quakers lost control of the

Pennsylvania legislature in 1756 over the issue of taxation to pay for a war against the Shawnee and the Delaware peoples.

Quaker leaders, now looking within rather than without, began to enforce such strict discipline upon their members that they became, in fact, a "peculiar people." Members were disowned or dismissed for even minor infractions; thousands were cut off for "marrying out of Meeting." Pleasure, music, and art were taboo; sobriety, punctuality, and honesty were demanded in all matters; dress was plain; and speech was biblical. They were "different" and dour; they gained few new converts and lost many old members during this period. A number of separate groups were formed as a result: the Hicksites in 1827, the Wilburites in 1845, the Primitives in 1861.

Influenced by revival movements of the nineteenth century, most Friends in the United States abandoned the quietism of an earlier generation and many engaged with other Christians in evangelism and the world missionary movement. Independently, various "Orthodox" yearly meetings started missions in Mexico, Cuba, Jamaica, and Palestine that combined emphases on evangelism, education, and economic development. In 1887, these yearly meetings gathered to issue a Declaration of Faith which reacted against two trends in American Quakerism. They opposed, on the left, a mysticism that seemed to disconnect the "inner Light" from the cross of Christ; and, on the right, they opposed use of outward rituals to celebrate baptism and communion. Friends traditionally view baptism and communion as purely inward and spiritual.

Service and Peace Work. Even during the quietistic phase of Quaker life, Friends continued to work for peace, public education, temperance, democracy, and the abolition of slavery. In 1688 the Friends of Germantown, Pennsylvania, announced that slavery violated the Golden Rule. It took nearly a century for Quakers to rid their own society of slavery. The writings of Friends John Woolman (1720–72) and John Greenleaf Whittier (1807–92) helped to further the abolition movement in American society.

During World War I, Friends from all branches of society were at work in the American Friends Service Committee (A.F.S.C.) in relief and reconstruction efforts abroad. The A.F.S.C. remains today one of the most effective of such agencies in the world. The A.F.S.C. and its British counterpart were jointly awarded the Nobel Peace Prize in 1947. Friends who enter military service are no longer disowned from membership, but many leave the society and join a church that does not profess pacifism. Conversely, pacifists brought up in other traditions often join the Friends in young adulthood. Peace conferences have had a prominent place in Friends' ministries.

Worship and Polity. The Inner Light is the heart of Quaker theology and practice. Friends believe that grace, the power from God to help humankind pursue good and resist evil, is universal among all people. They seek not holiness but perfection—a higher, more spiritual standard of life for both society and the individual—and they believe that truth is unfolding and continuing. They value the Bible but many prefer to rely on fresh individual guidance from the Spirit of God, which produced the Bible, rather than follow only what has been revealed to others.

Worship and business in the society are conducted in monthly, quarterly, and yearly meetings. The monthly meeting is the basic unit, made up of one or more meetings (groups) in a neighborhood. It convenes each week for worship and once a month for business. It keeps records of membership, births, deaths, and marriages; appoints committees; considers queries on spiritual welfare; and transacts all business. Monthly meetings join four times a year in a quarterly meeting to stimulate spiritual life and decide on any business that should be brought to the attention of the yearly meeting. The yearly meeting corresponds to a diocese in an episcopal system. In Friends' business meetings at every level, there often is frank inquiry into members' conduct of business and treatment of others.

Group decisions await the "sense of the meeting." Lacking unity of opinion, the meeting may have a "quiet time" until unity is found, or it may postpone consideration of the matter or refer it to a committee for study. Minority opinion is not outvoted, but convinced. Every man, woman, and child is free to speak in any meeting; delegates are appointed at quarterly and yearly meetings to ensure adequate representation, but enjoy no unusual position or prerogatives. Church officers, elders, and ministers are chosen for recognized ability in spiritual leadership, but they too stand on equal footing with the rest of the membership. A few full-time workers are paid a modest salary, and "recorded" ministers who serve as pastors in meetings that have programmed worship also receive salaries.

Worship may be either programmed or unprogrammed, but the two are not always distinct. The former more nearly resembles an ordinary Protestant service, although there are no outward sacraments. While Friends believe in spiritual communion, partaking of the elements is thought unnecessary. In unprogrammed meetings there is no choir, collection, singing, or pulpit; the service is devoted to quiet meditation, prayer, and communion with God. Any vocal contributions are prompted by the Spirit.

Friends World Committee for Consultation (F.W.C.C.), organized at Swarthmore, Pennsylvania, following the Second World Conference of Friends in 1937, functions as an agent, or clearinghouse, for interchange of Quaker aspirations and experiences through regional, national, and international inter-visitation, person-to-person consultations, conferences, correspondence, and a variety of publications. The F.W.C.C. maintains a world office in London, England, and as a nongovernmental organization (NGO) helps to operate a program at U.N. headquarters to forward world peace and human unity. Something of a world community has been set up in the Wider Quaker Fellowship, in which non-Friends in sympathy with the spirit and program of Quakerism may participate in the work without coming into full membership.

Suggestions for further reading:

Bacon, Margaret Hope. *Mothers of Feminism*. San Francisco: HarperSanFrancisco, 1986.

Barbour, Hugh and J. William Frost. *The Quakers*. New York: Greenwood Press, 1980.

Brock, Peter. *Pioneers of a Peaceable Kingdom : The Quaker Peace Testimony from the Colonial Era to the First World War*. Princeton, NJ: Princeton University Press, 1972.

Hall, Francis. *Friends in the Americas*. Philadelphia: Friends World Committee, 1976.

Hamm, Thomas D. *The Transformation of American Quakerism: Orthodox Friends: 1800–1907*. Bloomington: University of Indiana Press, 1988.

Stoneburner, Carol and John, eds. *The Influence of Quaker Women on American History*. Lewiston/Queenston, NY: The Edwin Mellen Press, 1986.

Weeks, Stephen B. *Southern Quakers and Slavery*. Baltimore: Johns Hopkins University Press, 1986.

EVANGELICAL FRIENDS INTERNATIONAL

Founded: 1990
Attendance: 39,913 in 288 meetings (2004)

This is the newest and one of the largest organizations of Friends meetings in the U.S. It grew out of the Evangelical Friends Alliance, which was formed in 1965 to encourage evangelical emphases and denominational unity. The Evangelical Friends represent one part of the general evangelical renewal that profoundly shaped American Christianity in the latter part of the twentieth century.

The Evangelical Friends are organized into six regions of the U.S., with commissions devoted to missions, education, youth ministry, and communication. Worship is programmed and includes Scripture readings, congregational singing, and a sermon by the pastor. The theology is generally conservative, and Evangelical Friends cooperate with other evangelical bodies. Of primary concern is the Great Commission (Matthew 28:19) to make disciples of all nations. Worldwide EFI has nearly 1,100 churches with over 150,000 regular attendees.

For more information: www.evangelicalfriends.org

Headquarters: 5350 Broadmoor Circle NW, Canton, Ohio 44709

FRIENDS GENERAL CONFERENCE

Founded: 1900
Membership: est. 34,000 in 650 meetings (2008)

Friends General Conference is an association of fourteen yearly meetings and regional associations and ten monthly meetings of Friends (Quakers) in the United States and Canada. It is less a denomination than a service organization that provides resources for yearly and monthly meetings. Most of these meetings are "unprogrammed," meaning that worshipers meet in silence, expecting that one or more Friends may be moved by the Spirit to speak. No pastors are employed; the responsibilities handled by pastors in other denominations are shared among the members of the meeting. This group of Friends emphasizes the Quaker belief that faith is based on direct experience of God and that God is found in every individual.

Friends General Conference serves the members of affiliated meetings by preparing and distributing educational and spiritual materials, providing opportunities for Friends to share experiences and strengthen the Quaker community, and helping monthly and yearly meetings to nurture and support the spiritual and community life of Friends in North America. It is best known for the annual "Gathering of Friends," which attracts between 1,500 and two thousand Quakers from all over North America. Friends General Conference offices are in Philadelphia, Pennsylvania. The Conference publishes various books and religious education materials and a newsletter.

For more information: www.fgcquaker.org
Headquarters: 1216 Arch St, #2B, Philadelphia, PA 19107

FRIENDS UNITED MEETING

Founded: 1902
Membership: 41,184 in 472 meetings (2002)

Friends United Meeting was formed in 1902 as the umbrella for Friends mission activities and the communications arm for a broadly Christian understanding of the Quaker movement. Friends United Meeting is an international association of twenty-six yearly meetings (regional bodies of Quaker meetings) the purpose of which is "to energize and equip Friends through the power of the Holy Spirit to gather people into fellowships where Jesus Christ is known, loved, and obeyed as Teacher and Lord." (www.fum.org) Friends United Meeting includes Friends meetings with both pastor-led services and those that practice traditional unprogrammed silent waiting on God.

The international work of Friends United Meeting includes medical, educational, and children services in Kenya, Palestine, and the Caribbean as well as a pastoral leadership training through the Friends Theological College in Kaimosi, Kenya. Of the 172,000 members of Friends United, 128,000 are in in East Africa. The headquarters in Richmond, Indiana, houses departments of Global Ministries and Communications, which includes a bookstore, press, denominational magazine, and internet outreach.

For more information: www.fum.org

Headquarters: 101 Quaker Hill Drive, Richmond IN 47374

Brethren and Pietist Churches

An international religious revival began in Germany in the late 1600s with the writings of Philipp Jakob Spener (1635–1705). Spener decried the barren intellectualism, theological factionalism, and general ineffectiveness of the Protestant churches of his day. He called for a new type of Reformation that would complete the promise of Luther's Reformation. Luther had reformed the church doctrinally and liturgically; Spener wanted to reform it morally and spiritually. He called for pastors to find ways to make the doctrine of the priesthood of all believers effective in the hearts and souls of the people.

To do this, Spener proposed that pastors form small groups of believers to meet for study, prayer, and mutual encouragement. The staples of modern church life, such as Sunday school, youth fellowship, and women's circle meetings, grew out of this idea. Also, Spener urged pastors to leave polemics aside and concentrate on edifying preaching that could transform individuals from sinners to laborers for God. This "religion of the heart" spread throughout Protestant Germany and profoundly influenced John Wesley's (1703–1791) early Methodist* movement. When Pietism, as it was called in Germany, came to the U.S. in the 1740s, it helped to fuel the First Great Awakening.

In the 1750s Philip Otterbein (1726–1813), a German Reformed pastor of Pietist leanings, began his career as an evangelist in Pennsylvania and Maryland. His activities led to the formation of the United Brethren Church, later called the Evangelical United Brethren (EUB). This body was one of the groups that eventually formed The United Methodist Church* in 1968. Although there are only a few relatively small denominations in the U.S. that emerged out of German Pietism, American Christianity in all its varieties has been influenced by this spiritual movement.

Many Pietist bodies use the name "Brethren" in various forms. For them, the church is primarily a company of brothers and sisters in Christ joined together by the Holy Spirit for mutual edification. The inner spiritual life, piety, is cultivated in prayer and study of Scripture and through association with fellow believers. For most Brethren, the local church is central, but they are often bound in close-knit national communities. The church claims their primary loyalty and is understood more as a community of people who love God and one another than as part of an organization or a body that formulates doctrine.

Brethren do not emphasize rigid doctrinal standards; rather, the Spirit of God within each person, which binds them together in love, takes precedence for them. Some place emphasis on prophecy and direct inspiration from the Holy Spirit. They usually live a simple, unadorned life. In their early decades in Europe and the United States, most Brethren were separatists from the state and conventional churches. While not manifesting a judgmental attitude, they devoted themselves to a moral purity that set them apart from other Christians as well as from general society.

Many Pietist groups took the New Testament literally and endeavored to put its teachings into practice, even in the minute details of their daily living. At the heart of their religious ritual was the love feast, or agape, and the serving of the Lord's Supper, preceded by a ceremony of foot washing. They saluted one another with a kiss of peace, dressed in simple clothing, covered women's heads at services, anointed their sick with oil for healing and consecration, refrained from worldly amusements, and refused to take oaths, go to war, or engage in lawsuits. Those Pietist groups that were not Brethren tended to be more embracing of the secular world.

Many of the Brethren churches stem from the work of Alexander Mack, Sr. (1679–1735), in Schwarzenau in Wittgenstein, Germany. After his experience of conversion, Mack was convinced of the need for those who had experienced regeneration to form separate communities modeled on the early church's practice of sharing goods in common. Exiled from the Palatinate for preaching separatism, Mack gathered a company of fellow refugees and in 1708 took the bold, and at that time illegal, step of rebaptizing adult believers. Eventually persecution in Germany led these German Baptists (see NORTH AMERICAN BAPTIST CONFERENCE) to immigrate to the U.S.

They were known for years simply as German Baptist Brethren, but that title has largely disappeared, except in the case of the Old German Baptist Brethren, who were also known as "Dunkers." The terms "Brethren" and "Dunker" have been the cause of much confusion. Dunker is a direct derivation of the German *tunken*, or, "to dip or immerse," and is identified with the peculiar method of immersion employed by this group of churches in which the new believer is immersed three times, face forward, in the name of the Father, the Son, and the Holy Ghost.

Several communal societies in American history were established by Pietist groups. Such communes were an intense expression of the Pietist ideal of brotherhood and sisterhood, and in many cases were inspired by the vision of the New Jerusalem in the book of Revelation. Among the most important were the Ephrata Cloister and Bethlehem in Pennsylvania; Salem in North Carolina; and Amana in New York (and later Iowa). Amana survived as a commune until 1932. At that time the organization was divided between the Amana Business Society and the Amana Church Society. The latter continues as a small denomination in Iowa that does not have an ordained ministry.

Suggestions for further reading:

Atwood, Craig D. *Community of the Cross: Moravian Piety in Colonial Bethlehem.* Pennsylvania University Press, 2004.

Bach, Jeff. *Voices of the Turtledove: The Sacred World of Ephrata.* Pennsylvania State University Press, 2003.

Brown, Dale. *Understanding Pietism.* Grand Rapids: Wm. B. Eerdmans, 1978,

Durnbaugh, Donald F., ed. *The Brethren Encyclopedia.* 3 vols. Philadelphia: Brethren Press, 1983–84.

Durnbaugh, Donald F. *The Church of the Brethren Past and Present.* Elgin, IL, 1971.

Hoestetler, John A. *Hutterite Society.* Baltimore: Johns Hopkins University Press, 1974.

Longenecker, Steve. *Piety and Tolerance: Pennsylvania German Religion, 1700-1850.* Metuchen, NJ: Scarecrow Press, 1994.

Stoeffler, Ernst, ed. *Continental Pietism and Early American Christianity.* Grand Rapids, MI, 1976.

Wittlinger, Carlton O. *Quest for Piety and Obedience: The Story of the Brethren in Christ.* Nappanee, Ind., 1978.

BRETHREN CHURCH (ASHLAND)

Founded: 1882
Membership: 10,287 in 117 congregations (2002)

In 1882 the Church of the Brethren* voted to expel a member for advocating Sunday schools, missions, a paid clergy, congregational polity, and more freedom in dress and worship. The supporters of such changes withdrew and formed the Progressive Convention of the Tunker Church in Ashland, Ohio. The following year it was officially organized as the Brethren Church. Most Brethren churches are still found in Ohio, Pennsylvania, and Indiana. The church has historic, relational, and functional ties to both a university and a seminary located in Ashland, Ohio.

Theologically, the Brethren Church tries to seek a balance between the Calvinist and Arminian perspectives on salvation; however, for the Brethren, style of life is more important than doctrine. The believing community of faith leads believers into the path proposed in the Sermon on the Mount. Nonetheless, the church suffered a schism during the fundamentalist*/modernist controversy that gripped American Christianity in the 1920s and 1930s. The more conservative ministers formed the Fellowship of Grace Brethren Church*. The church has two ministry councils that provide oversight over ministries in the United States and internationally. An Executive Board is responsible for governance on behalf of the churches. The church collaboratives with other churches and agencies for the purpose of church health, missional outreach at home and abroad, as well as with relief activities worldwide.

For more information: www.brethrenchurch.org
Headquarters: 524 College Avenue, Ashland, Ohio 44805

BRETHREN IN CHRIST CHURCH

Founded: 1778
Membership: 20,739 in 232 congregations (2002)

This church began as a result of a spiritual awakening that took place in Lancaster, Pennsylvania, in the 1760s, inspired by the preaching of Philip Otterbein (1726–1813) and Martin Boehm (1725–1812). The group that gathered along the Susquehanna River was called simply the River Brethren until the Civil War. Primarily of Mennonite* descent, the River Brethren separated from the Mennonites over the issue of triple immersion in baptism. The River Brethren were pacifists, and with the outbreak of the Civil War and the institution of a national military draft, it became necessary for the Brethren to obtain legal recognition as an established religious organization in order to protect the objectors. A council meeting in Lancaster County, Pennsylvania, in 1863 adopted the name Brethren in Christ Church, but the group was not legally incorporated until 1904. In addition to typical Protestant doctrines, the Brethren in Christ insist on temperance and modesty of apparel. Many Brethren wear "plain dress" similar to that worn by the Amish*. The Brethren in Christ remains a "peace church," but members are not excluded from membership if they serve in the military.

While the government of this church is largely in the hands of the local congregations, there are eight regional conferences and a general conference, which is the ultimate authoritative body. Its publishing arm, Evangel Publishing House, is in Nappanee, Indiana. The church has two institutions of learning: Messiah College at Grantham, Pennsylvania, and Niagara Christian College at Fort Erie, Ontario. Missionaries are at work in Africa, India, Japan, London, Colombia, Nicaragua, Venezuela, and Cuba and are engaged in Mennonite Central Committee work around the world.

For more information: www.bic-church.org
Headquarters: P.O. Box A, 431 Grantham Rd., Grantham, PA 17027-0901

CHURCH OF THE BRETHREN

Founded: 1708
Membership: 134,844 in 1,069 churches (2002)

The Church of the Brethren, the largest of the Brethren churches, was formed in 1708 in Schwarzenau, Germany, with the work of Alexander Mack. The early Brethren were influenced by the Anabaptists as well as by Pietism, and they covenanted to be a people shaped by personal faith in Christ, prayer, and study of Scripture. They stressed daily discipleship and service to neighbor. Severe persecution and economic conditions prompted virtually the entire movement to migrate to North America between 1719 and 1729. Commonly known as German Baptist Brethren, or even Dunkers or Dunkards, in its bicentennial year, 1908, the group adopted "Church of the Brethren" as its official name. "Brethren" was seen as a New Testament term that conveyed the kinship and warmth of Jesus' early followers.

The Brethren emphasize right living more than right doctrine, and their current website invites those who are "fed up with doctrine and still hungry" to try the Brethren way, which includes "open-minded consideration of Jesus, the scriptures, and our own hearts." True to Pietist principles, the Brethren develop their understanding through community discussion and study, using Jesus' own teaching as a guide for modern living. Although non-creedal, the Church of the Brethren has held firmly to basic tenets of the Free Church, or Believers Church, tradition. Among the most distinctive Brethren practices are the baptism of confessing believers by threefold immersion and the anointing of the ill for spiritual and bodily health. The Last Supper is observed with a service of foot washing that symbolizes servanthood, a fellowship meal that symbolizes family, and the commemorative Eucharist that symbolizes Saviorhood.

Brethren have long held an official peace witness, expressed often in conscientious objection to military service. During World War II, Civilian Public Health camps were maintained for religious objectors who performed work in the national interest. During and after the war, many of the programs were continued under the alternative service provisions of Selective Service, and voluntary service abroad, a forerunner of the Peace Corps, was introduced. Also growing out of the peace concern was a worldwide program of relief, reconstruction, and welfare, conducted by the Brethren Service Commission and later by the World Ministries Commission, as a service of love to those suffering from war, natural disasters, or social disadvantage. Since 1948, Brethren Volunteer Service has enlisted nearly five thousand men and women for one or two years of social service at home and abroad. Work with migrant laborers, inner-city dwellers, prison inmates, refugees, and victims of abuse exemplify the types of activity undertaken. Increasingly, older volunteers have enrolled in the program, quite often after they have reached retirement age.

Numerous projects initiated by the group have become full-scale ecumenical enterprises. Among them are the Heifer Project International; Christian Youth Exchange; Christian Rural Overseas Program (CROP); Sales Exchange for Refugee Rehabilitation Vocation (SERRV), an organization which sells handcrafts for Third World producers; and International Voluntary Service. Other pioneering ventures were agricultural exchanges that began with Poland in the 1950s and with China in the 1980s and ecumenical exchanges with the Russian Orthodox Church in the 1960s.

In polity, the Brethren combine both congregational and presbyterian practices, with final authority vested in an Annual Conference of elected delegates. The General Board of elected and ex officio members is the administrative arm of the church. Congregations are organized into twenty-three districts in thirty-six states, usually with one or more full-time executives in each district. The heaviest concentration of churches is in Pennsylvania, Virginia, Maryland, Ohio, Indiana, and Illinois.

The Brethren are related to six accredited liberal arts colleges: Bridgewater College in Virginia; Elizabethtown and Juniata colleges in Pennsylvania; University of LaVerne in California; Manchester College in Indiana; and McPherson College in Kansas. The church sponsors one graduate school, Bethany Theological Seminary, in Richmond, Indiana. General offices are in Elgin, Illinois, which is also the home of Brethren Press, which produces the monthly publication *Messenger* and various books and curriculum resources.

For more information: www.brethren.org

Headquarters: 1451 Dundee Ave., Elgin, IL 60120

CHURCH OF THE UNITED BRETHREN IN CHRIST

Founded: 1800, with roots to 1767
Membership: 22,740 in 217 congregations (2002)

This group had its origins in the Pennsylvania awakening led by Philip Otterbein (1726–1813) and Martin Boehm (1725–1812) in the 1760s. In 1800 the ministers of the Brethren officially adopted the name United Brethren in Christ and elected Otterbein and Boehm as the first bishops. In 1815 they adopted a confession of faith based on one that Otterbein had written in 1789. The United Brethren took a strong stand against slave holding in the 1820s; thus they did not spread in the South, but did make the western U.S. a mission area. In 1841 a constitution was adopted. When the constitution was changed in 1889, some members viewed the changes as unconstitutional and separated from the main body. The main body of United Brethren eventually merged with the United Methodists*, leaving the name "United Brethren" to the smaller group.

United Brethren believe in the Trinity and in the deity, humanity, and atonement of Christ. Observance of "scriptural living" is required of all members, who are forbidden consumption of alcoholic beverages and membership in secret societies. Baptism and the Lord's Supper are observed as ordinances. Local, annual, and general conferences are held. The highest governing body, the General Conference, meets quadrennially. General church offices are located in Huntington, Indiana; the majority of local churches are found in Pennsylvania, Ohio, northern Indiana, and Michigan. Both men and women are eligible for the ministry and are ordained only once as elders. Missionary societies administer evangelism and church aid in the U.S. and in Costa Rica, El Salvador, Honduras, Hong Kong, India, Jamaica, Macau, Mexico, Myanmar, Nicaragua, Sierra Leone, and Thailand. There are over thirty-six thousand members worldwide. The United Brethren Church maintains a college and a graduate school of Christian ministries at Huntington, Indiana, with secondary schools in Sierra Leone.

For more information: www.ub.org

Headquarters: 302 Lake St., Huntington, IN 46750

EVANGELICAL CONGREGATIONAL CHURCH

Founded: 1894 and 1928, with roots to 1800
Membership: 19,337 in 150 congregations (2007)

This denomination traces its origin to the work of Jacob Albright (1759–1808), a Pietist and Methodist* evangelist among the Germans of Pennsylvania in the early 1800s. Albright helped to organize the Evangelical Association that later became the Evangelical Church, which eventually merged with the United Brethren Church to form the Evangelical United Brethren Church. A division within the church in 1891 was healed by a merger in 1922, but some congregations in the Ohio River valley region objected and continued their separate existence. They chose the name Evangelical Congregational Church in 1928. This church, like its parent Evangelical Church, is "Methodist in polity, Arminian in doctrine." (www.eccenter.com) Emphasis is on the inspiration and integrity of the Bible and "fellowship of all followers of Christ." The church lists its Core Values as "Passion for Christ, Compassion for the Lost, Servant Leadership, Healthy Ministries, and Unity in the Body of Christ."

Each congregation owns its property, determines its membership, manages its affairs, and chooses its ecclesiastical affiliation. There is a National Conference that supervises conference ministers. The stationing committee, composed of the bishop and conference ministers assigns pastors to churches. The Global Ministries Commission supervises the missionary programs. Church headquarters, the Evangelical Theological Seminary, and the New Dawn Christian Community Services are located at Myerstown, Pennsylvania.

For more information: www.eccenter.com

Headquarters: 100 West Park Ave., Myerstown, PA 17067

EVANGELICAL COVENANT CHURCH

Founded: 1885
Membership: 107,379 in 689 congregations (2003)

The Evangelical Covenant Church is not a Brethren church but grew out of Pietism in Sweden. It traces its roots from the Protestant Reformation through the biblical instruction of the Lutheran state church of Sweden to the great spiritual awakenings of the nineteenth century. The Covenant Church was founded by Swedish immigrants in the Midwest and adheres to the affirmations of the Reformation regarding the Holy Scriptures as the only perfect rule for faith, doctrine, and conduct. It has traditionally valued the historic confessions of the Christian church, particularly the Apostles' Creed, but emphasizes the sovereignty of the Word of God over all creedal interpretations.

The Covenant Church's evangelical emphasis includes the necessity of the new birth, the ministry of the Holy Spirit, and the reality of freedom in Christ. It values the New Testament emphasis on personal faith in Jesus Christ as Savior and Lord and the church as a fellowship of believers that recognizes but transcends theological differences. Baptism and the Lord's Supper are seen as divinely ordained sacraments. While the denomination has traditionally practiced the baptism of infants, it has also recognized the practice of believer baptism.

The local church is administered by a board elected by the membership; its ministers, ordained by the denomination, are called, generally with the aid and guidance of the denominational Department of the Ordered Ministry and the conference superintendent. Each of the ten regional conferences elects its own superintendent. The highest authority is vested in an annual meeting composed of ministers and laypeople elected by the constituent churches. An administrative board, elected by the annual meeting, implements its decisions. The Covenant Church sponsors churches in Burkina Faso, Cameroon, Central African Republic, Central Asia, Colombia, the Czech Republic, the Democratic Republic of Congo, Ecuador, Equitorial Guinea, France, Germany, Japan, Laos, Mexico, Spain, Taiwan, and Thailand. Educational institutions include North Park University and North Park Theological Seminary in Chicago, Illinois. The church maintains fifteen retirement communities and nursing homes in seven states, two hospitals, three homes for adults with developmental disabilities, a children's home, a ministry for victims of domestic violence, and several camps and conference centers across North America.

For more information: www.covchurch.org

Headquarters: 5101 North Francisco Ave., Chicago, IL 60625

EVANGELICAL FREE CHURCH OF AMERICA

Founded: 1950, with roots to the nineteenth century
Membership: est. 336,000 in 1273 congregations (2004)

The Evangelical Free Church traces its origin to the Pietist revivals in Scandinavia in the late nineteenth century. Immigration brought members of various "free" churches to the U.S. A number of Swedish-speaking evangelical congregations, centered in Iowa, formed a fellowship of "free" congregations to be known as the Swedish Evangelical Free Mission in 1884. In that same year, two Norwegian-Danish groups began fellowshipping, one on the east coast and one on the west. In 1912, these merged to form the Norwegian-Danish Evangelical Free Church Association. In 1950 the Swedish denomination merged with the other Scandinavian bodies to form the present Evangelical Free Church, with headquarters in Minneapolis, Minnesota.

Doctrinally, the church endorses a variation on the popular Pietist statement: "In essentials, unity. In non-essentials, charity. In all things, Jesus Christ." (www.efca.org) In 1950 the merged denominations adopted a twelve-point doctrinal statement, which is now incorporated into the constitution of most local congregations. The constitution stresses faithfulness to evangelical beliefs while avoiding disputes over minor matters. Affirming both the rational and the relational dimensions of Christian faith, the church maintains that sound Christian doctrine must be coupled with dynamic Christian experience, facilitating a ministry of love and reconciliation. It includes belief in the premillennial return of Jesus and biblical inerrancy.

Local congregations are autonomous, but the church maintains administrative offices in Minneapolis, Minnesota. The president works with various boards and leadership teams to guide the several ministries of the denomination. Some six hundred missionaries serve stations in over forty countries around the world. The church sponsors Trinity International University, which includes Trinity Evangelical Divinity School, with the main campus located in Deerfield, Illinois; other campuses of the university are maintained in Chicago, Illinois; Miami, Florida; and Santa Ana, California.

For more information: www.efca.org

Headquarters: 902 East 78th St., Minneapolis, MN 55420-1300

FELLOWSHIP OF GRACE BRETHREN CHURCHES

Founded: 1939
Membership: 30,371 in 260 congregations (1997)

This body was part of the Brethren Church (Ashland) that separated from the main Church of the Brethren* in the early 1880s. During the fundamentalist*/modernist controversy of the 1920s and 1930s that church divided further. In 1939 the Ashland group and the Grace group went their separate ways. In 1969, the Grace group adopted its own statement of faith that expressed the church's beliefs which include the primacy of the Bible; the Trinity; the church as made up of believers; the Christian life as a way of righteousness; the ordinances of baptism and the threefold Communion service (including foot washing and the love feast); the reality of Satan; the Second Coming of Jesus; and the future life. The group was separately incorporated in 1987 as the Fellowship of Grace Brethren Churches and a new constitution was adopted in 1997.

Grace Brethren churches are grouped geographically into districts, which hold annual conferences. The entire church holds an annual conference, often held at Winona Lake, Indiana, where the group's headquarters are located. This conference, made up of delegates from Fellowship churches, elects a board of directors, known as the Fellowship Council, and general church officers. The church supports both international and North American missionary and relief efforts, and it maintains Grace College and Seminary in Winona Lake.

For more information: www.fgbc.org
Headquarters: P.O. Box 386, Winona Lake, IN 46590

MORAVIAN CHURCH (UNITAS FRATRUM)

Founded: 1458; came to the U.S. in 1735
Membership: 40,341 in 160 congregations (2008)

The Moravian Church is one of the few pre-Reformation Protestant churches (the Waldensians* are another). Its roots go back to John Hus (ca. 1372–1415), a Czech reformer who was burned at the stake at the Council of Constance in 1415. A young man named Brother Gregory grew dissatisfied with the lifestyle and worship of the major Hussite church, and in 1457/58 he organized a community dedicated to living according to the Sermon on the Mount and the example of the early church. They called their pacifist, communitarian body *Jednota Bratrska*, or "the Unity of the Brethren." At times they used the Latin form, *Unitas Fratrum*, which remains the official name of the church. In 1467 the group established an independent episcopacy and clergy.

Persecution under the Hapsburgs almost exterminated the church, but in 1722 refugees settled on the estate of Count Nicholas Ludwig von Zinzendorf (1700–60), one of the leaders of German Pietism, in Saxony. There they built the town of Herrnhut, a highly structured religious community that would be the model for similar communities in the U.S. Under the direction of Zinzendorf, the Moravians carried out an extensive mission enterprise, beginning with work among the slaves on St. Thomas in the Virgin Islands. In the 1730s the Moravians became the first church to ordain women of African descent as pastors and evangelists. The Moravian evangelist David Zeisberger (1721–1808) had great success among the native tribes of the northern United States, but that effort was virtually destroyed by the massacre of Moravian Indians at Gnaddenhutten, Ohio, in 1782 by an American militia.

The Moravians attempted to establish a settlement in Georgia in the 1730s, but the only lasting result of that work was the conversion of John Wesley (1703–1791) to "heart religion." Permanent work was established in Pennsylvania and North Carolina. In the nineteenth century, the church supported work among German and Scandanavian immigrants in the upper Midwest. Recent growth in the United States comes mainly from immigration from Central America and the Caribbean, where the Moravians have long had a strong presence.

The major doctrinal statement of the church is *The Ground of the Unity*, which emphasizes the love of God manifested in the life and death of Jesus, the teachings of Christ, the inner testimony of the Spirit, ecumenism, and Christian conduct in everyday affairs, including the pursuit of social justice. There has not been a schism in the church since 1495. In addition to infant baptism and Holy Communion, the Moravians observe the practice of the love feast, a simple meal taken communally. In the U.S., Moravians are most famous for the Easter Sunrise Service and Christmas Eve love feast and candle service.

There is only one Moravian Church worldwide, but it is divided into twenty governing units, called provinces. The provinces in North America are the Northern (including Canada), Southern, and Alaska provinces. The highest administrative body in each is the provincial synod, which meets every four years to direct missionary, educational, and publishing work and to elect a Provincial Elders' Conference, which functions between synod meetings. Bishops, elected by provincial and general synods, are the spiritual, not the administrative, leaders of the church. There are several female bishops in the church, and until recently the head of the Unity was Angelina Swart of South Africa.

Missionary work has always been a primary concern. There are nearly eight hundred thousand Moravians worldwide, more than half in Tanzania and South Africa. Always committed to education, the church founded Moravian College and Theological Seminary in Bethlehem, Pennsylvania, and Salem College in Winston-Salem, North Carolina. The church is also known for its distinctive musical heritage.

For more information: www.moravian.org
Headquarters: P.O. Box 1245, Bethlehem, PA 18016-1245

OLD GERMAN BAPTIST BRETHREN

Reorganized: 1881
Membership: 6,299 in 56 districts (2007)

While the Brethren Church left the Church of the Brethren because the latter body seemed too conservative in the early 1880s, the Old German Baptist Brethren left because they considered the Church of the Brethren not conservative enough. The dissenters stood for the old order and traditions. The salient point in their opposition lay in their suspicion of Sunday schools, salaried ministers, missions, higher education, and church societies. The basic objections still hold but with certain modifications. Children are not enrolled in Sunday schools, but are encouraged to attend the regular services of the church and to join the church by baptism during their teens; however, the decision is left entirely to the individual. Many congregations list a majority of members between fifteen and fifty years of age. The church today is not completely opposed even to higher education; most of the youth enter high school and some take training in college or professional schools.

The church stands for a literal interpretation of the scriptures in regard to the Lord's Supper and practices closed Communion, which excludes all but its own members. While it advocates compliance with the ordinary demands of government, it opposes cooperation in war. Any member who enters into military service will fall under the judgment of the church. Non-cooperation in political and secret societies is required; dress is plain, and all amusements deemed worldly are frowned upon. The group has no salaried ministers and enforces complete abstinence from alcoholic beverages; the members refuse to take oaths or engage in lawsuits; the sick are anointed with oil; the heads of the sister are veiled; and wedding ceremonies are not performed for previously divorced persons while their former spouses are living.

There are no missions, except the witness portrayed in their daily life. An annual conference that rules on matters on which the scriptures are silent is held each year at Pentecost; a brotherhood council is vital to their church body. Most of the members live in Ohio, Indiana, Pennsylvania, Virginia, California, and Kansas.

For more information: www.cob-net.org

Contact: 6952 N. Montgomery County Line Rd., Englewood, OH 45322-9748

SCHWENKFELDER CHURCH

Founded: 1782, with roots to 1519
Membership: est. 2,800 in six congregations (2000)

This church predates the Pietist movement, but shares so many Pietist features that it is included in this section as a "forerunner" of the movement. Though small in size, it represents such a unique branch of the Protestant Reformation that it merits inclusion in this *Handbook*. The church is named for Caspar Schwenckfeld von Ossig (1489–1561), a Silesian nobleman who experienced a spiritual awakening in 1518. Disappointed in his hope to help reform the Roman Catholic Church from within, he played a leading role in the Reformation. He broke with Luther over the issue of the Lord's Supper, insisting that the bread remains bread, and he insisted on complete separation of church and state. Espousing a "Reformation of the Middle Way," Schwenkfelder and his followers emphasized the supremacy of the Spirit over literalistic interpretations of Scripture. By the end of the sixteenth century, the movement numbered several thousand, but the group was persecuted by other religious bodies and remained small and rather dispersed.

Schwenkfelders arrived in Philadelphia in six migrations between 1731 and 1737. Unable to find land for common purchase, the immigrants spread out and settled in the region between Philadelphia and Allentown, Pennsylvania. The Society of Schwenkfelders was formed in 1782, and the Schwenkfelder Church was incorporated in 1909. Although descendants of the original settlers live in all regions of the U.S., the remaining Schwenkfelder churches are found within a fifty-mile radius of Philadelphia. All theology, the members hold, should be constructed from the Bible, but Scripture is considered dead without the indwelling Word. They believe that Christ's divinity was progressive, his human nature becoming more and more divine without "losing its identity." Faith, regeneration, and subsequent spiritual growth change human nature, but justification by faith must not obscure the positive regeneration imparted by Christ; thus the theology is Christocentric.

For more information: www.schwenkfelder.com
Headquarters: 105 Seminary St., Pennsburg, PA 18073

Baptists

The Baptists comprise one of the largest and most diverse groupings of Christians in the United States. Technically, there are no such things as Baptist denominations, because Baptists are strongly congregational in polity: each local congregation is independent; however, Baptist churches are commonly grouped into larger associations for purposes of fellowship. National conventions have been established to carry on educational and missionary work and to administer pension plans. For the purposes of this *Handbook,* these national conventions are considered denominations.

Most state and regional conventions meet annually with delegates from all Baptist churches in a given area. These conventions receive reports, make recommendations, and help to raise national mission budgets; but they have no authority to enforce their decisions. Baptists have insisted on freedom of thought and expression in pulpit and pew. They have insisted, too, on the absolute autonomy of the local congregation; each church arranges its own worship and examines and baptizes its own members. There is no age requirement for membership, but the candidate is usually of an age to understand and accept the teachings of Christ. Candidates for the ministry are licensed by local churches and are ordained upon recommendation of a group of sister churches.

Doctrine and Polity. Despite their emphasis on independence and individualism, Baptists are bound together by an amazingly strong "rope of sand" in allegiance to certain principles and doctrines based generally on the competency of each individual in matters of faith. Baptists generally agree on the following principles of faith: the inspiration and trustworthiness of the Bible as the sole rule of life; the lordship of Jesus Christ; the inherent freedom of persons to approach God for themselves; the granting of salvation through faith by way of grace and contact with the Holy Spirit; two ordinances (rather than sacraments), the Lord's Supper and the baptism of believers by immersion; the independence of the local church; the church as a group of regenerated believers who are baptized upon confession of faith; separation of church and state; life after death; the unity of humankind; the royal law of God; the need of redemption from sin; and the ultimate triumph of God's kingdom.

These overall doctrines have never been written into any official Baptist creed for all the churches, but they have been incorporated into two important confessions of faith. The Baptist churches of London wrote a Philadelphia Confession in the year 1689 that was enlarged by the Philadelphia Association in 1742. The New Hampshire State Baptist Convention drew up another confession in 1832. The Philadelphia Confession is strongly Calvinist, the New Hampshire Confession only moderately so.

Baptists in the United States. The Baptist movement in the United States grew out of English Puritanism in the early seventeenth century. Convinced that Puritanism needed further reform, Separatists began to teach that only self-professed believers were eligible for membership in the church. That is, the church is properly made up of only regenerated people. Fleeing persecution under James I, some of the English Separatists settled in Holland, where they encountered the Mennonites*. Many of the Mennonites' principles agreed with their own convictions, including the beliefs that the Bible is the sole authority for faith and practice, that church and state should be completely separated, and that church discipline should be rigidly enforced in business, family, and personal affairs. Before long the congregation of John Smyth (ca. 1570–1612) accepted another bedrock Mennonite principle and adopted the practice of "believer's baptism"—that is, baptism only of adults who make a profession of faith. Smyth rebaptized himself and his followers in 1609. Smyth's people eventually moved back across the channel and established a Baptist church in London.

The first churches were General Baptist churches, which means that they believed in a general atonement for all persons. In the course of time there arose a Particular Baptist Church, which held to the doctrine of predestination associated with the teachings of John Calvin (see REFORMED, CONGREGATIONALIST, AND PRESBYTERIAN CHURCHES). The first British Particular Baptist churches date back to 1638.

In 1631, Roger Williams (ca. 1603–1683) came to America and soon became the first great champion of freedom for faith and conscience in North America. Williams was a Separatist minister when he arrived. Preaching against the authority of the Puritan magistrates, Williams was forced to leave the Massachusetts Bay Colony, and he established the town of Providence on Rhode Island. There he organized the first Baptist church in America. John Clarke (1609–1676) established another Baptist church at Newport around the same time. Many scholars date the Providence church to 1638, and the Newport church to 1644.

The Baptist movement grew rapidly during the First Great Awakening of the 1740s, but a dispute soon arose among Baptists over the question of conversion. The Old Lights, or Regulars, distrusted the emotionalism of revivals, while the New Lights insisted on an experience of rebirth as a condition for membership in their churches. Despite internal disagreements Baptists continued to agitate for religious freedom in the new land and played a significant role in the adoption of the First Amendment.

Landmark Baptists. Many Baptists in America hold to the belief that the Baptist Church has existed since the days of John the Baptist in the first century CE. Of particular interest in this regard are the Landmark Baptists. The name originated with the writings of James Madison Pendleton (1811–1891) and James Robinson Graves (1820–1893) in Kentucky and Tennessee in the latter part of the nineteenth century. The four distinguishing tenets of Landmarkism are the following:

(1) The church is always local and visible. While members of Protestant churches may be saved, they are not members of true churches.

(2) The commission was given to the church; consequently, all matters covered by it must be administered under church authority. Clergy of other denominations are not accepted in Landmark Baptist pulpits.

(3) Baptism, to be valid, must be administered by the authority of a New Testament (Baptist) church. Baptisms administered by any other authority are not accepted.

(4) There is a direct historic succession of Baptist churches from New Testament times. Baptist churches have existed in practice, though not in name, in every century.

These principles are held primarily by the churches of the American Baptist Association and Baptist Missionary Association*, though an estimated one and a half million members of different Baptist churches hold to the Landmark position and doctrine, the largest concentration being in the South and the Southwest. More than fifteen Bible institutes and seminaries are supported by these churches.

Black Baptists. Baptist preachers were particularly effective in converting African Americans to Christianity before emancipation. The great majority of African Americans in pre-Civil War days were either Baptist or Methodist*. In 1793 there were nearly seventy-five thousand Baptists in the United States, one-fourth of them black. When the Battle of Bull Run was fought in 1861, there were 150,000 black Baptists, most of them slaves.

The church was one place where slaves and free, black and white had social interaction, but slaves usually had to sit in the galleries of white churches. White Baptist preachers, sometimes assisted by black helpers, moved from one plantation to another, holding services more or less regularly. Occasionally a black preacher was emancipated so he could work full time among blacks. The first black Baptist church was organized at Silver Bluff, across the Savannah River, near Augusta, Georgia, in 1773. Other churches followed in Petersburg, Virginia, 1776; Richmond, Virginia, 1780; Williamsburg, Virginia, 1785; Savannah, Georgia, 1785; and Lexington, Kentucky, 1790.

The slave rebellion led by Nat Turner in 1831 appears to have been fueled by Christian rhetoric of freedom and divine justice. Whites were so frightened by the rebellion that laws were passed in most Southern states making it illegal to teach blacks to read. The book that the masters feared was the Bible, with its message of liberation of the oppressed. The story of the Exodus inspired hope in the enslaved population that God would send a new Moses to free his people. The story of Jesus, who was flogged like a slave, also inspired hope for those suffering under the bondsman's lash. Jesus was more than the Lamb of God who takes away the sin of the world; he was suffering servant who shared the burdens of those who suffer.

Almost everywhere slave meetings were monitored by owners, lest unrest be fomented, but slaves continued to conduct their own meetings hidden from sight and sound of the masters in "the invisible institution." Slaves developed a distinctive type of Gospel music, called Spirituals, and sang about freedom, justice, and salvation. Evangelism and justice have always gone hand in hand in Black theology. After the Civil War, Baptist congregations divided along racial lines, and countless black Baptist congregations emerged throughout the South. Thus it is not uncommon to see two churches named "First Baptist," one white and the other black, in Southern towns. Aided by the Freedman's Aid Society and various

Baptist organizations, nearly one million black Baptists were worshiping in their own churches by 1880.

Emancipation did lead to the Promised Land for African Americans, but the church helped blacks endure decades of segregation. Large numbers of African Americans moved to Northern cities in the late nineteenth and early twentieth centuries, and they took their faith with them. The black church served as an anchor for many people living in growing metropolises, and national conventions were organized to coordinate Baptist ministries.

Baptist Missions. Strongly evangelical in theology, the Baptists were early participants in foreign missions, following the lead of English Baptist William Carey (1761–1834), who went to India in 1793. In 1814, Baptists in the United States organized their own General Missionary Convention of the Baptist Denomination in the United States of America for Foreign Missions. This convention, representing a national Baptist fellowship, marked the first real denominational consciousness. It was followed eventually by other organizations that welded them firmly together: general Baptist conventions; a general tract society, later called the American Baptist Publication Society; various missionary societies for work at home and abroad; an education society; and the Baptist Young People's Union.

These organizations were on a national scale, but divided over the issue of slavery. In 1845, there was a dispute over whether a missionary could own slaves. Many Baptists had come to the conclusion that owning another human being was inconsistent with Christian faith. In response, Southerners defended slavery on biblical grounds. When a compromise could not be reached, they formed their own Southern Baptist Convention. The SBC took a literal view of the Bible, especially passages that defended slavery, and insisted that the church focus on evangelism and personal morality rather than social justice issues. The Northern Baptist Convention was not officially organized until 1907 and is now called the American Baptist Churches in the U.S.A.

Some of the divisions caused by slavery and the Civil War have healed. The Baptist Joint Committee on Public Affairs—supported by the American Baptist Churches in the U.S.A., some Southern Baptist churches, and some other bodies—is housed in Washington, D.C. This committee serves mainly to spread Baptist convictions on public morals and to safeguard the principle of separation of church and state. The Baptist World Alliance, organized in 1905, now includes more than forty million Baptists. It meets every five years to discuss common themes and problems and is purely an advisory body.

The twentieth century brought new conflicts in the Baptist family, which resulted in the formation of new denominations. First was the Fundamentalist/Modernist controversy in the 1920s. Baptist theology respects the right of individuals to read and interpret the Bible on their own, but the methods of modern biblical criticism disturbed many Baptist preachers. Baptists divided over how literally one should read the Bible. Since World War II, Baptists have argued over the church's role in society. Should the church encourage the expansion of civil rights to all people or should the church insist on traditional gender roles? In 2008 a new initiative called the New Baptist Covenant was launched by prominent Baptists, most notably former President Jimmy Carter, who teaches Sunday school in a Baptist church in Plains, Georgia. The New Baptist Covenant is an attempt to reunite all Baptist churches in a common expression of faith focused on the redeeming work of Christ and God's plan for justice in the world.

Suggestions for further reading:

Ammerman, Nancy T. *Baptist Battles: Social Change and Religious Conflict in the Southern Baptist Convention.* New Brunswick, NJ: Rutgers University Press, 1990.

Balmer, Randall. *Mine Eyes Have Seen the Glory: A Journey into the Evangelical Subculture of America.* New York: Oxford University Press, 1989.

Brackney, William H. *The Baptists.* New York: Greenwood Press, 1988.

Dayton, Donald W., and Robert K. Johnston, eds. *The Variety of American Evangelicalism.* Downer's Grove, IL: InterVarsity Press, 1991.

Fitts, Leroy. *A History of Black Baptists.* Nashville: Broadman Press, 1985.

Lincoln, C. Eric, and Lawrence H. Mamiya. *The Black Church in the African-American Experience.* Durham, NC: Duke University Press, 1990.

Gardner, Robert. *Baptists of Early America: A Statistical History, 1639-1790.* Atlanta: Georgia Baptist Historical Society, 1983.

Hill, Samuel and Robert G. Torbet. *Baptists: North and South.* Valley Forge, Pa.: Judson Press, 1964.

Hill, Samuel S, ed. *Encyclopedia of Religion in the South.* Macon, Ga.: Mercer University Press, 1984.

Leonard, Bill J., ed. *Dictionary of Baptists in America.* Downers Grove, IL: InterVarsity Press, 1994.

Leonard, Bill J. *God's Last and Only Hope: The Fragmentation of the Southern Baptist Convention.* Grand Rapids, Mich.: Eerdmans, 1990.

MacBeth, Leon. *The Baptist Heritage.* Nashville: Broadman Press, 1987.

Matthews, Donald G. *Religion in the Old South.* Chicago: University of Chicago Press, 1977.

McLoughlin, William G. *Soul Liberty: The Baptists' Struggle in New England, 1630-1833.* Hanover, NH: University Press of New England, 1991.

Pelt, O. D. and R. L. Smith. *The Story of the National Baptists.* New York: Vantage Press, 1960.

Sernett, Milton C., ed. *Afro-American Religious History: A Documentary Witness.* Durham, NC: Duke University Press, 1985.

Wardin, Albert W. *Baptists Around the World: A Comprehensive Handbook.* Nashville: Broadman and Holman Publishers, 1995.

ALLIANCE OF BAPTIST CHURCHES

Founded: 1987
Membership: est. 65,000 in 127 churches (2007)

The Alliance of Baptists is a confederation of Baptist congregations and individuals who separated from the Southern Baptist Convention* during the conservative/moderate conflict of the 1980s. The Alliance stress the historic Baptist principles of individual and congregational autonomy, particularly in regard to biblical interpretation and missions. The Alliance churches encourage the use of modern methods of biblical study, theological education, and free inquiry into the history of Christianity. Most important, the Alliance has dedicated itself to social and economic justice and equity. Women are encouraged to seek ordination and assume leadership roles in the Alliance and in congregations. Leadership of the Alliance is composed of three elected officers who serve no more than two years and a thirty-four-member Board of Directors. The annual meeting of the Alliance is held each spring and reviews all decisions of the Board. There are nine standing committees that supervise such areas as women in ministry and interfaith dialogue.

For more information: www.allianceofbaptists.org
Headquarters: 1328 16th NW, Washington, D.C. 20036

AMERICAN BAPTIST ASSOCIATION

Founded: 1905
Membership: 280,987 in 1867 churches (ARDA, 2000)

Organized in 1905 as the Baptist General Association, the group adopted its present name in 1924. Teaching that the Great Commission of Christ (Matthew 28:18-20) was given only to a local congregation, members believe that the local church is the only unit authorized to administer the ordinances (baptism and communion) and that the congregation is an independent and autonomous body responsible only to Christ. Because of their belief that no universal church or ecclesiastical authority is higher than a local congregation, members of the American Baptist Association claim that those Baptists organized in conventions are not faithful to Bible mission methods.

Maintaining that their own way is the true New Testament form, they hold themselves separate from all other religious groups. They strongly protest the trend of many Baptist groups to identify themselves with Protestantism, since they believe that their faith preceded the Protestant Reformation, and indeed has a continued succession from Christ and the apostles. They do not accept as valid

167

baptisms performed in other Baptist churches, and they serve communion only to members of the local congregation.

The Association's doctrine is strictly fundamentalist (see FUNDAMENTAL-IST AND BIBLE CHURCHES) and includes the verbal inspiration of the Bible, the Triune God, the virgin birth and deity of Christ, the suffering and death of Christ as substitutionary, and the bodily resurrection of Christ and all his saints. The Second Coming of Jesus, physical and personal, is to be the crowning event of the gospel age and will be pre-millennial. There is eternal punishment for the wicked; salvation is solely by grace through faith, not by law or works. There must be absolute separation of church and state and absolute religious freedom. Members denounce abortion on demand, homosexuality, and premarital sex as being contrary to biblical teachings.

Government of both the local congregation and the annual meeting of the association is congregational in nature. Missionary work is conducted on county, state, interstate, and international levels, the program originating in the local church; and missionaries are supported by the cooperating churches. Educational work is pursued through the Sunday schools, five seminaries, three colleges, and twenty-seven Bible institutes. The greater strength of this group is found in the South, Southeast, Southwest, and West, but much new work has begun in recent years in the East and the North.

A comprehensive publishing program includes fourteen monthly and semi-monthly periodicals, Sunday school literature designed to cover the entire Bible in a ten-year period, and literature for young people and vacation Bible schools. National and state youth camps are held annually, as are pastors' and missionaries' conferences on regional and national levels.

For more information: www.abaptist.org

Offices: 4605 N., State Line Ave., Texarkana, TX 75503

AMERICAN BAPTIST CHURCHES IN THE U.S.A.

Founded: 1814 or 1845
Membership: 1,358,351 in 5,558 churches (2007)

This body has had several changes in name over the decades. It traces its origins to May 1814, when representatives from various Baptist associations and churches met in Philadelphia to organize the General Missionary Convention of the Baptist Denomination in the United States of America for Foreign Missions. This body quickly became known as the Triennial Convention and was the first national Baptist organization in the United States. The American Baptist Publication Society and the American Baptist Home Mission Society were established in 1824 and 1832 respectively. By 1841, sectional and theological differences centered around the issue of slavery began to erode the unity of the foreign mission board. In 1845, one year after the final meeting of the Triennial Convention, the Northern and Southern groups met and reorganized separately. The Northern group became the American Baptist Missionary Union and the southern group became the Southern Baptist Convention*. The women of the Northern churches formed their own home and foreign missionary societies in the 1870s.

Separate appeals for funds to support these competing societies created confusion and dissatisfaction, leading eventually to the formation of the Northern Baptist Convention in 1907. This convention was actually a corporation with restricted powers in conducting religious work, receiving and expending money, and affiliating itself with other bodies. The Convention reorganized in 1950, changing its name to the American Baptist Convention. In 1955, the two women's missionary societies joined administratively with their counterparts, the older foreign- and home-mission societies. In 1950 the first general secretary was elected.

In 1972 the convention adopted its third and present name and restructured to strengthen the representational principle and to integrate more fully the national program bodies into the larger organization. A larger (200-member) general board composed of election-district representatives and at-large representatives makes up the policymaking body. A general council of chief executives and staff of national program boards, chief executives of regions, and other American Baptist bodies serves to coordinate the corporate affairs of the denomination under the leadership of the general secretary.

The denomination is at work in twenty children's homes and special services, seventy-seven retirement homes and communities, twenty-seven hospitals and nursing homes, nine theological seminaries, and sixteen senior colleges and universities. Judson Press is its publishing arm. The Board of National Ministries has workers in thirty-six states. This board supports Bacone College for Native Americans in Oklahoma and carries on widespread work among African Americans, Native Americans, and Asians in the United States The Board of International Ministries currently supports missionaries in six countries in Asia (China, India, Japan, the Philippines, Singapore, and Thailand), two countries in Africa (South Africa and Zaire), and seven countries in Latin America and the Caribbean (Bolivia, Costa Rica, the Dominican Republic, El Salvador, Haiti, Mexico, and Nicaragua).

In matters of faith, American Baptist Churches hold to typical Baptist doctrines described above. They have historically taken a stand on such controversial issues as abolition, temperance, racial and social justice, and the ordination of women. They have traditionally been a denomination with diversity of race, ethnicity, culture, class, and theology. The ordinances of baptism and the Lord's Supper are considered aids more than necessities for salvation. Generally it may be said that Baptists represented in the American Baptist Churches in the U.S.A.

are less conservative in thought and theology than those in the Southern Baptist Convention. American Baptists are represented in the National Council of the Churches of Christ in the U.S.A. and the World Council of Churches; Southern Baptists are represented in neither. American Baptists have made gestures toward union with General Baptists, Southern Baptists, the National Baptist Convention, Seventh-Day Baptists, Disciples of Christ, Church of the Brethren, and the Alliance of Baptists and have welcomed Free Baptists into full fellowship. Like many historic Protestant denominations, American Baptists struggle with declining membership.

For more information: www.abc-usa.org

Headquarters: P.O. Box 851, Valley Forge, PA 19482-0851

ASSOCIATION OF REFORMED BAPTIST CHURCHES OF AMERICA

Founded: 1997
Membership: statistics unavailable; 69 churches (2009)

This association held its first annual General Assembly, in Mesa, Arizona, on March 11, 1997. The pastors and elders from twenty-four Reformed Baptist churches in fourteen states were present. Reformed Baptists have their origin in the Particular Baptists of the seventeenth century and have been heavily influenced by the nineteenth century Baptist theologian and popular preacher Charles Haddon Spurgeon (1834-92). During the mid-twentieth century the works of another Baptist theologian and writer, A.W. Pink, were the catalyst for the resurgence of "five-point Calvinism" that gave rise to the modern Reformed Baptists.

Member churches subscribe to the Second London Baptist Confession of Faith of 1689, and agree with the doctrines of the Synod and *Canons of Dort* (1618-19) and the *Westminster Confession of Faith* (1646), except in the areas of church government and infant baptism. They profess belief in total human depravity, unconditional election, limited and definite atonement, irresistible (or effectual and invincible) calling, and the final perseverance of all true saints. The Reformed Baptists believe that the Bible presents a Baptist understanding of Covenant Theology (in contrast to a Presbyterian view). The church rejects Dispensationalism, which is taught in some Baptist churches. The church gives prominence in worship to preaching believes that prophecy ceased with the and apostles.

As with many Baptist churches, the ARBCA churches resist any idea of denominational control over the member churches. Each member church is fully self-governing, yet voluntarily is accountable to sister churches through the

Association. The ARBCA has no mission board per se. An ARBCA mission- ary's home church is his mission board and his primary sending agent. Member churches assist one another in sending evangelists to accomplish the call of mis- sions at home and abroad. The four main arms of this association are Foreign Missions, Home Missions, Publications, and Ministerial Education. The ARBCA operates the Institute of Reformed Baptist Studies in Escondido, California, in cooperation with Westminster Theological Seminary.

For more information: www.arbca.com

Headquarters: P.O. Box 289, Carlisle, PA 17013

BAPTIST GENERAL CONVENTION OF TEXAS

Founded: 1848
Membership: 2,372,733 in 5,700 churches (2008)

Baptists came to Texas in the 1830s when it was still part of Mexico. The church grew rapidly during the days of the Republic, and the Baptist State Convention was formed in 1848 in Anderson, Texas. Because of the size of the state and theologi- cal diversity among the Baptists, other conventions, such as the Baptist General Association, were formed in various regions of the state. In 1886 the Baptist State Convention and Baptist General Association merged and adopted the name Bap- tist General Convention of Texas. In 1933 the fundamentalist preacher J. Frank Norris separated from the BGC and formed the Premillennial Missionary Baptist Fellowship, but the controversy between modernism and fundamentalism contin- ued within Baptist General Convention in Texas. The BGC was part of the South- ern Baptist Convention* until the SBC adopted a new Baptist Faith and Message statement in 2000. The Baptist General Convention rejected the new statement and reaffirmed the 1963 Baptist Faith and Message as its standard. The church stresses what it calls Baptist Distinctives: "the soul's competency before God, the priesthood of each believer and all believers, the autonomy of the local church, and a free church in a free state." (www.bgtc.org) Part of the controversy was over the ordination of women, which the new statement condemned. In 2007 the BGC of Texas elected its first female president. The church gives special attention to spiritual formation, servant leadership, and being inclusive of all people. The Con- vention operates Baptist Way Press, which publishes a variety of educational and devotional materials. The primary focus of the Convention is on evangelism and church planting, but it also has an active disaster response ministry. Over one thousand congregations are primarily Spanish speaking. The church is part of the Baptist World Alliance.

For more information: www.bgct.org

Headquarters: 333 N. Washington, Dallas, TX 75246-1798

CONSERVATIVE BAPTIST ASSOCIATION
OF AMERICA (CBAmerica)

Founded 1947
Membership: est. 200,000 in 1200 churches (2007)

The Conservative Baptist Association is described as a "voluntary fellowship of sovereign, autonomous, independent, 'Bible-believing' Baptist churches." The founders of this association of churches were active in the Fundamentalist* Fellowship that was started within the Northern Baptist Convention in 1920 (See AMERICAN BAPTIST CHURCHES). Doctrinal disagreement, which grew out of different views of the reliability and credibility of the scriptures, was aggravated by the "inclusive policy" by which both theologically liberal and conservative missionaries were sent to foreign and home fields.

The Conservative Baptist Foreign Mission (now CBInternational) was founded in 1943 for the purpose of sending only Bible-believing missionaries to the mission field. In 1947 the Conservative Baptist Association of America (now CBAmerica) was formed. Churches were free to belong to both this new association and the Northern Baptist Convention. The Conservative Baptist Home Mission Society (now Mission to the Americas) and the Conservative Baptist Theological Seminary (now Denver Seminary) were begun by the leaders of this new church association. Western Seminary of Portland, Oregon; Bethel Seminary of the East in Philadelphia, Pennsylvania; Southwestern College in Phoenix, Arizona; New England Bible College in Portland, Maine; and International College and Graduate School in Honolulu, Hawaii are associated with Conservative Baptist churches.

The ministry of CBAmerica through regional offices and the national office includes providing resources and counsel in the areas of Christian Education, church planting, women's ministry, pastoral placement, and church administration. Administering one benevolent fund for pastors, leaders and their families and another for churches in crisis are responsibilities of the Association. Endorsing and administrating military chaplains—in addition to hospital, prison and law enforcement chaplains—is a major focus of ministry.

The name "Conservative" was chosen to indicate the desire to conserve the basic doctrines of historic, biblical Christianity: the infallibility of the scriptures; God as Father, perfect in holiness, infinite in wisdom, measureless in power; Christ as the eternal and only begotten Son of God—His sinlessness, virgin birth, atonement, bodily resurrection, ascension and return to earth; the Holy Spirit as coming forth from God to convince the world of sin, of righteousness and of judgment; the sinfulness of all people and the possibility of their regeneration, sanctification, and comfort through Christ and the Holy Spirit; the church as the living body of Christ, with Christ as the head; the local church as free

172

from interference from any ecclesiastical or political authority; the responsibility of every human being to God alone; that human betterment is a direct result of the gospel; and the ordinances of believer's baptism by immersion and the Lord's supper. Members for the CBAmerica Board are elected through the eight regional offices. The offices of the Association of Churches are located in Littleton, Colorado.

For more information: www.CBAmerica.org

Headquarters: 3686 Stagecoach Road, Suite F, Longmont, CO 80504-5660

CONVERGE WORLDWIDE

Founded: 1852
Membership: 140,494 in 1075 churches (2008)

The history of what is now known as the Converge Worldwide began at Rock Island, Illinois, in 1852. Gustaf Palmquist, a middle-aged schoolteacher and lay preacher, had arrived from Sweden the previous year to become the spiritual leader of a group of Swedish immigrants who had been influenced by the Pietist* movement within the (Lutheran) state church of Sweden. At Galesburg, Illinois, he came in contact with Baptists, and early in 1852 he was baptized and ordained a Baptist minister. Visiting the Swedish people at Rock Island, Palmquist won his first converts to the Baptist faith and baptized three in the Mississippi River on August 18, 1852. There were sixty-five churches when the national conference of the Swedish Baptist General Conference of America was organized in 1879.

For several decades the American Baptist Home Mission Society and the American Baptist Publication Society of the American (then Northern) Baptist Convention* aided the new work among the Swedish immigrants, but gradually the church became self-supporting. A theological seminary was founded in Chicago in 1871, and the first denominational paper was launched the same year. From 1888 until 1944, foreign missionary activities were channeled through the American Baptist Foreign Mission Society. The Swedish Conference set up its own foreign-mission board in 1944 and today has more than 151 regular and dozens of short-term missionaries in India, Japan, the Philippines, Ethiopia, Mexico, Argentina, Brazil, the Ivory Coast, Cameroon, France, Belize, Cambodia, the Caribbean, Central Asia, the Muslim world, Senegal, Singapore, Thailand, Ukraine, and Uruguay.

Following World War I, with its intensified nationalistic conflicts, the transition from Swedish- to English-language church services was greatly accelerated and was practically completed in three decades. In 1945, Swedish was dropped from the name of the conference. With the language barrier removed, the growth of the conference has been rapid and far-reaching. Less than half of the pastors are of Swedish descent, and a large number of churches contain few members of that descent.

Converge partners with Bethel College and Seminary in St. Paul, Minnesota, a four-year college and a three-year theological school with campuses in St. Paul, San Diego, Philadelphia, New York City, and Washington, D.C. Also affiliated with the church are three children's homes, seven homes for the aged, and *Converge Point*, the official denominational publication. Harvest Publications offers Bibles, books, and Sunday school materials. Basically, the church's doctrine is theologically conservative, with unqualified acceptance of the Word of God, and holds the usual Baptist tenets. It is a strong fellowship of churches, insistent upon the major beliefs of conservative Christianity but with respect for individual differences on minor points.

For more information: www.covergeww.org

Headquarters: 2002 South Arlington Heights Rd., Arlington Heights, IL 60005

COOPERATIVE BAPTIST FELLOWSHIP

Founded: 1991
Membership: statistics not available; 1,800 churches (2000)

As with many Baptist groups, the Cooperative Baptist Fellowship (CBF) cannot quite be termed a denomination. It is a recently created and vital fellowship of Baptist churches, primarily in the South. The CBF was formed during the years of struggle within the Southern Baptist Convention* (SBC) between conservatives and moderates. Some of the moderates disapproved of the tactics of the conservatives and believed that the Convention itself was in danger of violating the historic Baptist affirmation of individual freedom. In 1991, the new CBF was formed as an alternative body to the SBC, although congregations are free to hold joint membership.

The mission of the Cooperative Baptist Fellowship focuses on ministry rather than theology, as indicated by their mission statement adopted in 2000: "We are a fellowship of Baptist Christians and churches who share a passion for the Great Commission of Jesus Christ and a commitment to Baptist principles of faith and practice. Our mission is to serve Baptist Christians and churches as they discover and fulfill their God-given mission."

With an annual budget of almost seventeen million dollars, the CBF focuses its work on global missions to the world's most neglected (the impoverished, homeless, victims of HIV/AIDS, and other marginalized peoples) and the least evangelized. It also fosters advocacy of historic Baptist values, such as local church autonomy, the priesthood of all believers, and religious liberty. The CBF has partnerships with fifteen seminaries and theological schools and has helped found new schools of theology in historical Baptist colleges in the South.

For more information: www.thefellowship.info

Headquarters: P.O. Box 450329, Atlanta, GA 31145-0329

DUCK RIVER (AND KINDRED) ASSOCIATION OF BAPTISTS

Founded: 1826
Membership: 10,188 in 99 churches (2000)

The Duck River Baptists originated in Tennessee as part of a protest within the old Elk River Association, which was strongly Calvinist. Duck River Baptists are liberally Calvinist in that they believe that Christ died for all rather than for the elect. In addition they believe that God will save those who come to him through Christ; that sinners are justified by faith; and that the saints will persevere in grace. In addition to the Lord's Supper and believers' baptism (by immersion), they view foot washing as a biblical ordinance. An 1843 dispute over missions divided the Duck River Baptists into two groups, which were formerly known as Missionary Baptists and Separate Baptists. They are congregational in polity and hold annual association meetings. In 1939, they and kindred associations formed the General Association of Baptists. They are found mainly in Tennessee, Alabama, Mississippi, and Georgia.

For more information: www.duckriverbaptistassociation.org

Headquarters: P .O. Box 820, Tullahoma, TN 37388

GENERAL ASSOCIATION OF GENERAL BAPTISTS

Founded: 1823; organized as denomination 1870
Membership: 61,500 in 698 churches (2007)

The General Association of General Baptists marks its beginning with the founding of Liberty Baptist Church by Benoni Stinson (ca. 1798–ca. 1870) in 1823 in the Howell neighborhood of Evansville, Indiana. Stinson proclaimed the principle from Hebrews 2:9 that Jesus Christ "by the grace of God should taste death for every man." This theological understanding of general atonement, which Stinson emphasized in the churches he helped start, can be traced back to the early 1600s when it was developed by John Smyth and Thomas Helwys in Europe. Those who adhered to this principle were labeled General Baptists, and Roger Williams is considered to be the first General Baptist minister in the American colonies.

Stinson's work spread to Kentucky, Illinois, Missouri, and Tennessee. Shortly after his death, these scattered associations of churches organized into a national denomination in 1870 called the General Association of General Baptists. Today, churches in this denomination reach from California to Florida and into New York City, though the bulk are in the "belt buckle" or the Bible Belt: Illinois, Indiana, Missouri, Kentucky, Tennessee, Arkansas. Mission work is active in China, Guam, Saipan, Jamaica, India, Honduras, the Philippines, and Mexico.

The General Baptist confession of faith is basically Arminian: Christ died for all; failure to achieve salvation lies completely with the individual; humankind is depraved and fallen and unable to save itself; regeneration is necessary for salvation; salvation comes by repentance and faith in Christ; Christians who persevere to the end are saved; the wicked are punished eternally; and the dead, both the just and the unjust, will be raised at the judgment. The Lord's Supper and believer's baptism by immersion are the only authorized ordinances, but some General Baptist churches practice foot washing.

Their polity is similar to that found in most Baptist groups, but a peculiar feature of the General Baptist church lies in the use of a presbytery into which the ordained members of local associations are grouped. They examine candidates for the ministry and for the diaconate. Ministers and deacons are responsible to this presbytery, which exists only on the local level.

The denomination maintains a liberal arts university in Oakland City, Indiana. Chapman Seminary for theological study is located on the campus. A publishing house, Stinson Press, is operated at Poplar Bluff, Missouri, where the monthly paper is issued. Also in Poplar Bluff are the denomination's Women's Ministries office and General Baptist Investment Fund office. The denomination has several facilities for the elderly and operates an adoption center in Oakland City.

For more information: www.generalbaptist.com

Headquarters: 100 Stinson Dr., Poplar Bluff, MO 63901

GENERAL ASSOCIATION OF REGULAR BAPTIST CHURCHES

Founded: 1932
Membership: 157,728 in 1,274 churches (2009)

Twenty-two Baptist churches of the American Baptist Convention* left that organization in May 1932 to found the General Association of Regular Baptist Churches. Their protest was against what they considered the Convention's modernist tendencies and teachings, the denial of the historic Baptist principle of independence and autonomy of the local congregation, the inequality of representation in the assemblies of the convention, and the control of missionary work by convention assessment and budget.

Basically fundamentalist* in outlook, the GARBC understands its mission "to champion the Biblical truth, impact the world for Christ, perpetuate a Baptist heritage, and advance the Association churches." (www.garbc.org) The association subscribes to the New Hampshire Confession of Faith (1832) with a premillennial interpretation of the final article of that confession. It holds to the infallibility of the Bible, the Trinity, the personality of Satan as the author of all evil, humankind as the creation of God, and humankind born in sin. Doctrines deal with the virgin birth, the deity of Jesus, and faith in Christ as the way of salvation through grace. The saved are in everlasting felicity; the lost are consigned to endless punishment. Civil government is by divine appointment. There are only two approved ordinances: baptism by immersion and the Lord's Supper.

Any Baptist church coming into the General Association is required to withdraw all fellowship and cooperation from any convention or group that permits modernists or modernism within its ranks. Dual fellowship or membership is not permitted. Church government is strictly congregational. Associated churches have the privilege of sending six voting messengers to an annual convention. A Council of Eighteen is elected (six members each year) to serve for three years. The Council makes recommendations to the association for the furtherance of its work and puts into operation all actions and policies of the association. The Council's authority depends completely on the will and direction of the association, but it does appoint a National Representative to oversee the denominational office in Schaumburg, Illinois, and to represent the Association to its churches and constituencies. The Regular Baptist Press publishes *The Baptist Bulletin*, a bi-monthly magazine.

For more information: www.garbc.org

Headquarters: 1300 North Meacham Rd., Schaumburg, IL 60173

INTERSTATE AND FOREIGN LANDMARK MISSIONARY BAPTIST ASSOCIATION

Founded: 1951, with roots to the mid-nineteenth century
Membership: 14,225 in 135 churches (2000)

This association traces its origins to the Landmarkian (see BAPTIST CHURCHES) controversy among Southern Baptists* in the middle of the nineteenth century when James Robinson Graves, James Madison Pendleton, and Amos Cooper Dayton challenged the accepted understanding of church history. They argued that the Baptist Church had begun during the time of Jesus and has had an unbroken history through the century. The Baptist Church is the only true church; therefore baptism and the Lord's Supper are only valid in the Baptist Church. Moreover, they argued that the only church is the visible, local congregation, and thus the great commission was given only to the local church

Landmark ideas had a strong impact on many Baptist groups in the South, especially the American Baptist Association and the Baptist Missionary Association. The Interstate and Landmark group developed from a split within the ABA. It seeks to promote cooperation among Landmark Baptists who support their ministries only through free-will offerings rather than regular salaries. Doctrinally, they follow typical Baptist teachings, but they do practice foot washing as an ordinance. They are strongest in the southern Mississippi River region but support missions in Mexico and the Philippines. They do not have salaried ministers.

NATIONAL ASSOCIATION OF FREE WILL BAPTISTS

Founded: 1935, with roots to colonial days
Membership: 185,798 in 2,369 churches (2007)

The rise of Free Will Baptists can be traced to the influence of Arminian-minded Baptists who migrated to the American Colonies from England. Unlike strict Calvinists, Arminians believe that Christ died for all people and each individual has the freedom to choose salvation. In other words, they reject the idea of predestination and preach that humans have free will in matters of faith.

The Southern line, or Palmer movement, began in 1727 when Paul Palmer (d. 1750) established a church at Chowan, North Carolina. The northern line, or Randall movement, began with a congregation organized by Benjamin Randall in 1780 in New Durham, New Hampshire. Both groups taught the doctrines of free grace, free salvation, and free will. There were gestures toward uniting the Northern and Southern groups until the outbreak of the Civil War.

The Northern body extended more rapidly into the West and the Southwest, and in 1910 this line of Free Will Baptists merged with the Northern Baptist denomination, taking along over 850 of its churches, all of its denominational property, and several colleges. In 1916 representatives of the 250 remnant churches from the Randall movement organized the Cooperative General Association of Free Will Baptists. By 1921 the Southern churches had organized into new associations and conferences, and finally into a General Conference. The division continued until 1935, when the two groups merged into the National Association of Free Will Baptists at Nashville, Tennessee.

Doctrinally, the church holds that Christ gave himself as a ransom for all, not just for the elect; that God calls all persons to repentance; and that whosoever will may be saved. Baptism is by immersion. One of the few Baptist groups that practice open communion, the Free Will Baptists also practice foot washing. Government is strictly congregational. There are two Bible colleges and two liberal arts colleges.

For more information: www.nafwb.org

Headquarters: P.O. Box 5002, Antioch, TN 37011-5002

NATIONAL BAPTIST CONVENTION OF AMERICA, INC.

Founded: 1895
Membership: statistics not available, but est. 1,700,000 in 6,716 churches (2000)

"National Baptist" has been the name of some aspect of organized black Baptist life since at least 1886. By 1876 all of the Southern states except Florida had a state missionary convention, but smaller bodies had existed since the 1830s in the Midwest; organized missionary efforts date back to that same period in the North. The first black Baptist group, the Providence Baptist Association of Ohio, was formed in 1836, and the first attempt at national organization occurred in 1880 with the creation of the Foreign Mission Baptist Convention at Montgomery, Alabama. In 1886, the American National Baptist Convention was organized at St. Louis, and in 1893 the Baptist National Educational Convention was begun in the District of Columbia. All three conventions merged into the National Baptist Convention of America in 1895 at Atlanta. For the next twenty years a single National Baptist body functioned through a variety of activities, such as the publication of Sunday school material. It sponsored foreign mission enterprises, especially to African and Caribbean countries; and it founded some colleges and provided support for others, several of which resulted from the church's dedication to providing education for the emancipated people.

In 1915 a division arose over the adoption of a charter and the ownership of the National Baptist Publishing Board. The group that rejected the charter continued to function as the National Baptist Convention of America. The group that accepted the charter became known as the National Baptist Convention, U.S.A., Inc.* The former is frequently referred to as "the unincorporated" (although it did eventually incorporate in 1986) and the latter as "the incorporated," but both trace their beginnings to the Foreign Mission Baptist Convention. In 1988, the NBCA broke its ties to the Board. Churches that wished to continue a relationship to the publishing house formed the National Missionary Baptist Convention.

The NBCA adopted a mission statement in 1991 that focuses on education, evangelism, benevolence, stewardship, publication, social and economic justice, and commitment to religious liberty and Baptist doctrine. Much of the denominational activity revolves around the annual meeting in September, which is followed by additional meetings in February and June. The June convention meeting lasts four days and focuses on instruction from an approved curriculum with qualified teachers.

The National Baptist Convention of America, Inc. has its greatest strength in Mississippi, Texas, and Louisiana, with large numbers of members also in Florida and California. It reports a membership of over three and a half million, but the figure cannot be verified. The church holds an annual convention, and officers are elected each year. Since 1985, the headquarters has been located in Shreveport, Louisiana.

For more information: www.nbcamerica.net

Headquarters: 1320 Pierre Avenue, Shreveport, LA 71103

NATIONAL BAPTIST CONVENTION, U.S.A., INC.

Founded: 1895
Membership: statistics not available but est. 5,000,000 in 9,000 churches

The largest body of black Baptists in the United States shared a common history with the National Baptist Convention of America* denomination throughout the formative years of the two groups. Its formal origins date from 1895, with many roots and predecessors stretching back to the period around 1840. Until the disagreement that arose over control of the publishing house of the denomination in 1915, there was a single National Baptist body. With the division the National Baptist Convention of America took control of the publishing house, and the National Baptist Convention of the U.S.A. assumed control of foreign missions.

In 1990 the Baptist World Center was opened in Nashville, Tennessee, where the Sunday School Publishing Board is also located. Nashville is also the home of the American Baptist College, which was opened in 1924 with the assistance of the Southern Baptist Convention*. The school is now entirely under the authority of the National Convention. The convention meets annually, and a Board of Directors directs the convention's business between its annual sessions.

The church has had several strong presidents—notably Joseph H. Jackson, who served from 1953–1982. Jackson promoted the theory and practice of racial uplift in the tradition of Booker T. Washington (1856–1915). "From protest to production" was Jackson's motto. He led the body to steer clear of political and social involvements on any large scale. That policy placed this group mostly outside the civil rights movement of the period 1954–1972, in which many black Baptist pastors and lay leaders worked for racial justice. As a result, another National Baptist schism occurred, out of which the Progressive National Baptist Convention* was formed in 1961. Since that period, however, the National Baptist Convention has shifted its practice and has been active in civil rights causes and voter registration drives.

This denomination, too, has been active in missionary, educational, and publication ministries. Recently it has established a ministerial pension plan. It has shown a particularly high degree of commitment to the support of colleges and seminaries, among them Morehouse School of Religion in Atlanta, Georgia, and Virginia Seminary in Lynchburg. The educational institutions are typically supported by Baptist churches and individuals rather than being affiliated officially with the Convention. The body supports missionary stations in the Bahamas, Jamaica, Panama, and Africa.

For more information: www.nationalbaptist.com
Headquarters: 1700 Baptist World Center Dr., Nashville, TN 37207

NATIONAL MISSIONARY BAPTIST CONVENTION OF AMERICA

Founded: 1988
Membership: statistics not kept, but claims 2,000,000 members

The recent origin of this body of black Baptists (which came into being in 1988) accurately suggests the degree of historical heritage it shares with the two older National Baptist bodies. Once again the issue of control over denominational publication ventures led to a rupture. When the National Baptist Convention of America* broke its ties to the National Baptist Publishing Board, this new fellowship maintained the old relationship. It was not opposed to the private control of the publishing board and the Sunday school congress.

The convention meets annually in September, and the governing boards hold two additional meetings. The National Missionary Baptist Convention is headquartered in Los Angeles, California, and many of its members live in the Pacific Coast states.

For more information: www.nmbca.com

Headquarters: 2018 South Marsalis Avenue, Dallas, Texas 75216

NATIONAL PRIMITIVE BAPTIST CONVENTION, U.S.A.

Founded: 1907
Membership: est. 53,630 in 547 churches (2000)

The black population of the South, throughout the years of slavery and the Civil War, generally worshiped with the white population in their various churches. The members attended white Primitive Baptist* churches until the time of emancipation, when their white co-worshipers helped them establish their own churches by granting letters of fellowship and character, ordaining deacons and ministers, and assisting in other ways.

The doctrine and polity are similar to that of other Primitive Baptists, though initially the members were opposed to all forms of church organization. There are local associations and a national convention, organized in 1907. Each congregation is independent, receiving and controlling its membership. Since 1900 this group has been establishing aid societies, conventions, and Sunday schools, over the opposition of some older and more traditional members. As with other Primitive Baptists, they call their pastors "elders," and they practice footwashing as an ordinance alongside Holy Communion.

For more information: www.natlprimbaptconv.org

Headquarters: P.O. Box 7451, Tallahassee, FL 32314

NORTH AMERICAN BAPTIST CONFERENCE

Founded: 1865
Membership: 64,000 in 416 churches (2008)

German Baptists first settled in New Jersey and Pennsylvania, where Quakers offered the religious freedom they sought. Few congregations continue to use the German language in worship. The scattered churches later became the North American Baptist Conference. The first local organizations were in the 1840s, and the local conference idea was enlarged as German immigration spread westward, and today is strongest in the upper Midwest, California, and Alberta. In 1865 delegates from the eastern and western conferences met in a General Conference in Wilmot, Ontario

Theologically, there is little variance from the basic Baptist position. In general, North American Baptists' 1982 statement of faith follows the New Hampshire Confession (1832), stressing the authority of Scripture, the revelation of God in Christ, regeneration, immersion, separation of church and state, and the congregational form of government. Membership is based on a personal experience of saving grace. The church teaches "soul liberty," which means that individuals do not need a mediator with God, and the church promotes separation of church and state.

The Triennial Conference is now the chief administrative unit, in which twenty associations meet annually. At the conference, clergy and lay representatives from all the churches superintend the work of publication, education, international missions, and church planting. A general council acts for the conference between sessions. German Baptists were a part of what is now Colgate-Rochester Divinity School, but in 1935, they established a seminary of their own, the North American Baptist Seminary, which relocated from Rochester to Sioux Falls, South Dakota, in 1949. The church supports ten homes for the aged and efforts at church planting in Japan, Brazil, Nigeria, Cameroon, West Africa, Russia, the Philippines, and Mexico.

For more information: www.nabconference.org
Headquarters: 1 South 210 Summit Ave., Oakbrook Terrace, IL 60181

OLD MISSIONARY BAPTIST ASSOCIATIONS

Founded: nineteenth century
Membership: est. 48,000 in 358 churches

There is no central body for Old Missionary Baptists, but they do have several local associations concentrated in the areas around the Mississippi River. Their roots go back to the nineteenth century debates about missions. The Old Missionary Baptists rejected many of the new evangelism methods adopted by other Baptist churches, and particularly objected to organizations beyond the local church. They base their doctrine and practice on the New Testament, and claim that their church was founded by John the Baptist and Jesus. Thus they are similar to Landmark Baptists and Primitive Baptists, but they do not practice footwashing. They place greater emphasis on a preacher's abilities than formal education. Most of the preachers (or elders) are bi-vocational. Preaching is extemporaneous and focuses on personal conversion. Most congregations have yearly revival meetings lasting up to two weeks. Old Missionary Baptists require a personal conversion experience for baptism and they generally practice closed communion. Congregations support missionaries directly rather than through an association. Since these Baptists reject denominational structures, there is no headquarters or official website.

OLD REGULAR BAPTISTS

Founded: 1825, named 1892
Membership: 15,218 in 326 churches (1995)

Old Regular Baptists trace their roots to the Second Great Awakening in eastern Kentucky in the early nineteenth century. Eight churches united to form the New Salem Association in 1825, and in 1892 they adopted the name Old Regular to distinguish them from the strictly Calvinist Primitive Baptists and the Arminian Free Will Baptists. They allow some diversity of belief on the issue of predestination, but emphasize the need for individuals to experience conversion, usually through a period of travail. Baptisms are performed in running water, and footwashing is an ordinance along with Holy Communion. They follow a strict patriarchal moral and social code based on New Testament teachings about men and women. Women have no formal voice in the church, but they do join in "shouting" during services. Women are forbidden to wear men's clothing, especially pants. Men are expected to own a home if they are married and to be master of the house. Formal education is not expected of ministers. There are seventeen regional associations and an annual convention which includes extended preaching. The church is located primarily in the Appalachian Mountains, and as late as the 1990s experienced a schism over the use of wine in communion. Old Regular Baptists are particularly known for their distinctive "lined-out" style of hymnody that preserves early American musical practice.

For more information: http://pages.suddenlink.net/orb/orb/index.htm

ORIGINAL FREE WILL BAPTIST CONVENTION

Founded: 1961, with roots to 1912
Membership: est. 40,000 in over 250 churches (2009)

This body shares much in common with other Free Will Baptists* and it traces its history back to the work of evangelist Paul Palmer (d. 1750) in the 1720s in North Carolina. In the early twentieth century, Free Will Baptists in North Carolina organized a state convention and in 1935 joined the National Association. However, the North Carolina churches followed a slightly different ecclesiology than the other Free Will congregations. In particular, they believed that the annual conference should have greater authority to discipline local congregations. They also established their own liberal arts school, Mt. Olive College (established 1920), rather than send students to the Association's Bible college in Nashville. The North Carolina group also wanted to establish a separate publishing house to produce Sunday school curriculum. In 1961, most of the North Carolina Free Will Baptists formed a separate denomination with headquarters in Ayden, North Carolina. In addition to the college and press, the Convention sponsors a children's home and supports missions in Bulgaria, India, Mexico, Nepal, and the Philippines.

For more information: http://www.ofwb.org
Headquarters: P.O. Box 159, Ayden, NC 28513-0159

PRIMITIVE BAPTISTS

Founded: 1827
Membership: est. 49,227 in 1,643 churches (2000)

Primitive Baptists have the reputation of being the strictest and most exclusive of all Baptist churches. Certainly they have held to the Baptist belief in local autonomy to an unusual degree. In fact, they have never been organized as a denomination and have no administrative body of any kind beyond the local church and local association. The movement originated in a nineteenth-century protest against money-based mission and benevolent societies. The Primitive Baptists maintained that there were no missionary societies in the days of the apostles and none are directed by Scripture; therefore, there should be none now. Spearheading this protest against new measures, in 1827 the Kehukee Association in North Carolina condemned all money-based and centralized societies as being contrary to Christ's teachings. Within a decade, several other Baptist associations across the country made similar statements and withdrew from other Baptist churches.

184

The various associations adopted the custom of printing in their annual minutes their articles of faith, constitutions, and rules of order. These statements were examined by the other associations, and, if they were approved, there was fellowship and an exchange of messengers and correspondence. Any association not so approved was dropped from the fellowship. Calvinism (see REFORMED AND PRESBYTERIAN CHURCHES) runs strongly through the Primitive Baptist doctrine. In general, the members believe that through Adam's fall, all humankind became sinners; human nature is completely corrupt, and humans cannot regain favor with God by their own efforts; God elected God's own people in Christ before the world began, and none of these saints will be finally lost; Christ will come a second time to raise the dead, judge all people, punish the wicked forever, and reward the righteous forever; and the Old and New Testaments are verbally and infallibly inspired. The authorized ordinances are the Lord's Supper, baptism of believers by immersion, and footwashing.

Pastors are to be called by God, come under the laying on of hands, and be in fellowship with the local church of which they are members in order to administer the two ordinances. No theological training is demanded of ministers. In spite of their opposition to missionary societies, their preachers travel widely and serve without salary, except when hearers wish to contribute to their support. The movement is concentrated in the South.

There are three traditional Primitive Baptist groups. The largest is the Old-Line Primitive Baptists (about forty-seven thousand members) who teach that Christians are responsible for the salvation given by God. The Predestinarian Primitive Baptists or Absoluters stress God's predestination of all things, not just salvation. The Universalist Primitive Baptists (No-Hellers) believe that God predestines all people to salvation. The latter two groups are small and declining, with only about two thousand members between them.

For more information: www.primitivebaptist.org

Headquarters: none

PROGRESSIVE NATIONAL BAPTIST CONVENTION, INC.

Founded: 1961
Membership: est. 2,500,000 in 1,800 churches (2004)

This group of Baptists came into being in 1961, after several years of tension and discussion, breaking away from the National Baptist Convention, U.S.A., Inc. In that year, Martin Luther King, Jr. (1929–68) nominated Gardner C. Taylor as president of the convention against longtime president Joseph Jackson, who was opposed to the protest movement of King. The National Baptist Convention, U.S.A.* followed a policy of disengagement from the civil rights movement and other social justice struggles during the revolutionary years following the 1954 Supreme Court decision concerning desegregation of public facilities.

Following the defeat of Taylor, who called for unity within the National Baptist Convention, U.S.A., the Rev. L. Venchael Booth, chairman of the Volunteer Committee for the Formation of a New National Baptist Convention, issued a call for a meeting at his church in Cincinnati, Ohio. One of the central objectives of the new convention was support for the "freedom fighters" in the civil rights movement. The first president was Dr. T. M. Chambers, who served until 1967, at which point Gardner Taylor was elected to that office.

Once the convention was established, it became a focal point of the civil rights movement, and many leaders of that movement assumed significant positions in the new convention. In addition to King and Gardner, this included the famous preachers Ralph David Abernathy (1926–90) and Benjamin Mays (1895–1984). From its inception, the Progressive body has taken a highly active role in civil rights, social justice, and political causes. It also took a strong stand against apartheid in South Africa. Recently it has focused on the HIV/AIDS crisis in Africa and the U.S.

The Progressive National Baptists are organized into four national regions. It claims more than two million members, but this cannot be verified. Eight departments include women, laymen, young adult women, young adult men, ushers, youth, moderator's council, and Christian education. From its beginning, the convention has been ecumenical in spirit, seeking to work harmoniously with other Christian denominations.

For more information: www.pnbc.org

Headquarters: 601 50th Street, NE, Washington, D. C. 20019

PROGRESSIVE PRIMITIVE BAPTISTS

Founded: twentieth century
Membership: est. 17,885 in 221 churches in three associations (2005)

There are three major bodies that can be termed Progressive Primitive Baptists since they come out of the Primitive Baptist* heritage while modifying some of the stricter tenants. The largest body (about eight thousand members) is the Progressive Primitive Baptist church. They maintain strict Calvinist teaching regarding predestination, but they have adopted such practices as Sunday school, musical instruments in worship, a mission to the Ukraine, and even support for institutions such as summer camps, conferences, nursing facilities, and a school for pastors. It is found mainly in Georgia.

Slightly smaller is the Eastern District Association of Primitive Baptists (over six thousand members), which was organized in 1848 and which is still found mainly in the Appalachian Mountains of Tennessee and Virginia. Though it allows musical instruments in worship and has a modified view of predestination, it holds to traditional Primitive Baptist attitudes toward camps, benevolent institutions, foreign mission programs, and similar extra-congregation activities.

In 1956 the Central Baptist Association separated from the Eastern District Association because of its acceptance of Arminianism and greater organization beyond the congregation. It teaches eternal security of the believer and practices footwashing, but it also has musical instruments in worship and supports a youth camp in Jasper, Virginia. In addition, the Association assists congregations in many ways, including Sunday School programming, worship planning, and evangelization.

For more information: www.freewebs.com/association/home.html
Headquarters: none

SEPARATE BAPTISTS IN CHRIST

Founded: ca. 1877 and 1912, with roots to the colonial period
Membership: 8,716 in 94 churches (2000)

The Separate Baptists emerged during the First Great Awakening in the mid-eighteenth century. By the end of the century most Separate Baptist churches had merged with Regular Baptists*. Some churches rejected the merger of Separate and Regular Baptists in Kentucky in 1803 and in 1806 formed their own association. Other local associations followed, and the first General Association was formed in 1877. It dissolved but was reestablished in 1912. By 1991 there were seven regional associations within the General Association, but then a split occurred over the issue of the millennium after Christ's return.

Along with many other Baptist groups, Separate Baptists do not claim to be Protestants: "We have never protested against what we hold to be the faith once delivered to the saints." Though officially non-creedal, Separate Baptists do have statements of faith in the infallibility of the scriptures and in the Trinity; regeneration, justification, and sanctification through faith in Christ; and the appearance of Christ on judgment day to deal with the just and the unjust. The election, reprobation, and fatality of Calvinism are rejected. These churches observe foot washing as well as baptism of believers by immersion only and the Lord's Supper as ordinances.

The General Association of Separate Baptists has incorporated a mission program called Separate Baptist Missions, Inc. Through this program, support is given to various mission fields and efforts, both in the United States and abroad.

For more information: www.separatebaptist.org
Contact: 787 Kitchen Rd., Mooresville, IN 46158

SEVENTH DAY BAPTIST GENERAL CONFERENCE

Founded: 1802, with roots to 1671
Membership: 6,200 in 96 churches (2006)

Differing from other groups of Baptists in its adherence to the seventh day (Saturday) as the Sabbath (see ADVENTIST AND SABBATARIAN CHURCHES), the Seventh Day Baptists first appeared as a separate religious body in North America in the Colonial period. Stephen and Ann Mumford came from England in 1664 and entered into a covenant relationship with those who withdrew from John Clarke's (1609–76) Baptist Church in order to observe the Sabbath. In 1671, they officially organized a congregation. Other churches were organized in Philadelphia and New Jersey. Other than the Sabbath observance, their beliefs are similar to other Baptists.

Local churches enjoy complete independence, although all support the united benevolence of the denominational budget. The highest administrative body is the General Conference, which meets annually and delegates interim responsibilities to its president, executive secretary, and general council. The denomination participates in the ecumenical movement at local, regional, national, and world levels. The Seventh Day Baptist conferences include those in Australia, Brazil, England, Germany, Guyana, India, Jamaica, Malawi, Mexico, Myanmar, the Netherlands, New Zealand, Nigeria, the Philippines, Poland, and South Africa as well as in the United States and Canada.

For more information: www.seventhdaybaptist.org
Headquarters: P.O. Box 1678, Janesville, WI 53547-1678

SOUTHERN BAPTIST CONVENTION

Founded: 1845
Membership: 16,266,920 in 44,696 churches (2007)

The largest Protestant denomination in the United States is the Southern Baptist Convention (SBC), whose membership, as its name suggests, is most numerous in the South. In recent years, however, the SBC has been expanding in all regions of the country. The name "Southern" has, therefore, become something of a misnomer.

The SBC came into being during the years leading up to the Civil War. Although there were significant disagreements between Baptists in the two regions over the question of centralized organization (the South favored one organization to control the various cooperative ministries), it was the issue of slavery that led directly to the formation of a separate Southern Baptist Convention. Specifically, the issue was whether slaveholders could be accepted as foreign missionaries. The mission board, located in Boston, refused to send slaveholders into the fields, and in May 1845, the Southern Baptist Convention (SBC) was organized in order to establish boards for foreign and home missions.

Along with the rest of the South, the Southern Baptist churches suffered great losses during the war. Homes, schools, churches, the livelihood of citizens—indeed, the very pattern of Southern society—were destroyed, with devastating effect on religious bodies. An anti-missionary movement further decimated Baptist ranks. Membership continued to decline when former slaves withdrew to form their own societies and conventions. The recovery of the Southern Baptist Convention was impressive, however. By 1890, there were over a million members, predominantly white.

On June 20, 1995, the SBC adopted a resolution to renounce its racist origins and to apologize for its founders' defense of slavery. In its apology to African Americans, the resolution declared that members of the church must "unwaveringly denounce racism, in all its forms, as deplorable sin" and repent of "racism of which we have been guilty whether consciously or unconsciously." (www.sbc.net) As of 2000, nearly two thousand SBC congregations were predominantly African American.

In 1997 the SBC was reorganized. Twelve denominational agencies work with thirty-nine state conventions and two fellowships. The North American Mission Board operates throughout the United States and its territories, with nearly five thousand missionaries active in the field. The International Mission Board sponsors more than four thousand missionaries in over 120 nations and operates over three hundred medical facilities. LifeWay Christian Resources (formerly the Sunday School Board) is the world's largest publisher of religious materials. It provides the literature for some thirty-seven thousand SBC churches. The SBC maintains six theological seminaries.

The SBC grew rapidly in the last quarter of the twentieth century, but growth has slowed dramatically in this century. The church grew more factional as conservatives exerted control over the seminaries, agencies, and boards that belong to the Convention. Conservatives distinguish their position as a commitment to biblical inerrancy. Others in the convention take their stand on what may be termed the infallibility of biblical authority and a commitment to the traditional Baptist principle of independence.

In the late 1990s, controversy arose over the issue of women's ordination. At the SBC annual convention in June 2000, delegates voted to amend the "Baptist Faith and Message" confession of faith first formulated in the 1920s. The convention stipulated that "while both men and women are gifted and called for ministry, the office of pastor is limited to men as qualified by Scripture." (www.sbc.net)The 2000 gathering also put the convention on record as supporting the death penalty in cases of murder and treason.

Earlier in 2000, a group of Southern Baptists opposed to "fundamentalist domination" of churches and state Baptist conventions met in Atlanta, Georgia, and formed the Network of Mainstream Baptists. Over one hundred representatives from fifteen states adopted the label "mainstream" to express their adherence to what they called traditional Baptist beliefs and practices. The tensions within the SBC and between the SBC and other Baptist churches increased in 2004 when the SBC voted to withdraw from the Baptist World Alliance. The SBC accused the Alliance of promoting the idea of women preachers, liberal theology, and anti-American attitudes.

For more information: www.sbc.net

Headquarters: 901 Commerce St., Suite 750, Nashville, TN 37203

SOVEREIGN GRACE BAPTISTS

Founded 1954
Membership: est. 5,000

The first "Sovereign Grace Bible Conference" was led by Rolfe P. Barnard in 1954 in Ashland, Kentucky. They maintain a loose fellowship of congregations and do not keep membership statistics, but they are held together by a common commitment to the First London Confession of 1646. Like the Reformed Baptists*, these congregations were strongly influenced by the neo-Calvinist movement of the mid-twentieth century. By the 1980s doctrinal differences led to a separation of the Sovereign Grace churches from the Reformed Baptists. The Sovereign Grace churches tend to place greater emphasis on the New Covenant than the Old Covenant and do not hold as strictly to observation of Sunday as a Sabbath day.

For more information: www.sovgrace.net

Headquarters: none

UNITED AMERICAN FREE WILL BAPTIST CHURCH

Founded: 1901, with roots to early nineteenth century
Membership: est. 50,000 in 816 churches (1995)

This African American denomination was organized as a separate institution in 1901, but its roots lie in the Free Will Baptist* tradition of the eighteenth century. Robert Taft was the first African American to be ordained as a minister in the church (1827). Freed slaves formed the first African American Free Will Baptist congregations in North Carolina in 1867 and the first convention was held in 1870. Unlike other Free Will Baptists, the UAFWB does limit local church autonomy. Quarterly, Annual, and General Conferences exercise authority over local churches and may exclude congregations from membership. The church's statement of faith is an interesting variation on the Apostle's Creed that clarifies the church's own doctrine: "We believe in the Holy Ghost, the Free Will Baptist Church, the Communion of Saints, the forgiveness of sins, the resurrection of the body, and eternal life for all true believers who persevere in holiness to the end." Although many members moved north in the twentieth century, the church remains strongest in the South.

For more information: www.uafwbc.org

Headquarters: 207 West Bella Vista Street, Lakeland, FL 33805

Methodist Churches

With the possible exception of the Reformed Churches*, the Methodists have been the most influential Protestant family of churches in the U.S. For many decades, the Methodists were the only church with a significant membership in virtually every county in the United States. Methodist churches range from small rural churches to large urban churches built like cathedrals. Hundreds of American denominations, service organizations, and educational institutions have their roots in the Methodist movement. Until it was eclipsed by the Catholic Church, the Methodist Church was the largest religious organization in the United States, and it still has the greatest geographical scope in the U.S. of any religious body. Methodist hymnody is heard in Protestant and Catholic congregations throughout the English-speaking world.

Beginning as part of the Pietist* movement within the Church of England in the 1730s, Methodism expanded greatly during the eighteenth century under the leadership of the Wesley brothers, John (1703–1791) and Charles (1707–1788), who preached and wrote hymns on the need for a personal experience of salvation and change of life. Methodism has been more concerned with ministry to the poor and disadvantaged than other forms of Protestantism, and Methodists often express their faith more in compassion for the suffering than in creedal statements. In a variety of ways, the witness of the Spirit among Methodists has been an impelling force for worship, love of neighbor, personal piety, and evangelization.

History. The origins of the Methodist Church can be traced to a small group of serious-minded students and fellows at Oxford University who were dubbed "Methodists" because of their strict regimen of prayer, fasting, Bible reading, and charitable works inspired by William Law's (1686–1761) *A Serious Call to a Devout and Holy Life.* Among the members of the group were the Wesleys and the future evangelist George Whitefield (1714–1770), all three of whom would be

191

ordained in the Church of England. After John and Charles Wesley left Oxford, they traveled to the colonies, arriving in Georgia in 1735. It was an unsuccessful and unhappy two years for John, but while aboard ship, he met a group of Moravians* and was deeply impressed by their piety and humble Christian way of life. After his return to London, he went to the meeting of a Moravian religious society in Aldersgate Street. There he felt his heart "strangely warmed" as the meaning of Luther's doctrine of "justification by faith" sank into his soul.

The Wesleys gradually separated from the Moravians and followed George Whitefield's example of preaching for conversion and holiness of life. When the Church of England closed its pulpits to them, they took to the open air and sought audiences among the large and ignored working class of the new industrial revolution. Converts came thick and fast, and they were soon organized into "societies." Between 1739 and 1744 the organizational elements of Methodism were instituted: a circuit system and itinerant ministry, class meetings and class leaders, lay preachers, and annual conferences. As early as 1739 John Wesley drew up a set of general rules that are still held by modern Methodists as an ideal delineation of biblical rules of conduct.

Methodism was primarily a lay movement, and John Wesley did his best to keep it within the Church of England. An evangelical party grew within that church that included such luminaries as hymn writer Isaac Watts (1674–1748) and the social reformer and abolitionist William Wilberforce (1759–1833). But it became evident that a separate Methodist organization was needed to deal with the large numbers recruited from among the unchurched. *A Deed of Declaration* in 1784 gave legal status to the yearly Methodist conference.

Methodists in the United States. By 1769, New York Methodists had built Wesley Chapel, now known as John Street Methodist Church. Captain Thomas Webb (ca. 1726–1796) established societies in Philadelphia. Devereux Jarratt (1733–1801), an Anglican minister, led a revival in Virginia that won thousands. Wesley sent Francis Asbury (1745–1816) and Thomas Rankin (1738–1810) to supervise work of Methodism in America. Rankin presided over the first conference in the colonies, called at Philadelphia in 1773. Since Wesley's pro-British attitude aroused resentment in the colonies, it is surprising that the work of Asbury prospered during the Revolution. By the end of the war, membership had grown to fourteen thousand, and there were nearly eighty preachers. It was now an American church, free of both England and the Church of England. Wesley accepted the inevitable and ordained ministers for the colonies. The Christmas Conference, held at Baltimore in December 1784, organized the Methodist Episcopal Church and elected Francis Asbury and Thomas Coke (1747–1814) as superintendents (later called bishops). *The Sunday Service* (an abridgment of *The Book of Common Prayer*) and Articles of Religion were adopted as written by John Wesley with the addition of an article that the Methodists should vow allegiance to the United States government.

Under Asbury's energetic direction, Methodism was adapted to the American rural setting. Circuit riders, preachers on horseback who traveled the expanding frontier, went to mountain cabins, prairie churches, schoolhouses, and camp meetings, preaching the need for conversion and regeneration. The Methodist Book Concern was established in 1789, putting into the saddlebags of the circuit riders religious literature that followed the march of the American empire south and west. The revivalistic flavor of the camp meeting, born among the Presbyterians,* was adopted by the Methodists. By the end of the Second Great Awakening there were over a million Methodists in the U.S.

Methodist evangelists had great success working with slaves and free blacks in the U.S. Initially the church opposed slavery, but eventually evangelists tolerated the practice in order to be allowed to preach to enslaved persons. Hundreds of thousands of African Americans converted before 1861. Only the Baptists had more black members. The Methodist Church adopted the Moravian* practice of using converted slaves as lay preachers and evangelists who worked under the authority of ordained whites. In the Northern cities, freed blacks were sometimes ordained as pastors. Between 1813 and 1917, large groups of African Americans formed independent churches: the African Methodist Episcopal Church*; the Union Church of Africans, now the Union American Methodist Episcopal Church*; and the African Methodist Episcopal Zion Church*.

The issue of slavery led to a devastating split between Southern and Northern Methodists in 1844. Bishop J. O. Andrew (1794–1871), a Georgian, owned slaves through inheritance, and his wife also was a slaveholder. The General Conference of 1844 requested that the bishop desist from the exercise of his office while he remained a slaveholder. Incensed, the Southern delegates rebelled. A provisional plan of separation was formulated, and the Southerners organized their own church.

The split that was not healed until 1939, when the Methodist Episcopal Church; the Methodist Episcopal Church, South; and the Methodist Protestant Church were reunited at Kansas City, Missouri, to form The Methodist Church. The uniting conference of that year adopted a new constitution in three sections: an abridgment of the Articles of Religion drawn up by John Wesley; the General Rules, covering the conduct of church members and the duties of church officials; and the Articles of Organization and Government, outlining the organization and conduct of conferences and local churches.

Another Methodist body with a distinct history was the Evangelical United Brethren Church, which had arisen from a series of mergers of two groups: United Brethren in Christ and the Evangelical Church (see BRETHREN AND PIETIST CHURCHES). The Evangelical Church, originally Evangelical Association, began as a result of the labors of Jacob Albright (1759–1808) among the German people of Pennsylvania. Preaching first as a Lutheran Pietist and then as a Methodist exhorter, Albright was made a bishop at the first annual conference of the Evangelical Association in 1807. The name "Evangelical Church" was adopted in 1922.

Another group, Church of the United Brethren in Christ, developed in a parallel manner through the preaching of the Pietists* Philip William Otterbein (1726–1813) and Martin Boehm (1725–1812) among the Germans in Pennsylvania, Maryland, and Virginia. They were elected bishops at a conference in September 1800. That conference created the Church of the United Brethren in Christ, which also was strongly Methodist in polity, doctrine, and practice. Each group had a *Discipline* modeled on that of the Methodists. The Church of the United Brethren in Christ and the Evangelical Church were merged into the Evangelical United Brethren Church (E.U.B.) at Johnstown, Pennsylvania, in 1946.

In April of 1968, the Methodist Church merged with the E.U.B. to form the United Methodist Church. Representatives from the African Methodist Episcopal Church, the African Methodist Episcopal Zion Church, the Christian Methodist Episcopal Church, and the United Methodist Church have met since the mid-1980s as the Commission on Pan-Methodist Cooperation. A newer body, the Commission on Union, was formed in 1996, again with representatives from the four churches. Members of the two bodies have recommended that the commissions be merged; the recommendation must be approved by the general conferences of each of the four churches before it can be adopted.

Beliefs and Practices. Methodists have stressed the foundational beliefs of Protestantism, including the doctrine of the Trinity; the natural sinfulness of humankind, its fall and the need of conversion and repentance; freedom of the will; justification by faith; sanctification and holiness; future rewards and punishments; the sufficiency of the scriptures for salvation; and the enabling grace of God. In terms of salvation, the church is Arminian, stressing the freedom of humans to choose grace. Two sacraments, baptism and communion, are observed; baptism is administered to both infants and adults, usually by sprinkling. Membership is based on confession of faith or by letter of transfer from another church; admission of children to membership is usually limited to those thirteen years of age or older, but in the South the age may be a few years younger.

Worship and liturgy are based on the English prayer book, with widespread modifications. The language of the prayer book is much in evidence in the sacraments of Methodist churches. In many forms of worship, however, each congregation is free to use or change the accepted pattern as it sees fit. There is wide freedom in the interpretation and practice of all doctrines, with some congregations more liberal and others more conservative. Methodists played major roles in many significant American religious movements, especially the Temperance Movement, the Social Gospel, the Holiness Movement, and the Ecumenical Movement. Some of these movements produced new denominations.

Polity. The local churches of Methodism are called charges. Clergy are appointed by the bishop at the Annual Conference, and each church elects its own administrative board that initiates planning and sets goals and policies on the local level. It is composed of staff members, chairs of various committees, those

Christianity

representing various program interests, and members at large. Charge, Annual, and General Conferences prevail in most Methodist bodies. While the government is popularly called episcopal, it is largely governmental, through this series of conferences. The Charge Conference meets at the local church or on the circuit, with the district superintendent presiding. It fixes the salary of the pastor, elects the church officers, and sends delegates to the Annual Conference.

Some areas have a district conference between the Charge and the Annual Conference, but it is not a universal arrangement. Annual Conferences cover defined geographical areas; they ordain and admit ministers, vote on constitutional questions, supervise pensions and relief, and exchange pastors with other Annual Conferences through acts of the bishop; and, every fourth year, elect lay and ministerial delegates to the General Conference. The General Conference is the lawmaking body of the church, meeting quadrennially; the bishops preside, and the work of the conference is done largely in committees whose reports then may be adopted by the General Conference.

Suggestions for further reading:

Bucke, Emory S., ed. *History of American Methodism.* Nashville: Abingdon Press, 1964.

Campbell, James T. *Songs of Zion: The African Methodist Episcopal Church in the United States and South Africa.* New York: Oxford University Press, 1995.

Heitzenrater, Richard P. *Wesley and the People Called Methodist.* Nashville: Abingdon, 1995.

Lincoln, C. Eric, and Lawrence H. Mamiya. *The Black Church in the African-American Experience.* Durham, NC: Duke University Press, 1990.

Langford, Thomas A., ed. *Doctrine and Theology in The United Methodist Church.* Nashville: Kingswood Books, 1991.

Matthews, Donald G. *Slavery and Methodism: A Chapter in American Morality, 1780-1845.* Princeton, NJ: Princeton University Press, 1965.

Marty, Martin E. *Protestantism in the United States: Righteous Empire.* 2nd ed. New York: Scribner; London: Collier Macmillan, 1986.

McEllhenney, John G. *United Methodism in America.* Nashville: Abingdon Press, 1992.

McKinley, Edward H. *Marching to Glory: The History of the Salvation Army in the United States, 1880-1992,* rev. ed. Grand Rapids, MI: Wm B. Eerdmans, 1995.

Richardson, Harry V. *Dark Salvation: The Story of Methodism as It Developed Among Blacks in America.* Garden City, NY: Anchor Press, 1976.

Smith, Timothy L. *Revivalism and Social Reform.* Baltimore, MD: Johns Hopkins Press, 1980.

Walls, William J. *The African Methodist Episcopal Zion Church: Reality of the Black Church.* Charlotte, NC: AME Zion Publishing House, 1974.

AFRICAN METHODIST EPISCOPAL CHURCH

Founded: 1814
Membership: 1,857,186 adults in 6,200 congregations (1999)

The African Methodist Episcopal Church (AME) is one of the oldest and largest Methodist bodies in the world. It was founded by Richard Allen (1760–1831), a former slave from Delaware who had bought his freedom. Allen had been converted to Christianity while still a slave, and he began preaching to freed African Americans in Philadelphia up to five times a day. He regularly attended St. George's Methodist Church, where African Americans were welcomed but segregated from whites. In 1787 Absalom Jones (1746–1818), who later became the first African American Episcopal priest, was kneeling in prayer when white trustees physically removed him to the back of the church. When the congregational leadership supported this discrimination, Allen and Jones led the black members out of the congregation. In 1793, Allen established the Bethel Church for Negro Methodists in Philadelphia.

Although Francis Asbury dedicated the chapel in Philadelphia and ordained Richard Allen as its minister, Bethel Church was a center of controversy within the Methodist system. The whites in the denomination tried to keep Allen and his congregation from controlling their own property, but in 1816 the Pennsylvania Supreme Court ruled in favor of Allen, setting an important legal precedent for black persons in the U.S. It was during the course of this struggle that the Bethel Congregation and five other predominantly black Methodist churches left the Methodist Church and formed the AMEC in 1814. Allen was consecrated by Asbury as the first bishop in 1816.

Around the same time, the AME Zion* church separated from the Methodist Church in New York. Bishop Allen held strongly to the connectional system of the Methodists and tried to bring the new Zion Church* under his umbrella after 1816, but the members of Zion preferred to create their own denomination. In the years preceding the Civil War, the AME Church was largely confined to the Northern states, but following the war its membership increased rapidly in the South. Today it is found all across the nation.

The church affirms traditional Methodist doctrine, but the worship style tends to be more exuberant than that found in predominantly white churches. The church is strongly evangelistic and has active social justice ministries. There are nineteen bishops (including the first woman bishop, who was elected in 2000), twelve general officers, and eighteen connectional officers in thirteen districts; a General Conference is held quadrennially. Foreign missions are supported in South Africa; West Africa; India; London, England; the Caribbean; and South America. The church supports six colleges and two theological schools. Journalism has been a central part of the church's work from its early years; the AME

Book Concern dates to 1816, and the weekly *Christian Reader* has been published since 1848.

For more information: www.ame-church.com

Headquarters: 1134 11th St. NW, Washington, DC 20001

AFRICAN METHODIST EPISCOPAL ZION CHURCH

Founded: 1821
Membership: 14 million in 3,337 churches (2007)

This church dates from 1796, when it was organized by a group of people protesting racial discrimination in the John Street Methodist Church in New York City. Their first church, named Zion, was built in 1800, and that word was later made part of the denominational name. The first annual conference was held in 1821, with nineteen preachers from six black Methodist churches in New Haven, Connecticut; Philadelphia, Pennsylvania; and Newark, New Jersey. James Varick (ca. 1750–1827), who had led the John Street dissension, was elected the first bishop. The present name was approved in 1848. The word "Zion" was included to distinguish this church from the African Methodist Episcopal Church* founded in Philadelphia. The church spread quickly over the northern states, and by 1880 there were fifteen annual conferences in the South. Departments of missions, education, and publications were created in 1892. AME Zion ministers were often spokesmen for African Americans in the decades following emancipation, and Bishop Alexander Walters helped found the National Association for the Advancement of Colored People (NAACP) in 1909. The church has always emphasized the importance of education, especially when educational opportunities were denied to black people. In addition to an extensive Sunday school network supervised by the Christian Education Department, the church founded several institutions of learning. Livingstone College, in Salisbury, North Carolina, the largest educational institution of the church, was established in 1879. The church also operates two junior colleges in the United States and one in Liberia. Hood Theological Seminary in North Carolina is its primary theological institution.

The church is heavily involved in evangelism and missions, and it has a particularly strong presence in Liberia and Ghana in Africa. AME Zion missionaries were among the first Protestant missions to Africa. In the twentieth century, some of the church's bishops were involved in the Pan African Congress of Marcus Garvey. The church has twelve episcopal districts in the United States and is governed by a board of bishops.

For more information: www.amez.org

Headquarters: 3225 Sugar Creek Road, Charlotte, NC 28269

CHRISTIAN METHODIST EPISCOPAL CHURCH

Founded: 1870
Membership: 850,000 in 3,500 churches (2006)

This body was established in 1870 in an amicable agreement between white and black members of the Methodist Episcopal Church, South. At the time of Emancipation there were at least 225,000 slave members of the Southern church, but following the Civil War, all but eighty thousand joined one of the two independent black bodies, the African Methodist Episcopal Church or the African Methodist Episcopal Zion Church. When the general conference of the Methodist Episcopal Church, South, met at New Orleans in 1866, a commission from the black membership asked to separate into a church of its own. The request was granted, and the Colored Methodist Episcopal Church was organized in Jackson, Tennessee. In 1954 the name was changed to Christian Methodist Episcopal Church.

The doctrine of the CME is Methodist, but this denomination adds a quarterly conference to the district, annual, and quadrennial conferences usual in Methodism. There are ten episcopal districts, each supervised by a presiding bishop, who together form the College of Bishops. Ten departments oversee the national work, each chaired by a bishop assigned by the College of Bishops. The general secretaries of the various departments are elected every four years by the General Conference, and the president of the Women's Missionary Council is elected every four years by the quadrennial assembly of the Missionary Council. The church issues two periodicals and supports five colleges, a theological seminary, a hospital, and several low-rent and senior-citizen housing complexes. In the latter decades of the twentieth century, the church encouraged economic growth for African Americans as part of its ministry.

For more information: www.c-m-e.org

Headquarters: 4466 Elvis Presley Blvd, Memphis, TN 38116-1212

CONGREGATIONAL METHODIST CHURCH

Founded: 1852
Membership: 14,738 in 187 churches (1995)

This church was established in Georgia in protest against certain features of the episcopacy and itinerancy of the Methodist Episcopal Church, South. In the late 1880s more than half of this body in turn withdrew to join the Congregational Church (see REFORMED and PRESBYTERIAN CHURCHES). The church grew in the twentieth century and sent out its first missionary in 1947. In 1972 the headquarters moved to its current location in Florence, Mississippi. It continues to be located primarily in the South. Theologically, it is close to both the Fundamentalist* and Holiness* traditions.

Local pastors are called by the local churches; annual conferences grant licenses, ordain ministers, and review local reports. Annual and general conferences are recognized as church courts, empowered to rule on violations of church law and to coordinate, plan, and promote general church activities. There is a missionary program among the Navajo in New Mexico and Mexico. The church founded Wesley College, which was accredited in 1976 and is located near the denominational headquarters in Florence, Mississippi.

For more information: http://congregationalmethodist.net

Headquarters: P.O. Box 9, Florence, MS 39073

EVANGELICAL CHURCH OF NORTH AMERICA

Founded: 1968
Membership: 15,011 in 135 congregations (2004)

When the Methodist Church merged with the Evangelical United Brethren to form the United Methodist Church* in 1968, a number of churches in the Brethren body withdrew to form the Evangelical Church of North America. The new church was organized at Portland, Oregon, and eventually came to include congregations across the country. In 1969 a union occurred with the Holiness Methodist Church. From 1982 to 1990 the Northwest Canada Conference was part of the Evangelical Church. In 1990 the Northwest Canada Conference united with the Missionary Church of Canada to form The Evangelical Missionary Church of Canada. The major mission fields are Bolivia, Brazil, and Navajo churches in New Mexico with cooperative ministries with national churches in Japan, Germany, Eastern Europe, and Russia.

The doctrinal position of the Evangelical Church is Wesleyan-Arminian. In polity the local church owns their own property while the clergy are assigned by the conference superintendent. Conference superintendents oversee each annual conference (six); the general administration is carried on by annual conference sessions and program committees. Every four years, a general conference is held, at which the general superintendent is elected and oversees the denomination.

For more information: www.theevangelicalchurch.com

Headquarters: 9421 West River Rd., Minneapolis, MN 55444

EVANGELICAL METHODIST CHURCH

Founded: 1946
Membership: 7,348 in 108 churches (2005)

The Evangelical Methodist Church is "fundamental in doctrine, evangelistic in program, and congregational in government." (www.emchurch.org) The denomination was formed just after World War II in Memphis, Tennessee, as a protest against the perceived liberalism of the Methodist Church*. The founders sought to preserve and apply the spirit and revivalistic fervor of "primitive Methodism" to the needs of modern American society. They oppose the "substituting of social, educational, or other varieties of cultural salvation for the gospel message." (www.emchurch.org) The denomination rejected the "autocracy" of bishops, and local churches own and control their own property and select their own pastors. Over the years, the denomination absorbed some smaller conservative Methodist churches, but there were also divisions within the church over the issue of entire sanctification. The more stridently fundamentalist pastors formed the Evangelical (Independent) Methodist Church in the 1950s. It has fewer than five thousand members. Other smaller splinter groups have formed over the years, usually more conservative than the main body. In 2008 the superintendent of the church proposed a plan for restructuring that would have provided a more typically Methodist structure. It was defeated.

For more information: www.emchurch.org
Headquarters: P.O. Box 17070, Indianapolis, IN 46217

KOREAN METHODIST CHURCH

Founded: 1884, est. in US in1921
Membership: statistics unavailable

Methodist missionaries began work in Korea in the 1880s, under the leadership of Robert Maclay and Henry Appenzeller. There were major revivals in the early twentieth century, with tens of thousands converting, and today there are over one and a half million Methodists in Korea. Hyupsung Theological College was established in 1907 to train Korean pastors and evangelists. The first bishop of the autonomous Korean Methodist Church was Rev. Ju-Sam Yang, who assumed office in 1930, and the next year the first female missionaries were ordained. The church has always tried to be "Authentically Korean" and "Authentically Methodist," and in the 1930s it adopted tenets of the Methodist Social Creed. The church suffered various forms of persecution during the thirty-five year long Japanese occupation of Korea. The church endured the division of the nation between the communist North, with an anti-Christian government, and the capitalist South, which was supported by the United States. The Methodist Church in South Korea grew rapidly as the country industrialized in the 1960s and 70s. The church has worked for reconciliation between the North and South for decades. By the beginning of the twenty-first century, the Methodist Church in Korea had become a major contributor to the evangelistic and mission activities of Methodism around the world under the banner of "Giving Hope to the World."

The first ethnically Korean Methodist Church in the United States was founded in Hawaii by Seung Ha-Hong in 1903 to minister to the Koreans laboring on the pineapple plantations. In 1921 a congregation was founded in New York by Rev. Chong-Soon Lee. The Korean Methodist Church in America grew rapidly with Korean immigration after 1965, and California has the most ethnic Korean congregations. As with most immigrant churches, many congregations have added English-language or dual-language services for members who were raised in the United States. Some Korean Methodist congregations remain under the authority of the national church in Korea, but most Korean-language congregations are part of the United Methodist Church*. In 1992 Rev. Hae Jong Kim was consecrated as the first Korean-American bishop in the UMC. The United Methodist Council on Korean American Ministries was established in 2000 to assist in congregational development and provide support for over two hundred Korean-American pastors in the United Methodist Church. Congregations tend to have under one hundred members. In general, Korean Methodist congregations are evangelical in worship and the pastors tend to be conservative theologically. However, Korean-American theologians, such as Kwok Pui-lan and Chung Hyung Kyung, have pushed both Asian and Western theologians to rethink traditional doctrines from the perspective of the oppressed. In particular, the Korean concept of *han* (suffering) has stimulated much theological reflection in Methodist seminaries in recent decades.

For more information: www.kmcweb.or.kr/

Headquarters: 633 W. 115th ST. New York, NY. 10025

THE SALVATION ARMY

Founded: 1880
Membership: 495,659 in 1,263 corps (2007)

The Salvation Army and its related organizations grew out of the Methodist Church's concern for outreach to the impoverished peoples of the growing metropolises in England. In order to bring the gospel to these neglected souls, a new type of religious organization was created. It is neither a traditional denomination nor a traditional service organization but a creative union of both.

William Booth (1829–1912), an ordained minister in the Methodist New Connexion in England, left that church in 1861 to become a freelance evangelist. In 1865 he dedicated his life to the poverty-stricken unchurched masses in the slum areas of London's East End. He first planned to supplement the work of the churches, but this proved impractical because many converts did not want to go where they were sent, and often when they did go, they were not accepted. Moreover, Booth soon found that he needed the converts to help handle the great crowds that came to his meetings.

He began his work under the name "Christian Mission," and in 1878 the name was changed to the Salvation Army. Booth first organized his movement along lines of Methodist polity, with annual conferences at which reports were made and programs planned. But when the name was changed, the whole organization became dominated by the new title. Articles of War (a declaration of faith) were drawn up, and soon the mission stations became corps, members became soldiers, evangelists became officers, and converts were called seekers. Booth was designated as general, and his organization was gradually set up on a military pattern, which provided a direct line of authority and a practical system of training personnel for effective action.

While the Salvation Army has a dual function of church and social agency, its first purpose is salvation by the power of God. Its social services are a means of meeting the needs of the "whole person," putting the socially disinherited—the needy both physically and spiritually—into a condition to be uplifted. The fundamental doctrines of the organization are stated in the eleven cardinal affirmations of its Foundation Deed of 1878. These statements include the Army's recognition of the Bible as the only rule of Christian faith and practice; God as the Creator and Father of all humankind; the Trinity of Father, Son, and Holy Ghost; Jesus Christ as Son of God and Son of man; sin as the great destroyer of soul and society; salvation as God's remedy for human sin and the ultimate and eternal hope made available through Christ; sanctification as the individual's present and maturing experience of a life set apart for the holy purposes of the kingdom of God; and an eternal destiny that may triumph over sin and death.

Administratively, the Army is under the command of a General. The primary unit of the Army is the corps, of which there may be several in a city. Each corps is commanded by an officer, ranging in rank from Lieutenant to Major, who is responsible to divisional headquarters. There are forty divisions in the U.S., with the work of each division under the direct supervision of a divisional commander. Divisions are grouped into four territories—Eastern, Central, Southern, and Western—with headquarters in West Nyack, New York; Des Plaines, Illinois; Atlanta, Georgia; and Long Beach, California, respectively. Territorial commanders are in charge of each territory, and the four territorial headquarters are composed of departments to facilitate all phases of Army work.

Basic training for each officer is a two-year, in-residence course at one of the Army's four schools in Suffern, New York; Chicago; Atlanta; and Rancho Palos Verdes. The chief source of officer candidates is the Salvation Army corps. A soldier who has served actively for at least six months may make application and, if accepted, may enter the School for Officers' Training, where the curriculum, in addition to formal study, includes field experience as well as orientation in all possible areas of Salvation Army service. The officer graduates from the school as a lieutenant and, following additional study, is eligible to attain the rank of Captain, Major, Lieutenant Colonel, Colonel, or Commissioner. Today there are 5,980 officers assisted by 64,093 employees with over three million volunteers.

Today the Salvation Army works in over 113 countries with over one million active members. The Army preaches the gospel in some 175 languages at over fifteen thousand evangelical centers; and operates more than five thousand social institutions, hospitals, schools, and agencies. The work of the Army in the U.S. includes about 140 rehabilitation centers, aiding over 148,000 annually. Each year, 81,468 people are served in fifty-three medical facilities; forty-seven camps provide camping facilities for more than 130,000 children, mothers, and senior citizens. The Army serves some forty-four million meals annually; and basic social services are offered to almost eighteen million. About 150,000 persons make life-changing spiritual decisions under the Army's ministry each year. There are also hotels and lodges for men and women, missing person bureaus, day-care centers, alcoholic care facilities, correctional service bureaus for prisoners and their families, programs for homeless persons, and other allied services. These services are given without respect to race, color, creed, or condition; the whole work is financed largely through voluntary subscriptions, federal funds, and annual appeals.

The national headquarters in Alexandria, Virginia, is the coordinating office for the entire country. The national commander is the chief administrative officer, official spokesperson, and president of all Salvation Army corporations in the U.S. Property and revenues are in the custody of a board of trustees, or directors, and citizen advisory boards assist in interpreting the work of the Army to the general public.

For more information: www.salvationarmy.org

Headquarters: 615 Slaters Lane, Alexandria, VA 22313

SOUTHERN METHODIST CHURCH

Founded: 1939
Membership: est. 6,000 in 101 churches (2006)

The Southern Methodist Church was formed by Southern Methodists who opposed the merger with the northern Methodist Episcopal Church in 1939 on grounds of the "alarming infidelity and apostasy found therein." (www.southern

methodist.org) There are no bishops, but there are the usual Methodist Annual and General Conferences and a president is elected every four years from the elders of the clergy. Laypeople and clergy have equal voice and voting privileges in the conferences. Local churches own and control their own property and buildings and call their own pastors, who must be approved by their Annual Conferences. There is one college and a publishing house, Foundry Press, both located at Orangeburg, South Carolina.

For more information: www.southernmethodist.org

Headquarters: P.O. Box 39, Orangeburg, SC 29116-0039

UNITED METHODIST CHURCH

Founded: 1968, with roots to 1784
Membership: 7,931,733 in 34,398 churches (2006)

The United Methodist Church is one of the largest religious bodies in the United States and has a major impact on American culture. In many ways, it is the quintessential American denomination, but it has been steadily losing members over the past two decades, which is symptomatic of changes in American religiosity.

Two mergers of major importance produced the United Methodist Church. The first merger was the reuniting of three separated Methodist groups in 1939 when the Methodist Episcopal Church, the Methodist Episcopal Church, South, and the Methodist Protestant Church were joined under a new name, the Methodist Church. This merger helped heal some of the wounds of the Civil War.

In 1968, this body merged with the Evangelical United Brethren (E.U.B.), a product of the German Pietist movement (see BRETHREN AND PIETIST CHURCHES), to form the United Methodist Church. Both the Methodist and the E.U.B. churches, across the years, had been deeply conscious of their common historical and spiritual heritage. Their doctrines were similar. Both were episcopal in government and traced their origins to John Wesley. They had similar books of discipline. Their preachers often exchanged pulpits and congregations, worked together, and shared the same buildings. The only major difference was that of language: German among the Brethren and English among the Methodists—but in time this barrier began to mean less and less. Conversations concerning a merger began as early as 1803; but the long-considered merger was not consummated until the two churches became the United Methodist Church at Dallas, Texas, on April 23, 1968.

There was some dissent at Dallas; fifty-one congregations and nearly eighty ministers of the Evangelical United Brethren withdrew from the Pacific Northwest

Conference to establish the Evangelical Church of North America*; eighteen E.U.B. congregations in Montana left to establish the Evangelical Church of North America in Montana. However, roughly 750,000 Brethren accepted the union, and their strength gave the new United Methodist Church a membership of nearly eleven million at its inception. In this union no significant changes were made in either doctrine or polity. The Confession of Faith of the Evangelical United Brethren Church, adopted in 1962, was placed beside the Methodist Articles of Religion. Similar systems of bishops and conferences were in use in both denominations, and the format is still maintained.

Above the sixty-four Annual Conferences are five jurisdictional conferences, established for geographical convenience in administrative matters. These meet quadrennially, at times determined by the Council of Bishops, to elect new bishops and to name the members of the larger boards and commissions. Outside the continental U.S., central conferences correspond to jurisdictional conferences; they meet quadrennially and, when authorized to do so, may elect their own bishops. All bishops are elected for life (except in some overseas conferences, where the term is four years), and a Council of Bishops meets at least once a year for the general oversight. The General Conference consists of one thousand delegates, half laity and half clergy, elected on a proportional basis by the Annual Conferences. The Judicial Council determines the constitutionality of any act of the General Conference that may be appealed, and it hears and determines any appeal from a bishop's decision on a question of law, in any district or annual, central, or jurisdictional conference.

In social ministries and education, the church operates or supports 225 retirement homes and long-term care facilities, seventy hospital and health-care facilities, fifty child-care facilities, thirty ministries for persons with disabilities, eight two-year colleges, eighty-two four-year colleges, ten universities, and thirteen theological schools. United Methodists give more than three and a half billion dollars annually for clergy support and benevolences, local church building and debt retirement, and operating expenses. The church also gives considerable financial support to the National Council of the Churches of Christ in the U.S.A. The World Methodist Council was organized in 1881. Headquartered at Lake Junaluska, North Carolina, the council is designed to draw the whole Wesleyan movement closer together in fellowship and devotion to the Wesleyan heritage.

The 1972 General Conference broadened the basis of doctrine in the church in the first restatement since the eighteenth century. The classic documents of the merging Methodist and Evangelical United Brethren churches were maintained, but the doctrinal door was left open to theological change and revision. A revised statement was adopted in 1988: "In theological reflection, the resources of tradition, experience, and reason are integral to our study of Scripture without displacing Scripture's primacy for faith and practice." (http://archives.umc.org/interior .asp?mid=1670)

Unusual among churches, The United Methodist Church has adopted a Social Creed that stresses human rights and ecological concerns. The church has considered the question of homosexuality at several General Conferences. At the 2000 conference, a substantial majority of lay and clergy delegates affirmed by vote that the practice of homosexuality is incompatible with Christian teaching and that no self-avowed practicing homosexual can be ordained as clergy or be given a pastoral appointment. This position was challenged several times after 2000 and remains controversial in the church.

For more information: www.umc.org

Headquarters: P.O. Box 320, Nashville, TN 37202-0320

VOLUNTEERS OF AMERICA, INC.

Founded: 1896
Membership: 14,000 employees, 70,000 volunteers, 1.8 million served (2003)

Volunteers of America (VOA) is a Christian church and a human-service organization founded in 1896 by Ballington (1857–1940) and Maud (1865–1948) Booth, son and daughter-in-law of William Booth, founder of the Salvation Army*. The mission of VOA is to reach and uplift all people, bringing them to the immediate knowledge and active service of God. VOA is one of the largest and most financially efficient service organizations in the world. Over eighty-five percent of its $770 million budget in 2003 went directly to those whom it serves. It is present in communities across the U.S., providing over 160 different human-service programs and opportunities for individual and community involvement. From rural areas to inner-city neighborhoods, VOA engages tens of thousands of professional staff and volunteers in operating programs that deal with today's most pressing social needs. It responds to individual community needs to help abused and neglected children, youth at risk, the frail elderly, the disabled, homeless individuals and families, and many others. Each year, it helps more than 1.8 million people in need.

Volunteers of America adheres to a defined set of beliefs, or Cardinal Doctrines, that conform to biblical teaching and traditional Christian thought and practice. Individuals who are commissioned as VOA ministers (having met all requirements for religious study and spiritual formation) become fully accredited clergy and may perform sacramental and evangelical functions. Volunteers of America is governed by both a religious body, the Grand Field Council, and a corporate body, the National Board of Directors. The Council is made up of all VOA clergy and represents the membership of the organization. The Council is responsible for framing the articles of incorporation, constitution, bylaws, and regulations and for electing its president. The National Board of Directors consists of thirty-one volunteer members and is responsible for the direction and effective functioning of the organization. The National Ecclesiastical Board is a smaller body of VOA clergy charged with ministerial affairs. The chief officer of Volunteers of America, Inc., elected for a five-year term, is president of the corporation as well as head of the church. The national office, in Alexandria, Virginia, provides technical and administrative support to local VOA programs and directs other strategic initiatives to address the organization's mission.

For more information: www.voa.org

Headquarters: 110 South Union St., Alexandria, VA 22314-3324

Native American Christianity

Contrary to popular belief, the largest single religion among the native peoples of North America today is Christianity in one form or another. As many as seven hundred thousand Native Americans profess Christian beliefs. Some of the oldest congregations in America are Native American. In fact, the oldest church building in the United States is the San Miguel in Santa Fe, built in 1610 by the Tlaxcalan people. The oldest church in continuous use as a house of worship is the Mission of San Esteban Rey on the Acoma pueblo in New Mexico. It was built by the Acoma tribe under the direction of Catholic missionaries from Spain in 1641 (forty years before the famous Old Ship Church in Massachusetts). Like all forms of Christianity, Native American churches incorporate elements of traditional religion and local culture with Christian symbolism and beliefs.

The earliest immigrants to North America probably came across a land bridge that once connected Asia and Alaska. These early settlers were tribal, but the details of their beliefs and ceremonies are lost in prehistory. Traditional tribal religions are still practiced throughout the U.S. wherever native peoples have communities. Since tribal religion is based on oral tradition, it is difficult to determine how much it has changed since contact with Europeans, but oral tradition has been the glue that has held tribes together in the face of white hostility. Suffice it to say that there is more variety than uniformity among traditional native religions in terms of both practice and belief.

Eventually, the Mayas, Aztecs, and Incas built large and prosperous empires that rivaled the ancient empires of Egypt and Mesopotamia in terms of technology and social organization. They had sophisticated religious systems with their own type of scholar-priests. One of the most famous dates in world history is 1492 when "Columbus sailed the ocean blue." The Italian explorer hoped to be the "Admiral of the Ocean Sea, Viceroy and Governor" of the Indes, and he felt a divine calling to spread the Catholic faith in pagan lands. Columbus hoped to find a shorter route to the riches of India by sailing West to reach the East. Instead he discovered an island in a New World and named it San Salvador in honor of Jesus Christ. Columbus assumed the inhabitants were Indians, and Native Americans have been stuck with the misnomer Indian ever since. Columbus forecast the history of European contact with Native Americans when he wrote: "How easy it would be to convert these people - and to make them work for us." (Quoted by Martin Marty in *Christianity in the New World: From 1500 to 1800*, pg. 15.) When he returned to Spain, he brought along six of the natives as slaves, but Isabella promptly released them and baptized them.

Tragically, the Aztec and Incan empires were no match for the military power of the European invaders, and hundreds of thousands of people were killed or enslaved. The Spanish conquistadores brought Christianity with them, and most of the native peoples in the Spanish empire converted to Catholicism*, sometimes under duress. The Catholic Church remains the dominant religious institution in Central and South America, but it is a Catholicism that has been shaped both by Spanish piety and the traditional practices of Native Americans (see Hispanic Catholicism).

When Bartolome de Las Casas came to America, he used natives as slaves on his plantation on the island of Hispanola, and by 1514 he was also serving as a priest. While preaching on a text from Ecclesiasticus (34: 18–20), "The sacrifice of an offering unjustly acquired is a mockery," he began to understand the situation of the natives in a new light. He realized he was mocking God by living off of the land and labor of the Indians. He returned to Spain to plead the cause of the native peoples and eventually Charles V gave Bartolome a colony on the coast of Venezuela where he could create a new type of Christian community. Unfortunately this first effort at establishing a church specifically for Native Americans failed. Bartolome retired to a monastery where he wrote "A Brief Relation of the Destruction of the Indies," detailing the devastation that European Christians brought to the natives of South America.

There were no native empires in North America like those in the South. Tribes in the North tended to be small and they had no written language. Thus, much of their history and heritage has been lost. Life in the woodlands and plains of North America was precarious and closely tied to natural rhythms. The phases of the moon, changes of the seasons, blessings of rain and sunshine were brought into an interpretative web of mythology and ritual that explained each tribe's unique place in world. Many of the tribes had religious leaders or shamans who experienced ecstatic trances and visions. Often they were skilled in healing arts, and thus were called "medicine men." Shamans were often adept at learning from other tribal religions and appropriating their magic. In this way Christian practices and symbols, such as the cross, were sometimes taken over into native religions. Europeans brought new technologies and gods to the natives.

Hernedez De Soto came to North America in search of gold. He brought along eight priests and four friars who unsuccessfully opposed the conquistadores' enslavement of natives. The Spanish pressed on through swamps and rivers until they reached the Mississippi. There De Soto failed to convince a local chief that he was a god. For his hubris and violence, De Soto was killed by natives in 1542. One of the first Catholic martyrs in the New World was Juan de Padilla who accompanied Coronado on his futile quest for the city of gold. In 1542, he and a couple of lay brothers left Coronado's band and set off without weapons into North America. The Wichita accepted him as a shaman, but were jealous of his efforts to convert their enemies, the Kansa. The Wichita eventually killed the defenseless missionary.

Catholic missionaries had greater success in what is now the American Southwest. In 1645, they reported that there were some 300,000 baptized natives in the Southwest and Mexico. One of the most successful missionaries was Eusebio Kino, an Austrian who wanted to emulate Francis Xavier. Kino became a Jesuit and spent twelve years preparing for a mission to China, but when his orders came, he was sent to Mexico instead. There he promoted a vision of a Catholic Empire stretching across North America. After years of failure, in 1687 he established a permanent mission at San Xavier del Bac, near Tuscon, which is still standing.

The piety of the Spanish missionaries was rigorous and focused on the suffering of Christ, which is still evident in some of the religiosity of the Southwestern tribes. Another area of mission focus was California. When Bering explored the Western coast of America for Russia in 1728, Spain became worried about Russian encroachment in New Spain. Missionaries, most notably Junipero Serra, were sent out to win the natives over to Spain through gentle persuasion and Christian conversion. From 1769 to 1784 Serra built a system of nine missions throughout California. At their peak, the California missions served some thirty thousand people. Little remains of Serra's mission but the preserved buildings.

In the east, the Iroquois formed a confederation of seven tribes. Women had a strong role in these tribes; they owned property, had the right of divorce and helped select the chiefs. Extended families would pass the winter in longhouses and tell myths about the origins of the world and their sacred tribe. Christianity was first brought to the Iroquois and Huron by French Catholic missionaries. In 1534, Francis I sent Jacques Cartier to the New World in an effort to establish a New France as a rival to New Spain in the South. Cartier was no priest, but he tried to convert the native peoples. Distracted by internal difficulties and wars of religion at home, it was sixty years before France made another serious effort at exploiting the New World. Champlain came to the northeast in 1608, and by 1713 there were about twenty-five thousand French Catholics in North America, primarily in Canada.

The most successful French missionary was Jean de Brebeuf who worked among the Hurons in Ontario. He baptized about a thousand natives and built five chapels. Brebeuf followed the practices of the pioneering Jesuit missionary, Francis Xavier, who argued that Christianity must be expressed in the idiom of the native peoples. Illustrative of this is a Christmas carol Brebeuf wrote in the Huron language: "Within a lodge of broken bark/ The tender Babe was found/ A ragged robe of rabbit skin/ Enwrapp'd His beauty round;/ But as the hunter braves drew nigh,/ The angel song rang loud and high/ Jesus your king is born, Jesus is born." (http://lyricsplayground.com/alpha/songs/xmas/jesuousahatonhiahuronchristmascarol.shtml) Brebeuf urged missionaries to live with the Indians and like the Indians. He was a gentle soul who was captured by the Iroquois in 1649 during a war with the Huron. The Iroquois were so impressed by his courage during his long and vicious torture that they ate his heart after he died.

The first woman missionary in the New World was Marie Guyart, a member of the Ursuline order in France. Her letters to Europe spread the challenge and romance of work with the natives and inspired several other women to join her community in Quebec. The stories of the Jesuit missionaries were circulated through an annual almanac called *Jesuit Relations*. Jacques Marquette read the *Relations* and adopted Francis Xavier as his patron saint. By 1666 he had made his way to Canada and soon was baptizing thousands at Sault Sainte Marie in Michigan. His travels around Lake Superior eventually led him on a mission of exploration down the Wisconsin River. He went as far as Arkansas, but returned when he found that the natives there were armed with guns gained from the Spanish. He died exhausted at the age of 38.

Protestant missions began in earnest with English colonization in New England and Virginia. Interest in missions among Congregationalists (see REFORMED, CONGREGATIONALIST, AND PRESBYTERIAN CHURCHES) began the day the Pilgrims landed at Plymouth. John Eliot spent seven years mastering Algonquian and translated the Bible. He also published a catechism in 1653, which was the first book to be printed in a Native American language. By 1674 there were about four thousand "praying Indians" in New England and twenty-four native preachers. These efforts were hampered by conflicts between settlers and natives, which were sometimes violent.

Protestants were generally less tolerant of native practices than Catholics and insisted that converts adopt European dress, languages, and behavior. As a result, few natives converted to Protestant churches until the arrival of Moravian* missionaries in the 1740s. The Moravians, led by David Zeisberger and John Heckewelder, worked within tribal society. They established several successful mission villages in Pennsylvania and New York, but hostility from whites virtually destroyed the Moravian work. In 1782 about ninety Moravian Indians were massacred by an American militia at Gnaddenhutten, Ohio. Forty years later the Moravians were unable to prevent the expulsion of the Cherokee from their lands in Georgia.

Once native peoples were confined on reservations and native children required to attend American schools, Protestant evangelical churches played an increasingly important role in Native American life. Many Native American Christian congregations today are evangelical in orientation, teaching that members must have a personal conversion experience. In the twentieth century, Pentecostal* evangelists had success working with Native Americans, in part because Pentecostalism is more tolerant of traditional native styles of worship, such as drumming, than earlier missionaries had been. Pentecostal churches have been actively engaged in efforts to curb alcoholism and drug abuse on reservations. Cook Christian Training School in Phoenix is an important institution for contemporary Native American missions.

Suggestions for further reading:

Bowden, Henry. *American Indians and Christian Missions: Studies in Cultural Conflict*. Chicago: Univ. of Chicago Press, 1981.

Gill, Sam. *Native American Religions*. Belmont, CA: Wadsworth, 1982.

La Barre, Weston. *The Peyote Cult*. Norman, OK: University of Oklahoma Press,1989.

Niehard, John G. *Black Elk Speaks: Being the Life Story of a Holy Man of the Oglala Sioux*. Omaha, NE: Univ. of Nebraska Press, 2000 (reprint), 1932 (original).

Wheeler, Rachel. *To Live Upon Hope: Mohicans and Missionaries in the Eighteenth-Century Northeast* (Ithaca and London: Cornell University Press, 2008).

NATIVE AMERICAN CHURCH

Founded: 1918 with roots to 1880s
Membership: est. 300,000

In the twentieth century there was a revival of interest in traditional beliefs and practices among the tribes, and schools have been established to preserve the languages in which the old stories are passed down. The 1978 American Indian Religious Freedom Resolution has made it easier for native peoples to practice traditional tribal religion on federal lands. Native American spirituality became a topic of great interest in the dominant culture, primarily through the so-called New Age movement. The book *Black Elk Speaks,* which was published in 1932 by John Neihardt, has been a major guide for whites and natives alike who are seeking to connect with a nature-based mysticism in which "Mother Earth" and all her inhabitants live in ecological and spiritual harmony. Shamanism, sweat lodges, vision quests, and other features of some tribal religions have become part of the American religious economy. This Native American spirituality is often an amalgam of many aspects of the different tribal religions.

There have also been attempts to create new types of indigenous religions that unite people across tribes without joining the European churches. Beginning around the turn of the last century, a group of Native Americans formed the Native American Church with principal concentration of membership in the Southwest. Its beliefs and practices are syncretistic, blending elements of Christianity with various traditional tribal practices. It was chartered in 1918 and reports about three hundred thousand members.

Popularly, but inaccurately, called the "peyote religion" because its ceremonies frequently make use of the button or crown of the hallucinogenic peyote, a plant in the cactus family, the Native American Church is a uniquely American religion dedicated to the Peyote spirit. Worshipers hold all-night ceremonies filled with chanting to the rhythms of a water drum, during which peyote is consumed. The reason for its use is not individual ecstasy but to serve as a communal ritual, to foster bonded relationships. Males perform the leadership functions; the central figure is the shaman, who is thought to be endowed with psychic abilities. A 1988 Supreme Court decision severely curtailed use of peyote as a sacrament. Despite its reputation as a "drug" church, the Native American Church is quite conservative and has been effective in dealing with drug and alcohol abuse among Native Americans.

For more information: www.ncai.org

Holiness Churches

The Holiness movement grew out of the Methodist* Church beginning in the mid-nineteenth century. Early Methodist ministry in the U.S. focused primarily on conversion and church extension, at times neglecting John Wesley's emphasis on sanctification and perfection. As Methodism became more established in the nineteenth century, there was renewed interest in the doctrine of perfection. One of the key figures in this revival of holiness teaching was the traveling evangelist and writer Phoebe Palmer (1807–1874), who experienced sanctification by the Holy Spirit in 1837. She worked tirelessly to bring others to a similar experience of holiness.

Toward the end of the nineteenth century, the Holiness movement had spread throughout the country, becoming a source of controversy in local Methodist churches. Congregations divided; holiness-minded preachers left the Methodist Church in order to work independently; and a wide-variety of small, often "storefront," churches sprang up in virtually every U.S. community. Over time, many of these independent congregations formed denominations. Holiness teaching generally rejects various forms of popular entertainment, such as dancing, movies, popular music, make-up, ornate clothing, gambling, drinking, and smoking. In many ways, the Holiness movement represents a countercultural movement in the U.S., but its adherents continue to live and work in the midst of the wider society.

Many Holiness churches use the word *Apostolic* in their names to emphasize their aim of returning to the life of the New Testament church, when the Holy Spirit was perceived to be particularly active. After 1900, many in the Holiness movement embraced further works of the Holy Spirit, such as speaking in tongues and physical healing (see PENTECOSTAL CHURCHES). Since the Holiness movement is focused more on lifestyle and an experience of conversion followed by sanctification, it is to be distinguished from the more doctrinally oriented fundamentalist* movement. However, there has been much cross-fertilization between these two forms of conservative Protestantism.

Suggestions for further reading:

Dieter, Melvin Easterday. *The Holiness Revival of the Nineteenth Century*. Metuchen, NJ: Scarecrow Press, 1996.

Dupree, Sherry Sherrod. *African-American Pentecostal Holiness Tradition: An Annotated Bibliography*. New York: Garland Publishing, 1995.

Jones, Charles Edwin. *Perfectionist Persuasion: The Holiness Movement and American Methodism, 1867-1936*. Metuchen: Scarecrow Press, 1974.

Kostlevy, William C. and Gari-Ann Patzwald, *Historical Dictionary of the Holiness Movement*. Lanham, MD: Rowman & Littlefield, 2001.

Niebuhr, H. Richard. *The Social Sources of Denominationalism*. New York, Meridian Books, 1957.

Sanders, Cheryl J. *Saints in Exile: The Holiness-Pentecostal Experience in African American Religion and Culture*. New York, 1996.

Smith, Timothy L. *Called unto Holiness: The Story of the Nazarenes: The Formative Years*. Kansas City, MO: Nazarene Publishing House, 1962.

Stanley, Susan C. *Holy Boldness: Women Preachers' Autobiography and the Sanctified Self*. Knoxville, TN: University of Tennessee Press, 2002.

Synan, Vinson. *The Holiness-Pentecostal Movement in the United States*. Grand Rapids: Eerdmans, 1971.

APOSTOLIC CHRISTIAN CHURCHES OF AMERICA

Founded: 1830s; came to the U.S. in 1847
Membership: 23,980 in 84 churches (2000)

This is the only Holiness group that originated in Europe. It began in Switzerland when S. H. Froehlich had a dramatic conversion experience that he felt marked the New Testament pattern of Christian experience. Froehlich's church first took the name Evangelical Baptist, but adopted the Apostolic title as it embraced the doctrine of holiness. Froehlich himself came to the U.S. in the 1850s and ministered to Swiss and German immigrants in the Midwest. By that time, another Swiss pastor, Benedict Weyeneth, already had organized the first congregation in the U.S. in upstate New York. The theology of the church reflects some of the concerns of German Pietism*.

The church consists of members who have been "reborn" and baptized, and who strive for sanctification along with "friends of the truth" who sincerely and earnestly strive to attain adoption by God in Christ. Members are noted for a life of simplicity, separation from worldliness, and obedience to the Bible, which is embraced as the infallible Word of God. Members may serve in the military, but they cannot bear arms since that would violate the commandment to love one's enemies. Though they strive to be good citizens, they do not swear oaths. There are no educational institutions for clergy, and they are not paid. A very close knit fellowship and strong sense of community exist throughout the denomination, evidenced in the observance of the kiss of peace. A smaller, related body is called the Apostolic Christian Church (Nazarene).

For more information: www.apostolicchristian.org

Headquarters: 3420 North Sheridan Rd., Peoria, IL 61604

APOSTOLIC OVERCOMING HOLY CHURCH OF GOD, INC.

Founded: 1916
Membership: 10,714 in 129 churches (2000)

Bishop W. T. Phillips (1893–1973), a former member of the Methodist Church*, became deeply concerned with the teaching of the doctrine of holiness and, after four years of study and preaching on the topic, organized the Ethiopian Overcoming Holy Church of God in 1916 in Mobile, Alabama. It is claimed that this church existed even from the days of Enos, when Christianity was known to be in existence in Abyssinia. "Ethiopian" was later changed to "Apostolic." Active in twenty-two states, the West Indies, Haiti, and Africa, the church's clergy, both men and women, are supported by tithes. Worship includes foot washing and divine healing. Services generally are emotionally expressive, with participants speaking in tongues and engaging in ecstatic dances. Marriage to the unsaved, the use of tobacco, foolish talking, jesting, and use of slang are forbidden. In doctrine, sanctification and holiness are stressed, along with the deity of Christ, the final resurrection of the dead, and the punishment of evil at the time of the last judgment at the Second Coming of Christ. A publishing facility is located in the headquarters building in Birmingham, Alabama.

For more information: www.aohchurch.com

Headquarters: 2257 St. Stephens Road, Mobile, Alabama 36617

THE CHRISTIAN AND MISSIONARY ALLIANCE

Founded: 1887
Membership: 420,006 in 2,009 churches (2007)

A. B. Simpson (1843–1919), a Presbyterian* minister in New York City, left that church to carry on independent evangelistic work in 1882. This led to the formation of two societies: the Christian Alliance, for home missions work, and the Evangelical Missionary Alliance, for work abroad. These merged in 1897, forming The Christian and Missionary Alliance. When the Assemblies of God* was founded, about one-tenth of that constituency resulted from the departure of people from the Christian and Missionary Alliance. The two groups have a close-knit history, are doctrinally similar, and maintain ties of fellowship. The Alliance remained a confederation for over seventy-five years, but it formalized its status with bylaws and a constitution in 1974.

Strongly evangelical, the Alliance believes in the inspiration and inerrancy of the Bible, the atoning work of Christ, the reality of supernatural religious experience, sanctification, and the premillennial return of Jesus Christ. It stresses the centrality of Christ as Savior, sanctifier, healer, and coming king. True to its original purpose, the Alliance sponsors foreign missions in eighty-one countries in Latin America, Africa, Asia, the Pacific Islands, the Middle East, and Europe. There are over one thousand Alliance missionaries and some fifteen thousand national pastors and workers ministering to nearly two million persons. Ethnic groups within the alliance include Cambodian, Dega, Haitian, Hmong, Jewish, Korean, Laotian, Native American, Hispanic, and Vietnamese. Each member church or group is engaged in missionary and evangelistic activities. An overall conference of delegates, the General Council, meets annually. The CMA in Canada became autonomous in 1980 but continues to support missions jointly with the U.S. Alliance.

For more information: www.cmalliance.org
Headquarters: P.O. Box 35000, Colorado Springs, CO 80935

CHURCH OF CHRIST (HOLINESS) U.S.A.

Founded: 1894
Membership: 11,468 in 148 churches (2007)

A Baptist preacher in Alabama and Mississippi, C. P. Jones, seeking a new church and faith that would make him a friend of God, founded this church. The body retained its Holiness emphasis when other early black churches moved into Pentecostalism*. The Church of Christ (Holiness) seeks to spread the gospel around the world, to reclaim those who have fallen away from the faith, to encourage believers to experience sanctification, and to support divine healing. The church has a strong eschatological focus as well.

Doctrinally, the church emphasizes original sin, the Holy Spirit as an indispensable gift to every believer, and Christ's atonement and Second Coming. There are two sacraments: baptism and the Lord's Supper. Foot washing and divine healing are employed as aids to the growth of spiritual life. The church has bishops who speak for the church, but its government is representative, with final authority vested in a biennial convention made up of elders, clergy, and local lay leaders. There are seven dioceses, each under a bishop's charge. Missionary work is conducted in the U.S. and in Liberia and Nigeria.

For more information: www.cochusa.com

Headquarters: P.O. Box 3622, Jackson, MS 39207

CHURCH OF GOD (ANDERSON, INDIANA)

Founded: 1881
Membership: 252,905 in 2,248 churches (2007)

The Church of God with general headquarters in Anderson, Indiana, grew out of the nineteenth century American Holiness Movement, but both Anabaptist* and Pietistic* emphases also influenced the Church of God. Daniel S. Warner (1842-1895) and several associates rejected denominational hierarchies and formal creeds. They understood unity as being a natural outgrowth of personal holiness, and holiness to be the basis of biblical unity. The Church of God's generally accepted doctrines include the divine inspiration of the scriptures; forgiveness of sin through the atonement of Christ and repentance of the believer; the experience of holiness; the personal (amillennial) return of Christ; the kingdom of God as the reign and rule of God in the human heart; resurrection of the dead; and a final judgment in which the righteous are rewarded and the wicked punished. Baptism by immersion is viewed as a witness to the new believer's regeneration by Christ and inclusion in the family of God. The Lord's Supper reminds participants of the grace experienced in the life of the believer. Foot washing is practiced in acknowledgement and acceptance of the servant ministry of Christians to each other and to the world. These New Testament practices are understood as divine ordinances of the church.

Local churches are responsible for their own way of functioning. As a result, one finds a wide variety of organizational structures among congregations. Ministers and lay leaders meet in voluntary state and regional assemblies for inspiration and instruction as well as to conduct business. The General Assembly meets in connection with the annual international convention held in Anderson. In 1996 and 1997 the assembly initiated a restructuring of the church's work in the U.S. The result was the formation of Church of God Ministries, Inc. The church's ministries emphasize outreach, congregational ministry, and service to pastors and others. Warner Press serves as the church's publisher of curriculum and other materials. There is no formal membership in the Church of God (Anderson), but persons are assumed to be members on the basis of conversion and holiness of life. Congregations are found mainly in the Midwest and Pacific Coast regions. The church supports Anderson University and its School of Theology along with Mid-America Christian University, Warner University, and Warner Pacific College. It carries on work in ninety countries, involving 859,589 worshippers.

For more information: www.chog.org

Headquarters: P.O. Box 2420, Anderson, IN 46018-2420

CHURCH OF GOD (HOLINESS)

Founded: 1886
Membership: est. 8,000 in approx. 140 churches (2000)

The Church of God (Holiness) is an association of autonomous congregations that was founded by former Methodists* who were active in the Southwest Holiness Association. They believe that entire sanctification is a biblical doctrine. They describe this as a second definite work of God's grace in the heart and life of the believer subsequent to regeneration, at which time the believer is cleansed of his or her sinful nature and is completely submitted to the controlling hand of the Holy Spirit.

The church today is concentrated in Missouri and Kansas. It is working increasingly among Hispanics in the U.S. and Mexico. The Home Missions Department also works with Haitian immigrants in New York City and sponsors a Navajo mission in the Southwest. World missions are concentrated in Ghana, Liberia, Nigeria, India, Myanmar, Nepal, the Caribbean basin, the Ukraine, Bolivia, and Colombia. In addition to Kansas City College and Bible School, the church operates The Herald and Banner Press, which produces Sunday school literature for all ages, devotional books, and a periodical. A General Convention is held annually.

For more information: www.cogh.net

Contact: Herald Banner and Press, 7407 - 7415 Metcalf Ave., Overland Park, KS 66204

CHURCH OF THE NAZARENE

Founded: 1908
Membership: 645,048 in 4,689 churches (2008)

The Church of the Nazarene is one of the largest and most influential of the Holiness bodies, and it is one that has self-consciously held to its Wesleyan roots. It is now an international body that includes nearly two million people. The church resulted from the merger of three independent Holiness groups in the U.S. In 1907, an Eastern Holiness body, the Association of Pentecostal Churches of America, joined with a California body, the Church of the Nazarene. Then in 1908, this body merged with a Southern group known as the Holiness Church of Christ. The current name was adopted in 1919. While many were involved in the founding of the church, perhaps the principal figure was Phineas F. Bresee (1838–1915), who became its first general superintendent.

The church's theological background is Wesleyan. Four of the first five general superintendents of the Church of the Nazarene, including Bresee, were former Methodist* ministers, and the church's *Manual* is similar to the Methodist *Book of Discipline*. The doctrine of the church is built around the justification and the sanctification of believers by faith. This includes a believer's entire sanctification as a second work of grace, subsequent to regeneration. All clergy, both men and women, and local church officials must profess this experience of entire sanctification. Other doctrines include belief in the plenary inspiration of the scriptures; the atonement of Christ for the whole human race (i.e., Arminianism); the justification, regeneration, and adoption of all penitent believers in Christ; the Second Coming of Christ; the resurrection of the dead; and the final judgment.

Members believe in divine healing but never to the exclusion of medical agencies. Nazarenes discourage use of tobacco and alcoholic beverages. Two sacraments, baptism by sprinkling, pouring, or (most often) immersion and communion are accepted as "instituted by Christ." Baptism of young children is allowed, but believer's baptism predominates. The General Assembly, the highest body of the church, elects six general superintendents whose terms last until the next General Assembly, and the General Board, consisting of an equal number of lay and clergy members. The General Board meets annually and oversees four administrative departments of the church: World Mission, USA/Canada, Sunday School & Discipleship Ministries, and the International Board of Education. The church is organized in 151 world areas and supports some six hundred missionaries. There is strong emphasis on evangelism. The church's International Center is located in Lenexa, Kansas.

Structurally, the Church of the Nazarene exists at the local, district, and general level, which is international in scope. All districts are represented at the General

Assembly on the same basis (based on district membership), and there are currently 433 districts worldwide, of which only seventy-seven are in the U.S. The year 1998 was the last year in which Americans and Canadians together made up fifty percent of the church membership. Today Americans make up only thirty-five percent. The denomination's worldwide membership is now at 1.9 million. Worldwide, the church supports ten liberal arts colleges, two graduate theological seminaries, forty-three Bible colleges, two hospitals, thirty-eight medical clinics, three nurse training colleges, one teacher training college, one junior college, and 430 primary and secondary schools that serve over fifty-one thousand children. The books, periodicals, and curriculum of the church are produced at the Nazarene Publishing House in Kansas City.

For more information: www.nazarene.org

Headquarters: 17001 Prairie Star Parkway, Lenexa, KS 66220

CHURCHES OF CHRIST IN CHRISTIAN UNION

Founded: 1909
Membership: 11,164 in 227 churches (2007)

This church began when five ministers and several lay persons withdrew from Christian Union* churches in 1909. The Christian Union had been founded in 1864 in Ohio "to promote fellowship among God's people, to put forth every effort to proclaim God's saving grace to the lost . . . and to declare the whole counsel of God for the edification of believers." (http://www.ohiocu.org/index.php?option=com_content&view=article&id=48&Itemid=55) Some of the clergy in the Christian Union felt that key doctrines were being neglected, and so the Churches of Christ in Christian Union was organized as a holiness church dedicated to the teachings of John Wesley. The first council was held that year at Jeffersonville, Ohio. The Reformed Methodist Church merged with the Churches of Christ in Christian Union in September 1952.

Churches in this body are generally evangelistic in faith and work; camp meetings, revivals, and soul-winning campaigns are held regularly throughout the denomination. Worship follows simple forms, with little prescribed ritual. A general council meets every two years at Circleville, Ohio, the body's headquarters. Circleville Bible College, established 1948, trains clergy and lay workers.

For more information: www.cccuhq.org

Headquarters: 1426 Lancaster Pike, Circleville, OH 43113

CHURCHES OF GOD, GENERAL CONFERENCE

Founded: 1830, name changed in 1975
Membership: 32,000 in 336 congregations (2000)

The Churches of God, General Conference originated with the preaching of John Winebrenner (1797-1860) in Pennsylvania in the 1820s. Winebrenner was ordained in the German Reformed Church, but some members objected to his use of revivalistic methods. Winebrenner adopted Arminianism, which contradicted the Calvinism of the German Reformed, and in 1828 he was removed from the pastoral roles. He continued to evangelize and his following increased. Soon he became convinced that believer's baptism was the only true baptism, and in 1830 he was rebaptized by an elder in his church. He and his colleagues formed the General Eldership of the Church of God, but they were popularly known as the Winebrennerians. In 1975 the current name was adopted.

The denomination is different from most Baptist churches because it has a presbyterial polity, organized by regions. The church recognizes three ordinances: baptism of believers, the Lord's Supper, and footwashing. The church is very evangelistic and Christocentric in piety. It encourages culturally relevant worship, but is critical of many aspects of modern American culture. It teaches that believers can and should live holy lives empowered by the Holy Spirit. The church's seminary is called Winebrenner Theological Seminary, which is on the campus of Findlay College in Ohio.

For more information: cggc.org

Headquarters: 700 E. Melrose Ave.,P.O. Box 926, Findlay, OH 45840

FREE METHODIST CHURCH OF NORTH AMERICA

Founded: 1860
Membership: 77,171 in 979 congregations (2007)

The Free Methodist Church was formed as part of the abolitionist movement prior to the Civil War. Its founder was the Reverend B. T. Roberts (1823–1893) who objected to "new school" Methodism, which he and his associates believed compromised the Wesleyan standards of the church. They called for a return to stricter doctrine and lifestyle in the Methodist Church*, which included the abolition of slavery, abolishing the practice of pew rentals, opposition to secret societies, and more freedom in worship. They were "read out" of their churches and organized the Free Methodist Church in Pekin, New York.

Doctrinally, the Free Methodists stress the virgin birth, the deity of Jesus, and his vicarious atonement and resurrection. No one may be received into

220

membership without undergoing confession and forgiveness of sin, and the experience of entire sanctification is sought in all members.

The church is connectional in a basic Methodist pattern, with a board of four bishops who supervise the four basic geographic areas of the church, a General Conference that meets every four years, Annual Conferences, and districts. The publishing arm of the church is Light and Life Communications. The church operates six four-year colleges and a seminary and maintains a seminary foundation that maintains cooperative relationships with several seminaries. Social services include a health care foundation, pregnancy and adoption services, retirement and nursing facilities for the elderly, day-care centers for children, homeless shelters, drug and alcohol abuse recovery ministries, a boarding high school, and many services for the poor and disenfranchised.

The Free Methodist Church is a world fellowship, consisting of fourteen General Conferences (Brazil, Burundi, Canada, Congo, Democratic Republic of Congo, Dominican Republic, Egypt, Japan, Mozambique, Philippines, Rwanda, South Africa, Zimbabwe and the U.S.) with a common constitution. Free Methodist churches are found in eighty countries, and the membership outside the U.S. is over 650,000.

For more information: www.freemethodistchurch.org

Headquarters: P.O. Box 535002, Indianapolis, IN 46253

NEW APOSTOLIC CHURCH OF NORTH AMERICA

Founded: 1863
Membership: 38,778 in 314 churches (2008)

The New Apostolic Church of North America is an international Christian church that developed from the Catholic Apostolic Church. It is led by apostles and its foundation is the Holy Scriptures. The New Apostolic Church recognizes three sacraments: baptism, Holy Sealing, and Holy Communion. They practice believer's baptism with water. Through the act of Holy Sealing, the baptized believer is filled with the Holy Spirit through prayer and laying on of the hands of an apostle. The idea of the return of Christ is a central component of New Apostolic doctrine. The church also emphasizes the importance of personal accountability of its members for their actions. The gospel of Christ and values inherent in the Ten Commandments provide orientation for behavior. The church is politically neutral and independent. The Catholic Apostolic Church was founded by Edward Irving (1792–1834), a Presbyterian pastor in London who expected the imminent return of Christ. In preparation for the eschaton, the founders recreated the apostolic offices of the church. The twelve apostles held their first conference in 1835. In a dispute over the appointment of new apostles to fill vacancies left by attrition, Bishop Schwarz of Hamburg was excommunicated from the Catholic Apostolic Church in 1862. To lead the dissenting body, a priest named Preuss was elected to the office of apostle "through the spirit of prophecy," and Bishop Schwarz served under him until his own elevation to the apostolic office. Under Preuss and Schwarz, the New Apostolic Church spread from Europe to North America, where today it is organized into districts under apostles, bishops, and elders. The church stresses mission work, and worldwide there are about eleven million Christians who profess the New Apostolic faith.

For more information: www.nak.org

Offices: 3753 Troy St., Chicago, IL 60618

WESLEYAN CHURCH

Founded: 1843
Membership: 138,164 in 1,626 churches (2007)

The Wesleyan Church was formed in 1968 through the merger of the Pilgrim Holiness Church and the Wesleyan Methodist Church. Many beliefs of the Wesleyan Church are based on doctrines set forth by the Dutch theologians, Jacobus Arminius and John Wesley (see METHODIST CHURCHES). The Wesleyan Methodist Church was the first Holiness denomination founded in the U.S. as a protest against slavery. Orange Scott (1800-1847) was a leading abolitionist Methodist preacher, and when Methodist bishops urged silence on the subject of slavery as the country was moving towards Civil War, Orange and his associates organized a separate Wesleyan Methodist Connection. Many of the Wesleyan Methodists of that day were activists in what came to be known historically as the underground railway before the Civil War.

Following the Civil War and emancipation, the Wesleyan Methodist Connection embraced the Holiness movement, which promoted the doctrine of sanctification as taught by John Wesley, with an uncompromising commitment to a temperate lifestyle. In 1947 the word "Connection" was changed to "Church." By the late nineteenth century several holiness groups had formed into functioning, autonomous, ecclesiastical bodies as a result of the holiness revival that spread through much of Protestantism. In 1897 a process was begun that resulted in one organized church in 1922, which adopted the name "Pilgrim Holiness Church." In 1966 the decision was made by the respective General Conferences to merge the Pilgrim Holiness Church and the Wesleyan Methodist Church as their doctrine and church polity were so similar. This merger was accomplished in June of 1968 and took place on the campus of Anderson University in Anderson, Indiana. Today, the Wesleyan Church has a presence in seventy-six countries with a worldwide membership of over three hundred thousand. There are over eleven thousand men and women involved in ministry either as ordained ministers or credentialed laymen.

For more information: www.wesleyan.org

Headquarters: PO Box 50434, Indianapolis, IN 46250

Christian and Restorationist Churches (Stone-Campbellite Tradition)

Protestantism, with its emphasis on the Bible alone as the basis of faith and practice, has always sought to remain true to the church of the apostles in the New Testament. Most Protestants have been willing to accept some historical development of the church and its doctrine in the post-biblical period (reciting the Nicene Creed, for example). There have been others, though, who have seen the history of Christianity as the story of a decline from New Testament purity. These Christians have attempted to "restore" original or "primitive" Christianity by purging the church of all non-biblical elements, including creeds and confessions of faith. The restorationist impulse has run throughout the history of Christianity, most notably among the Waldensians* and Brethren*.

During the Second Great Awakening of the early nineteenth century, this restorationist impulse grew particularly strong. In politics, the U.S. had "restored" Greek democracy, and many people thought that Americans could also restore the structure and doctrine of the original church in the new land. By returning to the New Testament alone, without recourse to creeds or rituals, the restorationists hoped to end fraternal strife among churches.

Thomas Campbell (1763–1854) was a Scottish Presbyterian who left his church in Ireland to come to western Pennsylvania in 1807. Campbell was convinced that the historical creeds and confessions of the church were a source of Christian division rather than union, and he preached that all Christians should share in the Lord's Supper together. When his views led to a censure from the Presbyterians* in 1809, Campbell formed the Christian Association of Washington County, Pennsylvania, and published the *Declaration and Address*, which was to become the Magna Carta of the Restorationist movement. In that document he argued that schisms in the church were anti-Christian, and produced confusion. God has spoken clearly, Campbell declared, and laid down the rules for church practices in the New Testament. "Where the Scriptures speak, we speak; where the Scriptures are silent, we are silent." (http://www.cccdisciples.org/TCampbell.html) With that phrase, Campbell abolished many traditional church practices, including the use of musical instruments in worship. Soon the Campbells adopted believer's baptism.

Campbell's son, Alexander (1788–1866), was less scholarly than his father, but more dynamic and consistent in his application of his father's principles. He fought many public battles against atheism, Mormonism, Unitarianism, creedalism, sectarianism, emotionalism, and even slavery, but he was singularly unsuccessful in bringing about church unity. His non-creedal church became one of the first independent denominations to be born in the United States.

The other major branch of the nineteenth-century Restorationist movement had its origins in the convictions of James O'Kelly (1757–1826), a Methodist minister; Abner Jones (1772–1841), a Baptist; and Barton Stone (1772–1844), a Presbyterian. When the Second Great Awakening swept through Tennessee and Kentucky in the early 1800s, preaching focused on the need for conversion rather than denominational or doctrinal distinctions. Barton Stone was instrumental in the famous Cane Ridge, Kentucky, revival, which began on August 7, 1801. Somewhere between ten thousand and twenty-five thousand people appeared during the weeklong revival in which preachers from a variety of churches took part. The revival convinced Stone that salvation has little to do with church affiliation and that deeds are worth more than creeds. The egalitarian promise of the American Revolution was being felt in Cane Ridge and other Western "camp meeting" revivals, but the controversy over them led to a schism in the Presbyterian Church.

The groups led by O'Kelly, Jones, and Stone engaged in a long series of conferences that resulted in agreement on six basic Christian principles: (1) Christ, the only head of the church; (2) the Bible, sufficient rule of faith and practice; (3) Christian character, the measure of membership; (4) a right, individual interpretation of the Scripture as a way of life; (5) "Christian," the name taken as worthy of the followers of Christ; (6) unity, Christians working together to save the world.

By 1832 the "Stoneites" and the "Campbellites" had come together for a meeting in Lexington, Kentucky. Stone used the word *Christian* to designate his group, feeling that all of God's children should be known as such. Alexander Campbell used the phrase "Disciples of Christ." After 1832, some of the Christians and the Disciples of Christ merged; both names are still used. Very soon thereafter, differences arose among the restorationists, and, over time, distinct fellowships emerged, most of which go by the name "Christian Churches."

Suggestions for further reading:

Garrison, W. E., and A. T. DeGroot. *The Disciples of Christ: A History*. St. Louis: Bethany Press, 1958.

Harrell, David E., Jr. *A Quest For Christian America, 1800-1865: A Social History Of The Disciples Christ*, 2 vols. Tuscaloosa, Ala.: University of Alabama Press, 2003.

Harrell, David E., Jr., ed. *The Churches of Christ in 20th Century America*. Tuscaloosa, Ala.: University of Alabama Press, 2000.

Hughes, Richard T. *Reviving the Ancient Faith: The Story of Churches of Christ in America*. Grand Rapids: Eerdmans, 1996.

McAllister, Lester G. and William E. Tucker, *Journey in Faith: A History of the Christian Church (Disciples of Christ)*. St. Louis, 1975.

Williams, D. Newell. *A Case Study of Mainstream Protestantism: The Disciple's Relation to American Culture, 1880-1989*. Grand Rapids, MI: Wm. B. Eerdmans, 1991.

CHRISTIAN CHURCH (DISCIPLES OF CHRIST)

Founded: 1832 or 1812
Membership: 689,507 in 3,731 congregations (2007)

The Disciples of Christ were organized primarily by Alexander Campbell and preserve the original ecumenical aim of Campbell more fully than other restorationist bodies. The first national convention of the Disciples of Christ and the first missionary society (American Christian Missionary Society) were organized in 1849, but state conventions and societies had begun to meet in 1839. The group grew rapidly in the nineteenth century in the Midwest. Differences between conservatives and progressives over such matters as the organization of missionary societies and instrumental music in the churches led to the separation of the Churches of Christ* and Disciples by the end of the century.

In matters of belief, the church allows for freedom in interpretation, stemming from the conviction that there is no creed but Christ and no saving doctrines save those of the New Testament. Faith is a matter of personal conviction, but there are areas of general agreement and acceptance. The Lord's Supper is served at every Sunday service, and baptism is by immersion for adult believers. The Disciples are firm in their belief in immortality. They do not accept the doctrine of original sin, but they do teach that all people are of a sinful nature until redeemed by the sacrifice of Christ. They are not concerned with speculation about the Trinity and the nature of a triune God. They have no catechism and no set orders of worship. Faith in Christ as Lord is the only requirement.

For more than a century Disciples of Christ were strictly congregational in polity, but in the twentieth century it was felt that such an arrangement needed restructuring in the interests of efficiency and economy. A new organization was adopted at Kansas City in 1968. The whole church works under a representative government referred to as "three manifestations"—local, regional, and general. The local church is still the basic unit, and each congregation manages its own affairs, but the congregations are grouped in thirty-five regions, organized to provide help, counsel, and pastoral care to members, ministers, and congregations. The General Assembly of the church meets every two years, and the Administrative Committee, with forty-four voting members, meets twice annually. The Office of Communication is located in Indianapolis, Indiana; the church's publishing arm, the Christian Board of Publication, is in St. Louis, Missouri.

The changes adopted in 1968 completed a long process of separation between moderates and conservatives in the Campbellite tradition. Those pastors who held to the original congregational polity and who had reservations about the liberalism of the Disciples formed a loose confederation of independent congregations known as the Christian Churches and Churches of Christ*. All three major branches of the old denomination (the Churches of Christ split in 1906) saw a severe decline in membership after the split.

There are now twenty-one colleges and seminaries in covenant relation with the Disciples, the largest of which is Texas Christian University, in Fort Worth, Texas. The church's National Benevolent Association operates eighty-three facilities and programs in twenty-two states, serving over thirty thousand people a year in residential facilities and community-based programs. True to their founding principles, the Disciples emphasize the importance of community, reconciliation, and laboring to make the kingdom of God visible in the world. Alexander Campbell was an early opponent of slavery and modern Disciples continue to oppose discrimination in its many forms.

For more information: www.disciples.org

Headquarters: P.O. Box 1986, Indianapolis, IN 46206-1986

INDEPENDENT CHRISTIAN CHURCHES AND CHURCHES OF CHRIST

Founded: 1830s
Membership: est. 1,439,253 in 5,471 churches (2008)

Even more so than most Baptist* groups, these independent churches reject the designation as a denomination, and they do not keep denominational statistics. Until 1968, these congregations were listed as part of the Christian Church (Disciples of Christ)*, but the reorganization of that denomination resulted in a formal separation. The Christian Churches and Churches of Christ are more of a fellowship of independent congregations with roots in the Restorationist movement, especially the Barton Stone tradition, than a denomination. However, they do distinguish themselves from the other Churches of Christ* that separated in 1906 over the issue of instrumental music.

Though the final straw for separation was the move toward centralization in the 1960s, there were theological issues involved as well. During the fundamentalist*/modernist controversy in the 1920s, many Christian Churches and Churches of Christ tended toward fundamentalism and believed that the Disciples were too liberal in theology. The more evangelical pastors formed the North American Christian Convention* in 1927, and this gathering served as the organizing unit of the later Christian Churches and Churches of Christ.

Key doctrines include the divinity of Christ; the authority of the Bible; the indwelling of the Holy Spirit for the believer; future reward or punishment; and God as a loving, prayer-answering deity. They baptize by immersion and observe the Lord's Supper in open communion every Sunday. Many Christian Churches and Churches of Christ still maintain the nineteenth-century practice of the extended revival, known as the "camp meeting."

The various congregations support over twenty related colleges, most of which are preacher-training schools insulated from liberal influences. Standard Publishing, in Cincinnati, Ohio, is identified with this group as well. The North American Christian Convention, an annual preaching and teaching assembly, draws as many as twenty thousand attendees to an annual gathering each July. Active in foreign missions, with a missionary presence in about a dozen foreign countries and a domestic missionary presence as well, these churches sponsor a National Missionary Convention that meets each fall, with an attendance of between three and five thousand. The Christian Churches and Churches of Christ remains strongest in the Midwest, but grew on the West Coast towards the end of the twentieth century. There are thirty-nine colleges associated with the Restorationist movement.

For more information: www.christian-church.org

Contact: P.O. Box 1232 Rapid City, SD 57709-1232

CHRISTIAN CONGREGATION, INC.

Founded: 1887
Membership: 122,181 in 1,496 churches (2004)

The philosophy and work of the Christian Congregation, formed in Indiana in 1887, revolve around the "new commandment" of John 13:34-35. Unlike many other descendents of the Restorationist movement, the Christian Congregation is pacifist and opposes all war and sectarian strife. The origins of the group go back to Barton Stone, but in 1887 a number of ministers desired greater coordination of activities and formally organized a church. Inspired by the preaching of John Chapman and John L. Puckett, the Christian Congregation insists that Christ's church is not built on creeds or rituals but solely on the relationship of the individual to God. Because of its teachings concerning the sanctity of life, the church condemns abortion, capital punishment, and all warfare. They believe that the ethical demands of the Scripture transcend all national and racial barriers and should unite all persons in activism for peace.

The church remains strongest in the areas where Barton Stone preached and the original Christian Congregation groups were located: Kentucky, the Carolinas, Virginia, Pennsylvania, Ohio, Indiana, Tennessee, and Texas. The greater part of the group's work is carried on in rural and mountain areas. Polity is congregational.

Headquarters: 812 W. Hemlock St., La Follette, TN 37766.

CHURCHES OF CHRIST

Founded: 1906, with roots to 1804
Membership: est. 1,639,495 in over 13,000 churches (2006)

The Churches of Christ represent the most conservative branch of the Restorationist movement. They are located throughout the nation but are concentrated in the South and the Southwest. They reject the idea of denominationalism and have no central headquarters; therefore, accurate statistics are impossible to attain, but they appear to have declined since 1970. This group has no governing bodies, but members cooperate voluntarily in international radio programs.

Like other Restorationist groups, the Churches of Christ are anti-creedal and look for a Christian union based on the Bible alone. Some of the participants in the Cane Ridge revival adopted the name "Church of Christ" to emphasize their belief that they were directly descended from the original church founded in 33 A.D. In the nineteenth century, the leaders of the Churches of Christ followed the more conservative Stone tradition rather than the leading of Campbell. Stressing a strict adherence to the New Testament pattern of worship and church organization, they refused to join any inter-congregational organization, such as a missionary society. Worship was simple, and they opposed the use of instrumental music on the grounds that the New Testament did not authorize it and that the early church did not use it. Those who called themselves "Disciples of Christ" adopted the use of musical instruments and encouraged ecumenical activities. Around the beginning of the twentieth century, the differences between the conservative and the more liberal wings of the restoration movements became evident, and in the 1906 there was a formal split. In the 1906 census of religious bodies, Churches of Christ were listed separately for the first time.

Key doctrines of Churches of Christ include belief in the Father, the Son, and the Holy Ghost as members of one Godhead; in the incarnation, virgin birth, and bodily resurrection of Christ; and in the universality of sin after the age of accountability. They teach that the only remedy for sin is the vicarious atonement of the Lord Jesus Christ. Strong emphasis is also laid on the church as the body and bride of Christ. A figurative, rather than literal, view is prevalent with reference to the book of Revelation. Church membership is contingent upon an individual's faith in Jesus Christ as the only begotten Son of God, repentance, confession of faith, and baptism by immersion for the remission of sins. Church attendance is stressed. Churches of Christ maintain that the final judgment of all religious groups is reserved to the Lord. This view, however, still allows for a vigorous evangelism that finds unacceptable the "doctrines, practices, names, titles, and creeds that have been grafted onto the original practice of Christianity."

The most conservative congregations reject instrumental music and use only a capella singing in worship, but that practice appears to be declining. There are some pastors who espouse premillennial theology, but only about twelve thousand persons are members of those congregations. Increasingly Churches of Christ congregations are adopting the style of other American evangelical denominations.

Clergy are ordained rather than licensed, and they hold tenure in their pulpits under mutual agreement with the elders of the churches in which they preach. Ministerial authority is essentially moral; the actual governance of the church is vested in its elders. A vigorous missionary program is carried on in over ninety nations outside the U.S. Churches of Christ support twenty-four Bible colleges, liberal arts colleges, and universities and twenty-seven high schools and/or elementary schools in the U.S. They also sponsor numerous facilities for care of the aged. The church publishes over one hundred periodicals, newspapers, and magazines.

For more information: www.church-of-christ.org

Contact: P.O. Box 726, Kosciusko, MS 39090

INTERNATIONAL CHURCHES OF CHRIST

Founded: 1979
Membership: est. 79,161 in 99 churches (2008)

The International Churches of Christ is the most controversial body to emerge from the Restorationist movement, and many of its former members describe it in negative terms. It was founded by Kip McKean (1955–) while he was serving as pastor of the Lexington Church of Christ in Massachusetts. McKean was an evangelist in the Crossroads movement, which Charles Lucas began in Gainesville, Florida, in the 1960s. The ICC utilizes many of the principles of Crossroads evangelism. This includes intensive recruitment of members, especially among college students and other young adults without a church community. They call their evangelical method "discipling," which means that members of the church commit themselves as disciples and vow to bring new disciples into the fold. Discipling is based on strict obedience to the "discipler." All personal decisions, including dating and marriage, are subject to the approval of the discipler. Members are expected to confess all of their sins, which may be recorded for future reference.

Members are carefully instructed in scripture according to the interpretation provided by McKean, who serves as the top of a pyramid structure of authority and obedience. The ICC, unlike the other Restorationist churches, is not congregational in polity. All congregations are linked in a pyramid structure with McKean's Los Angeles congregation at the top. The ICC teaches that believers' baptism by immersion is necessary for salvation. Those not baptized into the International Churches of Christ are considered damned, and members are urged to sever ties with those not baptized. All members are expected to devote their personal time to evangelism and discipling of new members.

For more information: www.icoc.org

Headquarters: 530 Wilshire Blvd., Ste. 1750, Los Angeles, CA 90010

Adventist and Sabbatarian (Hebraic) Churches

Throughout the history of Christianity there have been communities and individuals who have awaited the return of Jesus Christ with eager anticipation. From the evidence of the New Testament, it appears that the expectation of the imminent return of the resurrected Christ was widespread among the first generation of Christians. As the apostolic age passed without the Second Coming, hope in the immediate return of Christ waned and the church adjusted to the delay of the return of Christ. In place of the earlier fervent hope in the end of history and the consummation of the messianic mission, the church placed its faith in the ongoing presence of the risen Christ through Scripture, sacrament, and faith. However, when the New Testament canon was sealed in the fourth century, it included many writings about the end of time, the most famous of which is the book of Revelation, also known as the Apocalypse. The symbolic language of the Apocalypse, combined with the speculations of Paul in the letters to the Thessalonians, apocalyptic statements by Jesus in the Gospels, and the Old Testament book of Daniel, gave ample scope for the imagination of the faithful for centuries.

The hope that Christ would soon return to rule the world in justice and peace was particularly strong in the United States following the American Revolution. Even the phrase "the New World" conjured up images of the millennial kingdom long awaited. Ordinary farmers and merchants had defeated the world's greatest military power, had thrown off the rule of the king, and were creating a new nation. It seemed to many, even men such as John Adams, that the millennial age was dawning and that Christ would soon appear to take up his rightful throne. The Second Great Awakening, a series of revivals that swept across the Western frontier in the early decades of the nineteenth century, added fuel to this fire as reports about the phenomenal activity of the Holy Spirit in converting lost souls circulated around the nation.

The Adventist family of churches in the United States was born in this era of new possibilities and great hopes. Today regarded as conservative Protestants, Adventists were originally seen as dangerous radicals because of their intense focus on the Second Advent (or Second Coming) of Jesus Christ. By 1844, Adventist groups could be recognized as a distinct religious body separated from the traditional Protestant churches. Modern Adventism began as an interchurch movement whose most vocal proponent was William Miller (1782–1849) of New York, a veteran of the War of 1812. Miller had experienced conversion from skeptical deism to evangelical Christianity in 1816, during the Second Great Awakening. He became an ardent student of Scripture. Using a Bible that contained the famous chronology of Archbishop Ussher (1581-1656), Miller concentrated his attention on the prophecies of the end time in Daniel and Revelation.

Accepting the usual interpretation that the symbolic day of Bible prophecy represents one year, Miller concluded that the 2,300 days of Daniel 8:14 started concurrently with the seventy weeks of years of Daniel 9, which he claimed referred to 457 B.C.E., the year of the command to rebuild and restore Jerusalem. Miller believed that the 2,300 "days" would end in or about the year 1843, as calculated by Jewish reckoning. Miller thought that the sanctuary mentioned in Daniel 8:14 was the earth (or the church), which would be cleansed by fire at the Second Advent and that this cleansing would occur sometime between March 21, 1843 and March 21, 1844.

Miller's writings struck a chord in the popular culture of the 1830s. A New England pastor published an entire hymnal, *The Millennial Harp*, devoted to the theme of the imminent return of Christ and the restoration of paradise on earth. Miller himself made speaking tours in which he used elaborate charts and chronologies to support his reading of end-time prophecies. All of his research supported his central claim that the Advent would occur in the spring of 1844. Between fifty and one hundred thousand people in the United States believed in Miller's calculations and looked forward to the great day when the world would be cleansed and the righteous would meet Christ.

When March and April passed, and this expectation failed to materialize, some devotees left the movement and returned to their former churches. However, Miller's associates, on the basis of the study of Old Testament typology, arrived at a second date, October 22, 1844. This was to be the great Day of Atonement, prefigured in the Mosaic Law. When October 22 also passed with no Second Coming, vast numbers faced up to what has been termed "the Great Disappointment." Many gave up on Adventism; some gave up on the Christian faith itself; others simply gave up the desire to fix a date for the Advent. Out of the ashes of the disappointment, new Adventist bodies arose, divided over the relevance of Miller's original interpretations.

The largest group concluded that the 2,300 years in the prophecy of Daniel 8 would end sometime in the unknown future. They formed a loosely knit organization in Albany, New York, in 1845, and held generally to Miller's teaching. This included the personal and premillennial character of the Second Advent, which means that Christ will return in person, not in spirit, before the millennial kingdom comes into being. They also taught that the resurrection of the dead happens in two stages. The faithful are to be raised at Christ's coming, but the rest of humanity will rise a thousand years later. Furthermore, the earth will be redeemed and restored as an eternal abode of the faithful. Known at first as the American Millennial Association, a portion later came to be called the Evangelical Adventist Church. That church has now dwindled to the point of obscurity. The churches discussed in this section of the *Handbook* developed out of the minority bodies that formed after the Disappointment.

Despite the differences between the various groups, Adventism as a whole is based on the conviction that the Second Advent of Christ is the sole hope of the world. The present age is evil and irredeemable, except through the direct action of God. Adventism holds that humanity's nature is fallen because of sin and that those who rebel against the government of God will be ultimately destroyed, while believers, by God's grace, will be saved. After that cataclysmic event, Jesus Christ will reign in triumph through the thousand-year period, or millennium, of Revelation 20:1-6. This idea became central to Fundamentalism*.

Adventists are pessimistic about the present age, but they are filled with confidence and hope for God's future. In the meantime, they teach that God's people must be righteous, devout, and disciplined. Those who would be saved should practice a wholesome personal and family life, as well as a life of obedience to God. They should also work diligently toward the evangelization of the whole world in preparation for the return of Christ. There are still differing understandings among Adventists. Are the dead conscious or unconscious as they await the resurrection? Who are to arise: both the righteous and the wicked or only the righteous? Is there to be eternal punishment or ultimate annihilation for the wicked? What is the nature of immortality? Does the cleansing of the sanctuary in Daniel 8 refer to a sanctuary in heaven or to one on earth? Answers to these questions have served to divide various Adventist groups.

Though Adventism looks to the future, it has encouraged people to examine the Old Testament. In general, the different Adventist groups have viewed the Old Testament as prefiguring the coming millennial kingdom. Therefore it gives a reliable guide to God's will for the church. As a result, many of those influenced by Adventist teaching in the nineteenth century adopted many features of the Mosaic Law; some observe the Jewish Sabbath; others use the name "Jehovah" for God.

Suggestions for further reading:

Beckford, James A. *The Trumpet of Prophecy: A Sociological Study of Jehovah's Witnesses.* Oxford: Basil Blackwell, 1975.

Bull, Malcolm and Keith Lockhart. *Seeking a Sanctuary: Seventh Day Adventism and the American Dream.* San Francisco: Harper Row, 1989.

Davidson, James West. *The Logic of Millennial Thought: Eighteenth Century New England.* New Haven: Yale University Press, 1977.

Dick, Everett N. *William Miller and the Adventist Crisis, 1831-1844.* Berrien Springs, Mich.: Andrews University Press, 1994.

Doan, Ruth A. *The Miller Heresy, Millennialism, and American Culture.* Philadelphia: Temple University Press, 1987.

Gausad, Edwin, ed. *The Rise of Adventism: Religion and Society in mid-nineteenth Century America.* New York: Harper and Row, 1974.

Neufeld, Don. F., ed. *Seventh-Day Adventist Encyclopedia.* Rev. ed. Washington, DC: Review and Herald Publishing, 1961.

Penton, James. *Apocalypse Delayed: The Story of Jehovah's Witnesses.* Toronto: University of Toronto Press, 1985.

ADVENT CHRISTIAN CHURCH GENERAL CONFERENCE

Founded: 1860
Membership: 23,629 in 294 churches (2007)

The Advent Christian Church grew out of the main body of Adventists* who reorganized in 1845 following the Great Disappointment. While William Miller was not directly involved in the founding of this church, his preaching and teachings concerning the Second Coming of Christ formed the basis for Advent Christian theological, biblical, and organizational thought. They reject the prophecies of Ellen Harmon White (see SEVENTH-DAY ADVENTIST) and accept the Bible as the only source of authoritative teaching. The denomination maintains no formal creedal statement, but does have a declaration of principles. Two sacraments are observed: baptism (of adults by immersion) and the Lord's Supper. Worship is held on the first day of the week rather than on the Sabbath.

Like several Adventist groups, they teach the doctrine of conditional immortality, which states that only the redeemed receive everlasting life. The dead await the resurrection in an unconscious state; when Christ returns, all will rise and face the final judgment. The righteous will be given immortality, but the wicked will suffer eternal extinction as opposed to eternal torment. After the final judgment and destruction of the wicked, Christ will restore the earth and make it the eternal home for the just.

The first Advent Christian General Conference in 1860 was followed closely by the founding of publications, missions societies, and Aurora University. In 1964, Advent Christian Church merged with Life and Advent Union. Congregational in polity, the church is grouped in five regional districts in the U.S. and Canada. The General Conference meets every three years and maintains denominational offices in Charlotte, North Carolina, which oversee work in missions, urban ministries, church growth, Christian education, publications, administration, women's ministries, and public relations. The denomination also maintains missions in Japan, Mexico, India, Nigeria, Ghana, South Africa, Honduras, the Philippines, and Malaysia.

For more information: www.adventchristian.org

Headquarters: P.O. Box 23152, Charlotte, NC 28227

BRANCH DAVIDIANS

Founded: 1942
Membership: less than 5,000

Largely unknown before 1993, the Branch Davidians became world famous through their fifty-one-day standoff against federal authorities. Relatively unimportant in the current scope of American Christianity, the Davidians remain of historical and social interest. The events of April 19, 1993, which ended in the fiery deaths of over eighty members, including children, is one of the most tragic and spectacular episodes in American religious history. The members who lived at Mt. Carmel Center, a compound near Waco, Texas, followed their self-proclaimed messiah, David Koresh (1959–1993). Koresh commanded resistance against government officials whom he saw as the armies of the antichrist inaugurating the final apocalyptic battle. It is generally accepted that it was Koresh himself who ignited the fire that took the lives of almost all Davidians still living there. The anniversary of the conflagration has become an important date for anti-government extremist groups unrelated to the Davidians. It figured in the terrorist attack in Oklahoma City that killed over two hundred persons, including dozens of children in a day-care center.

This group of radical sectarians is a subset of one offshoot of the Adventist movement. They trace a lineage to 1930, when Victor T. Houteff, a Seventh-day Adventist church member in Los Angeles, expounded his new and, he claimed, divinely inspired message in a book, *The Shepherd's Rod*. Houteff found that his prophecies were not acceptable to the Seventh-day Adventist leadership, and in 1935 he took his followers to central Texas. Living under theocratic rule, Houteff's followers awaited the Second Coming of Christ, who would assume the leadership of the Davidic kingdom on earth. The group broke completely with the Seventh-day Adventists in 1942, and Houteff named his group the Davidian Seventh-day Adventists. In the decades following, various power struggles and disappointments over failed prophecies led to further divisions among the Davidians. Houteff died in 1955, and eventually the group in Waco became known as the Branch Davidians, apparently from one leader's statement that members should move onto a living branch.

David Koresh assumed the mantle of leadership over the Waco group in 1986, and the community became ever more isolated and defensive. He associated the events of the twentieth century with the prophecies of Revelation and urged his followers to prepare for the coming cataclysm, which would destroy and purify the earth as part of the final judgment. Influenced by the "survivalist" literature that proliferated during the Cold War era and fueled militia movements, Koresh and his followers began stockpiling food and arms as they prepared to fight for the "Lamb of God" (i.e. Koresh himself). Reports of the acquisition of a large cache of weapons and of the sexual abuse of children sparked the interest of the

U.S. Attorney General. After a lengthy siege, during which Koresh proclaimed his messianic rule, the compound was consumed by fire.

The General Association of the Branch Davidian Seventh Day Adventists has repudiated Koresh and his teaching. They are headquartered in Kingsland, Texas.

For more information: www.the-branch.org

Headquarters: The Branch, P.O. Box 1004, Kingsland, Texas 78639

CHRISTADELPHIANS

Founded: 1844
Membership: est. 15,000 in 170 ecclesias (2000)

Though Adventist and Unitarian* in theology, the Christadelphians actually have their roots in the Disciples of Christ*. When John Thomas (1805–1871) came to the United States from England in 1832, he joined the Disciples, but he eventually decided that the Disciples neglected many important biblical doctrines. In 1844, he founded a number of societies that preached the need for a return to primitive Christianity. Loosely organized, those various societies bore no name until the outbreak of the Civil War, when their members' doctrine of nonresistance forced them to adopt a name in order to avoid the draft. They chose the term *Christadelphians*, or Brothers of Christ.

Christadelphians reject belief in the devil and maintain that the scriptures teach that Christ was not pre-existent but was born of Mary by the Holy Spirit, that is, by the power of God. Humankind is mortal by nature, and Christ is the only means of salvation. Eternal life comes only to the righteous. In the U.S., some Christadelphians, called Unamended, believe Christ will raise only those who died in the faith; all other persons will simply remain dead, without consciousness. Other Christadelphians, known as Amended, believe that Christ will raise all responsible persons, rewarding the righteous and annihilating the wicked. Both groups believe the faithful will be gathered together, and the world will be ruled from Jerusalem for a thousand years. They hold the Bible to be the inspired Word of God, inerrant in its original text.

The church is congregational in policy; local organizations are known as ecclesias. Membership is by profession of faith, and baptism is by immersion. There are no paid or ordained ministers in the usual sense. Women take no part in public speech or prayer, though all vote equally in the affairs of the ecclesia. Christadelphians do not vote in civil elections or participate in war, and they refuse to accept public office. There are no associations or conventions, but there are fraternal gatherings for spiritual inspiration. Many meetings are held in rented halls, schools, or private homes, though a number of ecclesias have their own buildings. Foreign missions and ecclesias are found in sixty countries.

235

For more information: www.christadelphia.org
Headquarters: 1000 Mohawk Dr., Elgin, IL 60120-3148

CHURCH OF GOD (SEVENTH DAY)

Founded: 1863
Membership: est. 11,000 in 185 churches (1999)

Like the larger Seventh-day Adventist Church*, the founders of the Church of God believed that Christians should observe the Sabbath; however, this body rejected Ellen Harmon White's visions (see SEVENTH-DAY ADVENTIST) and separated in 1858 from other Sabbath-keeping Adventists. A similar group of anti-White Sabbatarians who had organized themselves in Iowa in 1860 joined the Michigan branch in 1863. Several denominational designations were used in its early history, including Church of Christ and Church of Jesus Christ. The present name was chosen in 1884, and the words "Seventh Day" were added in 1923.

In 1933, owing in part to disparate views on polity and administration, the church divided into two groups. An attempted merger in 1949 led to some realignment of membership and the relocation of the headquarters to Denver, Colorado. Those who did not join the merger maintained their headquarters at Salem, West Virginia and use "7th Day" rather than "Seventh Day" in its name. The Salem body claims a membership of about a thousand in seven churches. Both groups follow basic Adventist teaching on the reign of Christ and the extermination of the wicked. In addition to baptism and the Lord's Supper, this body practices footwashing. The Salem body also claims a "Biblical organization," which means that the numbers 7, 12, and 70 have particular relevance in church organization. They also teach that the physical Church of God (7th Day) is the "true church." The national organization headquartered in Denver supports Spring Vale Academy, a residential high school in Michigan, and the Summit School of Theology in Denver.

For more information: www.cog7.org
Headquarters: P.O. Box 33677, Denver, CO, 80233

CHURCH OF GOD AND SAINTS OF CHRIST

Founded: 1896
Membership: est. 40,000 in approx. 200 congregations (1999)

The Church of God and Saints of Christ is a Christian body that tries to live according to a literal understanding of Old Testament law. As such, they are sometimes called "Christian Israelites" or "Black Jews"; however, they have no direct relationship to historical Judaism.* Though not properly Adventist, they do share similarities with Adventists groups that emphasize the Mosaic Law and continuing relevance of prophecy.

The church was begun by William Saunders Crowdy (1847–1908), who was born to slave parents in Maryland. After serving in the Union Army, Crowdy bought a farm near Guthrie, Oklahoma. Active in the Baptist church, in 1893 Crowdy began having disturbing visions and hearing voices. He dreamed of tables covered in filth, each of which had the name of a denomination. Then he saw a clean table that came down from heaven; on it was the name "Church of God and Saints of Christ." Crowdy began preaching on the streets in towns and villages in the Midwest and in November of 1896 he formally organized his church in Lawrence, Kansas. Arrested numerous times because of his ministry, he made converts in prison as well.

In a vision, he received "The Seven Keys," which form the core set of doctrines: repentance of sin; baptism by burial into water upon confession of faith; unleavened bread and water for Christ's body and blood; foot washing by elders; obedience to the commandments; the holy kiss; and the Lord's Prayer. In Philadelphia he founded a church and also several businesses; the Church of God and Saints of Christ continues to stress the importance of individual enterprise and business acumen as marks of religious life.

Crowdy taught that his followers should celebrate a number of Jewish holy and feast days. Of particular importance are the observance of the Sabbath, Passover, the Day of Atonement, and the Jewish New Year. Members believe their church is built on the patriarchs and prophets of the Jewish tradition, and "Jesus the Anointed" is their chief cornerstone. They differentiate between prophetic Judaism from "legalistic" Judaism. They accept the Decalogue as the standard of conduct for all humankind. Men and women are instructed to wear particular clothing on the Sabbath according to the season of the year, and men are expected to wear the yarmulke and a tallith.

An executive bishop stands at the head of the church and of the bishops' council; the church maintains headquarters in Cleveland, Ohio. The *Newsletter*, published every two weeks, serves to inform members through sermons, lectures, and announcements. An a cappella choir formed of members of the church has released recordings of gospel music to critical acclaim.

For more information: www.cogasoc.net

Headquarters: 100 South Mulberry Street, Hagerstown, MD 21740

CHURCH OF GOD GENERAL CONFERENCE

Founded: 1921, with roots to the 1840s
Membership: 7,634 in 162 churches (2004)

This church is the outgrowth of several independent local groups of similar faith, some in existence as early as 1800; others date their beginnings from the arrival of British immigrants to this country around 1847. These diverse groups shared in general Adventist theology. A national organization was instituted at Philadelphia in 1888 and 1889; however, because of strong convictions relating to congregational rights and authority, the national body ceased to function until 1921, when the present general conference was formed at Waterloo, Iowa. The corporate name today is Church of God General Conference, Morrow, Georgia.

Members of the Church of God General Conference accept the Bible as the supreme and literal standard of faith. They teach that when Christ returns, he will establish a literal kingdom of God on earth. The Church of God is Arian, teaching the absolute oneness of God and that Christ as the Son of God did not exist prior to the birth of Jesus. The Holy Ghost is the power and influence of God on earth until the return of Christ. The church also promotes the belief in the restoration of Israel as a kingdom at the time of restitution. As with many other Adventist groups, the Church of God General Conference denies the immortality of the soul. The righteous will receive their reward on earth, but the wicked will be completely destroyed in a second death.

Due to the congregational nature of the church's government, the general conference exists primarily as a means of mutual cooperation and development of yearly projects and enterprises. The general conference supports Atlanta Bible College for the training of pastors; a Publishing Department; and an Outreach and Church Development Department, which promotes youth work, mission, and evangelism in preparation for the return of Christ on earth. Mission stations are located in India, Mexico, the Philippines, Malawi, Mozambique, Great Britain, and Peru.

For more information: www.abc-coggc.org
Headquarters: P.O. Box 100, Morrow, GA 30260-7000

GRACE COMMUNION INTERNATIONAL (ORIGINALLY THE WORLDWIDE CHURCH OF GOD)

Founded: 1934
Membership: est. 43,000 (2007)

Formerly known as the Worldwide Church of God, this church has one of the most distinctive histories in American Christianity. The original WCG divided into several bodies in the last decades of the twentieth century. The largest group, which retained legal right to the name Worldwide Church of God, has become a typical evangelical church and adopted a new name in 2006, but the Worldwide Church of God was originally characterized by the adoption of many Sabbatarian and Mosaic practices.

Originally known as the Radio Church of God, the WCG began its work in 1934 under the leadership of Herbert W. Armstrong (1892–1986). The mission of the church was to proclaim the gospel of Jesus Christ around the world and to help members grow spiritually. The church grew rapidly from 1964 to 1974, but controversy erupted in the 1970s. Garner Ted Armstrong, the founder's son, was "disfellowshiped" on four occasions for adultery, and in 1978 he took part of the membership with him when he founded the rival Church of God International, which never flourished. The original church weathered another bitter legal battle over control of finances, and its situation became more unstable in the 1980s. After Herbert Armstrong's death in 1986, Joseph W. Tkach became Pastor General. Tkach and his son, Joseph W. Tkach, Jr., led the church through an experience nothing short of religious conversion in the late 1980s and 1990s. The church officially repudiated many of Armstrong's most distinctive teachings.

The elder Armstrong saw himself as the apostle-messenger of the Last Days and so assumed absolute authority in the organization. Congregations generally worshipped in rented facilities or private homes rather than building separate structures. At the time of his death, he left a church with some 120,000 members, a budget of two hundred million dollars, and a publication, *Plain Truth*, with a circulation of eight million copies a month. His organization was a worldwide ministry, with churches in a hundred countries and territories, carried out from a headquarters in Pasadena, California.

The Worldwide Church of God held to some traditional Christian teachings, but it maintained several distinctive theological ideas. Accepting a number of Jewish (see JUDAISM) observances as scripturally mandated, the church observed the Lord's Supper, or Passover of Jesus Christ, annually as a memorial of the death of Jesus. The Sabbath (Friday sunset to Saturday sunset) was honored as a day of worship. Seven annual holy days were kept, and certain "unclean" meats were avoided. Holidays, such as Halloween, Easter, and Christmas, were condemned as pagan. The three ordinances of baptism, the Lord's Supper, and foot washing were practiced. Such was Armstrong's theological conviction that he did not acknowledge as Christian those who failed to keep the Sabbath.

Under the leadership of the Tkaches, the Worldwide Church of God made a dramatic theological turn, essentially moving to an evangelical position. Key changes included an affirmation of the Trinity (1993) and renunciation of Old Testament covenant laws (1994). The church issued formal apologies for "doctrinal errors" to the wider Christian community, and in 1997 it was accepted as a member of the National Association of Evangelicals. The wholesale transformation of the WCG into an evangelical church is one of the singular events in American religious history. The church practices believer's baptism by immersion and does not promote Pentecostal practices.

The church recently changed its name to Grace Communion International to reflect its new identity and to reduce confusion with other "Church of God" bodies. The church acknowledges that it "has changed radically from what we once were to what we are today." (www.graceci.org) Many adherents were disillusioned by the changes following Armstrong's death, and thousands left the church (see PHILADELPHIA CHURCH OF GOD). Hundreds of staff were laid off, finances and programs were depleted, radio and television ministries were cut back, and the church's educational institution, Ambassador University, was closed. In 1996, Plain Truth Ministries separated from the WCG to form an independent non-profit media ministry that publishes *The Plain Truth* and offers online ministry. It has no legal connection to the church. Grace Communion International publishes *Christian Odyssey* magazine and provides video programs on its website. It offers online undergraduate courses through Ambassador College of Christian Ministry and graduate training online through Grace Communion Seminary.

For more information: www.graceci.org

Headquarters: P.O. Box 5005, Glendora, CA 91740

JEHOVAH'S WITNESSES

Founded: ca. 1870
Membership: 1,005,789 in 12,635 congregations (2008)

The Jehovah's Witnesses are among the most zealous religious bodies in terms of promotion of their beliefs. Meeting in Kingdom Halls (not in churches), members witness and publish their faith in a remarkably comprehensive missionary effort. They do not believe in a separation of clergy and laity, since "Christ Jesus did not make such a separation," and they never use titles like "Reverend." All members are expected to give generously of their time in proclaiming their faith and teaching in private homes. Called "publishers of the Kingdom," they preach only from the Bible. Pioneers, or full-time preachers, are required to give at least seventy hours per month; special pioneers and missionaries donate a minimum of 140 hours per month and are sent to isolated areas and foreign lands where new congregations can be formed. All pioneers provide for their own support, but the society gives a small allowance to some, in view of their special needs. This missionary activity has made Jehovah's Witnesses one of the most widely known (although not widely understood) churches in the U.S.

It was Charles Taze Russell (1852–1916) who established the Witnesses, and until 1931 they were known as Russellites, Millennial Dawn People, or

International Bible Students. Russell, the first president, is acknowledged not as founder (there is no human founder) but as general organizer. Witnesses claim they have been on earth as an organization for more than five thousand years (based on Isaiah 43:10-12; Hebrews 11; John 18:37).

Russell was deeply influenced by Adventist thought, which captivated American attention around the middle of the nineteenth century. He developed his own Adventist ideas based on personal study of the Bible, and his lectures attracted huge crowds. To date, some thirteen million copies of his books have been circulated, and they have profoundly influenced the Witnesses.

The first formal Russellite group was organized in Pittsburgh, Pennsylvania, in 1870, and soon after a board of directors was elected by vote of all members who subscribed ten dollars or more to support the work (a practice discontinued in 1944). In 1884, Zion's Watch Tower Tract Society was incorporated. In 1939, the name of this corporation was changed to Watch Tower Bible and Tract Society of Pennsylvania, and it remains one of the world's largest publishers. When Russell died in 1916, Joseph F. Rutherford (1869–1942), known widely as Judge Rutherford, became president. He had been a lawyer and occasionally sat as a circuit court judge in Missouri. His numerous books, pamphlets, and tracts supplanted those of Russell, but his neglect of some aspects of Russell's teaching brought dissension.

The vast literature of the Witnesses (all circulated without bylines or signatures) quotes extensively from the Bible and relates the eschatological teachings of the church. Witness theology is based on the idea of theocracy, or rule of God. It teaches that there is only one God, Jehovah; Jesus is not God. In the beginning, the world was under the theocratic rule of the Almighty. At that time all was "happiness, peace, and blessedness." But Satan rebelled and became the ruler of the world, and from that moment, humankind has followed his evil leading. Then Jesus, the first creation of Jehovah, came to earth as a human being. Jesus was "the beginning of the creation of God" (Rev. 3:14, KJV), as the prophets had predicted, to end Satan's rule.

Witnesses maintain that Jesus' heavenly rule, after he paid the ransom sacrifice of his death on earth, began in 1914. Russell had seen World War I as the final apocalyptic struggle that would usher in the return of Christ. When that did not happen, Rutherford reorganized the movement and announced in 1918 that Christ then "came to the temple of Jehovah." With Jesus now enthroned in the temple of Jehovah, the rule of Satan was nearly over, and so Rutherford began to send out his followers to preach the good news in the final days.

God, according to Witness belief, will take vengeance on wicked human beings in our time. God is now showing great love by "gathering out" multitudes of people of goodwill, to whom God will give life in the new world that is to come after the battle of Armageddon. This is to be a universal battle; Christ will lead the army of the righteous, composed of the "host of heaven, the holy angels," and they will completely annihilate the army of Satan. The righteous of the earth will watch the battle and the suffering of God's enemies, but they will not participate.

After the battle, Witnesses teach, the believers in God and God's servants will remain on the earth. Those who have proven their integrity in the old world will multiply and populate the new earth with righteous people. A resurrection of the righteous will also take place, as an additional means of filling the cleansed earth with better inhabitants. After the Great Tribulation, "righteous princes" will rule the earth under Christ, "King of the Great Theocracy." One special group—the 144,000 Christians mentioned in Revelation 7 and 14—will become the "bride of Christ" and rule with him in heaven.

The governing body today is in the hands of older and more "spiritually qualified" men who base their judgments on the authority of Scripture. This is not considered a governing hierarchy, but an imitation of early apostolic Christian organization. Under direction of the leaders at headquarters, local congregations of Witnesses (always called congregations, never churches) are arranged in circuits, with a traveling minister who spends a week with each congregation. Approximately twenty congregations are included in each circuit, and circuits are grouped into districts, with more than forty in the U.S.; circuit organizations are now found in over two hundred countries and islands around the world.

The headquarters is located at Bethel Home in Brooklyn, New York. Staff engage primarily in editorial and printing work and receive an allowance of forty-five dollars a month, in addition to room and board. They write, print, and distribute literature in almost astronomical proportions. The official journal, *The Watchtower*, has a circulation of 25.6 million. More than one billion Bibles, books, and leaflets have been distributed since 1920; they are made available in nearly three hundred languages.

Although expectations of Armageddon have repeatedly been disappointed, Witnesses maintain their belief in its imminence. They have been especially active in opposing what they consider the three allies of Satan: false teachings of the churches, tyranny of human governments, and oppression by big business. This "triple alliance" of ecclesiastical, political, and commercial powers has misled humankind, the Witnesses claim, and must be destroyed at Armageddon before the new world can be born. They refuse to salute the national flag, bear arms in war, or participate in the political affairs of government, not because of pacifist convictions, but because they desire to remain apart from what they consider expressions of Satan's power over humankind.

This attitude has brought them into conflict with law enforcement agencies; they have also endured whippings, assaults by mobs, stonings, being tarred and feathered, the burning of their homes, imprisonment, and detention in concentration camps. All of this they have accepted in a submissive spirit. Their position is that they will obey the laws of the earth when those laws are not in conflict with the laws of God.

For more information: www.jw.org
Headquarters: Watch Tower Society, 25 Columbia Heights, Brooklyn, NY 11201-2483

PHILADELPHIA CHURCH OF GOD

Founded: 1989, with roots to 1934
Membership: over 5,000 in about 100 churches

The Philadelphia Church of God is one of the larger groups that remained committed to the teachings of Herbert Armstrong after the Worldwide Church of God adopted a more traditional evangelical perspective in the 1980s. George Flurry organized the PCG in 1989 to hold strictly to Armstrong's teachings, especially as outlined in the book *Mystery of the Ages*. Armstrong founded the Radio Church of God in 1934, and he viewed himself as the apostle-messenger of the Last Days. Eventually the name of the church was changed to the Worldwide Church of God. Armstrong believed this church was the Philadelphian church described in Revelation 3:7-13 as the true church, and so Flurry adopted the name Philadelphian for his group. At the time of his death, the Worldwide Church of God had about one 120,000 members and a budget of over two hundred million dollars (see GRACE COMMUNION INTERNATIONAL). Armstrong's magazine *Plain Truth* had a circulation of eight million copies a month. When his successor Joseph Tkach repudiated some of Armstrong's beliefs, several splinter groups were formed.

Armstrong held to many traditional Christian teachings, but he also promoted several distinctive theological ideas. For instance, he taught that there is one God, who is the Father. Jesus was accepted as part of God's family and is divine, but Armstrong rejected the idea of the Trinity. The Holy Spirit was not a distinct person. Concerning human nature, the inspiration of the scriptures, Christ's bodily resurrection, and baptism, the church held traditional positions. Like many Adventist* groups, they took a strong stand against bearing arms and the taking of human life, and they rejected the concept of everlasting conscious torment in hell for the unsaved.

Armstrong also taught a number of Jewish (see JUDAISM) observances as scripturally mandated; the church observed the Lord's Supper, or Passover of Jesus Christ, annually as a memorial of the death of Jesus. The Sabbath (Friday sunset to Saturday sunset) was honored as a day of worship. Seven annual holy days were kept, and certain "unclean" meats were avoided. Holidays, such as Halloween, Easter, and Christmas, were condemned as pagan. The three ordinances of baptism, the Lord's Supper, and foot washing were practiced. Such was Armstrong's theological conviction that he did not acknowledge as Christian those who failed to keep the Sabbath. The church is also opposed to the theory of biological evolution.

The death of Herbert Armstrong caused a crisis in the Worldwide Church of God, and under the leadership of Joseph Tkach the church adopted more traditional Evangelical doctrines. Several splinter groups, such as the Global Church of God, United Church of God, and Restored Church of God, were formed to promote Armstrong's teaching. The Philadelphia Church of God holds strictly to Armstrong's teaching, including Armstrong's rejection of medical treatment. In 1995 several pastors left the PCG to form the United Church of God*. The PCG broadcasts on television and radio and publishes magazines and booklets.

For more information: www.pcog.org

Headquarters: P.O. Box 37000, Edmond, OK 73083.

SEVENTH-DAY ADVENTIST CHURCH

Founded: 1863
Membership: 1,004,419 in 4,958 churches (2007)

The Seventh-day Adventists have about seventeen million members in over two hundred countries. They hold to the doctrine of the Trinity and the Reformation emphases of *sola scriptura*, *sola fides*, and *sola gratias*. Their understanding of biblical teachings is encapsulated in *28 Fundamental Doctrines* which can only be modified by vote of the world assembly (called the General Conference Session), which meets every five years. The name of the church enshrines the heart of their beliefs and practices. Strongly committed to obedience to the teachings of the whole Bible, they observe the seventh day, Saturday, as the day of worship. As Adventists, they expect the near return of Jesus to this earth. Since their organization as a church, they have distanced themselves from efforts to set a date for the Second Coming.

The Seventh-day Adventist Church is the largest of the Adventist churches that arose during the upsurge in millennial anticipation in the United States in the early nineteenth century. William Miller, a farmer-preacher, predicted that Christ would return on October 22, 1844. The faithful prepared, prayed, and waited, but their hopes of seeing the returning Lord were dashed. One of the small Adventist groups that emerged from the Disappointment was a seventh-day Sabbath group that reinterpreted the events of October 1844. It was not an earthly event that took place on that prophesied day, but an event in heaven itself.

As early as 1844, a small group of Adventists near Washington, New Hampshire, had begun to observe the Sabbath on the seventh day. A pamphlet written by Joseph Bates in 1846 gave the issue wide publicity and created great interest. Shortly thereafter, Bates, together with James White, Ellen Harmon (later Mrs.

James White), Hiram Edson, Frederick Wheeler, and S. W. Rhodes, with the aid of regular publications, set out to champion the seventh-day Sabbath, along with the imminence of the Second Advent. In the 1850s they set up headquarters at Battle Creek, Michigan, and began publishing a weekly magazine called *Review and Herald*. In 1860 the name Seventh-day Adventist was officially adopted, and in 1903 the headquarters was moved to Washington, D.C. Its present location is in Silver Spring, Maryland.

Ellen Harmon White (1827-1915) was the key figure in this rejuvenation of Adventism, and the church believes that she had the gift of prophecy. When she was only in her teens, she began having visions and receiving messages from heaven. Her visions contributed to the development of the new Seventh-day Adventist Church, doctrinally and structurally. She counseled, preached, taught, traveled, and wrote extensively (almost twenty-five million words). White believed that the Bible is the judge and test of all other revelations.

Seventh-day Adventists believe in creation by divine fiat and recognize the fall of the human race through the sin of Adam. They teach that humans are by nature mortal, but may receive immortality through divine grace and the redemption effected through the atoning work of Jesus Christ. They believe that the dead await the resurrection in an unconscious state until the whole person (body, mind, and soul) is resurrected on the last day when Christ will return in person. The righteous will then receive immortality, while the wicked are destroyed by fire. When Christ returns a new earth will be created out of the ruins of the old, and this will be the final home of the redeemed. Adventists practice baptism of adults by immersion and the practice of foot washing in preparation for Holy Communion. They also encourage members to tithe their income for support of the church.

The church strongly emphasizes health and wellness, not as a means to salvation, but as a part of glorifying God in all of life. The church recommends following a vegetarian diet when possible. Adventists own and operate 168 hospitals and nearly six hundred other medical facilities worldwide. In addition, the church operates a network of health food factories and promotes public health. The church's Loma Linda University in Southern California is noted for its research and medical care.

Adventists operate an extensive worldwide system of elementary and secondary schools and own more than one hundred colleges and universities. They own more than sixty publishing houses, and their radio and television broadcasts reach nearly every country. The church broadcasts twenty-four hours a day from its global satellite system, the Hope Channel. The Adventist Development and Relief Agency (ADRA) distributes food and clothing around the world, particularly when disasters strike. The organization also drills wells, educates mothers on baby care and nutrition, helps farmers become self-sufficient, and ministers to those infected with HIV/AIDS.

For many years the church has been noted for its promotion of religious liberty and the separation of church and state. Through the International Religious Liberty Association, Adventists organize symposiums, congresses, meetings of experts, and large gatherings called Festivals of Religious Freedom. Adventists have also been involved in interchurch relationship for years. They are invited as observers to the meetings of the World Council of Churches and belong to the Conference of Secretaries of the Christian World Communions.

The church is organized in a representative form of government consisting of four steps. First is the local church made up of individual believers. Next is the local conference that covers a state or local territory. The union conference is a united body of local conferences. The General Conference embraces the worldwide church. Union conferences send delegates to the world session of the General Conference. The chaplain of the U.S. Senate, Admiral Barry Black, is a member of the church.

For more information: www.adventist.org

Headquarters: 12501 Old Columbia Pike, Silver Spring, MD 20904-6600

UNITED CHURCH OF GOD

Founded: 1995, with roots to 1934
Membership: 15,000 (est.) in 230 churches (2008)

The United Church of God is the largest denomination that still holds to the teachings of Herbert Armstrong, the founder of the Worldwide Church of God (see GRACE COMMUNION INTERNATIONAL). It was founded by several leaders in the Philadelphia Church of God* in 1995 who objected to the leadership of George Flurry. The United Church of God is open to the idea of salvation outside of its own denomination, and it has various accountability structures in place for finances and church administration. The church's mission is "to announce the coming of God's Kingdom, not to establish it." (www.ucg.org)

Like all of the descendents of the original Radio Church of God, the UCG makes extensive use of all forms of media, especially internet, to promote its message, which is grounded in the thought of Armstrong. The church is strongly Adventist, believing that the Second Coming is imminent, and it is the mission of the church to prepare people to live in the Kingdom of God as godly people. This includes the adoption of many practices in the Mosaic Law, particularly the observance of Saturday as the Sabbath. The church also teaches that Anglo-Saxon peoples are descendents of the biblical patriarch Joseph, and are thus really Israelites. The church is an international fellowship that operates in over fifty countries. Its primary publication is *Good News Magazine*, which is published in four languages. As with most Adventist groups, the church believes strongly that biblical prophecies will be fulfilled in history, and it interprets contemporary events in light of prophecy.

For more information: www.ucg.org

Headquarters: P. O. Box 541027, Cincinatti, OH 45245-1027

Unitarians and Universalists

Unitarianism and universalism represent two quite distinct theological ideas that were brought together with the formation of the Unitarian Universalist Association of Congregations in 1961. It is helpful to look at the separate history of these two movements before discussing the new institution that was established in the twentieth century.

Unitarian: The basic tenet of Unitarianism is that there is only one God and Jesus was thus not divine in essence. Unitarians often claim that their thought reaches back into the early Christian centuries before the concept of the Trinity was developed. Unitarianism as we know it today, however, began with the Protestant Reformation, among anti-trinitarians such as Michael Servetus (ca. 1511–1553) and Faustus Socinus (1539–1604). Some Anabaptists* in Switzerland, Hungary, Transylvania, Holland, Poland, and Italy held ideas similar to Unitarianism. In England Unitarianism was championed by the scientist and mathematician Isaac Newton (1642–1727), the philosopher John Locke (1632–1704), and the poet John Milton (1608–1674), but no attempt was made to organize the movement until late in the eighteenth century.

American Unitarianism developed in New England Congregational (see UNITED CHURCH OF CHRIST) churches that were known as Liberal Christian. The split within Congregationalism came into the open in 1805 when Henry Ware (1764–1845), a Unitarian, was appointed professor of theology at Harvard University, the bastion of Congregationalist education. The split widened in 1819 when William Ellery Channing (1780–1842) of Boston preached his famous Baltimore sermon outlining the Unitarian view. Channing defined the true church in these words: "By his Church our Savior does not mean a party bearing the name of a human leader, distinguished by a form or an opinion. . . . These are the church—men made better, made holy, virtuous by his religion—men who, hoping in his promises, keep his commands."

There are several Pentecostal* bodies, known as "Jesus Only" churches that espouse a form of Unitarian theology, but they are to be distinguished from Unitarians. Unitarians are generally very liberal theologically, politically, and socially. They reject the idea of the divinity of Jesus in favor of the oneness of

God unlike the "Jesus only" Pentecostals who proclaim that the one God was incarnate in Jesus.

Unitarians played a prominent role in nineteenth century reform movements such as abolition, women's suffrage, prison reform, and interreligious dialogue. Prominent Unitarians include Elizabeth Cady Stanton, Susan B. Anthony, John and Abigail Adams, Dorothea Dix, and Oliver Wendell Holmes. Almost half of the signers of the famous *Humanist Manifesto* were Unitarians, causing a division within the movement between theists and non-theists that was eventually healed.

Eventually Unitarian Congregationalists organized the American Unitarian Association in 1825 in order to work for the Kingdom of God and promote the religion that Jesus preached: love to God and love to humankind. Included in the plan was the expansion of liberal religion around the world. Independent local churches were grouped in local, county, district, state, and regional conferences and were united in an international association for purposes of fellowship, counsel, and promotion of mutual interests. In 1961, there were four Unitarian seminaries, two preparatory schools, 386 churches, and approximately 115,000 members.

Universalist. There are many forms of universalism, but in general the term refers to the belief that all persons will be saved regardless of religious belief or non-belief. Universalists find evidence of their thinking and philosophy in many cultural streams, and the teaching has much in common with several religions throughout the world. Universalists claim roots in the early Christian gnostics Origen of Alexandria (185-254 C.E.), certain Anabaptists, and radical Pietist* mystics such as Jacob Boehme (1575-1624).

In 1759, James Relly (1722-78) of England wrote *Union,* in which he opposed the Calvinistic doctrine of election of the few. Relly's conviction of universal salvation deeply influenced John Murray (1741-1815), a Wesleyan evangelist who came to New Jersey in 1770 and found groups of universalist-minded people scattered along the Atlantic coast. He became minister to one such group in Gloucester, Massachusetts, and later served briefly as a Revolutionary War chaplain in the armies of Washington and Greene. His Independent Christian Church of Gloucester became the first organized Universalist church in the U.S. in 1779.

A group of Universalists met at Philadelphia in 1790 to draft their first declaration of faith and plan of government. They promoted pacifism, abolition of slavery, testimony by affirmation rather than by oath, and free public education. This Philadelphia declaration was adopted by a group of New England Universalists in 1793. At about the same time, Hosea Ballou (1771-1852), a school teacher and itinerant preacher in Vermont, was ordained in the Universalist ministry. He broke radically with Murray's thought. His 1805 *Treatise on Atonement* gave Universalists their first consistent philosophy. In addition to the rationalist rejection of endless punishment in hell, the Trinity, and miracles, Ballou taught that God recognized humanity's heavenly nature and loved the human race as God's own offspring. The meaning of the atonement was not found in bloody sacrifice to appease divine wrath, but in the heroic sacrifice of Jesus, who wanted to win all persons to God's love.

Like the Unitarians, Universalists in the nineteenth century were active very early in reform movements for prison inmates and working women. They opposed slavery, stood for separation of church and state, and have maintained a continuing interest in the fields of science, labor, management, civil rights, and human concern. Universalists founded several non-sectarian colleges and universities, including Tufts, St. Lawrence, Goddard, and the California Institute of Technology. At the time of the merger, there were 68,949 members in 334 churches.

Suggestions for further reading:

Buehrens, John A., et al. *A Chosen Faith: An Introduction to Unitarian Universalism*. Boston: Beacon Press, 1998.

Robinson, David. *The Unitarians and the Universalists*. Westport, Conn. Greenwood Publishing, 1985.

Williams, George H. *American Universalism: A Bicentennial Historical Essay*. Boston: Universalist Historical Society, 1971.

AMERICAN UNITARIAN CONFERENCE

Founded: 2000
Membership statistics not available

This organization represents a rare institutional split in American Unitarianism, and it is still unclear how this new denomination will develop as an institution. The AUC developed from Carl Scovel's concern that the Unitarian Universalist Association's embrace of humanism and Eastern religious beliefs was crowding out Unitarian theism, which was the traditional understanding of the denomination. The AUC remains committed to the Unitarian principle of freedom in religion and tolerating a wide variety of religious beliefs while promoting monotheism. Central to the ethos of the AUC is that faith, reason, science, and religion should be seen as collaborative rather than competitive activities.

Among the denomination's principles are that God's presence is known in different ways and that revelation is continuing; religion should be a responsible search for meaning; that free will is a gift from God and religion should assist in the development of human ethics; that both reason and faith lead to humility and humility leads to tolerance; and finally the religious quest should lead to greater mercy and compassion in a world filled with suffering.

For more information: www.americanunitarian.org

Headquarters: 6806 Springfield Dr., Mason Neck, VA 22079

UNITARIAN UNIVERSALIST ASSOCIATION

Founded: 1961
Membership: 221,476 in 1,046 churches (2007)

In May 1961, the Unitarian and Universalist churches in the U.S. and Canada were consolidated as the Unitarian Universalist Association of Congregations in North America, one of the most influential liberal churches. The two bodies had separate and interesting origins and history (see above). In this association, flexibility, freedom of conscience, and local autonomy are prime values. No minister, member, or congregation is required to subscribe to any particular creed or statement of belief.

The aims of the association were set forth in 1985 in a revised statement that promotes human dignity, social justice and compassion, the free and responsible search for truth, democracy, the goal of global community, and respect for the environment. Increasingly since the merger in 1961 the UUA has embraced Eastern as well as Western religious practices, beliefs, and traditions.

In recent years the Association has been heavily involved in numerous causes and concerns: the issue of racial and cultural diversity; the rise of feminist consciousness; scholarship in church history and process theology; inner-city ministries; and the rights of gay, lesbian, and bisexual persons. The Unitarian Universalist Service Committee provides leadership and materials in the field of social change. The denomination has dozens of independent affiliate organizations that advocate and provide resources for various causes.

A General Assembly, with clergy and lay representatives, is the overall policy-making body, meeting annually. The officers of the Association are elected to four-year terms and serve together with other elected members as a Board of Trustees that appoints the executive and administrative officers and generally carries out policies and directives. In 2001, the UUA elected William Sinkford as its first African American head.

The headquarters are in Boston, and twenty-three district offices have been established. Principal numerical strength lies in the Northeast, the Midwest, and the Pacific West Coast. Foreign work is now conducted through the International Association for Religious Freedom. Beacon Press, which produces fifty new titles each year and is one of the most distinguished independent publishing houses in the U.S., is owned under the auspices of the UUA. There are two UUA seminaries, Meadville Lombard Theological School in Chicago and Starr King School for Ministry in Berkeley.

For more information: www.uua.org
Headquarters: 25 Beacon St., Boston, MA 02108

Pentecostal Churches

Pentecostalism is a modern American Christian movement that emerged out of the Holiness* movement around the turn of the twentieth century. Two key figures in the genesis of Pentecostalism were Charles Fox Parham (1873–1929), the founder of Bethel Bible College in Topeka, Kansas, and William J. Seymour (1870–1922), an African American Holiness evangelist from Louisiana. Through his study of Paul's letters, Parham became convinced that the gifts of the Holy Spirit that were evident in apostolic times are available to Christians in modern times as well. Of particular interest was speaking in tongues, the first incidence of which occurred at Bethel Bible College in 1901. Five years later, Seymour, who had studied at Bethel with Parham, led a revival on Azusa Street in Los Angeles that lasted for several months. Participants experienced a "baptism in the Holy Ghost." Some were healed of illnesses, while others spoke in tongues. Thousands from across the U.S. traveled to Azusa Street and carried the message back to their home states.

The movement eventually became known as "Pentecostal" because of its similarity to the first Pentecost, fifty days after Christ's resurrection, when the Spirit came upon the early Christians and enabled them to speak in unfamiliar languages. There are a great variety of Pentecostal churches, most of which are theologically and socially conservative. In general, Pentecostals are in the evangelical tradition and teach that the Holy Spirit continues to act as it did at the first Pentecost. Convinced that contemporary Christians can receive the same spiritual gifts that the apostles did, many Pentecostal churches use the word *apostolic* in their names.

Seeking and receiving the gift of tongues is regarded as a sign of the baptism of the Holy Spirit, and in many Pentecostal churches this is a requirement for full membership. Other spiritual gifts, such as healing, love, joy, prophecy, and answers to prayer, also make up Pentecostals' experience of God. Like the Baptists*, many Pentecostal churches refer to rites such as baptism as "ordinances" rather than as "sacraments." Pentecostals are generally less bound to traditional forms of worship than are other churches, and many have adapted contemporary music for evangelistic purposes.

The term "Neo-Pentecostalism" is often used to describe churches that embrace charismatic worship practices, such as speaking in tongues, but not the Holiness (see HOLINESS CHURCHES) tradition of the older Pentecostal bodies. In the 1960s Pentecostal beliefs and practices made in-roads in many liturgical churches, including the Roman Catholic* and Episcopal* Churches, but the term "charismatic" is used in mainline churches rather than "pentecostal." Charismatics tend to be less sectarian in orientation than Pentecostals, and they generally restrict overt displays of the gifts to private gatherings rather than public worship.

In general, Pentecostal denominations are Protestant and evangelical, but many were influenced by the fundamentalist* movement. They commonly hold to beliefs in original sin, salvation through the atoning blood of Christ, the virgin birth and deity of Jesus, the divine inspiration and literal infallibility of the scriptures, pre-millennialism (the return of Jesus Christ prior to his thousand-year reign on earth), and future rewards and punishments. Most Pentecostal churches practice baptism of believers (usually by immersion) and the Lord's Supper, but some of the smaller bodies also observe foot washing. Pentecostals are generally trinitarian; but they place greater emphasis on the direct action of the Holy Spirit, which is manifested in a "baptism in the Spirit" accompanied by spiritual gifts, rather than in creation.

Originally strongest among the rural peoples of the South and the Midwest, early Pentecostalism also found a home among the urban poor in the 1930s. Now the movement has spread to all fifty states and represents a cross-section of American society. For the most part, Pentecostal bodies do not have educational requirements for clergy. More important for them is evidence of the Spirit in a preacher's life and ministry. Many Pentecostal associations serve primarily as accrediting bodies for freelance ministers, and they tend to have far more clergy than congregations listed since many clergy do not have churches. In the 1980s and 1990s many Pentecostals in America grew prosperous, and several members of Pentecostal churches, such as former Attorney General John Ashcroft, rose to positions of prominence in national government.

The Pentecostal movement spread internationally after World War II, particularly in Latin America and Africa, because of the immediacy of spiritual experience. Pentecostal churches typically have little institutional structure and can sprout up quickly if there is enthusiastic local leadership. Pentecostal worship tends to focus on the immediate physical and spiritual needs of the worshipers. Although statistics are hard to gather and verify, there is little doubt that this is the fastest spreading form of Christianity around the world.

Suggestions for further reading:

Anderson, Robert Mapes. *Vision of the Disinherited: The Making of American Pentecostalism*. New York: Oxford Univ. Press, 1979.

Blumhofer, Edith. *Aimee Semple McPherson: Everybody's Sister*. Grand Rapids, Mich.: Eerdmans, 1993.

Blumhofer, Edith. *Restoring the Faith: The Assemblies of God, Pentecostalism, and American Culture*. Urbana, IL: InterVarsity Press, 1993.

Cox, Harvey. *Fire From Heaven: The Rise of Pentecostal Spirituality and the Shaping of Religion in the 21st Century*. Reading, Mass.: Addison-Wesley Publishing, 1994.

Dayton, Donald. *Theological Roots of Pentecostalism*. Grand Rapids, MI: Francis Asbury Press, 1987.

Faupel, David W. *The American Pentecostal Movement*. Wilmore, KY: B. L. Fisher Library, 1972.

Harrell, David E. *All Things Are Possible: The Healing and Charismatic Revivals in Modern America*. Bloomington, IN, 1985.

Synan, Vinson. *The Holiness-Pentecostal Movement in the United States*. Grand Rapids: Eerdmans, 1971.

APOSTOLIC FAITH MISSION CHURCH OF GOD

Founded: 1906
Membership: 9,120 in 18 churches (2007)

This mission was a fruit of the Azuza Street Revival in Los Angeles and the preaching of William Seymour. F. W. Williams experienced the outpouring of the Holy Spirit during that revival and founded the Apostolic Faith Mission in Mobile, Alabama, to spread the revival. Bishop Williams incorporated the church in 1915 under the present name. The church spread to Georgia and Florida. Pastors are called bishops in this church. The headquarters is called Ward's Temple in Cantonment, Florida.

Headquarters: 806 Muscogee Rd., Cantonment, FL 32533

APOSTOLIC WORLD CHRISTIAN FELLOWSHIP

Founded 1970
Membership: statistics unavailable, but est. 135 churches

W. G. Rowe founded the AWCF as a way to heal the divisions among the various Pentecostal churches in the U.S. and the world. It is not a denomination, but a fellowship of black and white Pentecostal churches and organizations that work cooperatively. In addition to typical evangelical and Pentecostal teachings, the AWCF places great emphasis on Jesus' high priestly prayer (John 17) in which he prays that the world will be one. For the AWCF, this unity comes through the Holy Spirit, whose gifts are still evident. In 1991 leadership passed to Samuel Smith and the headquarters moved to Evansville, Indiana. Its most unusual feature is that two white bishops and two black bishops serve as the principal officers of the church.

For more information: www.awcf.org

Headquarters: 11 West Iowa St., Evansville, IN 47710

ASSEMBLIES OF GOD INTERNATIONAL

Founded: 1914
Membership: 2,863,265 in 12,362 churches (2007)

The General Council of the Assemblies of God is actually a group of churches and assemblies that joined together at Hot Springs, Arkansas, in 1914. The founders were former pastors of evangelical persuasion who wished to unite in the interest of doctrinal unity, more effective preaching, and an enlarged missionary crusade.

Theologically, the Assemblies of God is Arminian (after Jacobus Arminius, 1560-1609), stressing Christ's atoning death for all persons, the freedom of human will, and the need for conversion. There is also a strong belief in the infallibility and inspiration of the Bible, the fall and redemption of the human race, baptism in the Holy Spirit, a life of holiness and separation from the world, divine healing, the Second Coming of Jesus and his millennial reign, eternal punishment for the wicked, and eternal bliss for believers. Two ordinances, baptism and the Lord's Supper, are practiced. Assemblies of God members are especially insistent that baptism in the Holy Spirit be evidenced by speaking in tongues. They hold that all the gifts of the Spirit should be evident in a church modeled after that of the New Testament.

The government of the assemblies is an unusual mixture of Presbyterian and congregational systems. Local churches are independent in polity and in the conduct of local affairs. District officers have a pastoral ministry to all the churches and are responsible for the promotion of home missions. Work is divided into fifty-eight districts in the U.S. and Puerto Rico, including eleven foreign-language districts, each with a district presbytery that examines and recommends credentialing of ministers. The General Council consists of all ordained ministers and lay representatives from local churches. The biennial General Council (business meeting) elects general officers, sets doctrinal standards, and provides for church expansion and development. The General Superintendent and other general church officers serve at the national headquarters in Springfield, Missouri.

The denomination's publishing arm, the Gospel Publishing House, produces curriculum and other resources and several periodicals, including the weekly *The Pentecostal Evangel*, which has a circulation of approximately 230,000. In the U.S., the Assemblies of God International sponsors a seminary in Springfield and eighteen colleges around the country. Missionary work is conducted under the guidance of a central missionary committee; there are nearly two thousand foreign missionaries at work in some two hundred nations. The church sponsors hundreds of bible schools abroad.

For more information: www.ag.org
Headquarters: 1445 Boonville Ave., Springfield, MO 65802

ASSEMBLIES OF THE LORD JESUS CHRIST

Founded: 1952
Membership: statistics unavailable; 413 churches (2001)

Three Pentecostal groups—the Assemblies of the Church of Jesus Christ, Jesus Only Apostolic Church of God, and the Church of the Lord Jesus Christ—formulated a merger in 1952, adopting the name "Assemblies of the Lord Jesus Christ." The Assemblies promotes many basic Pentecostal doctrines, including the infallibility and direct divine inspiration of Scripture, the fall of humankind, salvation by grace, a pre-millennial tribulation, water baptism and baptism in the Holy Spirit, Holy Communion, the service of foot washing, divine healing, and holiness in life.

The church teaches that the "one True God manifested Himself in the Old Testament in diverse ways, in the Son while he walked among men, as the Holy Ghost after the ascension." (www.aljc.org) Baptism is in the name of Jesus only. Members are forbidden to attend dances or theatrical events, even in public schools; thus private Bible schools are preferred. Another distinctive teaching of the church is that Christians are to obey the government in all matters except for the bearing of arms. Members are thus conscientious objectors.

The Assemblies of the Lord Jesus Christ has churches in thirty-five states, with particular strength in the Midwest and the South. It maintains offices in Memphis, Tennessee. Administration includes a general superintendent and three assistant superintendents. The church maintains Parkersburg Bible College in West Virginia and the Memphis School of Ministries in Tennessee; it supports missions in eight countries outside the U.S.; and it carries out prison ministry, ministry to Native Americans, and church building programs throughout the U.S.

For more information: www.aljc.org
Headquarters: 875 N. White Station Rd., Memphis, TN 38122

BIBLE WAY CHURCH OF OUR LORD JESUS CHRIST, WORLD WIDE, INC.

Founded: 1957
Membership: est. 300,000 in 350 churches worldwide (1995)

The Bible Way Church is an organization of primarily African American Pentecostal churches formed in 1957 when Apostle Smallwood Edmond Williams led some seventy churches out of the Church of Our Lord Jesus Christ of the Apostolic Faith* to form the Bible Way Church, World Wide. The vision of the founder was to promote evangelistic goals. The church's basic beliefs include Christ's resurrection and pre-millennial Second Coming, the resurrection and translation of the saints, the priesthood of all believers, and the final judgment of humankind. Baptism is by immersion, and baptism of the Holy Spirit is necessary for second birth. Foot washing is also practiced.

Phenomenal growth was reported by the church in the late twentieth century, but precise numbers are difficult to obtain. The Bible Way Church has twenty-seven dioceses, six of which lie outside of the United States. A board of bishops directs the church, and individual bishops preside over the various dioceses. A general conference is held annually in July, and the church sponsors various convocations. A publishing house at Washington, D.C., circulates periodicals, religious pamphlets, and recordings.

For more information: www.biblewaychurch.org

Headquarters: 261 Rochester Ave. Brooklyn, NY 11213

INTERNATIONAL FELLOWSHIP OF CHRISTIAN ASSEMBLIES

Founded: 1948
Membership: 7,200 in 96 churches (1999)

This church has had several names. From 1963-2008 it was known as the Christian Church of North America, but it was originally known as the Italian Christian Church. This body originated in a gathering of Italian Pentecostal ministers held in 1927 at Niagara Falls, New York. The leader was Luigi Francescon (1866–1964) who had left the Roman Catholic Church in 1892, joining the First Italian Presbyterian Church in Chicago (see WALDENSIANS). He embraced believer's baptism in 1903 and established the first Italian American Pentecostal congregation in 1907 in Chicago. When the church was incorporated in 1948 at Pittsburgh, it took the name "Missionary Society of the Christian Church of North America." The IFCA holds to basic Pentecostal beliefs, emphasizing the infallibility of Scripture, the Trinity, and salvation through faith in Jesus Christ. Although affirming the experiences of salvation and spirit baptism, the body does not teach the doctrine of entire sanctification. Headquarters are in Transfer, Pennsylvania.

For more information: www.ccna.org

Headquarters: 1294 Rutledge Rd., Transfer, PA 16154-9005

CHURCH OF GOD (CLEVELAND, TENNESEE)

Founded: 1886; name changed in 1907
Membership: 1,067,106 in 6,666 churches (2008)

The Church of God (Cleveland, Tennessee) claims the distinction of the being the oldest Pentecostal body. It traces its founding to 1886 in Monroe County, Tennessee, when the Christian Union* was organized by Richard Spurling (1810–91), a Baptist*, and his son, R. G. Spurling (1857–1935). The Spurlings had been led to the Bible to stem the tide of what they considered to be a growing accommodation to modern culture and spiritual indifference. In 1892 a second church was formed in Cherokee County, North Carolina, under the leadership of William F. Bryant (1863–1949); four years later, this group experienced speaking in tongues for the first time. R. G. Spurling met with the North Carolina group and others, and two more congregations were added over the next few years. The small organization was renamed the Holiness Church in 1902.

In 1903, Ambrose J. Tomlinson (1865–1943) of the American Bible Society joined the Holiness Church. In January of 1907 the name was changed once more, to Church of God, and headquarters were moved to Cleveland, Tennessee. Tomlinson was elected general overseer in 1909, and the church began publishing *The Church of God Evangel* the following year. The Church of God embraced Pentecostal practices and grew rapidly across the South and Midwest.

A crisis occurred in 1923 that raised concerns over the personal role of Tomlinson (see CHURCH OF GOD OF PROPHECY) and, more important, the nature of the church's government and the leader's authority. The majority, those with whom the Church of God (Cleveland, Tennessee) is continuous, rejected Tomlinson's leadership and selected F. J. Lee as overseer.

The church's major doctrines blend many Protestant themes with those that are specifically Pentecostal: justification by faith, sanctification, baptism of the Holy Spirit, speaking in tongues, the need to be born again, fruitfulness in Christian living, and a strong interest in the pre-millennial Second Coming of Christ (Christ to return before reigning on earth for a thousand years). The Church of God professes reliance on the Bible rather than a creedal statement. It practices divine healing; condemns the use of alcohol and tobacco; opposes membership in secret societies; and accepts baptism, the Lord's Supper, and foot washing as ordinances.

The Church of God elects its officers at a biennial General Assembly. The administration of the church includes a general overseer, three assistant overseers, a secretary general, and an eighteen-member International Executive Council which is responsible for the day-to-day operations of the church. Administrative divisions include education, world evangelism, church ministries, care ministries, and support services. Pathway Press is the publishing arm of the church, producing resources for Christian education and books for ministers and lay people. The Church of God operates Lee University and the Church of God School of Theology in Cleveland, Tennessee; a school of ministry; and a preparatory school. Its foreign missions enterprise is extensive, serving in 168 nations, with an international membership of over seven million.

For more information: www.churchofgod.org

Headquarters: P.O. Box 2430, Cleveland, TN 37320-2430

CHURCH OF GOD IN CHRIST

Founded: 1897
Membership: est. 5,500,000 in 15,300 churches (unverifiable)

Generally acknowledged to be the largest African American Pentecostal body in the U.S., the Church of God in Christ was founded after ministers Charles H. Mason (1866–1961) and Charles P. Jones were expelled by Baptist* groups in Arkansas for what was considered an overemphasis on holiness. Together they founded the Church of Christ (Holiness) U.S.A. in 1895. This church stressed the doctrine of entire sanctification. Mason also organized a congregation in Lexington, Mississippi, in 1897, to which he gave the name Church of God in Christ. In 1907 Mason went to Azusa Street in Los Angeles, California, to observe the Pentecostal revival taking place there. While in attendance, he had his first experience of speaking in tongues.

Subsequently, Mason raised the issue of Pentecostal experience in a gathering of leaders of the Church of Christ (Holiness) U.S.A. Charles P. Jones and others did not share Mason's enthusiasm for the Pentecostal movement and withdrew fellowship from him. Mason then called for a meeting in Memphis, Tennessee, of ministers who endorsed Pentecostal doctrine. With this group, he organized a general assembly of the Church of God in Christ, of which he was named general overseer and chief apostle. Mason remained head of the church until his death in 1961.

Church of God in Christ is trinitarian and stresses repentance, regeneration, justification, sanctification, speaking in tongues, and the gift of healing as evidence of the baptism of the Spirit. The sanctifying power of the Holy Spirit is considered a prerequisite to living a holy life, separate from the sin of the present world. Ordinances include baptism by immersion, the Lord's Supper, and foot washing.

The Church of God in Christ is governed by executive, legislative and judicial bodies. The executive branch is composed of the General Board, which is chaired by the Presiding Bishop. Executive officers are chosen at a general assembly that meets every four years. Clergy consist of bishops, district superintendents, pastors, evangelists and evangelist missionaries. The denomination has its headquarters in Memphis, Tennessee, which is also the location of the publishing house and All Saints Bible College. Atlanta, Georgia is the home of the church's Charles H. Mason Theological Seminary, which is a founding member of the Interdenominational Theological Center. The church has established ministries in over fifty countries and every state in the U.S.

For more information: www.cogic.org

Headquarters: P.O. Box 320, Memphis, TN 38101

CHURCH OF GOD OF PROPHECY

Founded: 1923
Membership: 91,106 in 1,858 churches (2008)

Church of God of Prophecy is one of the churches that grew out of the work of A. J. Tomlinson (1865–1943). At his death, his son M. A. Tomlinson was named general overseer, a position he held until 1990. He emphasized church unity and fellowship unlimited by social, racial, and political differences.

From its beginnings, the church has based its beliefs on "the whole Bible, rightly divided" and has accepted the Bible as God's Holy Word, inspired, inerrant, and infallible. The church affirms that there is one God, eternally existing in three persons. It believes in the deity, virgin birth, sinlessness, miracles, atoning death, bodily resurrection, ascension to the Father, and physical second coming of Christ. The church professes that salvation results from grace alone through faith in Christ, that regeneration by the Holy Spirit is essential for the salvation of sinners, and that sanctification by the blood of Christ makes personal holiness possible. The church stresses the ultimate unity of believers, based on John 17, and the sanctity of marriage and family. Other official teachings include baptism by the Spirit with the speaking of tongues as evidence; divine healing; the pre-millennial Second Coming of Christ; baptism by immersion; abstinence from tobacco, alcohol, and narcotics; and holiness in lifestyle. In addition to the Lord's Supper, the church practices foot washing.

The church is racially integrated on all levels, and women play a prominent role in church affairs, including serving in pastoral roles. The General Oversight Group consists of at least two bishops who, along with the General Overseer, are responsible for setting the vision for the entire church body. Doctrinal and business concerns of the church are addressed at the biennial General Assembly.

For more information: www.cogop.org

Headquarters: P.O. Box 2910, Cleveland, TN 37320-2910

CHURCH OF OUR LORD JESUS CHRIST
OF THE APOSTOLIC FAITH, INC.

Founded: 1919
Membership: est. 30,000 in 450 churches (1998)

This church was organized in 1919 at Columbus, Ohio, by Robert C. Lawson as a continuation of the revival begun on Pentecost. Lawson moved to New York City later that year, where he founded Refuge Temple, which he pastored until his death in 1961. He also led the wider organization as chief apostle until his death. He was succeeded as pastor of the church (now Greater Refuge Temple) by William L. Bonner, who later also became chief apostle of the Church of Our Lord Jesus Christ of the Apostolic Faith, Inc.

Church doctrine is held to be the same as that of the biblical apostles and prophets, with Christ as the cornerstone. The basic emphases are Christ's resurrection and pre-millennial Second Coming, the resurrection and translation of the saints, the priesthood of all believers, and the final judgment of humankind. The church is non-trinitarian, maintaining belief "in the oneness of God, who was the Father in creation, the Son in redemption, and today, He is the Holy Ghost in The Church." Baptism is by immersion, and baptism of the Holy Spirit is necessary for second birth. Foot washing is practiced, but not as an ordinance.

The Church of Our Lord Jesus Christ of the Apostolic Faith, Inc. has congregations in thirty-two states, the British West Indies, Africa, the Philippines, Haiti, the Dominican Republic, and London, England. It operates a Bible college in New York City, where general offices are maintained, and carries out various ministries of caring in the communities in which it serves. A national convocation meets every year. National officers include a chief apostle, a presiding apostle, a board of apostles, a board of bishops, and a board of presbyters.

For more information: www.cooljc.org

Headquarters: 2801 Adam Clayton Powel Blvd., New York, NY 10029

CHURCH OF THE LIVING GOD,
CHRISTIAN WORKERS FOR FELLOWSHIP

Founded: 1889
Membership: est. 20,000 in 120 temples (2002)

This body claims to be the first black church in the U.S. that was not begun by white missionaries. The Church of the Living God, Christian Workers for Fellowship came out of an organization formed in 1889 at Wrightsville, Arkansas, by

William Christian (1856–1928), a former slave. At a time when many white Christians treated blacks as less than human, Christian began a group that maintained that many of the prominent people of the Bible, including Jesus and David, were black. Christian held the office of "Chief" in the new church, and was succeeded in the office by his wife and, eventually, by their son.

Christian held to trinitarian doctrine and accepted Pentecostal practices, such as speaking in tongues, without requiring that members speak in tongues. He insisted that inspired speaking must be in recognizable languages. The Church of the Living God, Christian Workers for Fellowship observes three ordinances: water baptism, washing of feet, and the Lord's Supper celebrated with water and unleavened bread.

Christian was also fascinated by Freemasonry, and he developed a church structure that resembled a fraternal organization. He insisted that his "organism" be known as "operative Masonry" and characterized the three ordinances as the "first three corporal degrees." A chief bishop is the presiding officer of the organization. Members tithe their incomes to support their churches, which they call temples. The church's leaders are currently in the process of removing the Masonic aspects of the denomination.

Headquarters: 430 Forest Ave., Cincinnati, OH 45229

CONGREGATIONAL HOLINESS CHURCH

Founded: 1921
Membership: est. 18,000 in 250 churches (2008)

The Congregational Holiness Church traces its roots to the Wesleyan holiness revival and the Pentecostal movement (Pentecostal Churches) of the early twentieth century. The church affirms basic evangelical, Wesleyan, and Pentecostal doctrines including salvation, sanctification, the baptism of the Holy Spirit with speaking in tongues as evidence, divine healing, the imminent rapture of the church, and the imminent second coming of Christ. The ordinances are baptism by immersion, the Lord's Supper and foot washing.

Church government is congregational. Congregational Holiness Church pastors are elected by a majority vote of the congregation to which they are called. Both women and men are ordained. In the early days of the denomination, there were no full-time elected leaders. This arrangement continued until 1935. Today a full-time elected General Superintendent, who is given the honorary and lifetime title of Bishop, along with a full-time World Mission director and Mission USA administrator serve the church. A General Executive Board consisting of the General Superintendent, First Assistant Superintendent, Second Superintendent, Secretary, and Treasurer direct the monthly operations of the denomination. The local churches are now grouped into eight geographical districts in the southeast region of the U.S. as well as a Hispanic Conference that includes Hispanic congregations nationwide. Each district has a presbytery of five members, which licenses and ordains ministers. Between Quadrennial General Conferences, the church is governed by a General Committee that consists of the General Executive Board, all national department heads, and district presbytery members. The General Conference is the highest ruling body of the church. *The Gospel Messenger* is the official monthly publication of the church. The denomination conducts missions in nineteen countries, primarily in Latin America. Worldwide there are about seven thousand congregations. The International Headquarters is in Griffin, Georgia.

For more information: www.chchurch.com

Headquarters: 3888 Fayetteville Highway, Griffin, GA 30223

ELIM FELLOWSHIP

Founded: 1947
Membership: est. 20,000 in 100 churches (2004)

This body is an outgrowth of the missionary-oriented Elim Ministerial Fellowship, formed in 1933, and the work of graduates of the Elim Bible Institute in Lima, New York, founded in 1924 by Ivan and Minnie Spencer. The group was incorporated in 1947 as the Elim Missionary Assemblies; the present name was adopted in 1972.

Members of the Elim Fellowship hold to basic Pentecostal tenets of belief, beginning with affirmation of the Bible as the inspired and infallible Word of God. The fellowship espouses the trinitarian understanding of the Godhead, the atoning death and resurrection of Jesus Christ, salvation, sanctification, water baptism, the celebration of Communion among believers, the baptism of the Holy Spirit as evidenced in charismatic gifts and ministries, divine healing, and resurrection of the saved and unsaved for eternal reward or punishment.

The organizational pattern of Elim Fellowship is congregational, with individual churches autonomous in decision making. An annual assembly meets in Lima, where the General Chairman maintains offices. Over eight hundred ministers have credentials through Elim Fellowship and over 150 missionaries affiliated with the fellowship are at work in Africa, Asia, Europe, and South America.

For more information: www.elim.edu

Headquarters: Elim Bible Institute, 7245 College St., Lima, NY 14485

FIRE BAPTIZED HOLINESS CHURCH OF GOD

Founded: 1898
Membership: statistics unavailable, est. 170 churches (2004)

The Fire Baptized Holiness Church of God was founded by William Edward Fuller, Sr. It is closely related to the International Pentecostal Holiness Church and shares a common history in Southern African American Pentecostalism. Coming out of the Methodist Holiness tradition, it is an episcopal church, but in addition to baptism and Holy Communion, its members practice foot-washing. The church maintains that there is no distinction between male and female in the eyes of Christ; therefore it was one of the early churches to ordain women as preachers and pastors. The church holds to basic evangelical, holiness, and Pentecostal teachings, but it also provides a list of things that it opposes. This includes Unitarianism*, Mormonism*, Islam*, Psychics, Spiritualists*, and the Seventh-Day Adventists'* doctrines.

For more information: www.fbhchurch.org

Headquarters: 901 Bishop William Edward Fuller, Sr. Highway, Greenville, S.C.

FULL GOSPEL FELLOWSHIP OF CHURCHES AND MINISTERS, INTERNATIONAL

Founded: 1962
Membership: 432,632 in 1,273 churches (2007)

This fellowship was founded in Dallas, Texas, at a meeting called by Gordon Lindsay to support, encourage, and promote apostolic, Pentecostal ministry. As Lindsay and others envisioned it, the organization would give expression to the essential unity of those who believe in Christ and in the active work of the Holy Spirit. It was not to be a denomination as such but a fellowship of ministries. The organization also made it easier for independent churches to have tax-exempt status with the Internal Revenue Service.

Although individual churches or groups of churches affiliated with the Full Gospel Fellowship have doctrinal and ecclesial autonomy, certain core beliefs form the basis for fellowship. Among the suggested tenets of faith are belief in: the Bible as the inspired Word of God, the Trinitarian understanding of the Godhead, the atoning death and resurrection of Jesus Christ, the need for personal salvation and sanctification, the return and reign of Jesus Christ, and heaven and hell. The fellowship strongly advocates baptism by the Holy Spirit, as evidenced by the gift of speaking in tongues.

Regional conventions and an annual international convention are held; and various cooperative ministries, including curriculum development, are facilitated by the organization.

For more information: www.fcfcmi.org

Headquarters: 4325 W. Ledbetter Dr., Dallas, TX 75233

INDEPENDENT ASSEMBLIES OF GOD, INTERNATIONAL

Founded: 1922
Membership: statistics not available

This group is to be distinguished from the Assemblies of God*, but it shares a common heritage in the early Pentecostal movement. It traces its origins to the Azusa Street revival in Los Angeles in 1906 that soon spread across the country and across ethnic lines. In 1918, Scandinavian Pentecostals, who were particularly concerned to preserve the principles of Congregationalism*, formed the Scandinavian Assemblies of God in the United States, Canada, and Foreign Lands. This group operated essentially as a fellowship of like-minded churches until 1935, when they merged with the Independent Pentecostal Churches to form the Independent Assemblies of God, International.

Doctrinally, the church's statement of faith includes the common tenets of Pentecostalism, such as belief in the Bible as the inspired and infallible Word of God, in the Trinity, in the reality of Satan, and in the need for baptism by the Holy Spirit as evidenced through speaking in tongues. Ordinances include baptism by immersion and the Lord's Supper.

The churches in this assembly are autonomous but work together on common ministries. The leadership of the Assemblies of God International includes a general overseer, an assistant general overseer, and an international mission director. The offices are in Santa Ana, California, and the organization supports missionaries and national pastors in Africa, Central America, South America, Mexico, India, and the Philippines.

For more information: www.iaogi.org

Headquarters: P.O. Box 2130, Laguna Hills, CA 92645-2130

INTERNATIONAL CHURCH OF THE FOURSQUARE GOSPEL

Founded: 1927
Membership: 353,995 in 1,875 congregations (2006)

Founded during the evangelistic work of Aimee Semple McPherson (1890–1944), this church is a tribute to the organizing genius and striking methods of its founder. Born in Ontario in 1890, McPherson was converted under the preaching of her first husband, Robert Semple, an evangelist. Semple died while they were serving as missionaries in China, and Aimee Semple returned to the U.S. in 1911, where she conducted evangelistic crusades throughout North America. In 1918, after her remarriage, Aimee Semple McPherson and her children, Roberta and Rolf, settled in Los Angeles. With the help of her followers, she built Angelus Temple, which was dedicated on January 1, 1923. She also founded the Echo Park Evangelistic Association, the Lighthouse of International Foursquare Evangelism (L.I.F.E.) Bible College, and the International Church of the Foursquare Gospel.

With her speaking ability and faith in prayer for the sick, McPherson attracted thousands to her meetings. Her critics felt that the meetings were too much like a spectacle, but others appreciated her presentation. Her followers showed great interest in the sick and the poor; more than a million and a half are said to have been fed by Angelus Temple during the Great Depression. McPherson was president of the church during her lifetime and, together with a board of directors, oversaw the denomination's expansion. Upon her death in 1944, her son Rolf Kennedy McPherson became president and led the church until 1988.

The "four-fold gospel" refers to four central Pentecostal teachings that predate McPherson but that she popularized nationally. They are (1) salvation, (2) baptism by the Spirit, (3) divine physical healing, and (4) the Second Coming of Jesus Christ. The broader teaching of the church is set forth in a *Declaration of Faith* written by McPherson. It also stresses the return of Christ prior to his reign on earth, personal holiness, and the trinitarian conception of God. The Bible is affirmed as "true, immutable, steadfast, unchangeable, as its author, the Lord Jehovah." (www.foursquare.org) Baptism with the Holy Spirit, with the initial evidence of speaking in tongues, is subsequent to conversion, and the power to heal is given in answer to believing prayer. The ordinances of baptism and the Lord's Supper are observed in the church.

The official business of the church is conducted by a board of directors, a missionary cabinet, and an executive council made up of corporate officers. The highest seat of authority is the annual Foursquare Convention, which alone has the power to make or amend the bylaws of the church and which elects the president of the church to a four-year term. District supervisors are appointed for ten districts in the United States and are ratified by pastors of the respective districts every four years. Pastors are appointed by the board of directors of the denomination and are assisted by a local church council. Congregations are subordinated units of the denomination and contribute monthly to home and foreign missionary work. The official publication of the church is the *Foursquare World ADVANCE* magazine, published bimonthly.

While membership is highest on the West Coast, there are Foursquare churches in all fifty states. Overseas, the Foursquare Gospel is preached in 107 countries, with over three million members. In addition to L.I.F.E. Bible College in Los

Angeles and L.I.F.E. Bible College East in Christiansburg, Virginia, the church supports numerous Bible colleges and institutes around the world. There is also an extensive youth camping program. The church sponsors radio station KFSG-FM in Los Angeles.

For more information: www.foursquare.org

Headquarters: PO Box 26902, Los Angeles, CA 90026-0176

INTERNATIONAL PENTECOSTAL HOLINESS CHURCH

Founded: 1911
Membership: 257,758 in 2,010 churches (2007)

The International Pentecostal Holiness Church traces its origins to an organization founded in 1898 at Anderson, South Carolina, by a number of Holiness* associations. At that time the group was called the Fire-Baptized Holiness Church. In the same year, in Goldsboro, North Carolina, another group was organized as the Pentecostal Holiness Church. In 1907, G. B. Cashwell (1862–1916), a participant in the Azusa Street revival, led a Pentecostal revival in North Carolina and brought these two groups into Pentecostalism. The two bodies united in 1911 as the Pentecostal Holiness Church; and a third body, the Tabernacle Pentecost Church, joined them in 1915. The present name was adopted in 1975.

The theological standards of Methodism* prevail in the International Pentecostal Holiness Church, with certain modifications. The denomination accepts the pre-millennial teaching of the Second Coming, holding that Christ's return will precede his thousand year reign on earth, and believes that provision was made in the atonement for healing of the human body. Divine healing is practiced, but not to the exclusion of medicine. Three distinctive experiences are taught: two works of grace—justification by faith and sanctification—and Spirit baptism, attested to by speaking in other tongues. Services are often characterized by "joyous demonstrations." Two ordinances are observed: water baptism and Holy Communion.

The church's general executive board is elected by a quadrennial conference. There is a general superintendent and directors of World Missions, Evangelism, Church Education, Stewardship, and representatives from the different regions. Twenty-nine conferences or regional judicatories cover the U.S. IPHC sponsors Emmanuel College in Georgia and Southwestern College of Christian Ministries in Oklahoma, both four-year accredited colleges. The church operates a children's home at Falcon, North Carolina; a children's convalescent center at Bethany, Oklahoma; and a home for the aged. Foreign mission work takes place in one hundred countries with more than 3.75 million members worldwide.

For more information: www.iphc.org

Headquarters: P.O. Box 12609, Oklahoma City, OK 73157

OPEN BIBLE STANDARD CHURCHES, INC.

Founded: 1935
Membership: est. 45,000 in 302 churches (2007)

This association of churches was originally composed of two revival movements rooted in the Azusa Street meetings of 1906: Bible Standard, Inc., founded in Eugene, Oregon, by Fred Hornshuh in 1919 and Open Bible Evangelistic Association, founded in Des Moines, Iowa, by John R. Richey in 1932. The Pacific Coast group, with activities centered in Oregon, spread through Washington, California, and into the Rocky Mountain areas of the West; the Iowa group expanded into Illinois, Missouri, Ohio, Florida, and Pennsylvania. Similar in doctrine and government, the two groups joined on July 26, 1935, taking the combined name Open Bible Standard Churches, Inc., with headquarters in Des Moines. There are now churches in thirty-seven states.

The teachings of the Open Bible Churches are "fundamental in doctrine, evangelical in spirit, missionary in vision, and Pentecostal in testimony." (www.open bible.org) They emphasize the infallibility of the Word of God, the blood atonement of Christ, baptism by immersion, personal holiness, baptism of the Holy Spirit, divine healing, and the return of Jesus Christ. Open Bible Churches are grouped into five geographical regions and subdivided into twenty-seven districts. Individual churches are congregationally governed, locally owned, and affiliated by charter with the national organization. The highest governing body is the general convention, which meets biennially. The church has over one thousand credentialed ministers.

Internationally, the association ministers in thirty-eight countries and sponsors ten Bible institutes serving some 1,400 students. Mission emphasis is on the training of nationals for ministry. Institute of Theology by Extension (INSTE), a nontraditional educational program, operates in about thirty countries with over twelve thousand students, both in Open Bible and other denominational churches. The program is translated in or being translated into ten languages. In the United States, Open Bible Churches sponsors Eugene Bible College in Oregon, Master's Commission discipleship and leadership development groups in Iowa and Washington, and many INSTE groups serving 1,400 students studying in Spanish or English.

For more information: www.openbible.org
Headquarters: 2020 Bell Ave., Des Moines, IA 50315

PENTECOSTAL ASSEMBLIES OF THE WORLD, INC.

Founded: 1907
Membership: est. 1,500,000 in 1,750 churches (2006)

Tracing its origin to the Azusa Street revival in 1906, this body is the oldest "oneness" Pentecostal body, meaning that it baptizes in the name of Jesus only.

The goal of the Pentecostal Assemblies of the World, Inc., is to spread the message that Jesus Christ is Lord to all people. From its beginning, the group, including its leadership, has been interracial; however, the church is predominantly African American today. Two of it most influential leaders were G. T. Haywood, who directed the church during a period of consolidation from 1924 until his death in 1931, and Samuel Grimes, a former missionary, who led the church through a period of expansion from 1937 until his death in 1967.

Basic Pentecostal and Holiness* doctrine and practice are followed, except for rejection of the trinitarian understanding of God. The church stresses holiness of life, holding that believers must be wholly sanctified to fully participate in salvation. Strict codes governing dress and leisure pursuits are maintained. Water baptism and the Lord's Supper are practiced, with wine used in the latter. Only the King James Version of the Bible is accepted as the true Word of God.

The Pentecostal Assemblies of the World hosts two major conferences annually, to which its constituents come from around the globe to worship God and for fellowship with one another. The church is headed by a presiding bishop who guides its members spiritually. There is also an executive board, including an assistant presiding bishop, a general secretary, a general treasurer, and lay directors. The organization's administrator and staff handle its business affairs from general offices in Indianapolis, Indiana. This body is heavily concentrated in urban areas, such as Chicago, Detroit, and Indianapolis, but there are ministers serving in all fifty states.

The Aenon Bible College, located in Indianapolis, Indiana, serves to train Pentecostal Assemblies ministers and lay members. The college has affiliate institutes all over the U.S. and two foreign affiliates in Liberia: the Samuel Grimes Bible Institute and the Haywood Mission.

For more information: www.pawinc.org

Headquarters: 3939 Meadows Dr., Indianapolis, IN 46205

PENTECOSTAL CHURCH OF GOD

Founded: 1919
Membership: 90,030 in 1,158 churches (2007)

This body was organized in Chicago under the name "Pentecostal Assemblies of the U.S.A." in order to better organize early Pentecostalism in the Midwest for evangelism and to preserve congregations from unethical preachers pretending to be Spirit-filled. When the church was reorganized in 1922, the name was changed to "Pentecostal Church of God." For a number of years "of America" was a part of the name, but this was dropped in 1979. The Pentecostal Church of God is evangelical and Pentecostal in faith and practice. The doctrines of salvation, divine healing, baptism in the Holy Spirit (with the evidence of speaking in tongues), and the Second Coming of Christ are strongly emphasized. Ordinances include water baptism, the Lord's Supper, and foot washing.

A General Convention of the church meets biennially. Executives of the denomination include a general superintendent, a general secretary, a director of world missions, a director of home missions/evangelism, and a director of (American) Indian missions. Headquarters are located in Joplin, Missouri. The church has six regional divisions, each presided over by an assistant general superintendent. Most of the divisions have annual conventions. The Pentecostal Church of God conducts mission work in about fifty countries in Europe, Asia, Africa, and the Americas. Some five thousand churches have been established outside the U.S., and over 2,500 national ministers have been commissioned. The group sponsors twenty-two Bible schools, fifty-seven training centers, and fifty-one day schools across the globe. Messenger College, Messenger Publishing House, and Messenger Towers, all in Joplin, are supported by the church. *The Pentecostal Herald* is the official publication.

For more information: www.pcg.org

Headquarters: P.O. Box 850, Joplin, MO 64802

PENTECOSTAL FREE WILL BAPTIST CHURCH, INC.

Founded: 1959
Membership: est. 28,000 in 150 churches (1998)

The Pentecostal Free Will Baptist Church came into existence through the merging of four Free-Will Baptist conferences in North Carolina in 1959. These various groups traced their origins as Free Will Baptists* to the work of Paul Palmer (d. 1750) in the Carolinas during the first half of the eighteenth century. The Pentecostal aspect of the church's doctrine was developed in response to the preaching of G. B. Cashwell (1862–1916), who had participated in the Azusa Street revival of 1906 in Los Angeles, California. Cashwell launched a series of meetings in North Carolina on New Year's Eve, 1906; in response, many Free Will Baptist individuals and churches adopted Pentecostal doctrine and practice.

The church's doctrine is a mixture of Baptist* and Pentecostal beliefs. Central affirmations include the inerrancy of the Bible, regeneration through faith in the shed blood of Christ, sanctification as a second definite work of grace (subsequent to regeneration), Pentecostal baptism of the Holy Spirit as evidenced through speaking in tongues, divine healing, and the pre-millennial Second Coming of Christ. Ordinances include baptism by immersion, the Lord's Super, and foot washing.

269

A general meeting of the Pentecostal Free Will Baptist Church is held biennially in August; lay and ministerial representatives attend. Church officials include a general superintendent, a general secretary, and a general treasurer. Offices are maintained in Dunn, North Carolina, where Heritage Bible College was established in 1971. Most of the group's churches are in eastern North Carolina, but mission work is carried on in nine foreign countries and Bible institutes are operated in Mexico, the Philippines, and Venezuela.

For more information: www.pfwb.org

Headquarters: P.O. Box 1568, Dunn, NC 28355

UNITED HOLY CHURCH OF AMERICA, INC.

Founded: 1886
Membership: statistics not available, but est. 100,000

The United Holy Church claims to be "the oldest black Pentecostal church in America." (www.uhcoa.org) The church was first organized in 1886 in Method, North Carolina, as a regional body. An organizing convention was held in Durham, N.C. in 1900. Known originally as the Holy Church of North Carolina, it was reorganized in 1918 as the United Holy Church of America, Inc. In the following decades, the church established seven districts covering different regions of the country. The church seeks to establish and maintain holy convocations, assemblies, conventions, conferences, public worship, and missionary and educational efforts. The church's famous logo features a cross in the intersection of three circles in a triangle.

Articles of faith contain statements of belief in the Trinity, the record of the revelation of God in the Bible, redemption through Christ, justification with instantaneous sanctification, baptism of the Holy Spirit, divine healing, and the ultimate reign of Christ over the earth. Baptism by immersion, the Lord's Supper, and foot washing are observed as ordinances. The United Holy Church believes in speaking in tongues and views Spirit baptism as normative, although it shares the position held by many Pentecostal groups that speaking in tongues is not required for full membership, full discipleship, or even spirit baptism.

The church maintains headquarters in North Carolina, but it is now an international body with congregations in the Caribbean and Africa. The chief officer is the General President. Other officials include two general vice presidents, a general recording secretary, a general financial secretary, and a general treasurer. Each district has its own president. A board of bishops supervises the work of the church. The United Holy Church's primary publication is *The Holiness Union*.

For more information: www.uhcoa.org

Headquarters; 312 Umstead Street, Durham, NC 27702

UNITED PENTECOSTAL CHURCH INTERNATIONAL

Founded: 1945
Membership: 646,304 in 4,358 churches (2006)

The United Pentecostal Church International (UPCI) was founded in 1945 by the union of the Pentecostal Assemblies of Jesus Christ and the Pentecostal Church, Inc. Each of those bodies was itself the result of mergers of other Pentecostal bodies in the 1930s. All the constituent members were "oneness" ("Jesus only") Pentecostals who withdrew from the Assemblies of God in 1916. The doctrinal views of the UPCI reflect most of the beliefs of the Holiness-Pentecostal movement, with the exception of the "second work of grace." Holiness of life is understood to be an aspect of God's salvation of an individual, not the result of a subsequent experience.

Theologically, the church is non-trinitarian. The oneness view held by the UPCI asserts that God "revealed Himself in the Old Testament as Jehovah and in the New Testament revealed Himself in His Son, Jesus Christ." (www.upci.org) Jesus Christ is thus the one true God manifested in flesh and the Holy Ghost is the Spirit of God/the resurrected Christ. Baptism is carried out in Jesus' name only. The church embraces the Pentecostal view that speaking in tongues is the initial sign of receiving the Holy Spirit. For the UPCI, the Bible is the inerrant and infallible Word of God, and the church rejects all extra-biblical revelations and writings, such as church creeds and articles of faith.

UPCI polity is essentially congregational, with autonomous local churches. The General Conference of the church meets annually to elect officials. A general superintendent, two assistants, and a secretary-treasurer are members of a general board that also includes district superintendents, executive presbyters, and division heads. Denominational offices are located at Hazelwood, Missouri, as is World Aflame Press, the church's publishing house. The press publishes books, Sunday school materials, and a wide variety of religious literature. *The Pentecostal Herald* is the official organ of the UPCI, and there are various divisional publications. The church also sponsors "Harvest Time," an international radio broadcast.

UPCI's foreign missions program sponsors work in 170 countries outside the U.S. and claims an international membership of four million. Within the U.S., the church supports seven Bible colleges and opened a graduate school of theology in St. Louis, Missouri, in 2001. Other UPCI ministries include children's homes in Tupelo, Mississippi and Hammond, Louisiana; a chaplaincy program for persons in prison; and a chaplaincy program for the armed services.

For more information: www.upci.org

Headquarters: 8855 Dunn Rd., Hazelwood, MO 63402

VINEYARD CHURCHES INTERNATIONAL

Founded: 1983
Membership: est. 155,000 members in 529 churches (2008)

The Vineyard movement began as part of the Calvary Chapel* movement in California in the 1970s and grew rapidly in the late twentieth century. Kenn and Joanie Gulliksen served in a Calvary Chapel in Los Angeles, and around 1974 they began to emphasize the gifts of the Spirit. In 1982, the congregation changed its name to Vineyard to distinguish it from Calvary Chapel because the Vineyard congregation promoted public expressions of glossolalia, healing, exorcisms, and prophecy while Calvary Chapel saw such things as private gifts of the Spirit. Another Calvary Chapel minister, the former rock musician John Wimber (1934-1997), teamed up with Gulliksen to promote charismatic gifts among the younger generation. Wimber was the major public figure of the church until his death in 1997.

Wimber's "Signs and Wonders" course at Fuller Theological Seminary in Pasadena attracted many younger ministers to the movement despite the controversy it evoked. He called his movement the Third Wave of Pentecostalism and urged his followers to adopt Power Evangelism, using miracles to attract people to the faith. Christian rock music was also used effectively in evangelical outreach through recordings and radio broadcasts. The church embraces evangelical and charismatic/Pentecostal theology regarding the infallibility of Scripture, the fall of the human race, the need for an experience of salvation, and the spiritual gifts of healing and speaking in tongues. The Vineyard also emphasizes informal worship and provides fellowship for disaffected youth.

Contrary to the original anti-establishment character of the movement, Wimber had already begun the process of denominationalization before his death in 1997. His death was a serious blow to a movement that was centered on the idea that prayer produces healing. It has also become evident that Wimber's own personality was an important aspect of the church, and the movement has been struggling with issues of organization, leadership, and future direction. In 2000 Bert Waggoner, a successful Vineyard pastor, was appointed national director.

For more information: www.vineyard.org

Headquarters: 5340 E. LaPalma Ave., Anaheim P.O. Box 17580, Anaheim, CA 92817

Fundamentalist and Bible Churches

Representing the most conservative form of Protestantism, socially and theologically, fundamentalism was one of the most potent forces within American

Christianity in the twentieth century. Fundamentalism is a form of conservative evangelical Protestantism, but may be distinguished from other types of evangelical churches by its intense opposition to modern scientific theories and many aspects of popular culture. Doctrinally, fundamentalists place great stress on the fulfillment of the apocalyptic prophecies of the books of Daniel and Revelation. According to fundamentalist teaching, the world is divided between the forces of God and Satan. Satan will exert ever greater control over the world until the cataclysmic moment when Christ returns and destroys the forces of the Antichrist.

It is difficult to categorize and study fundamentalist churches because of the variety within fundamentalism and the fact that fundamentalism exerts an influence beyond its membership rolls. Fundamentalist churches tend to be congregationalist and Baptist* in orientation; therefore, structure exists primarily on the local level. Pastors tend to found their own congregations. Some preachers, like the late Jerry Falwell, build their congregations into major bodies that are loosely joined to like-minded congregations. Rather than having traditional denominational structures, fundamentalist churches generally establish a variety of cooperative ministry programs, such as radio and television ministries, sponsorship of foreign missions, and educational programs. Bible colleges, often associated with local congregations, are one of the backbones of fundamentalism. Graduates of these Bible colleges often serve in denominations that are not in themselves fundamentalist.

Fundamentalism grew out of nineteenth-century American evangelicalism and revivalism. Dwight L. Moody (1837–1899), founder of Moody Bible Institute, was one of the key figures in the formation of fundamentalist organizations, but the roots of the movement go back to the Plymouth Brethren* in England. The early Brethren dismissed with clergy and encouraged any members with spiritual gifts to preach, evangelize, and offer the sacraments. One of the key preachers was John Nelson Darby (1800–1882), who stressed the importance of biblical prophecy, especially that found in the apocalyptic books, for understanding human history. Drawing on Dutch Reformed theologians of the seventeenth century, Darby taught that history was divided into seven dispensations described in the Bible. The first six ended in a cataclysm, such as the expulsion from Eden and the great flood. The seventh dispensation will be the millennial age that Christ will inaugurate. Cyrus Scofield (1843–1921) made Darby's theory the centerpiece of his popular reference Bible early in the twentieth century. According to this scenario, life on earth will grow increasingly violent and sinful, as in the days before the flood.

Fundamentalism thus runs directly counter to modern trends in biblical scholarship and scientific theories about the origin, age, and evolution of the universe. It also rejects the modern idea of social progress in favor of a view of declension. Since biblical truth is under attack, according to fundamentalists, true believers must defend the Bible–especially those passages that support apocalyptic eschatology and dispensationalism. *The Fundamentals: A Testimony to the Truth* was a popular pamphlet series designed to defend the Bible from critics. It appeared between 1910 and 1915 and included nearly one hundred articles that sought to defend the deity of Christ, the virgin birth, the historical resurrection, the inerrancy of Scripture as the Word of God, and the reality of sin and Satan. Though many of the authors of these pamphlets were conservative evangelicals rather than fundamentalists, the movement got its name from these publications. Though some fundamentalist bodies were originally connected to the Holiness* movement, most have roots in the Baptist* and Presbyterian* churches.

World War I put the fundamentalist controversy on hold as Christians of all kinds joined in the war effort, but by 1920, the fundamentalist controversy heated up as Baptist* and Presbyterian* fundamentalists fought to preserve their churches from modern theology and biblical scholarship. This early period culminated in the famous Scopes "Monkey Trial" of 1925 over the teaching of evolution in the public schools. Following that celebrated trial, fundamentalists began organizing separate congregations, schools, and inter-church organizations. It appeared that the fundamentalists had lost the struggle and were retreating from society, but public ridicule merely confirmed the fundamentalists' conviction that America was an apostate nation.

By the end of the twentieth century, Protestant fundamentalists had successfully created a significant sub-culture in American society. World events fueled the growth of fundamentalism. In particular, the formation of the State of Israel in 1948 seemed to confirm the fundamentalists' prediction that the Jews would return to the Promised Land shortly before the return of Christ. Plus, the threat of nuclear destruction during the Cold War gave renewed vigor to fundamentalist preaching and writing. A number of best-selling books, such as Hal Lindsey's *The Late Great Planet Earth*, popularized the fundamentalists' view of human history. The Supreme Court's decision to extend separation of church and state to the public schools (banning school-sponsored prayers and other expressions of religion) galvanized the fundamentalist movement in the 1950s. Fundamentalists also objected loudly to the feminist movement, civil rights movement, peace movement, and gay rights movement.

Though prone to fractures and doctrinal disputes, fundamentalists since the Second World War have increasingly established cooperative ministries with other evangelicals. Some of the major fundamentalist associations are discussed below, but it should be noted that separatism is part of the nature of fundamentalism and many bodies only keep records of individual pastors who participate. Though hostile to modern science, fundamentalists have made very effective use of modern technology to communicate their message far beyond the membership of fundamentalist churches.

A fairly reliable estimate of total membership in fundamentalist congregations in the U.S. is close to one million, but the influence of fundamentalism extends more broadly in conservative evangelicalism in the U.S. Pastors in many evangelical denominations have been trained in fundamentalist educational institutions, such as Dallas Theological Seminary, and the Scofield Study Bible and its descendents are widely used. Jerry Falwell, who became famous through his Old Time Religion television show, brought fundamentalism into national conservative politics in the 1970s with his Moral Majority. The best-selling *Left Behind* fiction series written by Jerry B. Jenkins has introduced millions to fundamentalist pre-millennial eschatology while making allies in the anti-abortion and anti-gay rights effort.

In the 1980s and 90s, fundamentalist pastors in the Southern Baptist Convention* gained authority over many of aspects of the denomination, including control of its theological seminaries. However, the association of the word "fundamentalist" with Islamic radicalism has led many conservative Protestants to distance themselves from the word fundamentalist. It is not always easy to distinguish between conservative evangelicals, holiness churches, and fundamentalists.

Suggestions for further reading:

Balmer, Randall. *Mine Eyes Have Seen the Glory: A Journey into the Evangelical Subculture of America.* New York: Oxford University Press, 1989.

LaHaye, Tim. *The Battle for the Family.* Old Tappan, NJ: Fleming H. Revell, 1984.

Lawrence, Bruce B. *Defenders of God: The Fundamentalist Revolt Against the Modern Age.* San Francisco: HarperSanFrancisco, 1989.

Lindsey, Hal. *The Late Great Planet Earth.* Grand Rapids, Mich.: Zondervan, 1970.

Longfield, Bradley J. *The Presbyterian Controversy: Fundamentalists, Modernists, and Moderates.* New York: Oxford University Press, 1991.

Marsden, George M. *Fundamentalism and American Culture: The Shaping of Twentieth-century Evangelicalism, 1870–1925.* New York: Oxford University Press, 1980.

Marty, Martin and R. Scott Appleby. *The Glory and the Power: The Fundamentalist Challenge to the Modern World.* Boston: Beacon Press, 1992.

Marty, Martin and R. Scott Appleby, eds. *The Fundamentalism Project,* 5 vols. Chicago: Univ. of Chicago Press, 1991-1995.

Sandeen, Ernest. *The Roots of Fundamentalism.* Chicago: Univ. of Chicago Press, 1970.

AMERICAN EVANGELICAL CHRISTIAN CHURCHES

Founded: 1944
Membership: 17,400 in 192 churches (2006)

The American Evangelical Christian Churches (AECC) are less a denomination than an inter-church organization that offers credentials for ministers.

Congregations associated with the AECC are autonomous but agree to a fundamentalist statement of belief. Clergy credentialed by the AECC serve in a variety of capacities, including prison ministry, military and hospital chaplaincy, as well as outreach to truckers, bikers, and others without a permanent Christian community. Ministerial applicants must subscribe to "Seven Articles of Faith": (1) the Bible as the written Word of God; (2) the virgin birth; (3) the deity of Jesus Christ; (4) salvation through the atonement of Christ; (5) the guidance of life through prayer; (6) the return of Christ; and (7) the establishment of the millennial kingdom. Upon completion of training, ministerial students are granted licenses enabling them to perform all the functions and offices of the ministry, with the exception of officiating at marriages. Full ordination is withheld until the licentiate has become pastor of a regular congregation or is engaged in full-time evangelistic or missionary work. Twelve regional offices in the U.S. and one in Canada supervise the work of the organization.

For more information: www.aeccministries.com

Headquarters: P.O. Box 47312, Indianapolis, IN 46227

BAPTIST BIBLE FELLOWSHIP INTERNATIONAL

Founded: 1950
Membership: est. 525,165 in 3,294 churches (2000)

Baptist Bible Fellowship was founded by some one hundred Baptist ministers and missionaries to promote fellowship among independent Baptists in three main areas of church life: evangelism, education of church workers, and the founding of churches. Many of the founders had been part of the World Fundamental Baptist Missionary Fellowship (today known as the World Baptist Fellowship)*, which had roots in the Baptist Bible Union, founded in 1921. The Baptist Bible Fellowship's statement of faith was based on that of the Baptist Bible Union. It is strongly fundamentalist in character, emphasizing the inerrancy of Scripture, the virgin birth, the deity of Christ, the substitutionary atonement, the resurrection of the body of Christ, biblical miracles, and the literal millennial kingdom on earth. Ministers and members of the fellowship use only the King James Version of the Bible in English-speaking churches.

The Baptist Bible Fellowship also teaches that Jesus was a Baptist in his thinking and work. They recognize baptism by immersion only, participate in Holy Communion only with members of their own church, and are adamantly opposed to dancing, drinking, smoking, movies, gambling, and sex outside of marriage. No formal membership statistics are kept, and the above figures are estimates based on attendance figures. There are churches in every state, but the greatest concentration is in the Great Lakes region and the South. Almost one third of the congregations have dual affiliation with other fundamentalist bodies.

Baptist Bible College in Springfield, Missouri, and Baptist Bible College East in Boston, Massachusetts, are owned and supported by these independent Baptists. Recently the Baptist Bible Graduate School of Theology was founded in Springfield, Missouri. Other schools supported by the fellowship are Pacific Coast Baptist Bible College and Spanish Baptist Bible Institute in Miami, Florida.

For more information: www.bbfi.org

Headquarters: P.O. Box 191, Springfield, MO 65801

BAPTIST MISSIONARY ASSOCIATION OF AMERICA

Founded: 1950
Membership: 177,463 in 1,306 churches (2007)

Organized at Little Rock, Arkansas, as the North American Baptist Association, this group changed its name to Baptist Missionary Association of America in 1968. It concentrates on fostering and encouraging missionary cooperation. There are workers in home missions and missionary work abroad in Mexico, Japan, Brazil, Taiwan, Portugal, Cape Verde Islands, Uruguay, Guatemala, Costa Rica, Nicaragua, Australia, Italy, France, Africa, India, Bolivia, Honduras, Korea, and the Philippines. A strong publications department issues literature for Sunday school and training classes as well as pamphlets, books, tracts, and magazines in both English and Spanish. The association also owns and operates a printing business in Brazil, where literature is printed in Portuguese for use in Africa and Europe. A worldwide radio ministry is also maintained.

The members are thoroughly fundamentalist in conviction, placing strong emphasis on the verbal inspiration and accuracy of Scripture, direct creation, the virgin birth and deity of Jesus, his blood atonement, justification by faith, salvation by grace alone, and the imminent personal return of Christ to earth. The Lord's Supper and baptism are accepted as ordinances, and baptism is considered "alien" unless administered to believers by the divine authority as given to the Missionary Baptist churches. With its roots in the American Baptist Association, this body carries on the Landmark Baptist movement (see BAPTIST CHURCHES), holding to the historic succession of independent Baptist churches from the time of Christ.

Churches are completely autonomous in the Baptist tradition and, regardless of size, have an equal voice in the cooperative missionary, publication, evangelical, and educational efforts of the association. Member churches must, however, conform to the doctrinal standards of the association. Three junior colleges and several orphans' homes are maintained on a state level, and a theological seminary is located in Jacksonville, Texas.

For more information: www.bmaam.org
Headquarters: P.O. Box 30910, Little Rock, Arkansas 72260

BEREAN FUNDAMENTAL CHURCH

Founded: 1947
Membership: est. 12,000 in 55 churches (2005)

In the mid-1930s, Dr. Ivan E. Olsen became the first pastor of the Berean Fundamental Church, an independent congregation in North Platte, Nebraska. Following the biblical principle of evangelism found in Acts 1:8, Olsen assisted in planting sixteen other churches in surrounding communities. In 1947 these churches formed the Berean Fundamental Church Council, Inc. The member churches possess a common constitution, stressing the basic doctrines of Christianity and the verbal, plenary inspiration of Scripture (the inerrancy of the Bible in all matters of faith and morals); the virgin birth of Christ; the deity of Christ; the blood atonement; the bodily resurrection of Christ; and the return of Christ to earth, following the rapture and preceding the millennial kingdom. The local assemblies are also Bible centered and evangelistic. Berean Fundamental churches support a variety of independent faith missions, draw their pastors from various seminaries and Bible institutes, and freely choose their own Sunday school curricula and church literature. The Berean Fundamental Church Council, Inc., supports its own Maranatha Bible Camp and Conference Grounds near North Platte.

For more information: www.bereanchurchfellowship.org
Headquarters: P.O. Box 1264, Kearney, NE 68848

BIBLE FELLOWSHIP CHURCH

Founded: 1858
Membership: 7,605 in 60 churches (2007)

This body was formed in the 1850s when Mennonite* leaders in Pennsylvania resisted the more evangelical style of some of the younger generation. The evangelical Mennonites formed their own group. Originally it was called the Evangelical Conference, but the name was changed in 1959 when a new confession of faith was adopted. The church now has a more fundamentalist outlook, but retains some of its Mennonite heritage. Bible Fellowship Church's doctrinal emphases include salvation through the death and resurrection of Christ, transformation of life through new birth by the Holy Spirit, the authority and trustworthiness of the Bible as the Word of God, the culmination of history in the Second Coming of

Jesus (pre-millennialism), and a shared life in the church of believers, with every member being responsible for the propagation of the gospel through evangelism and missions. Churches are found mainly in Pennsylvania, New Jersey, New York, and Ontario, Canada. The churches support missions on five continents, in addition to the Pinebrook Junior College, the Victory Valley Camp for children and youth, a home for the aging, and Pinebrook-in-the-Pines, a conference and retreat center—all in Pennsylvania.

For more information: www.mybfc.org

Headquarters: 3000 Fellowship Drive, Whitehall, PA 18051

BIBLE PRESBYTERIAN CHURCH

Founded: 1938
Membership: est. 10,000 in 32 congregations (2000)

On June 11, 1936, during the fundamentalist/modernist controversy, a group of about three hundred people, led by Princeton professor J. Gresham Machen (1881–1937), formed a new Presbyterian church based on their belief "that the great battle in the world today is the faith of our fathers versus modernism, compromise, indifferentism, and worldliness. With all our hearts we throw our strength into the great task of winning lost souls to Jesus Christ by the Gospel of the Grace of God." (http://www.bpc.org/about/history.html) It soon became apparent that the new church was actually composed of two groups with divergent views; therefore, on September 6, 1938, one group formed the Bible Presbyterian Church, and the other subsequently took the name Orthodox Presbyterian Church*.

The BPC is fundamentalist* but subscribes to the Westminster Confession of Faith and the Shorter and Larger Westminster Catechisms. Local congregations may call their pastors "without interference" from presbyteries or synods. Among its approved agencies are Western Reformed Seminary, Cohen Theological Seminary, Faith College of the Bible, and two Independent Boards for Presbyterian Missions.

For more information: www.bpc.org

Headquarters: P.O. Box 26164, Charlotte, NC 28221-6164.

BOB JONES UNIVERSITY

Founded: 1927
Membership: 4,000 students in 1 campus (2009)

One of the most successful of the first generation of fundamentalist preachers was Bob Jones, Sr. (1883-1968), who grew up in poverty in Alabama. His mother was a Primitive Baptist* and his father was a Methodist*. After a conversion experience and baptism at the age of twelve, Jones became superintendent of the Sunday school in his Methodist congregation and was a child evangelist. By the time he was fifteen, he was licensed as a Methodist circuit preacher, and by the 1920s was almost as famous as the revivalist Billy Sunday. Like Sunday, Jones was a prohibitionist. He was also a pioneer in religious broadcasting, and in 1927 he became one of the first preachers to have a nation-wide radio network. In 1944 he founded and directed National Religious Broadcasters, an organization that helped conservative evangelical and fundamentalist preachers get air time. Broadcast media became one of the major forms of ministry for fundamentalist churches.

After the infamous Scopes Monkey trial in 1925, Bob Jones decided it was time for fundamentalist Christians to establish their own schools, which would be untainted by secular humanism and the theory of evolution. He began Bob Jones College in Florida in 1927, claiming that the donors insisted on naming the school for him. The school's creed was grounded in Calvinism, but stressed the inerrancy of Scripture and abstinence from alcohol. The school struggled to survive during the Depression and World War II, and eventually was moved to Greenville, South Carolina, in 1947. At that time the name was changed to Bob Jones University, and Bob Jones, Jr. (1911-1997) became chancellor even though he only held a bachelor's degree. The school was not accredited as a university until 2005 after it changed its racial policies. Bob Jones, Sr., was an ardent segregationalist, and the university reflected his politics for decades. The school has had over thirty-five thousand graduates, many of whom are fundamentalist preachers.

Bob Jones, Jr. was more stridently fundamentalist than his father and famously criticized Billy Graham's revivals for being too accepting of American culture. He also criticized Jerry Falwell and other fundamentalist leaders for working with Catholics and Jews. Bob Jones, Jr. supported Ian Paisley, the Irish Protestant leader who encouraged violence against Catholics, and he maintained that the pope was the antichrist. Interestingly, he was also an accomplished Shakespearean actor and a collector of European art. He was succeeded as head of BJU in 1971 by his son Bob Jones III, who retired in 2005. The school is now led by Stephen Jones, but it continues to promote fundamentalism, including opposition to abortion, women's rights, and gay marriage.

The Jones family also established a complete pre-K through high school educational system and a retirement facility so that individuals can spend their entire life within the church. BJU operates an art museum and its own press.

For more information: www.bju.edu

Headquarters: Bob Jones University, Greenville, SC 29614

GRACE GOSPEL FELLOWSHIP

Founded: 1945
Membership: est. 60,000 in 128 churches (1992)

Dispensational and pre-millennial, this fellowship had its beginnings as a pastors' fellowship at a conference of pastors and missionaries at the Berean* Bible Church in Indianapolis, Indiana, in 1943. A year later, at Evansville, Indiana, its purpose was defined in a constitution: "to promote a fellowship among those who believe the truths contained in [our] doctrinal statement and to proclaim the Gospel of the Grace of God in this land, and throughout the world." (www.ggfusa.org)

That doctrinal statement includes belief in the Bible as infallibly inspired by God; in the total depravity of the human race; in redemption by God's grace through the blood of Christ by means of faith; in eternal security for the saved; in the gifts of the Spirit (as enumerated in Ephesians 4:7-16); and that the human nature of sin is never eradicated during this life. Its members believe in baptism by the Holy Spirit but hold that, while water baptism is biblical, it is not relevant to the present dispensation. Any church may vote to become affiliated with Grace Gospel Fellowship, provided it meets the doctrinal standards. The constitution was revised in 1995 and now the church is divided into ten regions.

The church is present in Zaire, Puerto Rico, India, the Philippines, Australia, South Africa, Tanzania, and South America. Grace Bible College and the headquarters of the Fellowship are located in Grand Rapids, Michigan. Closely connected to Grace Gospel Fellowship are Grace Ministries International, Grace Publications, and Grace Youth Camp in Indiana.

For more information: www.ggfusa.org

Headquarters: Fellowship, 2125 Martindale SW Box 9432, Wyoming, Michigan 49509

GREAT COMMISSION CHURCHES

Founded: 1983, with roots to 1965
Membership: est. 43,000 in 60 churches (2005)

In 1965 a young man name Jim McCotter attempted to recreate the church of the New Testament in Greely, Colorado. He began a housechurch based on the Book of Acts, and soon was attracting students from the University of Northern Colorado. McCotter's family had ties to the Plymouth Brethren* and McCotter shared the Brethren's attitudes toward church discipline. The church recruited aggressively on college campuses across the United States and Canada in the 1970s in a campaign they called The Blitz. Eschewing traditional church labels, the denomination was formally organized as Great Commission International in 1983, with a focus on campus ministry and publication. Currently the organization is called Great Commission Churches.

The church is very conservative theologically and socially, especially in terms of gender roles. Over the years, McCotter's movement was frequently criticized for adopting some cult-like practices, especially authoritarian leadership methods. McCotter resigned from the church in 1986 amid allegations of abusive practices in the church. In the 1980s former members of the church began Wellspring Retreat and Resource Center to assist people who felt they were victims of "religious abuse," and in 1991 the church issued a formal apology for some of its teachings and practices. Since then, it has become part of the National Association of Evangelicals.

For more information: www.gccweb.org

Headquarters: P.O. Box 29154, Columbus, OH 43229

IFCA INTERNATIONAL

Founded: 1930
Membership: 61,655 in 659 churches (1999)

Originally known as the Independent Fundamental Churches of America, this body was organized at Cicero, Illinois, to safeguard fundamental doctrine. Members must agree with doctrines of the verbal plenary inerrant inspiration of the Bible; the virgin birth, deity, and sinless life of Jesus Christ; the death, burial, and resurrection of Christ to provide salvation for all; the person and work of the Holy Spirit; the reality of Satan and his destructive work today; the personal and bodily return of Jesus Christ; and the bodily resurrection of all people, some to eternal life and some to "everlasting punishment." The name was changed in the 1990s to disassociate the group from "radical fundamentalists," such as snake handlers.

This body is less a traditional denomination than a sponsoring agency for autonomous churches and ministries. It has a strong commitment to various forms of chaplaincy, particularly military and prison ministries, and it publishes *Voice* magazine and other materials devoted to evangelical/fundamentalist ministries. There are five Bible camps, seven Bible institutes, and two children's homes. The president of the body presides over an annual conference in which the members have voting power; an executive committee of twelve serves for three years. The constituent churches are completely independent but are required to subscribe to the statement of faith of the organization. A home office is maintained in Grandville, Michigan.

For more information: www.ifca.org

Headquarters: P.O. Box 810, Grandville, MI 49468

INDEPENDENT BAPTIST FELLOWSHIP INTERNATIONAL

Founded: 1984
Membership: statistics not available; 647 churches (1999)

Raymond Barber broke with the World Baptist Fellowship in 1984 after having served as president of that body. Barber was a pastor in Fort Worth, Texas, and a professor at Arlington Baptist College, a fundamentalist school. After the split he founded Norris Bible Baptist Institute and began a publication to promote his views. The IBFI is strongest in Texas and Oklahoma, but it has a presence in Michigan, Ohio, and Florida and supports about twenty-five missionaries. Though its directory lists over six hundred churches, about two thirds of them have membership in other fundamentalist associations as well.

For more information: www.ibfi-nbbi.org

Headquarters: 724 North Jim Wright Frwy., Ft. Worth, TX 76108

INDEPENDENT FUNDAMENTALIST BAPTIST CHURCHES

Founded: roots to 1920s
Membership: est. over 150,000 in 1,400 churches

It is impossible to give accurate statistics for membership in the many independent fundamentalist churches because so many maintain dual membership in various state and regional associations. Some of the independent churches maintain fellowship in the New Testament Association of Independent Baptist Churches and the Fundamental Fellowship. Many of these bodies separated from the Northern Baptist Convention (see AMERICAN BAPTIST CHURCHES) in the 1920s during the Modernist controversy and formed the Fundamental Fellowship of the Northern Baptist Convention. In the 1940s some of the members created the Conservative Baptist Association* with foreign and homeland mission societies. Some of the more fundamentalist pastors criticized the Conservative Baptists for supporting the Billy Graham crusades and other "neo-evangelical" activities.

A number of organizations were founded such as the Fundamental Baptist Fellowship (which has over one thousand individuals representing some eight hundred churches) and the New Testament Association of Independent Baptist Churches (1,400 members in about 120 churches). Conservative Baptist state conventions in Minnesota, Illinois, Indiana, and Montana-Wyoming are basically fundamentalist. In a number of states the fundamentalists among the Conservative Baptist formed their own associations.

PLYMOUTH BRETHREN (CHRISTIAN BRETHREN)

Founded: 1820s
Membership: est. 86,000 in 1,200 churches (2003)

The Plymouth Brethren is a widely used, but unofficial, designation for a loose grouping of churches with early nineteenth-century roots in the British Isles. Within these churches, the common terminology is simply "Brethren" or "Christian Brethren," but they are to be distinguished from Brethren* churches associated with the Pietist movement. Similar to the Restorationist bodies in the U.S., the early Brethren envisioned a basis for Christian unity by forsaking denominational structures and names in order to meet simply as Christians. The autonomy of the local congregation is another feature of the movement.

The weekly hour-long "remembrance meeting" is probably the surest way to identify a Brethren assembly. In accordance with the meaning of "priesthood of believers," the service is unstructured and participatory. Brethren have consistently refused to restrict the administration of baptism or the Lord's Supper to ordained ministers, thus effectively eliminating a clergy/laity distinction and the traditional concept of ordination. A preacher may serve full-time with a congregation, but will not be identified as clergy or be given control of the congregation.

The Brethren are committed to all the fundamentals of conservative Christianity, including the verbal inspiration of Scripture. They emphasize gospel preaching and the necessity for personal conversion. Except for the weekly breaking of bread and the absence of collections at other meetings, their services are much like those of evangelical Baptist* and Bible churches.

Among American evangelicals, Brethren have had an influence out of proportion to their numbers. Their pre-millennial theology helped to shape evangelicalism, especially in the proliferation of independent churches and mission boards. In recent years, many have responded to the Brethren emphasis on plurality of leadership and participatory worship in the local church. Brethren are also characteristically found in leadership positions in interdenominational evangelistic campaigns and the founding and operation of nondenominational Bible schools, colleges, seminaries, and parachurch organizations. They have only one multiple-year, college-level institution, Emmaus Bible College in Dubuque, Iowa.

As a result of a division in England in 1848, there are two basic types of assemblies, commonly known as exclusive and open. Led in the beginning by John Nelson Darby (1800–82), the exclusive assemblies produced most of the movement's well-known Bible teachers, such as William Kelly, F. W. Grant, and C. H. Macintosh. They operated on the premise that disciplinary action taken by one assembly was binding on all. As a result, once started, a division often spread worldwide, until by the end of the century the exclusive Brethren were divided into seven or eight main groups. Recent mergers have reduced that number somewhat, and an important American group has merged with the open assemblies.

Open assemblies were led by George Müller (1805–95), well known for his orphanages and life of faith. Their strength has always been in evangelism and foreign missions. Lacking the exclusive disciplinary premise, local disputes spread only as far as there was interest and involvement; thus open assemblies have never experienced worldwide division.

Contact: John H. Rush, 2872 Illinois Ave., Dubuque, IA 52001

SOUTHWIDE BAPTIST FELLOWSHIP

Founded: 1956
Membership: at least 100,000 in 500 churches

Lee Robinson, pastor of Highland Park Baptist Church in Chattanooga, Tennessee withdrew from the Southern Baptist Convention* in 1955 and formed the Southern Baptist Fellowship the following year. In the previous decade he had established Tennessee Temple Schools, which had four campuses and which taught premillennialist theology. In 1948 he founded the Tennessee Pre-millennial Fellowship out of which the SBF developed. In 1960 he helped establish Baptist International Missions which today includes over one thousand missionaries worldwide. The doctrine and practices of the fellowship are similar to other fundamentalist churches, and nearly half of the members are also in other fundamentalist associations. In the 1990s the denomination adopted more lenient attitudes toward dress and hair style. Some congregations adopted contemporary music in worship as a way to increase attendance. This may indicate a movement away from strict fundamentalism.

For more information: www.wayoflife.org

Contact: Marcus Pointe Baptist Church, 6205 North "W" Street, Pensacola, FL 32505

THOMAS ROAD BAPTIST CHURCH (JERRY FALWELL MINISTRIES)

Founded: 1956
Membership: 17,500 in 1 church (2009)

Jerry Falwell (1933-2007) founded the Thomas Road Baptist Church in Lynchburg, Virginia, with thirty-five members meeting in an elementary school. Within months, he began preaching on the local radio and began videotaping the

Old Time Gospel Hour, which became one of the most popular television ministries nationwide. Falwell made very effective use of the medium of television. The Old Time Gospel Hour brought traditional Southern revivalism, with its distinctive music and conversion-oriented preaching, to the airwaves, but the show also included interviews with people whose lives had been changed through the gospel. Particularly important was Falwell's personable and direct conversations with viewers, which included appeals for money. Within a decade the church had grown to over two thousand members.

Like many fundamentalists after World War II, Falwell was upset by the Supreme Court decision outlawing prescribed prayer in public schools as well as the forced desegregation of public schools. He was associated with a number of segregationist politicians in the 1960s, most notably Lester Maddox. In 1967 he founded Lynchburg Christian Academy as an alternative to secular humanist education. The school does not teach the theory of evolution as scientific fact, for instance. In 1971 Falwell founded Liberty University, which remains one of the premier academic institutions associated with the fundamentalist movement. Liberty is fully accredited, and it offers a counseling program that relies on the Bible rather than Freud for guidance. The university now has some thirty-eight thousand students.

Falwell became a national political figure in the 1970s as he used his media network to oppose liberalism in society. Unlike some fundamentalists, Falwell made patriotism a cornerstone of his preaching, and he was a strong supporter of the military. He was also a fervent supporter of Zionism and had close ties to many Israeli officials. Like most fundamentalists, Falwell was particularly opposed to the feminist movement, insisting that Scripture mandates norms for both sexes. He aggressively pushed a "pro-life" agenda and joined Anita Bryant's campaign against gay rights.

In 1979 he formed the Moral Majority, a network for social conservatives, and Thomas Road Baptist Church provided a forum for conservative politicians. The Moral Majority helped Ronald Reagan defeat Jimmy Carter in the 1980 presidential election, even though Carter was a "born again" Baptist who taught Sunday school. Many people viewed the Moral Majority as the "praying arm" of the Republican Party, but its influence waned over the years, especially after 2001 when Falwell blamed the 9/11 attacks on "pagans, and the abortionists, and the feminists, and the gays and lesbians." (http://www.msnbc.msn.com/id/6601018/)

Jerry Falwell's death was a major blow to the more populist wing of the fundamentalist movement. His son Jonathan assumed the role of pastor of the Thomas Road Baptist Church in 2007, which continues to promote the vision of its founder.

For more information: www.trbc.org

Headquarters: 1 Mountainview Rd., Lynchburg, VA 24502

WORLD BAPTIST FELLOWSHIP

Founded: 1932, 1950
Membership: statistics not available; 998 churches (2001)

One of the most famous and controversial leaders of the early fundamentalist movement was J. Frank Norris (1877-1952), who in 1932 founded the Premillennial Baptist Missionary Fellowship, which was renamed World Baptist Fellowship in 1950. Norris was pastor of the First Baptist Church of Fort Worth, Texas, and he led his congregation out of the Southern Baptist Convention* in protest against what he perceived as liberal trends in the convention. He was also a vigorous proponent of dispensationalist theology, which is taught at Arlington Baptist College, the WBF's theological institution.

The denomination does not keep statistics of overall membership, but it does list pastors who are in fellowship. About sixty percent of the congregations represented are also counted in other fellowships and associations of fundamentalist and conservative Baptist churches. The WBF officially promotes the primacy of the local church, but Norris' autocratic leadership led to splits in the WBF, the most notable being the formation of the Baptist Bible Fellowship International*. The WBF continues to publish *The Fundamentalist*, a paper started by Norris in 1917 to combat modernism and promote premillennial dispensationalism. It also supports some 150 missionaries, primarily in Latin America.

For more information: www.wbfi.net

Headquarters: P.O. Box 13459, Arlington, TX 76094-0459

COMMUNITY AND
NEW PARADIGM CHURCHES

One of the most important trends in American Christianity since 1980 has been the rapid increase in the number and size of congregations with few or no ties to traditional denominations. Some authors have gone so far as to call this a third (or fourth) Great Awakening. These churches report dramatic increases in worship attendance since 1980.

As the U. S. population shifted from rural and urban areas to the suburbs, the residents of new neighborhoods, like their ancestors who settled the frontier, sometimes took it on themselves to establish a local church and hire their own minister without consulting with denominational authorities. Increasingly in the 1980s and 90s, energetic and entrepreneurial ministers responded to population shifts by establishing congregations that reflected the musical and social tastes of the "baby boomer" generation. Some of these dynamic congregations have become "mega-churches" that are larger than some denominations in this *Handbook*. Most are located in the West and South in cities with populations greater than 250,000.

Some of these new-style churches officially have a denominational connection (and their statistics are included in those denominations), but for the most part they are functionally independent. They resemble other New Paradigm or Community Churches more than they do congregations in their own denomination. Doctrine is rarely the defining feature of the churches in this category. In general, the new paradigm churches stress personal transformation and spiritual growth more than traditional doctrinal themes or social justice.

In some ways, New Paradigm churches are not that new. The Community Church movement actually dates from the mid-1800s when Midwestern and Western communities took charge of their own church life. The first national organization of community churches was in 1933. Community Churches are a result of the desire to eliminate over churching in some communities; to replace the restrictiveness and divisiveness of denominationalism with self-determination and Christian unity; to refocus primary loyalty from organizations outside a community to the community itself; and, by addressing specific needs within a community, to make religious expression more immediately relevant.

There are several types of Community Churches. Federated and United Churches resulted from mergers of congregations previously affiliated with certain denominations. Some have continued alignments with two or more denominations; others have become entirely independent. However, the majority of Community Churches never have had denominational affiliation. Since each church is adjusted to the needs of a different community, there is great variety among Community Churches in worship, work and witness styles, and methods. They are generally more flexible in worship, more casual in dress, and more focused on family issues than denominational churches. Community churches depend heavily on active lay involvement in the work of the congregation, and pastors are expected to be resource persons rather than chaplains.

Even more than the typical community church, mega-churches depend on the entrepreneurial zeal and organizational skill of the head pastor. A mega-church usually has a large staff that encourages specialization. Thus there are pastors for children, youth, young adults, singles, young married people, families, and so forth. With congregations of one thousand members or more, most of the ministry of mega-churches takes place in small, intense "cell" groups inspired by Wesley's bands in early Methodism*. Although most Americans still worship in congregations of fewer than five hundred people, the number of mega-churches continues to grow. Over two million people worship in mega-churches each week. There are now over 1,300 mega-churches with more than a thousand worshipers, but more than half of these mega-churches are located in just four states: California, Texas, Florida, and Georgia.

Mega-churches may be compared to the shopping malls and warehouse stores that proliferated during the same period of American history. They offer a dazzling variety of services under one roof: counseling, worship, private schools, support groups, teen clubs, movie theaters, health centers, sports teams, travel agencies, and business associations. Increasingly they even have food courts with chain restaurants. Deliverance Evangelical Church in Philadelphia, for instance, financed its multi-million dollar facility in the 1990s in part through its profitable shopping mall, which in turn helped revitalize an economically troubled black community.

In many ways, though, mega-churches are simply an updated, institutionalized, and domesticated version of the nineteenth century camp meetings of the Second Great Awakening where thousands of people traveled from miles around for twenty-four-hour, seven days-a-week religious services including evangelistic preaching, baptisms, weddings, Bible studies, and fellowship. The key difference from the past is that New Paradigm churches make effective and creative use of sophisticated communication technologies and pastors tend to have a savvy business sense.

The theology and doctrine of community churches and mega-churches varies according the beliefs of the pastor, but in general they may be termed conservative evangelical. A personal decision of faith is expected from members who are then encouraged to bring others to faith. Most of the New Paradigm churches have "seeker" services and classes that introduce potential converts to basic Christian doctrine and discipleship. For the most part, they require adult baptism by immersion along with intensive "disciplining classes."

Some New Paradigm churches advertise themselves as churches "for people who do like church." Many community churches and mega-churches adopt some of the attitudes, style, and practices of the Pentecostal churches, but are less fervent in their promotion of the gifts of tongues, healing, and prophecy. New Paradigm churches focus almost exclusively on personal transformation and family issues rather than social justice. Some of the large churches, though, operate their own charitable organizations.

Because of their independent nature, it is difficult to give an adequate account of the number and variety of New Paradigm and Community Churches, but some of the most visible organizations are included below. Many of the pastors of these churches have national and international influence through their workshops, tapes, internet resources, radio and television ministries, and speaking engagements. Perhaps nowhere else is the American adage "nothing succeeds like success" more evident in religion than in the mega-churches.

Suggestions for further reading:

Miller, Donald E. *Reinventing American Protestantism: Christianity in the New Millennium.* Berkeley: University of California Press, 1997.

Pritchard, G. A. *Willow Creek Seeker Services: Evaluating a New Way of Doing Church.* Baker Books: Grand Rapids, Michigan, 1996.

Quebedeaux, Richard. *Worldly Evangelicals: Has Success Spoiled America's Born Again Christians?* San Francisco: Harper & Row: 1978.

Schaller, Lyle E. *The Very Large Church.* Nashville: Abingdon, 2000.

Schaller, Lyle E. *The Seven Day a Week Church.* Nashville: Abingdon, 1992.

Vaughan, John N. *Megachurches & America's Cities: How Churches Grow.* Grand Rapids: Baker Books, 1993.

Wuthnow, Robert. *The Restructuring of American Religion: Society and Faith Since World War II.* Princeton, NJ: Princeton University Press, 1988.

Thumma, Scott. "Megachurches Today: Summary of Data from the *Faith Communities Today Project*," http://hirr.hartsem.edu/org/faith_megachurches.html

CONGREGATIONS WITH OVER 15,000 MEMBERS

There are at least 250 Protestant congregations in the United States that have a membership of over five thousand, which is the minimum size for a denomination to be included in this *Handbook*. In other words, these congregations have more members than some of the denominations discussed in this volume. The following is a list of just those with at least fifteen thousand members. Catholic parishes in America typically have over one thousand members and are not included in this listing. The data was provided by the Faith Communities Today Project of Hartford Institute. Links to the websites of these congregations are available at http://hirr.hartsem.edu/megachurch/database.html. A star (*) indicates that there is a separate entry on this congregation in the *Handbook*.

*Lakewood Church (non-denominational/evangelical); Houston, Texas
    43,000 average attendance; pastor Joel Osteen

*Willow Creek Community Church (Community); South Barrington, Illinois
    23,500 members; pastor Bill Hybels

Second Baptist Church (Baptist); Houston, Texas
    23,100 members; pastor Edwin Young

*Saddleback Community Church (Community); Lake Forest, California
    22,000 members; pastor Rick Warren

Life Church (Evangelical Covenant); Edmund, Oklahoma
    19,907 members; pastor Craig Groeschel

*Southeast Christian Church (Christian); Louisville, Kentucky
    18,000 members; pastor Dave Stone

First Baptist Church (Baptist); Hammond, Indiana
    18,000 members; pastor Jack Schaap

North Point Community Church (non-denominational); Alpharetta, Georgia
    17,700 members; pastor Andy Stanley

* Thomas Road Baptist Church (Baptist/fundamentalist); Lynchburg, Virginia
    17,450 members; pastor Jonathan Falwell

* Calvary Chapel (Calvary Chapel); Ft. Lauderdale, Florida
    17,000 members; pastor Robert Coy

*The Potter's House (Pentecostal/non-denominational); Dallas, Texas
    17,000 members; pastor T. D. Jakes

Phoenix First Assembly of God (Assemblies of God); Phoenix, Arizona
    16,000 members; pastor Tommy Barnett

Fellowship of the Woodlands (Baptist/non-denominational);
    The Woodlands, Texas
    15,600 members; pastor Kerry Shook

Church of the Harvest (non-denominational); Los Angeles, California
    15,000 members; pastor Clarence Mcclendon

West Angeles Church of God in Christ (COGIC); Los Angeles, California
    15,000 members; pastor Charles E. Blake

*World Changers Ministries (Baptist/non-denomintional); College Park, Georgia
    15,000 members; pastor Creflo Dollar

New Birth Missionary Baptist (Missionary Baptist); Lithonia, Georgia
    15,000 members; pastor Eddie Long

ACTS 29 NETWORK

Founded: 2007
Membership: 7,500 (est.) in 7 "campuses"

The Acts 29 Network was started by Mark Driscoll who was twenty-five years old when he began the Mars Hill Church in his apartment in Seattle, Washington. From the beginning, Driscoll's church was directed at the so-called Generation X, which was born after the "Baby Boom." Driscoll's preaching is modeled on the style of aggressive stand-up comedians, like Chris Rock, and he speaks in the vernacular used by the disaffected youth of the Northwest. As a result, he is sometimes referred to as "the cussing preacher." Despite his "grunge" persona, Driscoll's preaching is grounded in traditional evangelical systematic theology.

The Mars Hill Church has an extensive educational program to promote its conservative theology, particularly in regards to gender roles in the church, family, and society. The church has a very web-based ministry, and Driscoll's blogs are read by as many as one hundred thousand people each week. In 2003, the church opened its first satellite congregation, and now it has seven locations. Services are often very lively, and Driscoll has had to employ bodyguards because of threats against him. In 2007, the church reorganized, making Jamie Munson the Lead Pastor and Driscoll the preaching pastor.

The Acts 29 Network is dedicated to planting new churches on the Mars Hill model, and it conducts "bootcamps" to train church planters. The church promotes Calvinist theology (see REFORMED, CONGREGATIONALIST AND PRESBYTERIAN CHURCHES). It distinguishes itself from both fundamentalists* and liberals, and believes that there are demonic forces in the world that must be overcome by prayer. There are twenty-eight chapters in the Book of Acts in the New Testament, which tells of the spread of Christianity and it ends with the Apostle Paul going to Rome. "Acts 29" refers to the mission of the church beyond the New Testament into the whole world.

For more information: www.acts29network.org
Headquarters: 1411 NW 50th St., Seattle, WA 98107

CALVARY CHAPELS

Founded: 1965
Membership: statistics not available, but at least 500,000
in 700 churches (2004)

The Calvary Chapels began as a single Calvary Chapel in Costa Mesa, California, in 1965 and has grown to over seven hundred related congregations, most of them also named Calvary Chapel, across the nation. The founder and head of Calvary Chapels is Chuck Smith (1927–), who began his ministry career in 1946 in the Foursquare Gospel Church*. Frustrated with the restrictions of that and other denominations, Smith went independent in the early sixties, with a focus on campus ministry. His focus was on addressing the everyday needs and concerns of his listeners. Two years after taking over the twenty-five member Calvary Chapel, he had increased attendance to over two thousand worshipers. Soon they built a much larger facility which regularly has over twenty-five thousand worshipers. It is the fountainhead for the Calvary Chapel network.

One of the hallmarks of Smith's ministry in the 1960s was reaching out to the "hippies" and drug users of the California beach culture. He was a leader of the "Jesus Freak" movement that encouraged people to "turn off to drugs and on to Jesus." Smith founded over a hundred "community houses" modeled on the original "House of Miracles" for recent converts who needed a supportive environment.

Smith was a pioneer in the adaptation of secular rock and roll music for Christian worship. He established the Maranatha Music and Calvary Chapel recording companies, which have had a major impact on contemporary Protestant music. This "praise music" uses guitar and piano rather than traditional church instruments and has an up-beat tempo that has become very popular on Christian radio stations. This informal, lively music corresponds to the practice of wearing casual clothing, and following very informal worship. Worship, fellowship, and study times may be very emotional since members are encouraged to express their love for Christ, love for one another, and offer their personal testimonies of salvation.

Calvary Chapels emphasize evangelism, conversion, and personal experience of the Holy Spirit, but try to do so in an invitational rather than confrontational way. Slightly fewer than fifteen percent of the members report that they had no previous church connection before joining a Calvary Chapel.

For more information: www.calvarychapel.com

Contact: 3800 S Fairview St. Santa Ana, CA 92704

COMMUNION OF CONVERGENCE CHURCHES

Founded: 1995
Membership: est. 200,000 worldwide

The Communion of Evangelical Episcopal Churches was founded in 1995 and became part of the Communion of Convergence Churches USA in 2006. Convergence Movement was inspired largely by the works of Lesslie Newbigin (1908–1998) of the Church of South India in the 1940s. Newbigin proposed that the fullness of the Body of Christ required a flowing together of several "streams" of Christianity: the Catholic emphases of incarnation and creation; the Protestant focus on biblical proclamation and conversion; and the Orthodox/Pentecostal experience of mysticism and the Holy Spirit. Newbigin's vision played a key role in the formation of the Church of South India out of five different churches that received apostolic succession through Anglican bishops in India. Thus, the Convergence Movement brings together liturgical and charismatic churches around the world, using the Lambeth Quadrilateral as a guiding principle (ANGLICAN CHURCHES).

In the United States, Robert Webber (1933–2007), a professor at Wheaton College, encouraged evangelical leaders to take the early church seriously as a model for the modern church. He personally moved from a fundamentalist evangelical background into the Anglican tradition. A handful of participants in the Vineyard* movement and other liturgically-minded charismatics and evangelicals gathered in 1993 to discuss the "streams of Christianity" idea. This led to more serious discussion, and Bishop Michael Owen agreed to be the chief consecrator for the first two bishops, Russell McClanahan and John Kivuva, at a service in Virginia in 1995. In 1997 it was incorporated as the Communion of Evangelical Episcopal Churches. Soon the movement spread to other countries.

For more information: www.theceec.org

Headquarters: 124 Broadwell Circle, Franklin, TN 37067

COWBOY CHURCHES

Founded: 1960s
Membership: statistics unavailable, but over 650 churches

Cowboy churches are not a separate denomination, but they form a distinctive sub-group of evangelical churches, especially in the Southern and Western states. Cowboy churches often meet in barns or other rural facilities, and members generally wear cowboy hats and boots to services. The music is rooted in American folk music, especially as popularized by "singing cowboys" such as Roy Rogers, in the twentieth century. Cowboy churches often sponsor rodeos that include revival services and spirited preaching by "cowboy evangelists," like Jeff Smith. They are the only churches known to incorporate mechanical bulls in ministry. Most cowboy churches are Baptist* but many are non-denominational. They have grown in popularity in the past decade, with hundreds of congregations established since 2000. Theologically, cowboy churches are traditionally evangelical, placing emphasis on converting sinners to Christ. They tend to be politically and socially conservative, too. The mission of the Cowboy Church Network is "impacting the cowboy culture by planting Cowboy Churches in every county." (www.cowboycn.org)

For more information: www.cowboycn.org

Headquarters: 11014 Sam Black Road, Midland, NC 28107

EMERGENT VILLAGE

Founded: 2001
Membership: statistics not available

Emergent Village is one of the most prominent examples of the emergent church (or emerging church) movement that gathered steam toward the end of the last century. Emergent Village is not a denomination. Rather it is a network of Christians seeking to find authentic expressions of the gospel in the twenty-first century. Theological writers such as Brian McLaren, Tony Jones, and Phyllis Tickle use the biological concept of "emergence" to describe the new type of Christian community that is being created out of older institutions. Emergent or emergence Christianity is one of the most creative responses to the challenges that all religious communities face in contemporary America.

By the end of the twentieth century, there was ample evidence that American society was entering a "post-denominational," perhaps even a "post-Christian," era. Many observers believe that Christian institutions are losing relevance outside their own structures. Instead of reacting negatively to this development, emergent churches embrace a future that is open-ended. They see the marginalization of Christian institutions as a way for Christians to reclaim Jesus' vision of living as a servant people. According to emergence theory, Christian communities must be open to a radical transformation of individuals, churches, and society through the gospel. Drawing on "post-modern" philosophy and literary theory, emergence theologians and pastors seek to dismantle those church structures that impede faithful living.

In general, emergent churches reject modern bureaucracies and prefer to build cohorts and virtual communities rather than boards and agencies. Emergent Village, for example, relies heavily on internet networking (podcasts, blogs, etc.) to build relationships across theological and social divides. Rather than defending the crumbling ramparts of denominational identity, emergent churches encourage congregations to create their own eclectic collage from the rich resources of the Christian past. Sometimes called the Ancient-Future church, emergent churches blend various Christian traditions with modern music and visual presentations. Many participants work within current denominations to revitalize worship and service.

The emergence movement has similarities to the Pietist* movement of the early Enlightenment in that the participants try to avoid doctrinal polemics that create schisms, noting that Jesus did not have a statement of faith. They advocate instead for a "generous Orthodoxy" that encourages conversation among different types of Christians. Instead of fearing post-modernity's rejection of objectivity and absolutism, emergence Christianity seeks to rediscover the transformative power of Biblical and liturgical narrative.

Several emergent communities have adopted "missional living," which means that the focus of life together is active engagement in service rather than merely

296

meeting for worship and prayer. Shane Claiborne's Potter Street Community in Philadelphia is a famous example of this "new monasticism." Much like the Mennonites* and Brethren*, emergence writers insist that the central teachings of Christianity are found in Jesus' teaching and example. As such, they tend to be critics of market capitalism, and they actively promote peacemaking as a central mark of faithfulness to the Good News of Jesus. They do so, however, without separating themselves from technology or contemporary thought.

For more information: www.emergentvillage.org

Headquarters: P.O. Box 390104, Minneapolis MN 55439

INTERNATIONAL COUNCIL OF COMMUNITY CHURCHES

Founded: 1950
Membership: 73,174 in 155 churches (2009)

Not a denomination in the traditional sense, the International Council of Community Churches provides services to several hundred independently organized and operated community churches in the U.S. and around the world. The stated purposes of the council are (1) to be an answer to Christ's prayer: "That they may all be one" (John 17:21 NRSV); (2) to affirm the worth and dignity of every person; (3) to attend to human need and suffering throughout the world; (4) to seek and share the truth; (5) to build toward a new world of peace.

The current organization resulted from a 1950 merger of two other councils: one composed of predominantly black congregations, the other of churches with predominantly white memberships. The council holds an annual conference to which every member church can send two voting members, at least one of which must be a lay person. This conference elects a president, an executive director, a board of trustees, and other officers who carry on the business of the council between conferences. The executive director and a small staff oversee the projects of the council on a daily basis; headquarters are in Frankfort, Illinois.

The Council's services include ecclesiastical endorsement, personnel placement, continuing education, direct and brokered consultation for help in various areas, and supportive networks for clergy and their spouses and children. Publications include *The Christian Community*, a monthly newspaper; *The Pastor's Journal*, a quarterly for professionals; and materials from the Community Church Press.

It should be noted that many of the Council's member churches do not use the word *Community* in their names. Moreover, many churches that do include this term in their names are affiliated with a denomination, are members of a national organization outside the historic movement, or are independent congregations.

For more information: www.icccusa.com

Headquarters: 21116 Washington Parkway, Frankfort, IL 60423

LAKEWOOD CHURCH

Founded: 1959
Membership: 40,000 (est.) in 1 church

Lakewood Church was founded by John Osteen in an old feed store north of Houston. Osteen was a popular preacher who made effective use of television to extend his ministry to some one hundred countries worldwide. His son Joel succeeded him as pastor in 1999 and quickly became one of the premier religious figures in America. Osteen is a leading proponent of what is sometimes termed the "prosperity gospel" that is a blend of the "positive-thinking" program of Norman Vincent Peale and traditional Pentecostal* ideas of spiritual health and healing.

The congregation grew so rapidly under the leadership of Joel Osteen and his wife Victoria that it moved into the former Compac Center, a sixteen-thousand seat sports arena that once housed the Houston Rockets, in 2005. Several millions of dollars were spent in renovating the facility to make it suitable for worship and other ministries. The church reports spending more than $30 million each year on its television ministry that has a viewership of over seven million in the United States alone. Osteen is the author of several popular books on the benefits of faith.

For more information: www.lakewood.cc

Church Office: P.O. Box 4600, Houston, TX 77210

POTTER'S HOUSE

Founded: 1996
Membership: 18,000 in 1 church

Thomas D. Jakes, Sr. is one of the most prominent figures in the history of African American Pentecostalism*. His website describes him as a "pastor, community advocate, humanitarian, author, songwriter, playwright, conference speaker and broadcaster." (www.thepottershouse.org) Like many Pentecostal preachers, Jakes started with a storefront church, but his keen entrepreneurial and preaching skills helped him create one of the largest inter-racial faith communities in American history. His Potter's House specializes in "ministry to the shattered" and has a number of vibrant ministries to the homeless, hopeless, and addicted in the Dallas area.

Jakes is probably best known for his television broadcasts on cable TV networks such as BET (Black Entertainment Television). The church's distinctive blending of economics and spirituality is evident in its mission statement which includes the desire "to become a global voice, along a lifelong journey of spiritual and economic hope, encouragement and empowerment to people locally, nationally and around the world." (www.thepottershouse.org) Theologically, the church affirms many common elements of conservative evangelicalism including the inerrancy of Scripture, the pre-millenial return of Christ, and everlasting punishment for unbelievers. Jakes leads an extensive network of like-minded pastors who have partnered with the Potter's House and use resources provided by the organization.

For more information: www.thepottershouse.org

Headquarters: 6777 W. Kiest Blvd, Dallas, TX 75236

SADDLEBACK CHURCH

Founded: 1980
Membership: 22,000 in 1 church

Saddleback Church has become a legend in American Protestantism. It was founded by a recent seminary graduate named Rick Warren in the Saddleback Valley of California in 1980 with two hundred people and has since grown to be one of the largest mega-churches in the country. Warren described his goal for the church as "a place where the hurting, the depressed, the confused can find love, acceptance, help, hope, forgiveness and encouragement." (www.saddleback.com) More than twenty-thousand people on average attend worship services and the church has more than two hundred ministries locally. Saddleback has helped establish over thirty "daughter congregations" around the country and appears to be moving towards becoming its own denomination.

Warren's 1995 book *The Purpose Driven Church* made Saddleback and its pastor internationally famous. The church reports that over 350,000 church leaders have been trained in his model of church growth. The book was praised in business journals as a guide to entrepreneurship. Another one of Warren's books, *The Purpose Driven Life*, was the #1 bestseller on the *New York Times* bestseller list for months. Warren also established internet resources to mentor pastors in his approach to church building and ministry. In this way, the Saddleback network of Rick Warren stretches across many denominations. In 2009 Pastor Warren offered the prayer at the inauguration of Barack Obama.

For more information: www.saddleback.com

Headquarters: 1 Saddleback Pkwy, Lake Forest, CA 92630

SOUTHEAST CHRISTIAN CHURCH

Founded: 1962
Membership: 18,000 in 1 church

The Southeast Christian Church started in 1962 as a fairly typical new church started in the Christian Church*, but when Robert Russell took over as pastor four years later the church developed a vision for facilities expansion. After having out-grown two sanctuaries, the congregation decided to build a massive campus off a major parkway in the 1990s. Over thirty million dollars were raised for the proj-ect, and now Southeast is one of the largest congregations in the U.S. and is now a major economic force in Louisville. The congregation's spectacular Christmas and Easter performances attract thousands of visitors each year. Over eight hundred members have participated in short-term mission programs.

The church offers a variety of ministries to all age groups as well as special pro-grams for blended families, disabled and deaf persons, and Spanish-language ser-vices. Their mission program includes an assertive messianic mission to Jews. The church's mission statement is "to evangelize the lost; edify the saved; minister to those in need; and be a conscience in the community." (www.southeastchristian.org) The statement of faith includes much of the Apostles' Creed, but adds a number of beliefs important to the Christian Church* such as believers' baptism by immersion and local congregational autonomy.

For more information: www.southeastchristian.org

Headquarters: 920 Blankenbaker Parkway, Louisville, KY 40243-1845

TRINITY UNITED CHURCH OF CHRIST

Founded: 1961
Membership: 8,500 (est.) in 1 church

Chicago's Trinity Church is one of the largest congregations in the United Church of Christ*, but its doctrine and practice is so distinctive from other UCC churches that it merits special attention in the *Handbook*. Trinity became famous during the 2008 presidential campaign because then-candidate Barack Obama was an active member of the church. Comments that a former pastor, the Rev. Dr. Jeremiah Wright, made during one of his sermons were the subject of intense me-dia scrutiny and controversy during the campaign. President Obama credits Rev. Wright with helping transform his life and teaching him the power of hope.

Trinity was founded during the civil rights movement with the original inten-tion that it would become an interracial congregation in the South Side of Chi-cago. As the dream of integration died in the 1960s, the leadership of Trinity grew increasingly interested in the Black Power movement, whose leading spokesman was Malcolm X. The church embraced a mission of being "unabashedly black" and endorsed Afrocentrism in worship, education, and self-understanding. In 1972 the church called an energetic young Baptist preacher named Jeremiah as pastor. Rev. Wright had masters degrees in English literature and divinity, and he combined brilliant oratory with sophisticated sociological analysis and biblical exegesis. Un-der Wright's leadership the church grew into one of the largest congregations in the UCC. Along with the theologian James Cone, Wright was one of the leaders of the Black Theology movement. More provocatively, he also established working relations with leading figures in the Nation of Islam*. Trinity Church played an active role in Chicago politics. Wright retired in 2008 and was succeeded by the Rev. Otis Moss III. The church maintains extensive ministry programming focusing on the African American community in the Chicago area.

For more information: www.tucc.org

Church Office: 400 West 95th Street, Chicago, IL 60628

UNIVERSAL FELLOWSHIP OF METROPOLITAN COMMUNITY CHURCHES

Founded: 1970
Membership: 15,666 in 115 churches (2006)

This Protestant denomination is unique among Christian bodies in that it was founded specifically to reach out to and affirm homosexual persons. The church holds the belief that theology is the basis to present the good news of God's love to a segment of society often excluded from, and sometimes ridiculed for, participation in church life. This awareness prompted Troy D. Perry (1940–) to create a denomination in which such marginalized people could find genuine acceptance in a context of Christian worship and service. Perry had been discharged from the Baptist* church he served as pastor and ostracized from his denomination. He called a congregation into being in Los Angeles, and soon churches were organized in other cities. In the summer of 1970, the first general conference was held.

Heterosexuals may and do belong to the church, but a large percentage of the membership is homosexual. The church faces the controversial nature of its existence by stating that its members accept homosexuality as a gift from God, just as heterosexuality is a gift from God. Nonetheless, it holds that sexuality is not and should not be the focal point of life. Everything in life, including sexuality, should be centered around a relationship with God. The denomination describes its ministry as a shared one—lay and clergy, women and men, privileged and underprivileged, lesbian, gay, and heterosexual. Forty-three percent of its clergy are women.

The church professes traditional Christian theology on such doctrines as Scripture, the Trinity, and the sacraments. The Bible, "interpreted by the Holy Spirit in conscience and faith," (www.mcchurch.org/BylawsandGovernance/December07/Bylaws07eng.pdf, p. 4) is the guide for faith and discipline. Since its members come from all types of Christian churches, the worship style, liturgy, and practice of congregations is eclectic and varied. Some congregations are more or less Pentecostal* while others are very liturgical. Baptism and Holy Communion are the sacraments.

301

The membership of this denomination is active in a variety of ministries, reflecting its primary orientation to the social gospel and liberation theology. In particular, it has sought to address the needs of the hungry, the homeless, and the powerless. It supports a freeze on nuclear weapons and is committed to eradicating sexism in its theology and in society at large. The civil rights of all people are a major concern. It also addresses the AIDS epidemic as a major social issue, partly because incidences of the disease are so prevalent among its own membership.

The government of the church is vested in a Board of Elders, which includes the Moderator and six regional elders. The denomination was restructured in 2002, and subsequently decentralized its offices. The church is an international body, with a strong presence in Canada and Australia. The last General Conference met in 2007. The church applied for membership in the National Council of the Churches of Christ in the U.S.A. in 1983 and was declined. It hopes eventually to become a part of that ecumenical organization, with which it remains in dialogue. It does participate as an official observer in World Council of Churches events.

For more information: www.mccchurch.org
Headquarters: P.O. Box 1374, Abilene, TX 79604

WILLOW CREEK COMMUNITY CHURCH

Founded: 1975
Membership: est. 23,000 in 1 church

Willow Creek is one of the most successful and famous community churches, and it has developed its own national network of similar growth-oriented non-denominational congregations. The church grew out of a popular youth ministry of the South Park Church in Park Ridge, Illinois, which included about one thousand teenagers. The group was led by Bill Hybels, the founding pastor of Willow Creek, who employed contemporary music and drama as a way to apply the Bible to the lives of American teenagers. In 1975 Hybels and his co-workers rented a movie theater to hold services directed toward youth. As attendance grew to over two thousand, the members purchased ninety acres of undeveloped land in South Barrington and built a state of the art auditorium in 1981.

The Willow Creek model for church development includes hundreds of small groups within the congregation that focus on different needs. Among them are "seeker groups" and discipleship groups. Evangelism is seen as the work of the entire congregation, and the large gatherings use the latest in stagecraft and musical technology. The doctrine of the church is basically evangelical Protestant. They practice believers' baptism but offer "infant dedication" ceremonies for children of baptized parents. Through the Willow Creek Association, the church is developing its own denominational identity, but the distinguishing characteristics are those of style and structure rather than doctrine or history. Currently there are about eight thousand congregations in the Association, but many of them have denominational affiliations as well. Tens of thousands of church leaders have been trained in the Willow Creek method.

For more information: www.willowcreek.org

Willow Creek Church, 67 East Algonquin Rd., South Barrington, IL 60010

WORLD CHANGERS MINISTRIES

Founded: 1986
Membership: 15,000 members

Since their marriage in 1986, Creflo Dollar and his wife Taffi have become one of the most popular ministry teams of the electronic church. They are attractive, charismatic, and engaging on television and in person. These qualities contributed greatly to the stunning growth of the World Changers Ministry they first established in the cafeteria of a Georgia elementary school that Dollar attended as a child. A decade later he dedicated the World Dome, an 8,500-seat worship facility complete with state of the art audio and video equipment. Dollar boasts that the facility "had not only been prayed for, but that was paid for." (www.worldchangers.org)

Dollar is most famous for his vigorous promotion of "Prosperity Theology" in addition to the more traditional Pentecostal* gifts of healing and speaking in tongues. A major theme of his addresses and his educational programs is that believers who tithe and live according to the Scripture will not only get out of debt but will grow financially prosperous. He points to his own prosperity, which includes two Rolls Royce cars and tailor-made suits, as evidence of the blessings of God on the faithful. The congregation's most famous member is the former heavy-weight boxing champion Evander Holyfield. A significant portion of the congregation's $80 million annual budget goes toward purchasing television time on cable networks such as BET (Black Entertainment Television).

For more information: www.worldchangers.org

Headquarters: P.O. Box 490124, College Park, GA 30349.

ISLAM

Islam is second only to Christianity in size and geographical scope among world religions, but it is only in the last quarter of the twentieth century that Muslims have been a significant presence in the United States. At the beginning of the twenty-first century, Muslims outnumber Episcopalians and many other denominations in the U.S. If current trends keep up, there will be more Muslims than Jews or Lutherans in a generation. Despite this increasing presence in American religious and social life, Islam is poorly understood in the U.S., and Muslims have been subject to unfair stereotyping. This has been particularly the case since the militant attacks of Al Qaida, which promotes a violent fundamentalist ideology. It is important to keep in mind that such militants are a small percentage of Muslims.

Islam is a monotheistic religion that has close historical and theological ties to Christianity and Judaism. Like them, it seeks to build a just and peaceful society based on a rational moral code. Islam has a long and glorious tradition. In fact, when the Christian West was in its so-called Dark Ages, Islamic countries were renowned for their science, art, and philosophy. But in the nineteenth and twentieth centuries, many Islamic regions were colonized by the industrialized Western nations. Their development was impaired by colonial rule, and for many Muslims anti-Western sentiment grew strong. For Muslims living in the U.S., there is the ever-present question of how much one can live like an American and remain faithful to the commandments of Allah. The question of how fully one can embrace American culture while remaining true to one's religious faith is, of course, common to all devout people in America, regardless of their religion.

History. The words "Muslim" and "Islam" are based on the Arabic root word meaning obedience. A Muslim is one who is obedient to God in his or her thoughts and deeds. According to Muslims, Islam began about four thousand years ago when God made a covenant with the Patriarch Abraham (Ibrahim). Abraham was obedient to God; therefore, Abraham was a Muslim—one who submits to the will of Allah. His was the true religion that later suffered corruption. The oldest son of Abraham was Ishmael (Ismail), whom the Arabs claim as their forebear. According to Muslims, it was Ishmael, the first born, whom Abraham willingly

305

offered to God rather than Isaac. According to the sacred text of Islam, the Holy Quran, Abraham and Ishmael built the first Ka'ba in Mecca as a place of worship for the one true God.

Historically, though, Islam as an organized religion developed out of Judaism six centuries after the birth of Jesus. Within a hundred years of Muhammad's famous *Hijrah* (see below) in 622, Muslims conquered much of the ancient Christian world: Syria, Palestine, Egypt, North Africa, and Spain. In addition to the astounding military success of the early Muslim armies, this represents one of the most rapid expansions of any new religious movement. After the initial expansion of Islam, though, the various Muslim principalities and sultanates became divided among themselves. Eventually many were conquered by the Mongols who in turn were conquered by the Turks. In 1453, the great Christian city of Constantinople fell to the Turks and became an Islamic capital, whose name was eventually changed to Istanbul. Now Muslims pray in mosques in Africa, Europe, America, much of Asia, and Indonesia. But it all began with one man.

Origins. Muslims around the world proclaim, "There is no God but Allah, and Muhammad is his prophet." This greatest prophet of Islam was a member of the Quraysh tribe of Mecca, which was an important center for trade and religion in Arabia. Mecca housed the Ka'ba, a very important shrine among the people of Arabia. Thousands made pilgrimage each year to visit the Ka'ba and see or touch the holy stone contained therein. They also left gifts before the idols located at that time in the shrine.

When he was twenty-five years old, Muhammad married a wealthy widow named Khadijah and managed her extensive holdings and trade. Every year during the month of Ramadan the family would leave the heat of the city to live in one of the cool caves nearby. During one of these family retreats, Muhammad received a call to be a prophet. He heard a voice that told him to read. When he protested that he could not read, the voice commanded him again. He then left the cave and saw the angel Gabriel (Jibril), who told him that he was to be God's messenger.

Later the angel revealed to Muhammad that he was called to reform the religion of the people of Mecca. They must get rid of their idols and worship only the true God of Abraham, Isaac, and Ishmael. Muhammad's first converts were Khadijah, his cousin Ali, and his friend Abu Bakr. Muhammad's reform plans offended his own tribe who profited from the pilgrimages and gifts to the idols in the Ka'ba. After some thirteen years of struggling to convert the people of Mecca, a group of pilgrims from Yathrib, now known as Medina, heard Muhammad preach and accepted him as Allah's prophet. Messianic hopes were high among the Jews in Yathrib, and for a brief period early Muslims and Jews were united in their hope for the millennial kingdom.

In Mecca, though, the anger against the prophet increased, and in 622 C.E. Muhammad fled to Yathrib in order to avoid assassination. This flight to Yathrib is known as the *Hijrah,* and it begins the Muslim calendar. Dates in Islamic lands are counted in years after the *Hijrah* (AH), just as Christian lands date events before and after the birth of Jesus. Because of its importance in the development of Islam, Yathrib became known as Al-Medina (*the* city). It was in Medina that Muhammad laid the foundation for the religion of Islam and became a great chieftain. Medina remains one of the sacred cities of Islam and is visited by millions of pilgrims.

Over the years Muhammad received many divine messages in a state of trance. These prophecies, called *surahs*, were written down by his hearers and later collected and edited in the book we know as the Quran, or simply the Reading. They are organized according to length rather than content or chronology. Islam teaches that the Quran is the faithful recording of the word of God as it was delivered to Muhammad. It is written in the beautiful and poetic Arabic of the time of Muhammad.

After several years organizing his followers in Medina, Muhammad entered Mecca as a victor. The residents converted, and the idols were destroyed. Soon afterward Muhammad became the virtual emperor of Arabia and outlawed all forms of idolatry. Only monotheists—Muslims, Jews, and Christians—were tolerated. Before Muhammad died in 632 C.E., it is said that he was taken by Gabriel to Jerusalem where he visited the Temple site. There Muhammad ascended into heaven and met Moses and Jesus. The rock from which he descended remains a holy site. One of the most beautiful buildings in the world, The Dome of the Rock, was built in 687 over the rock.

Shortly after this journey by night, Muhammad died. His death was a blow to his followers, but they remembered that he was a mortal and not a god. Muslims follow the teachings of Muhammad, but they do not worship him or view him as divine. The prophet was succeeded by his close companion and relative Abu Bakr. The early successors of the prophet are known as the Caliphs, which has much the same meaning as the English word "steward." A caliph (khalifah) acts on behalf of another. The first four Caliphs were instrumental in defining the nature of Islam and ensuring its long-term survival, and they are known to Muslims as the four "rightly-guided" Caliphs.

One of the early tasks of the Caliphs was to insure that the Quran was written in an authentic and unalterable form so that the words of the prophet would not be corrupted through the years. A single version of the Quran was approved and all others destroyed. Even today, there are not different versions of the Quran. Translations into modern languages are all considered interpretations of the Quran rather than the Quran itself. Devout Muslims, who no longer speak this form of Arabic, even in Arabia, learn the language of the Quran and commit much of the book to memory. Arabic, like Hebrew in Judaism, is one of the things that binds the worldwide Islamic community (the Umma) together.

During the period of the Caliphs, other sayings of Muhammad and remembrances of the prophet were collected and classified. These sayings or *sunnahs* are recorded in the *Hadith*. Though they are not considered sacred scripture equal to the Quran, they play an important role in helping to define Islamic practices and laws. The period of the "rightly guided" Caliphs was crucial in defining Islam, but it ended with the assassination of Ali, the last of Muhammad's original companions to lead the Muslims, in 662 C.E. The leadership of Islam passed to the Umayyad dynasty after a period of internal dispute, but their rule was rejected by many supporters of Ali. It was at this point that Shi'ite* Islam was born.

Theology and Practice. The basic idea of Islam is submission to the will of Allah. The will of God was expressed through the prophets, many of which are common to Judaism and Islam. According to Islam, there were five great prophets: Noah, Abraham, Moses, Jesus, and Muhammad. Many Christians are surprised to learn that the Quran teaches that Mary was a virgin when Jesus was conceived and that Jesus worked miracles. Muslims, like most Christians, believe that Jesus will return at the end of human history, but they do not believe that Jesus was divine nor do they accept the idea of the crucifixion and resurrection of Jesus.

Though there are different branches of Islam, some of which have been in conflict with each other, there are some things basic to all forms of Islam (excluding the Nation of Islam*). There are five major beliefs in Islam: (1) there is only one God; (2) there are angels; (3) there have been many prophets, but there is only one message; (4) there will be a final judgment; (5) it is possible to have knowledge of God and God's will.

Islam emphasizes the ability of ordinary people to know and understand the teachings of God; therefore, Islam emphasizes the intellect. Every faithful Muslim is a student. There is a Muslim saying that God's first creation was the pen. The first word God revealed to Muhammad was *read*. It is obligatory in Islam to read, study, and seek knowledge; therefore the ink of the scholar is considered to be more valuable than the blood of a martyr.

Even more important than these five fundamental beliefs are the Five Pillars of Islam. Every Muslim must follow these five pillars in order to attain heaven, but provisions are made for the weak, the poor, and the infirm. The demands of religion, in Islam, should never imperil the health of one's spouse and children. The Five Pillars are:

(1) *Shahada*: There is no God but Allah and Muhammad is his prophet. This is the foundation of Islamic monotheism combined with confidence that the words Muhammad spoke were a true revelation of the will of the one God.

(2) *Salat*: five prayers daily facing Mecca. The prayers are proscribed, as is the bodily posture. By praying five times a day and humbling oneself physically before God, Muslims are reminded that humans are to submit to God in all things, at all times, and in all places.

(3) *Zakat*: ritual almsgiving. Muslims are expected to give two and a half percent of their income to the needy. This is beyond the obligation to pay taxes, and the money must go to those in need rather than just any charitable organization.

(4) *Siyam*: a one-month fast during Ramadan. This is in imitation of the practice of Muhammad, and it makes Ramadan the holiest time of the year for

Muslims. The fast is a daytime fast, but exceptions are made for those who are elderly, pregnant, or in poor health. The Ramadan fast emphasizes that the true fast is to refrain from evil and to be humble enough to ask forgiveness for those one has wronged.

(5) *Hajj*: a pilgrimage to Mecca. Each Muslim is expected to make at least one journey to Mecca to pray at the Ka'ba during his or her life. More than two million people do so each year, at great cost to the Saudi Arabian government, which provides hospitality. Muslims are forbidden to borrow money for their *Hajj* or to impoverish their families.

The Five Pillars and the five basic tenets form the foundation of Islam, but there is much more to the Muslim life than these. Islam, like Judaism*, is an all-encompassing religion, and Islamic scholars through the centuries have offered guidance in how to live according to the commands of God. Muslims have always needed teachers to educate people about the law and to interpret the law so that it may be applied to every circumstance of life. These teachers and interpreters of the law are called *Muftis*. Those who help worshipers in the mosque understand and apply the law are called Imams or Mullahs.

Islam is a practical religion that gives guidance for daily life rather than encouraging asceticism. Moderation in all things, even religion, is stressed. Some things, like images, alcohol, and pork, are forbidden. Other things, like divorce, are permitted but discouraged. Thus there is some variation in Muslim customs because they reflect local traditions. Islam in the U.S. is different from Islam in Pakistan, for instance, but the Islamic ideal is that the whole world will become submissive to the will of God.

Islamic law is known as the *Sharia*, and it includes not only what Americans would consider criminal matters, such as theft, but also instructions on how family life and society should be organized. It also includes laws regarding religious observance, devotion, and worship. Sharia is based on the Quran and the Hadith of the prophet, but it also includes the work of legal scholars who faced the difficult task of applying teachings originally given in Arabia to the quite different situation of Muslims in many cultures. This process of interpretation of Sharia is called *ijtihad*. Sunni* and Shi'ite* Islam differ on important aspects of Sharia.

Islam in the United States. There were Muslims in America from the earliest days of European exploration and colonization. Some of these were Moors employed by the Spanish conquistadors; others were Africans brought as slaves. In the colonial period enslaved Africans in America were more likely to be Muslim than Christian. After the Civil War, Syrian and Lebanese immigrants left their farms in the Middle East in order to work in America's burgeoning metropolises. Some of the new arrivals were Christians, but many were Muslims. Muslim neighborhoods developed in New York City, Chicago, Detroit, and other major northern cities. As the Ottoman Empire slowly collapsed in the years leading up to World War I, more immigrants from the Middle East fled to America.

The most celebrated conversion of an American of European descent to Islam came in 1888 when Alexander Russell Webb, the U.S. Council to the Philippines, spoke the *Shahada*. He promoted his new faith and worked for greater toleration of Islam through his journal *The Moslem World*. He was also a featured speaker at the famous World's Parliament of Religions in Chicago in 1893, which brought the world's great religious traditions to the American public's attention.

Immigration laws enacted after World War I to restrict the immigration of non-whites slowed the growth of Islam in the U. S. With the changes made in American immigration policy in 1965, an average of thirty thousand Muslims a year immigrated. Muslim immigrants, like their Catholic and Jewish predecessors, settled primarily in the urban centers of the Northeast, the Midwest, and the West Coast. American Muslims come from over sixty different nations; therefore, there has been some difficulty in bringing together divergent cultural expressions of the religion in a single mosque. Slightly over one-fourth of U.S. Muslims emigrated from the Middle East, but almost as many came from Eastern European countries, especially the Balkans. Turkish Americans established numerous Divan Centers to preserve Turkish culture and introduce all Americans to Islamic and Turkish culture.

Because of the diversity of national origins, the architectural style of mosques, leadership styles, and attitudes toward gender roles differ widely among American Muslims. Despite the diversity of American Islam, certain things, such as learning Arabic, reciting the prayers, and reading the Qur'an unite Muslims of all national origins. In terms of personal behavior in public, though, Muslims share the values of conservative Jews and Christians. They urge both men and women to be modest in dress, monogamous in sex, respectful to others, and generous to the poor.

The major branches of Islam are represented in the U.S., but they are not organized as institutions the way Christian denominations are. There are Sunni mosques and organizations to promote and defend Sunnism, and there are similar organizations for the Shi'ites, but there are no headquarters for the different branches that maintain membership lists or statistics.

African American Muslims. In the twentieth century, Islam began attracting significant numbers of African American converts. Estimates range from five hundred thousand to over a million African American Muslims in the U.S. today. For many converts, Islam represented an alternative to Christianity, which they associated with slaveholders. Further, Islam represented a connection with their ancestors, for at least some of the Africans brought in bondage to these shores had been Muslims in their homeland. Finally, Islam offered a practical discipline and control over one's destiny that many felt was denied to them in the dominant culture.

It was Malcolm X (1925–65) who did the most to spotlight Islam in the African American community. He had originally been a leader in the Nation of Islam*; however, he rejected that organization after he made his *hajj* to Mecca and encountered Sunni Islam in its full international and interracial character. He saw that racism of every kind is condemned in Islam: all Muslims are equal in the eyes of God and will face the same judgment, just as all Muslims on *hajj* wear the same white robes of penitence and submission to Allah.

Malcolm X brought this message of racial equality back to the United States, but he was murdered just as he was establishing his own Islamic organization for African Americans. After his death, others followed his example and continued his cause. Among them were notable athletes who took Muslim names, such as Muhammad Ali and Kareem Abdul-Jabbar. W. Deen Muhammad has played a leading role in introducing African Americans to orthodox Sunni Islam. African American Muslims tend to establish their own mosques and publishing houses, but the same is true of Muslims who have recently immigrated. Perhaps a quarter of American Muslims today are of African descent.

Suggestions for further reading:

Armstrong, Karen. *Islam: A Short History.* New York: Modern Library, 2000.

Barks, Coleman, trans. *The Essential Rumi.* HarperOne, 1997.

Esposito, John L. *Islam: The Straight Path.* New York: Oxford University Press, 1988.

Esposito, John L, ed. *The Oxford Encyclopedia of the Modern Islamic World.* 4 vols. New York: Oxford University Press, 1995.

Haddad, Yvonne Yazbeck. *The Islamic Impact.* Syracuse, NY: University of Syracuse Press, 1984.

Haddad, Yvonne. *Muslims of America.* New York: Oxford University Press, 1993.

Malcolm X, with Alex Haley. *The Autobiography of Malcolm X.* New York: Ballantine, 1973.

McCloud, Aminah Beverly. *African American Islam.* New York: Routledge, 1995.

Nu'man, Fareed H. *The Muslim Population in the United States.* Washington D.C.: The American Muslim Council, 1992.

Turner, Richard B. *Islam in the African-American Experience.* Bloomington, IN: University of Indiana Press, 1997.

Westerlund, David, ed. *Sufism in Europe and North America.* RoutledgeCurzon, 2003.

SUNNI ISLAM

Founded: 622 (major influx in the U.S. after 1965)
Membership: est. 1.5 million in approx. 1,200 mosques (2000)

Ninety percent of the world's one billion Muslims are in one of the four orthodox branches of Sunni Islam*. The Sunni teach that the "gate of *ijtihad*," or the process of interpretation of the law, was closed in the tenth century. Before the gate of *ijtihad* was closed, four major schools of legal thought had developed in Sunni Islam. They are the Hanafi, Maliki, Shafi, and Hanbali legal traditions.

This is not the place to discuss the technicalities of the different schools, but it is important to recognize that the different schools impacted different areas of the Muslim world. The schools also differ in their level of strictness.

Hanafi is the oldest school and was the official teaching of the Abbasid dynasty. It continues to influence regions once controlled by the Abasids, such as Egypt, Syria, Jordan, India, and Turkey. The jurist Malik ibn Anas placed great weight on the Hadith in interpreting the law, and he also emphasized the law's role in promoting the common good. Maliki law has been influential in parts of Egypt, the Persian Gulf countries, and North Africa. Sharifi law is based on a more strict interpretation of the Quran and Hadith than the previous two, and it is suspicious of human legal reasoning. It has been influential in southern Arabia and Southeast Asia as well as East Africa. The latest and strictest interpretation of the law, the Hanbali, is also the smallest. But it has become very influential since it is promoted in central Arabia and forms the basis of Saudi Arabia's legal system.

Theoretically, each school accepts the others as orthodox, but from time to time charismatic religious reformers will promote one view to the exclusion of the others. Sunni Muslims are expected to follow the teachings of one of the four traditions faithfully rather than mixing them. This has been difficult in Western countries because Muslims from different regions of the world, following different schools of *Sharia*, often participate in the same mosques.

Membership figures for the Sunni in the U.S. are very rough estimates, since there are no central organizations for Muslims. Mosques are primarily places of prayer and study and generally do not keep or report statistics. The Islamic Society of North America (ISNA), located in Plainfield, Indiana, is the largest organization that provides support for Muslim ministries. In particular, it helps to establish full-time Islamic schools and reviews textbooks for Muslims. It also helps Muslims observe dietary laws while under U.S. government control (e.g., in the military or prison). The ISNA also has programs aimed at keeping youth involved in Islam and in training Islamic workers.

For more information: www.theislamiccenter.com

Contact: Islamic Center of Washington, 2551 Massachusetts Avenue NW, Washington, D.C. 20008

SHI'ITE ISLAM

Founded: 662
Membership: perhaps 100,000 in U.S. (2000)

About ten percent of the world's one billion Muslims (roughly one hundred million) are Shi'ite instead of Sunni. The split between the Shi'a and the Sunni came when the fourth Caliph, Ali, was assassinated by extremists who believed that he had fallen into unbelief because he had accepted human arbitration during a dispute rather than letting God settle the matter through warfare. With the sudden death of Ali, the Umayyad family seized power and established the first Muslim ruling dynasty.

Ali was a very pious man, and his followers rejected the worldliness of the Umayyads. The Shi'is, as his followers were called, viewed Ali as the First Caliph, rather than the Fourth, and they traced the line of true Caliphs through Ali's family. Ali's second son, Husain was put forward as the true successor when the first Umayyad ruler, Muawiyyah died in 680. In that year the Umayyad army surrounded Husain and his family on the plain of Kerbala near Kufa in modern day Iraq. Though it was a holy day of fasting, they were all murdered, with Husain dying while holding his infant son.

The murder of Husain and his family became a central aspect of Shi'ite devotion, and the shrine of Husain in Kerbala remains one of the most holy sites to Shi'ites. For centuries the story has been retold and even acted out as a "passion play," reminding Shi'ites of the importance of martyrdom. The Shi'ites grew strong in Iraq and Iran and developed a distinctive form of Islam.

The Shi'ite use the title "Imam" rather than "Caliph" to refer to the true leader of Islam. The clergy in Shi'ism generally have more authority to interpret Islamic law and observances than in Sunni Islam. Shi'ism has tended to be more flexible and more volatile than Sunni'ism since it allows for greater adaptation to changing social and historical conditions. In Yemen, the Zaydi legal tradition has been a force for moderation and social justice, but the last Zaydi Imam was overthrown by revolution in 1962.

Shi'ites tend to promote greater separation between politics and religion than the Sunni, and there is a strong mystical element to Shi'ite faith. Many Shi'ites expect a "Twelfth Imam" to appear at the start of the messianic age. Over the centuries, Shi'ite religious leaders have sometimes led popular resistant movements against regimes they found to be unjust. In 1979 the Shi'ites in Iran rebelled against the oppressive rule of the last Shah of Iran, whom many viewed as a pawn of Western powers.

Shi'ite Islam has produced a number of interesting sects that are not very visible in the U.S. The most important are the Ismali, who believed that the true line of Imams ran through the line of Ismail, the sixth imam rather than his brother. Over time the Ismaili (or Seveners) developed an esoteric religious faith often accused of antinomianism. In Turkey, the Druze sect developed as a millenialist movement in the eleventh century. The Druze teach reincarnation and other ideas taken from Persian Zoroastrianism that are contrary to traditional Islamic teaching.

SUFISM

Founded: eighth century; came to U.S. ca. 1910
Membership: statistics not available

Sufism is a mystical tradition in Islam that originated sometime before the tenth century. By its very nature, it has not developed denominational forms, and thus it is difficult to provide statistical information. There are many different Sufi orders in the United States, each associated with different Sufi masters. Historically, Sufism has been most popular in Muslim regions with large Christian populations, such as Turkey, because of its fundamental message of religious toleration. Jesus plays a major role in all Islamic thought, but many Sufi view him as the true founder of their order. For the Sufi, Jesus was the great ascetic teacher of mystical union with God. Those who follow the path of Jesus can achieve a union with the divine similar to his own.

The Sufi call upon Muslims to live and pray more like Jesus rather than focusing on external observation of the law. They called on Christians to focus less on worshiping Jesus and instead to seek the same mystical path of Jesus. In general, Sufism places less emphasis on legalism and more on religious experience and an embrace of all people in divine love. This has not always been acceptable to religious authorities, and over the centuries, a number of Sufi masters have been executed because of their violations of Islamic law.

In India, Sufism provided a middle group between Islam and Hinduism, and Sufism adapted techniques from the yogis. For the Sufi, religion is essentially an interior matter of the soul purified by God rather than outward observance. Hazrat Inayat Kahn brought a universalist form of Sufi mysticism from India to the West early in the twentieth century. He introduced Americans to several different Sufi orders, such as the Chisti, Naqshbandi, Qadiri, and Suharwardi order, arguing that all paths lead to the same divine reality. His followers formed the Sufi Order International in 1927. One of Kahn's disciples was Samuel L. Lewis, who adopted the name Sufi Ahmad Murad Chisti in 1926. He established a center, Sufi Ruhianat, in San Francisco.

One of the most important Sufi masters was the poet Rumi (1207-1273), whose writings were popularized in America by the poet Coleman Barks, who rendered them into English free-verse in the 1970s. Rumi's poems became very popular on American college campuses, and there is an annual Rumi festival in North Carolina. It is not accidental that Sufism has grown in popularity in the United States as the country has become more religiously pluralistic and ethnically diverse. Many Americans who were attracted to Sufi teachings studied in the historic centers of Sufism before establishing themselves as teachers. Sufism also appeals to many Americans who were interested in New Age and eastern religious thought. Others have been attracted to Sufi meditation, music, and dance for its therapeutic benefits.

The Sufi path is called the Sema, and it is a form of spirituality based in the body more than the mind. Unlike Sufism in the Middle East, women often participate with men in Sufi exercises in the United States. Sufism is similar to Hasidic Judaism* in its teaching that God is in all things, its focus on divine joy at all times, and its use of dancing to help induce religious experience. In Turkey, the Dervish developed Sufi mystical dance as the centerpiece of prayer. Unlike the Hasidim, though, the Sufi do not establish separate communities. Rather, Sufi masters teach the Sufi arts in any number of schools or religious orders.

The Sufi do not believe that their way is the right way for everyone; it is for those who are specially called. However, the teachings of the Sufi are available to all. Unlike the rationalism of most Islamic schools of thought, the Sufi self-consciously embrace paradox and parable. Sufi wisdom is often communicated through stories in which the fool is the one who is truly wise because he sees through the hypocrisy of the world. Poetry rather than didactic writing is the major medium of the Sufi.

One of the major Sufi teachers in the United States today is Pir Zia Inayat Khan. The Vision Statement of his Sufi Order International provides a nice summary of Sufism: "1. To realize and spread the knowledge of unity, the religion of love and wisdom, so that the bias of faith and beliefs may of itself fall away, the human heart may overflow with love and all hatred caused by distinctions and differences may be rooted out. 2. To discover the light and power latent within all human beings, that is the secret of all religion, the power of mysticism, and the essence of philosophy, without interfering with customs or belief. 3. To help to bring the world's two opposite poles, East and West, closer together by the interchange of thought and ideals, that the Universal Kinship may form of itself, and human being may see with human being beyond the narrow national and racial boundaries." (www.sufiorder.org)

For more information: www.sufiorder.org

Headquarters: Sufi Order International, P.O. Box 480, New Lebanon, NY 12125

WAHHABISM

Within Sunni* Islam, the Hanbali legal tradition is the most conservative, but the Wahabi movement of eighteenth century made the Hanbali law even more rigid. Muhammad Ibn 'Abd al-Wahhab (1703-1792) was the leader of an Arabian revivalist movement that sought to restore Islam to its original condition before various "corruptions" entered in. The Wahhabis viewed those who disagreed with their interpretation of Islam and Sharia as unbelievers. As such, they were a threat to true Islam. Convinced that Islam had become idolatrous, the Wahhabis violently attacked popular shrines, such as the tombs of Sufi saints and the sites sacred to the Shi'ites. They even tried to destroy the Ka'ba and its central stone. The Wahhabis were only concerned about Arabic Muslims and creating a true Islamic country. Through their alliance with the Saud family, the Wahhabis were able to make Saudi Arabia into a Wahhabbi state.

ISLAMIC FUNDAMENTALISM

"Fundamentalism" is a term taken from American Protestantism to describe several diverse extremist religious movements that arose in many parts of the world during the twentieth century. Some of these extremist movements have engaged in acts of violence that shocked the world. Unlike Christian and Jewish fundamentalism, Islamic fundamentalism developed as a response to the control of traditionally Muslim countries by Western commercial empires, especially Britain and the United States.

As the Ottoman Empire decayed, the British Empire expanded into the Middle East and North Africa, often with the complicity of the local rulers. Trade agreements were established that were more advantageous to Europeans and the ruling elites than to the general populations, and many of these countries grew weaker and poorer during the economic boom of the twentieth century. The Western powers encouraged, and at times, required that the traditional religious law be replaced by Western laws.

Inspired in part by the example of the Wahhabi movement in Arabia, a number of zealous young scholars and activists in Egypt, Iran, and elsewhere turned to a strict interpretation of Islam as the only hedge against Western hegemony. These early theorists, such as the Egyptian Abul Ala Mawdudi (1903-1979), tended to be more moderate and democratic than their followers, who were persecuted by despotic secularist regimes. Many fundamentalist leaders forged their extremist theories and agenda in prisons, labor camps, or in exile. Ironically, they often drew upon Western revolutionary ideology in formulating their ideas.

Mawdudi introduced a radical new element in Islamic thinking. He argued that the *jihad*, or struggle, was the central tenet of Islam. In traditional Islamic theology there are two *jihads*. The lesser *jihad* is the holy war that is sometimes required against idolatry, such as Muhammad had fought. The greater *jihad*, though, is the struggle against sin in oneself. Mawdudi, in contrast, argued that Muslims are required to engage in a *jihad* against the secular forces of oppression. The faithful must seize power from those who blaspheme against Allah and his laws, and then they must impose the *Sharia* on the nation. He founded the Muslim Brotherhood in order to resist the rule of General Nasser in Egypt.

Sayyid Qutb (1906-1966) was a devout young man who was profoundly influenced by Mawdudi. Qutb was able to study in an American university after World War II, and he was disgusted at the hedonism and unbelief he saw displayed in America. He became convinced that the West was intent on destroying the very basis of Islam: the belief in God and the desire to do God's will instead of pursuing one's own selfish pleasures. After returning to Egypt, he joined the radical opposition to Nasser, was arrested, and spent several years in prison where he wrote many of his most important works. Later Muslim extremists built on Qutb's critique of the West and his proposal to restore Islamic law in all Muslim lands.

Islamic fundamentalism grew more radical and violent in the 1970s and 80s as it was adopted by some Palestinian groups as a weapon in their struggle for an independent state. In the struggle with Israel, Islamic extremists adopted virulent anti-Semitic propaganda borrowed from Europe. Islamic radicals also adopted the terrorist tactics that had been employed in the Catholic-Protestant conflict in Northern Ireland. However, it was the Soviet invasion of Afghanistan that led to the most violent forms of Islamic extremism. The resistance to the Soviet Union was defined as a *jihad* by many of the mujahedeen, and their success against one of the world's most powerful armies emboldened the radicals.

By the end of the twentieth century, Islamic fundamentalism identified the United States as the great enemy of God's law in the world. American television and movies brought images of lust and violence and self-destruction into Muslim homes and villages. Americans controlled the world's economy to the detriment of Muslim countries, and American troops were stationed in Arabia. Osama Bin Laden, a member of a wealthy Saudi Arabian family, was a veteran of the anti-Soviet *jihad*, and in the 1990s he turned his attention to the United States. In 2001, members of his international terrorist organization, Al-Qaida, launched kamikaze attacks on the World Trade Center and the Pentagon, killing thousands.

LATTER-DAY SAINTS
(MORMONS)

Popularly known as Mormons, the Latter-day Saints are one of the most distinct religious groups in the Abrahamic tradition*. Their roots are clearly in the Christian tradition, but their scriptures, doctrine, and practices mark them as a unique religion. They were also one of the fastest growing religious movements of the twentieth century.

The Saints believe that the authentic church, having gone underground for many centuries, was restored with the revelations given to their great prophet Joseph Smith, Jr. (1805–1844) who published the *Book of Mormon* in the 1820s. In addition to the sacred scriptures of Judaism and Christianity (the Old and New Testaments), the Latter-day Saints base their beliefs on the *Book of Mormon* and two later works by Smith, *Doctrine and Covenants* and *The Pearl of Great Price*. In the Utah territory, they founded a religious community in what was once a desert. Few churches live with such clear identity and maintain such a high degree of loyalty and dedication. Today, the Saints are conservative politically and morally, giving a predominant place to family life.

History. The early years of the Latter-day Saints centered on the prophet Joseph Smith, Jr., who organized the movement with six charter members at Fayette, New York, in 1830. Smith grew up in the famous "Burned-over District" of upstate New York, so called because of the frequency and intensity of the religious revivals there during the Second Great Awakening. Smith claimed to have experienced a series of heavenly visitations, beginning with the appearance of God and Jesus Christ in 1820. During these visits he was informed that all existing churches were in error and that the true gospel was yet to be restored. It would be revealed to him, and he was to reestablish the true church on earth.

An angel named Moroni led Smith to a hill called Cumorah near Manchester, New York, where he found a book written on gold plates left there by an ancient prophet named Mormon. The angel also gave Smith a "seer stone" that gave him the knowledge to translate the mysterious hieroglyphic writings. The plates contained the sacred records of the ancient inhabitants of North America, righteous

Jews who had fled from Jerusalem in 600 B.C.E. and sailed to North America in a divinely designed ark. Smith returned the metal plates to the angel, but eleven other persons besides Smith claimed they had seen the book before it was returned.

The "priesthood of Aaron" was conferred upon Smith and his scribe, Oliver Cowdery (1806–50), by a heavenly messenger, John the Baptist, who instructed them to baptize each other. In 1829, a year before the founding of the church, three other divine visitors, Peter, James, and John, bestowed upon Smith and Cowdery the "priesthood of Melchizedek" and gave them the keys of apostleship.

Opposition arose as the church gained strength, and in 1831 the Mormons left New York for Ohio, where headquarters were established at Kirkland. Smith moved on to Independence, Missouri, in 1838, where he and his followers planned to build the ideal community, with a temple at its heart. Friction with other settlers there became so acute that they soon left Missouri and settled at Nauvoo, Illinois. Violence followed them and reached its peak when Joseph Smith announced his intention to run for the U.S. presidency. He and his brother, Hyrum Smith (1800–1844), were murdered by a mob at Carthage, Illinois, in 1844.

With Smith's death, the Quorum of the Twelve Apostles was accepted as the head of the church, and Brigham Young (1801–1877) was made president of the Quorum. Some objected that Young was not the legal successor to Smith, and they withdrew to form other churches. Some followed James J. Strang (1813–1856) to Wisconsin. The largest body of "anti-Brighamites" believed that the leadership belonged to direct descendants of Joseph Smith, and in 1847 these people, led by Joseph Smith III (1832–1914), formed the Reorganized Church of Jesus Christ of Latter-day Saints.

The majority of Saints followed Young, who had the administrative ability to save the church from disruption and further division. He led the Saints when they were driven out of Nauvoo in February 1846 and began their epic march to what is now Utah. They arrived in Salt Lake Valley in July 1847, and there they built the famous Mormon Tabernacle.

Some sources indicate that Joseph Smith, Jr., informed his associates in the 1840s that polygamous marriages were sanctioned and even commanded by God. Such marriages had been contracted secretly for some time before the practice was announced publicly by Brigham Young in 1852. Following the Civil War, the U.S. federal government mounted an increasingly intense campaign against Mormon polygamy. In 1882, the Edmunds Act provided stringent penalties against polygamy, and in 1887 the church was unincorporated and its properties confiscated. In 1890, the church's president issued a manifesto that officially discontinued the contracting of new polygamous marriages, paving the way for Utah to be granted statehood.

Beliefs and Practices. In some respects the Latter-day Saints today resemble conservative Protestant churches; but certain aspects of their doctrine depart dramatically from traditional Christian theology. The Saints believe that before his ascension into heaven, Jesus Christ appeared in North America where he preached to the Judeans who had fled before the Babylonian Captivity in 586 B.C.E. The Saints teach that there are three persons who comprise the Godhead: the Father, the Son, and the Holy Ghost. But the Father and the Son have bodies of flesh and bone. It is also maintained that persons will be punished for their own individual sins, not for Adam's transgression; however, those who have died may yet be saved through the atonement of Christ

Ordinances include faith in Christ, repentance, baptism by immersion for the remission of sins, the laying on of hands for the gift of the Holy Ghost, and the observance of the Lord's Supper each Sunday. Baptism is necessary for salvation. Like Pentecostal churches, they believe in the gift of tongues and of interpretation of tongues, visions, prophecy, and healing.

The Latter-day Saints also practice baptism for the dead, which is based on the conviction that persons who died without a chance to hear or accept the gospel cannot possibly be condemned by a just and merciful God. They find authority for this practice in the New Testament (1 Peter 4:6). The ceremony is performed with a living person standing proxy for the dead. The practice of baptizing Holocaust victims has become a source of controversy with Jewish groups.

Suggestions for Further Reading:

Allen, James B. and Glen M. Leonard. *The Story of the Latter-day Saints,* rev. ed. Salt Lake City: Desseret Book Co., 1992.

Arrington, Leonard J. *Brigham Young: American Moses.* New York: Alfred A. Knopf, 1985.

Brodie, Fawn. *No Man Knows My History: The Life of Joseph Smith, Mormon Prophet.* New York: Alfred A. Knopf 1945.

Hansen, Klaus J. *Mormonism and the American Experience.* Chicago: University of Chicago Press, 1981.

Ludlow, Daniel, ed. *The Encyclopedia of Mormonism,* 4 vols. New York: Macmillan, 1992.

Shipps, Jan. *Mormonism: The Story of a New Religious Tradition.* Urbana: University of Illinois Press, 1985.

CHURCH OF CHRIST (TEMPLE LOT)

Founded: 1867, with roots to 1830
Membership: est. 2,400 in 32 congregations (2000)

Though under five thousand members, the Temple Lot body is included in this *Handbook* because of its significance in Saints' history. It was formed after the death of Joseph Smith, Jr., in 1844, when some of the Saints who remained in the

Midwest became convinced that the church leaders were advocating new teachings quite at variance with the original doctrines. The group centered in Crow Creek, Illinois, functioned under the name Church of Christ, and they returned to Independence, Missouri, in response to a revelation given in 1864 through the presiding elder, Granville Hedrick, in the "appointed year" of 1867. They took possession of the land originally dedicated in 1831 by Joseph Smith, Jr., for the building of the Lord's Temple. They believe that the church cannot build until the appointed time, but they have a sacred obligation to "hold and keep this land free; when the time of building comes. The Church of Christ won court battles with other Saints' bodies to maintain control of these lots.

The church accepts the King James Version of the Bible and the *Book of Mormon* as its standards. It holds that all latter-day revelation, including that of Joseph Smith, Jr., must be tested by these scriptures; thus it does not accept all that was given through Smith. They prefer *The Book of Commandments* to *Doctrine and Covenants,* which includes changes in the original doctrine. For this reason, the doctrines of plural marriage, baptism for the dead, celestial marriage, and plurality of gods are not accepted.

For more information: www.churchofchrist-tl.org

Headquarters: P.O. Box 472, Independence, MO 64051-0472

THE CHURCH OF JESUS CHRIST OF LATTER-DAY SAINTS

Founded: 1830
Membership: 5,873,408 in 13,201 congregations (2007)

The main body of Latter-day Saints is headquartered in Salt Lake City, Utah, where the Salt Lake Temple and Tabernacle are located. They believe that Christ will return to earth to rule from his capitals in Zion and Jerusalem following the restoration of the tribes of Israel. According to the LDS church, revelation is not confined to either the Bible or the *Book of Mormon*; it continues today in the living apostles and prophets of the Latter-day Saints church. Members are to adhere to the official pronouncements of the living president (prophet) of the church. Subjection to civil laws and rules is advocated, together with insistence on the right of the individual to worship according to the dictates of conscience.

A distinctive teaching of LDS church is that marriage has two forms: marriage for time and marriage for eternity (celestial marriage). Members who are married by only civil authority still remain in good standing in the church, but marriage for time and eternity in one of the church's temples is regarded as a prerequisite for the highest opportunity for salvation. There are over one hundred temples around the world, and only members of the church may enter a temple.

Latter-day Saints recognize two priesthoods: (1) the higher priesthood of Melchizedek, which holds power of presidency and authority over offices of the church and whose officers include apostles, patriarchs, high priests, seventies, and elders, and (2) the lesser priesthood of Aaron, which guides the temporal affairs of the church through its bishops, priests, teachers, and deacons. The presiding council of the church is the First Presidency, made up of three high priests—the president and two counselors. Its authority is final in both spiritual and temporal affairs. The president of the church is "the mouthpiece of God"; through him come the laws of the church by direct revelation.

Next to the presidency stands the Council of the Twelve Apostles, chosen by revelation to supervise, under the direction of the First Presidency, the whole work of the church. The church is divided into areas and stakes (geographical divisions) composed of a number of wards (local churches or parishes). Members of two quorums of seventy preside over the areas, under the direction of the Twelve. High priests, assisted by elders, are in charge of the stakes and wards.

Members of the Melchizedek priesthood, under the direction of the presidency, officiate in all ordinances of the gospel. The stake presidents, ward bishops, patriarchs, high priests, and elders supervise the work within the stakes and wards of the church. The Aaronic priesthood is governed by three presiding bishops, known collectively as the Presiding Bishopric, who also supervise the work of the members of the priesthood in the stakes and wards. In 1978, it was ruled that "all worthy male members of the church may be ordained to the priesthood without regard for race or color."

Mission. The church influences all aspects of the life of every member; it supplies relief in illness or poverty and assists with education and employment when necessary. This church maintains, as part of a self-help welfare system, storehouses for community food and clothing. Members operate vegetable, seed, and wheat farms; orchards, dairies, and cannery processing facilities; sewing centers; soap-processing plants; and several grain elevators. Through this system the church donates thousands of tons of surplus clothing annually to needy populations around the world and sponsors water and agricultural projects in underdeveloped countries. The welfare system also includes sheltered workshops for persons with handicapping conditions and a variety of social services, including adoption and foster-care agencies.

Over fifty thousand young persons currently serve as full-time missionaries throughout the world without compensation; they devote eighteen months to two years to spreading the teaching of their church at home and abroad at their own expense. Only about a hundred persons in full-time leadership positions receive a salary or living allowance.

The Latter-day Saints grew tremendously in the twentieth century and in the last half of the century became influential in national politics. The church is strongest in the Western U.S., but now has more members outside the U.S. than in it.

The church's largest institutions are Brigham Young University in Provo, Utah, and Brigham Young University in Rexburg, Idaho. Some 525,000 secondary and post-secondary students worldwide are enrolled in seminary and institute classes, which provide religious instruction.

For more information: www.lds.org

Headquarters: Joseph Smith Memorial Building, 15 East South Temple St., Salt Lake City, UT 84150.

COMMUNITY OF CHRIST

Founded: 1860, with roots to 1830
Membership: 178,328 in 935 congregations (2007)

Formerly know as the Reorganized Church of Jesus Christ of the Latter-day Saints, this church claims to be the true continuation of the original church organized by Joseph Smith, Jr., with leadership passing to his son Joseph Smith III in 1860. It bases this claim of succession on the book of *Doctrine and Covenants*. Court actions on two occasions, in Ohio in 1880 and in Missouri in 1894, are cited in naming it the legal continuation of the original church.

The Reorganized Church rejected the claims of the group led by Brigham Young because of their abandonment of this rule of succession, along with other doctrinal disagreements. Those holding to the lineal succession eventually reorganized, and the first collective expression of this movement was a conference in Beloit, Wisconsin, in 1852. Joseph Smith III was chosen president in 1860 at Amboy, Illinois. All of his successors have been descendants of the founder. Since 1920, headquarters have been located in Independence, Missouri, where a temple was built late in the twentieth century.

The Reorganized Church held polygamy to be contrary to the teachings of the *Book of Mormon* and the book of *Doctrine and Covenants* of the original organization. It also differs from the larger body over the doctrine of the Godhead, celestial marriage, and baptism of the dead. Basic beliefs include faith in the universality of God the Eternal Father, Jesus Christ as the only begotten Son of the Father, the Holy Spirit, the worth and dignity of persons, repentance of sin, baptism by immersion, the efficacy of various sacramental ordinances, the resurrection of the dead, the open canon of scriptures and the continuity of revelation, the doctrine of stewardship, and the accountability of all people to God.

The work of the church is supported by tithes and free-will offerings. This is regarded as a divine principle, and the tithe is calculated on a tenth of each member's annual increase over needs and just wants. Church doctrines, policies, and matters of legislation must have the approval and action of a delegate conference held biennially in Independence. General administration of the church is by a

First Presidency of three high priests and elders, a Quorum of Twelve Apostles who represent the presidency in the field, and a pastoral arm under the high priests and elders. Bishops are responsible for church properties, the stewardship of members, and church finances.

The Community of Christ has been active in developing ministries and understanding as it has expanded since 1960 into non-Western cultures. With work in over thirty countries, it has a worldwide membership of nearly a quarter-million people. It sponsors several homes for the elderly, medical clinics, and educational facilities both in the U.S. and abroad. It seeks to dedicate itself to the pursuit of world peace and reconciliation. The ordination of women was approved in 1984, and by 2000 more than three thousand women had been ordained to ecclesiastical orders

For more information: http://cofchrist.org

Headquarters: 1001 W. Walnut, Independence, MO 64050-3562

FUNDAMENTALIST CHURCH OF JESUS CHRIST OF LATTER-DAY SAINTS

Founded: 1935
Membership: est. 6,000 in 7 communities

When Wilford Woodruff issued a manifesto banning plural marriage in the Church of Jesus Christ of Latter-day Saints* in 1890, some Mormons rejected the decree and held to the older teachings of Brigham Young. The towns of Hildale, Utah, and Colorado City, Arizona (formerly known as Short Creek), were particularly resistant to the change in doctrine. Some of the residents continued to practice plural marriage despite state laws banning the practice, and in 1935 they were excommunicated from the LDS church. A number of small fundamentalist Mormon churches were formed in the 1930s and 40s. Gradually the FLDS Church, led by John Y. Barlow, emerged as the largest body.

The church insists that men and women adopt "plain dress" that covers most of the body. Women are forbidden to wear make-up or short hair. The church sells appropriate clothing online. Children are generally educated by the community, and a disproportionate number of teenage boys are excommunicated for behavior deemed inappropriate. In addition to plural marriage, the leader of the church assigns brides to husbands in a practice called placement marriage. The church is apocalyptic and believes that it is the righteous remnant that will survive the war between Christ and the Antichrist.

In 1953, Arizona state police and National Guard troops raided the Short Creek community in an effort to stamp out polygamy. They arrested over four hundred people, including over two hundred children, but the raid backfired and generated widespread support for the polygamists. The FLDS church grew, and now there are satellite communities in Colorado, South Dakota, British Columbia, and Texas. In the 1980s Rulon Jeffs assumed leadership and took the title of prophet. He reportedly had twenty-eight wives and over sixty children, one of whom, Warren, succeeded him in 2002.

Soon after assuming leadership Warren Jeffs was arrested on charges of being an accomplice to rape since he helped arrange the marriage of a member of the church to an underage girl. This case brought unwanted publicity to the FLDS Church, and in 2004 the church purchased about 1,700 acres of land near Eldorado, Texas, where they established Yearning for Zion Ranch. The ranch is nearly self-sufficient and houses over seven hundred persons. The church constructed its first Temple on the ranch, and it was dedicated by Jeffs in 2005. Reports of plural marriage and underage marriage led Texas authorities to raid the ranch and take over four hundred children into protective custody. Most of the children have been returned to their mothers, but the case publicly raised difficult issues regarding separation of church and state. Jeff's sermons have also been criticized for their racism and implicit call to violence.

For more information: www.fldstruth.org

Headquarters: Yearning for Zion Ranch, Eldorado, TX 76936

ESOTERIC, SPIRITUALIST,
AND NEW THOUGHT BODIES

Some of the more interesting and controversial religious organizations in the U.S. endorse esoteric doctrines and practices. The word "esoteric" refers to hidden or secret teachings, and a common feature of esoteric groups is difficult for outsiders to gain a clear understanding of them. One needs to be initiated in order to fully learn their teachings. Despite this, esoteric bodies in the United States have been able to present some of their central beliefs publicly in an effort to recruit members or defend themselves from prejudice. With the Internet, there has been an explosion of esoteric religious web-sites and discussion groups. Complicating study of esoteric bodies is the great diversity of groups as well as their inter-relatedness.

Esoteric groups generally trace their origins back to the ancient world, especially to Egypt and Solomon's Temple. They believe that some of the original wisdom of God was transmitted by Egyptian and Israelite priests in their temple rituals, but much of that wisdom was lost. According to esotericists, some of the important secret knowledge was passed down through various individuals and organizations, such as Hermes Trismegistus, the Templars, Paracelsus, and the Rosicrucians. Esotericism draws from Renaissance neoplatonic philosophy, medieval alchemy, and ancient magic. Some of the radical Pietist sects used esoteric thought, as did the Masons, but for the most part, esotericism has been in the shadows of the Abrahamic tradition.

Closely related to esotericism is Theosophy, or divine wisdom. Theosophists view this divine wisdom as the universal perennial philosophy that underlies all religions. Thus it draws from both Eastern and Western philosophy and religious teachings. The chief founder of the modern Theosophical movement was Helena Petrovna Blavatsky (1831–1891), who was born in Russia and traveled over the world in search of knowledge of governing laws of the universe. She arrived in the U.S. and founded the Theosophical Society of New York in 1875. Her aim was "to form a nucleus of the Universal Brotherhood of Humanity, without distinction of race, creed, sex, caste, or color; to encourage the study of comparative religion, philosophy, and science; and to investigate the unexplained laws of nature and the powers latent in man." (http://www.theosophy.org.nz/HQAdmin/Consti.pdf) Blavatsky held that all religions stem from a hierarchy that includes Jesus, Buddha, and other master thinkers who have experienced a series of rebirths, or reincarnations, ultimately to attain divinity.

Reincarnation is a central theme in Theosophy. It is the method through which persons rid themselves of all impurities and unfold their inner potentials through varied experiences. Closely connected with the concept of reincarnation is that of karma, the law of cause and effect; each rebirth, then, is seen as the result of actions, thoughts, and desires brought from the past. The movement split after the death of Blavatsky in 1891. Spiritualism and theosophy generated great excitement and controversy early in the twentieth century, but its appeal declined significantly over the course of the century. This was due in part of the spread of unlicensed mediums and psychics whose unethical practices brought the movement into disrepute. It was also due to the dramatic rise of New Age religious groups among the "baby boomers."

Theosophy and esotericism influenced a number of religious thinkers and organizers, some of whom promoted less exotic and more practical versions of these beliefs. New Thought was influenced by New England Transcendentalism and draws upon both Eastern and Abrahamic esoteric traditions to help individuals learn new ways of thinking in order to overcome the dualism of mind and body. The key idea in the various forms of New Thought is that a person's physical, emotional, and spiritual health are inter-related. In other words, faith and right thinking are the path to health.

Suggestions for Further Reading:

Benz, Ernst. *Emanuel Swedenborg: Visionary Savant in the Age of Reason.* Tr. Nicholas Goodrick-Clarke. West Chester: Swedenborg Foundation, 2002.

De Witt, John. *The Christian Science Way of Life.* Boston: Christian Science Publishing Society, 1971.

Esoterica: The Journal. Published by the Michigan State University, East Lansing, MI.

Fuller, Robert. *Mesmerism and the American Cure of Souls.* Philadelphia: University of Pennsylvania Press, 1982.

Gibbons, B.J. *Spirituality and the Occult from the Renaissance to the Modern Age.* London: Routledge, 2001.

Nelson , Geoffrey K. *Spiritualism and society.* New York: Schoken Books, 1969.

Toksvig , Signe. *Emanuel Swedenborg, scientist and mystic .* New Haven: Yale University Press, 1948.

ASSOCIATION OF UNITY CHURCHES

Founded: 1886
Membership: est. 30,000 in 610 churches (2009)

Unity is a religious educational institution devoted to demonstrating that following the teaching of Jesus Christ is a practical, seven-day-a-week way of life. Unity teaches that "the true church is a state of consciousness in man." (www.unity.org) The Association of Unity Churches helps provide resources for congregations dedicated to Unity teachings. Unity has been described as "a religious philosophy with an 'open end,' seeking to find God's truth in all of life, wherever it may be." (www.unity.org) Unity has no strict creed or dogma; it finds good in all religions and teaches that people should keep their minds open to receive that goodness. Unity teaches that reality is ultimately spiritual and that realization of spiritual truth will illuminate, heal, and prosper humanity. Cultivation of health-conducive emotions such as love, confidence, and joy is encouraged. Overcoming health-inhibiting emotions such as anger, hatred, and despair is also encouraged. Unity has no rules concerning health but concentrates on spiritual goals, knowing that healthful living habits will follow. Some Unity students are vegetarians in the interest of health.

Unity began in 1886 when Charles Fillmore (1854–1948), bankrupt and crippled, and his wife, Myrtle (1845–1931), seriously ill with tuberculosis, discovered a way of life based on affirmative prayer. They studied a variety of Christian and Eastern theosophical and esoteric systems in creating their new approach to healing. The Fillmores held that "whatever man wants he can have by voicing his desire in the right way into the Universal Mind." (www.unity.org) It is through Christ, or the Christ consciousness, that the human gains eternal life and salvation. Salvation means the attainment of true spiritual consciousness, becoming like Christ. This transformation takes place not in any hereafter, but on this earth through a process of unfolding and regeneration. A person suffers no final death, but changes into increasingly better states until finally becoming like Christ.

Prayer and meditation are suggested for every human want and illness. The Unity way of prayer and meditation involves relaxation and affirmation of spiritual truth to develop the consciousness of the individual and silent receptivity to the "Divine Mind" for whatever the seeker needs. The Bible is used constantly and is highly valued, but is not considered the sole or final authority in faith and practice. People must be in direct, personal communion with God, not dependent upon such secondary sources as the scriptures.

The Association of Unity Churches ordains ministers, provides educational and administrative support, and is self-supporting. Unity School trains ministers in a two-year program. It also educates teachers and offers retreat programs. A large staff in Unity Village—near Kansas City, Missouri—is available to pray with people day and night. Workers answer an average of one million calls and nearly two million letters annually. Most calls come from members of various Christian churches, but correspondents are never asked to leave the churches to which they belong. Unity School publishes some 75 million copies of booklets, brochures, and magazines annually. These materials are used by many who never contact headquarters or become members of a Unity church.

For more information: www.unity.org

Headquarters: P.O. Box 610, Lee's Summit, MO 64063

CHURCH OF CHRIST, SCIENTIST
(CHRISTIAN SCIENCE)

Founded: 1879
Membership: approx. 2,200 churches (1998)

The Church of Christ, Scientist is one of the few denominations founded by a woman, and for a time it was very influential in American society. Mary Baker Eddy (1821–1910) was the founder of Christian Science. Her book *Science and Health with Key to the Scriptures* (1875, rev. 1883) and the Bible are the twofold textbooks of the church. She defined Christian Science as "the scientific system of divine healing," the "law of God, the law of good, interpreting and demonstrating the divine Principle and rule of universal harmony." (Science and Health with Key to the Scriptures, p. 13) Christian Science originated from Eddy's personal experience. Eddy had suffered from a form of paralysis much of her life until 1866 when, after reading the account of Christ's healing of a man with a form of palsy (Matthew 9:1-8), she recovered almost instantly. Convinced that God was the source of her healing, Eddy found confirmation of her ideas in the writings of both Emanuel Swedenborg and Phineas Quimby. She became an advocate for spiritual causation and mental healing, and she quickly demonstrated a rare ability to recruit and organize followers. Under her direction, the Church of Christ, Scientist, was established in her hometown of Lynn, Massachusetts, in 1879. In 1892 she built a large "Mother Church" in Boston, which became the headquarters for her rapidly-expanding denomination.

Christian Science is more closely connected to traditional Christianity than many bodies in this section of the *Handbook*. It teaches that God is the only "Mind"; God is "All-in-all," the "divine Principle of all that really is," "the all-knowing, all-seeing, all-acting, all-wise, all-loving, and eternal; Principle; Mind; Soul; Spirit; Life; Truth; Love; all substance; intelligence." (*Science and Health With Key to the Scriptures* p. 587) The Bible is seen as sacred scripture and the church proclaims faith in the Father, Son, and Holy Spirit. The crucifixion and resurrection of

Jesus are held as serving "to uplift faith to understand eternal Life, even the allness of Soul, Spirit, and the nothingness of matter."

The "allness" of spirit and "nothingness of matter" involve the basic teaching of Christian Science concerning reality. As *Science and Health* explains, "All reality is in God and His creation, harmonious and eternal. That which He creates is good, and He makes all that is made. Therefore the only reality of sin, sickness, or death is the awful fact that unrealities seem real to human, erring belief, until God strips off their disguise. They are not true, because they are not of God."

According to the Basic Tenets of the church, God forgives sin through destroying it with "the spiritual understanding that casts out evil as unreal." (Science and Health With Key to the Scriptures p. 497) The punishment for sin lasts as long as one's belief in sin endures. Adherents of Christian Science do not ignore what they consider "unreal"; rather, they seek to forsake and overcome error and evil through Christian discipleship, prayer, and progressive spiritual understanding of God's "allness" and goodness; they strive to see the spiritual "body," created in God's likeness, as the only real body.

Christian Scientists commonly rely wholly on the power of God for healing rather than on medical treatment. Healing is not held to be miraculous but divinely natural. Disease is understood to be basically a mental concept that can be dispelled by active Christian discipleship, spiritual regeneration, and application of the truths to which Jesus bore witness. Prayer is "an absolute faith that all things are possible to God—a spiritual understanding of Him, an unselfed love." (Science and Health With Key to the Scriptures, pg. 1) Baptism is not observed as a traditional ceremony, but is held to be a continuing individual spiritual experience.

The local Churches of Christ, Scientist employ their own forms of democratic government within the general framework of bylaws laid down by Eddy in the *Manual of the Mother Church*. Reading rooms, open to the general public, are maintained by all churches. The affairs of the mother church are administered by the Christian Science Board of Directors, which elects a president and other officers of the church.

There are two Readers in each branch church, usually a man and a woman, who are elected by the church members. In all services on Sundays and Thanksgiving Day, they read alternately from the Bible and from *Science and Health*. The "lesson sermons" of Sunday services are prepared by a committee and are issued quarterly by the Christian Science Publishing Society.

Practitioners devote their full time to healing and are listed in a directory in the monthly *Christian Science Journal*. A board of education consists of three members: a president, a vice president, and a teacher of Christian Science. Under the supervision of this board, a Normal class is held once every three years. Teachers are duly authorized by certificates granted by the board to form classes. Women practitioners outnumber male practitioners ten to one. Since World War

II, the denomination has experienced a significant decline in membership and a corresponding increase in average age of membership.

For more information: www.tfccs.org

Headquarters: 175 Huntington Avenue, Boston, MA 02115

THE GENERAL CHURCH OF THE NEW JERUSALEM (SWEDENBORGIAN)

Founded: 1897
Membership: 6,760 in 37 churches (2006)

One of the primary figures in both Spiritualism and Theosophy was Emanuel Swedenborg (1688–1772). He was born in Stockholm, Sweden, and was an Enlightenment-era scientist distinguished in the fields of mathematics, geology, cosmology, and anatomy before he turned seriously to theology. Although certain he was divinely commissioned to teach the doctrines of the "New Church," Swedenborg never preached or founded a church. His followers, however, felt that the need for a separate denomination was implicit in the new revelation given in Swedenborg's monumental work *Arcana Celestia,* in which, they believed, he unlocked the hidden meaning of Scripture and recorded his conversations with great figures long dead.

The Swedenborgian church centers its worship on the risen and glorified present reality of Christ and looks for the establishment of the kingdom of God in the form of a universal church on earth. In this new church all people will strive for peace, freedom, and justice. Swedenborgian bodies have often used the name "Churches of the New Jerusalem" to indicate the in-breaking of the eschatological reality described in the New Testament. The most famous Swedenborgian evangelist in America was John Chapman (Johnny Appleseed), and today J. Appleseed & Co. distributes books and pamphlets based on Swedenborg's writings.

Swedenborgians believe that the Bible has both a literal, historical meaning and a deeper, spiritual meaning. The church teaches that there is one God, known by many names, and that the Christian Trinity denotes aspects of this God. Human beings are believed to be essentially spirits clothed in material bodies, which are laid aside at death; the human spirit lives on in a spirit world, in a manner determined by its attitudes and behavior on earth.

The Faith and Aims of the church state that the "Lord Jesus Christ has come again, not in a physical reappearance, but in spirit and in truth; not in a single event only, but in a progressive manifestation of his presence among men." Adherents claim that tokens of Christ's coming appear in the burst of scientific development, the rise of the spirit of inquiry, the progress toward political and intellectual freedom, and the deepening sense of national and international responsibility that has characterized the modern era.

As an organization, the New Church arose in London in 1783 when Robert Hindmarsh (1759–1835), a printer, gathered a few friends to discuss the writings of Swedenborg. They formed a general conference of their societies in 1815. The first Swedenborgian Society in the U.S. was organized at Baltimore, Maryland, in 1792, and in 1817 the General Convention of the New Jerusalem in the U.S.A. was established. It was incorporated in 1861 and currently has about two thousand members.

The General Church of the New Jerusalem broke away from the original Swedenborgian body in 1890. It shares many of the doctrines of the larger body, but teaches that the writings of Swedenborg are divinely inspired. The General Church built a cathedral in Bryn Athyn, Pennsylvania. There are Swedenborgian theological schools in Newton, Massachusetts, and Bryn Athyn. The Swedenborg Foundation is in West Chester, Pennsylvania. At the end of the twentieth century, a new Swedenborgian church, the Lord's New Church, was established in South Africa and now has a handful of congregations in the U.S. Perhaps the most celebrated Swedenborgian in America was Helen Keller.

For more information: www.newchurch.org; www.swedenborg.org

Headquarters: P.O. Box 74311, Bryn Athyn, PA 19009

GNOSTICISM

Founded: twentieth century with roots to the first century
Membership: statistics unavailable

One of the major competitors of orthodox-Catholic Christianity until the rise of Islam was Gnosticism, so called because of its emphasis on esoteric "gnosis" (Greek for "knowledge"). There were many versions of ancient Gnosticism, most of which had roots in neo-platonic philosophy. Gnosticism was declared heretical by early Christian bishops and councils, and most Gnostic writings were lost. From time to time there were unsuccessful attempts to revive ancient Gnosticism based on fragmentary evidence, but interest in Gnosticism as a living religion increased dramatically after the discovery of numerous Gnostic manuscripts at Nag Hammadi in Egypt in the 1940s.

By the end of the twentieth century, there were a number of groups advocating Gnosticism as an ancient faith that combines belief in Jesus and esotericism. Most Christian Gnostic groups teach that Jesus revealed secret teachings to his disciples. Mary Magdalene figures prominently in Christian Gnosticism, and many Gnostics believe that she was the physical and spiritual spouse of Jesus. Dan Brown's best-selling and highly imaginative novel, *The DaVinci Code*, made the marriage of Jesus and Mary central to the plot, generating great interest in Gnosticism. Unlike ancient Gnosticism, which tended to be ascetic, American Gnosticism often celebrates sexuality as part of spirituality. Many Gnostic groups

333

are served by "wandering bishops," who claimed an apostolic succession from Jesus and Mary Magdalene parallel to that of the Catholic Church*.

For more information: www.gnosis.org

LIBERAL CATHOLIC CHURCH INTERNATIONAL

Founded: 1940s
Membership: est. 6,000 in 9 churches

This church has its roots in the Old Catholic* movement in England. The church endorses certain theosophical and esoteric principles and its worship incorporates many basic tenets of Eastern mysticism. Paramount in the thinking is a central inspiration from faith in the living Christ, based on the promises of Matthew18:20 and 28:20, which are regarded as "validating all Christian worship." (www.liberalcatholic.org) But special channels of Christ's power are found in the traditional seven sacraments of the church. Through such "spiritual labor," believers are able to come into a full realization of the divine Presence and grow into the true likeness of God. The Nicene Creed is generally used in Liberal Catholic services, but there is no requirement of submission to any creed, scripture, or tradition. Members seek to serve humanity through corporate worship in a common ritual rather than doctrinal uniformity. The church ordains women and permits gay marriage.

The church operates St. Alban Theological Seminary in Frisco, Texas, while the St. Alban Press is located in San Diego. There was a division in the Liberal Catholic (see LIBERAL CATHOLIC CHURCH, PROVINCE OF THE UNITED STATES) over the question of episcopal jurisdiction in the 1940s, and this body won a legal dispute in California over the use of the name Liberal Catholic Church. It added the word "International" to the name when it separated from the parent body in England.

For more information: www.liberalcatholic.org
Headquarters: 741 Cerro GordoAve., San Diego, CA 92102

LIBERAL CATHOLIC CHURCH, PROVINCE OF THE UNITED STATES

Founded: 1916
Membership: 5,800 in 21 churches (2006)

This church was founded in London by J. I. Wedgewood. It traces its holy orders to an apostolic succession that runs back to the Roman Catholic Church under the reign of Pope Urban VIII (1568–1644). The Liberal Catholic Church aims at a combination of traditional Catholic forms of worship with the utmost freedom of individual conscience and thought. The church adopted the name Liberal Catholic Church, Province of the United States in the 1940s during a dispute with what is now called the Liberal Catholic Church International*. As with the Old Catholic* churches, Liberal Catholic priests and bishops may marry, and they exact no fee for the administration of the sacraments; LCC priests are employed in secular occupations, but LCCI churches may offer a salary to their priests if financially able. The church endorses the Nicene Creed, and its Statement of Principles outlines additional theosophical principles, such as reincarnation. Clergy are expected to be in general agreement with the Statement, but laity are free to accept or reject these beliefs. The church also encourages members to adopt a vegetarian and alcohol-free lifestyle. The LCC, Province of the United States is in communion with the worldwide LCC headquartered in London. The denomination is governed by a General Episcopal Synod made up of thirty bishops from around the world. The Regionary Bishop for the United States is the Rt. Rev. William S. H. Downey.

For more information: www.lcc.cc/tlc/thelcc.htm

Headquarters: P.O. Box 598, Ojai, CA 93023

NATIONAL SPIRITUALIST ASSOCIATION OF CHURCHES

Founded: 1893
Membership: est. 3,000 in 136 churches (1999)

Spiritualism has had a broader impact on American culture than is evident from its institutional forms. The Spiritualist movement in the U.S. began in 1848 with the activities of Margeretta and Kate Fox in Hydesville, New York. The sisters claimed that they had succeeded in contacting the dead who communicate through strange "rappings." Central to the beliefs and practices of Spiritualism in its many forms is the ability to communicate with the spirits of those who have departed this earthly life. This may be done through such things as mediums, séances, and mystical rites. In recent years there has been greater interest in psychic experiments and extrasensory perception. Many Spiritualists hold to a belief in reincarnation and seek to reconnect with past-life experiences.

The older Spiritualist organizations in the U.S. remain closer to the Abrahamic tradition than the more recent New Age spiritual movements. Christ is often regarded as a master medium; the annunciation is seen as a message from the spirit world; the transfiguration was an opportunity for materialization of the spirits of Moses and Elias; and the resurrection was evidence that all people live on in the spirit world.

Spiritualists often call the soul the astral body. At death the material body dissolves, and the soul, or the body of the spirit, progresses through a series of spheres to a higher and higher existence. In two lower spheres, persons of bad character or sinful record are purified and made ready for higher existences. Most of the departed are to be found in a third sphere, the summer land. Beyond this are the philosopher's sphere, the advanced contemplative and intellectual sphere, the love sphere, and the Christ sphere. All reach the higher spheres eventually; Spiritualists do not believe in heaven or hell or that any people are ever lost.

Spiritualists in general profess belief in Infinite Intelligence and that natural phenomena are expressions of that Intelligence. True religion includes a correct understanding of the expressions of the Infinite Intelligence and learning how to live in accordance with the Infinite Intelligence. The personality of each individual lives on after death, which is just a change in state, and that the living can and do contact those who have passed beyond. The moral code of Spiritualism is Jesus' Golden Rule, and happiness or unhappiness depends on whether people obey or disobey Nature's physical and spiritual laws. Spiritualism, like Pentecostalism*, believes that prophecy and healing are still spiritual gifts.

Services or séances are held in private homes, rented halls, or churches. Most Spiritualist churches have regular services with prayer, music, selections from writings by various spiritualists, a sermon or lecture, and spirit messages from the departed. Churches and ministers are supported by free will offerings; mediums and ministers also gain support from classes and séances in which fees are charged. Attendance at church services is invariably small, averaging twenty to twenty-five.

Administration and government differ slightly in the various groups, but most have district or state associations and an annual general convention. All have mediums, and most have ministers in charge of the congregations. Requirements for licensing and ordination also differ, but a determined effort is being made to raise the standards of education and character in the larger groups.

The National Spiritualist Association of Churches was organized in Chicago around the time of the World's Parliament of Religions, which had heightened American interest in Eastern religions and esoteric philosophies. This association furnishes literature for the whole American Spiritualist movement. In 1994, the Association established the Center for Spiritual Studies, NSAC in Lily Dale, New York, that offers a course of study for members, licentiates, healers, mediums, National Spiritualist Teachers, and ordained ministers, leading to an Associate of Arts in Religious Studies.

The National Spiritualist Alliance separated from the NSAC in 1913 in a dispute over reincarnation. TNSA is primarily located in New England, but its influence is broader than its membership. The alliance stresses paranormal and impersonal manifestations and intercommunication with the spirit world. A board of directors steers the work of ministers and certified mediums; college training

336

is not required, but a minister must have passed a course of study arranged by the alliance. Mediums may baptize, but only ministers may officiate at ceremonies of ordination and marriage. A distinctive feature of the Alliance are its Psychic Fairs, held in various locations, which display psychic literature and phenomena.

For more information: www.nsac.org

Headquarters: P.O. Box 217, Lily Dale, NY 14752-0217

BAHÁ'Í FAITH

Founded: 1844 (came to the U.S. in 1894)
Membership: 163,858 registered in 1,086 assemblies (2009)

The Bahá'í Faith is one of the few religions to emerge in modern times; however, like many other religious bodies, it has roots in the ancient traditions of Western monotheism that can be traced back to the biblical patriarch Abraham. Now recognized as an independent religion, the Bahá'í Faith was born in the milieu of Shi'a Islam in mid-nineteenth century Persia (present-day Iran). Bahá'ís see all of the great religions of the world, Eastern as well as Western, as part of a single process of "progressive revelation" through which God reveals His will to humanity. The founders of the world's major religions, including Abraham, Krishna, Moses, Zoroaster, Buddha, Jesus, and Muhammad, are recognized as "Manifestations of God," peerless individuals who are seen as reflections of God's attributes who appear in each age to guide and educate humanity. The founder of the Bahá'í Faith, Bahá'u'lláh, claimed to be the most recent, but not the final, manifestation of God in this ongoing process of divine revelation.

According to Bahá'í teachings, claims of exclusivity and finality by the followers of the various religions have been a prolific source of violence and contention in the world. These conflicts can be resolved through the recognition of the progressive nature of religious truth. Throughout the ages, all the religions have reaffirmed the same core spiritual and ethical principles, but their social and temporal teachings have differed in response to the evolving needs of an ever-advancing civilization.

Bahá'ís believe that there is only one God and one human race, and that all the manifestations of God have come to help move humankind gradually closer to God. Bahá'u'lláh taught that in this day humankind is reaching its long-awaited stage of maturity, when the global unity and oneness of the human race can be recognized and established. He laid down principles, laws and institutions for a world civilization, including the abandonment of all forms of prejudice, the full equality of men and women, the elimination of the extremes of poverty and wealth, universal compulsory education, the abolition of the clergy and the responsibility of each person to search independently for truth, the harmony of science and religion, and the establishment of a world federal system based on the principles of collective security.

The Bahá'í Faith originated with the teachings of Mirza Ali Muhammad (1819-50), called "the Báb" (Arabic, for "gate" or "door"), who suffered persecution and was martyred in 1850. The Báb emphasized a messianic theme in Islamic thought: that the Madhi (or "Messiah") would soon appear to inaugurate an age of peace and justice on earth. It was a message of hope for thousands of the disenfranchised in Persia (modern day Iran), but the Báb's preaching threatened the Persian authorities, who feared that the prophecies about the Madhi might inspire revolution. Thus the Báb was arrested, imprisoned, and executed. As many as 20,000 of his followers, known as Bábis, were also slain during the early years of the new faith.

As so often happens in the history of religious persecution, the death of the prophet did not stop his message. One of the Báb's followers was a nobleman, Mirza Husayn-'Ali (1817-1892), long admired for his philanthropy and selflessness. In 1852, he was stripped of his possessions and cast into an underground dungeon in Tehran. While in prison, he experienced the descent of the Holy Spirit, an event that Baha'is compare to God's revealing himself to his earlier messengers: Moses before the Burning Bush; the Buddha under the Bodhi tree; when the Holy Spirit, in the form of a dove, descended upon Jesus; and when the Archangel Gabriel appeared to Muhammad. When he was released, he was banished from Persia and spent the rest of his life as a prisoner and exile, first in Baghdad, then in Istanbul, and finally in the prison-city of Akko in Ottoman Palestine. He took the title "Bahá'u'lláh," which means "the Glory of God" in Arabic.

In 1863 Bahá'u'lláh announced publicly that he was the one about whom the Báb had prophesied, the messenger sent by God with a new revelation for the coming age. His words were to prepare a new world order. Beginning that year Bahá'u'lláh issued a series of weighty letters to the kings and rulers of the world to inform them of the coming new world order and urge them to assist in the next stage of human development. He maintained that the nations of the world should reduce their armaments, reconcile their differences, and seek justice for all of the world's people. In addition to these letters to the kings and rulers, Bahá'u'lláh revealed thousands of epistles, prayers, mediations, poems, and books that address every aspect of human existence and which are considered the revealed Word of God.

When Bahá'u'lláh passed away in 1892, his remains were buried in a small room near the mansion of Bahji, an estate just north of Akko. Known as the Shrine of Bahá'u'lláh, this burial place has since been further developed is a pilgrimage site for Bahá'ís today. Before his passing, Bahá'u'lláh appointed his eldest son, Abbas Effendi (1844-1921), as the Center of His Covenant, to whom his followers would turn for guidance after his passing. Subsequently, Bahá'u'lláh's great grandson, Shoghi Effendi, was appointed head of the Faith and promoted the development of the Bahá'í community until shortly before the first election of the Universal House of Justice in 1963.

While efforts have been made to create breakaway sects, all but a few Bahá'ís today are part of a single world community united by an administrative structure ordained by Bahá'u'lláh. This structure consists of consultative assemblies elected from among the adult believers at the local, national and international levels. The international governing body of the Bahá'í Faith is an elected council of nine members known as the Universal House of Justice, which operates from its seat at the Bahá'í World Center in Haifa, Israel. The Bahá'í Faith is established in virtually every country and in many dependent territories and overseas departments of countries. Most nations and a few territories have a National Spiritual Assembly elected by the Bahá'ís of that jurisdiction. Bahá'ís live in some one hundred thousand localities around the globe. More than ten thousand of these localities have a local Spiritual Assembly. About 2,100 indigenous tribes, races, and ethnic groups are presented in the Bahá'í community

Abbas Effendi, known to Bahá'ís as Abdu'l-Bahá ("Servant of the Glory"), was released in 1908 when the Ottoman Empire collapsed in the aftermath of the Young Turk Revolution. Between 1911 and 1913 he undertook a series of historic journeys to Egypt, Europe, and North America to proclaim his father's message. At Wilmette, Illinois, in 1912, he laid the cornerstone of the first Bahá'í house of worship in the West. The headquarters of the National Spiritual Assembly, the administrative body in the United States, is in that vicinity.

In 1953 the building was dedicated to the unity of God, the unity of the prophets, and the unity of humankind. Worship services are conducted frequently and are not restricted to weekly programs. Bahá'í Houses of Worship follow a design principle in which the number 9, symbolic of unity, is repeatedly emphasized. The temples have nine entrances on nine sides surmounted by a single dome. While in the future these temples will be built in every locality where Bahá'ís reside, at present there are only seven in the world. In addition to the Wilmette temple, Bahá'í Houses of Worship are located in Panama, Uganda, Germany, Australia, Western Samoa, and India. Ground has been broken for an eighth temple in Santiago, Chile.

These temples are mostly used for private prayer and meditation. There are no rituals, sacraments, or sermons. Devotional programs are held to commemorate Bahá'í Holy Days and other occasions, during which selections from the scriptures of all the major religions may be recited. In the temple auditorium, the display of pictures or statues is forbidden, as is the use of musical instruments. Only the human voice may be used to sing, chant, or recite.

The chief purpose of the Bahá'í Faith is to help unite humanity in a peaceful and just world order. Its chief principle is the oneness and the wholeness of the human race. Other dominant principles are recognition of the divine foundation of all religions, independent investigation of the truth, the essential harmony of science and religion, universal compulsory education, equality of men and women, a spiritual solution for economic problems, the need for a universal auxiliary language, universal peace based on a world federation of nations, elimination of all prejudice, and recognition of the essential unity of humanity. Not surprisingly, Bahá'ís view the creation of the United Nations as a significant step toward the establishment of universal peace and justice.

Unlike many new religious movements, the Bahá'í Faith stresses the importance of secular education and the equality of women with men. The oppression of women around the world, Bahá'u'lláh declared, is the cause of much of the world's suffering, and he made the education of women a cardinal teaching. Bahá'ís see the achievement of equality between the sexes and the integration of women into every field of human endeavor—in government, academia, and professional life— as an essential prerequisite to peace and human progress. In fact, Bahá'ís hold that if a family has the means to send only one child to school, the daughter should be given precedence, since the daughter will be the first educator of the future generations. When it comes to sexual morality, the Bahá'í are rather traditional and conservative. Sex is to be only within the confines of a marriage between a man and a woman. Divorce is discouraged, but permitted under certain circumstances.

Bahá'ís are also instructed to obey their government, to avoid alcohol and narcotics except for medicinal purposes, and to use prayer and fasting as a means of elevating the soul. Bahá'í teachings condemn idleness, exalt any work performed in the spirit of service, and prohibit slavery and other forms of oppression. Bahá'í teachings also prohibit certain religious practices, most notably confession of sins, asceticism, and monasticism. Each man and woman is expected to live in a happy and productive family, working for the cause of peace and harmony.

The Bahá'í Faith has no prescribed rituals or clergy. Marriage and funeral services are simple and flexible. Bahá'í communities organize devotional and prayer services, public lectures, study classes, children's classes, youth groups, and discussion groups for inquirers, which are offered by unpaid teachers. Other Bahá'í community meetings include electoral conventions for the election of the National Spiritual Assembly and summer and winter schools and institutes. Permanent Bahá'í schools are located in Maine, California, and Michigan.

The Bahá'í calendar is composed of nineteen months of nineteen days each, with four "intercalary days" from February 26 to March 1. The final month of the year, from March 2 to 20, is a time of spiritual renewal and fasting, when Bahá'ís avoid food and drink between sunrise and sunset. The fast is followed by the Bahá'í New Year on the vernal equinox. The Bahá'í day starts and ends at sunset.

The focal point of Bahá'í community life is the Nineteen-Day Feast, held on the first day of each Bahá'í month, which contains three central elements: spiritual devotion, administrative consultation, and fellowship. Other than these, the details of the Feast embody local cultural norms for food and celebration. The central aspect of the Nineteen-Day Feast is not food, however, but rather spiritual fellowship and communion.

Although forbidden from aggressively seeking converts, Bahá'ís do enthusiastically teach their religion to others as part of the effort to foster an ever-advancing civilization founded on the principle of unity in diversity. Since 1963 there has been marked growth in the number of adherents to the religion around the world. The Bahá'í Faith grew rapidly in the United States during the 1960s and 70s as many youth sought out new avenues of spirituality, and the religion has grown moderately since then.

Although still a small movement in the United States, the Bahá'í Faith claims five million believers in some 230 countries, making it one of the most geographically diverse religions in history. There are approximately 11,740 local assemblies and 182 national assemblies. Within this world fellowship are people of all races, nationalities, and creeds, including former Muslims, Hindus, Christians, and Jews. The writings of the Bahá'í Faith have been translated into more than eight hundred languages.

For more information: International Bahá'í community: www.bahai.org; www.bahai.us

Headquarters: Bahá'í National Center, 1233 Central St., Evanston, IL 60091

Suggestions for further reading:

Bahá'í Prayers, Wilmette, IL: Bahá'í Publishing Trust, 2002

Bahá'u'lláh, *Gleanings from the Writings of Bahá'u'lláh*. Wilmette, IL: Bahá'í Publishing, 2005.

Bowers, Kenneth E., *God Speaks Again*. Bahá'í Publishing, 2004.

Stockman, Robert. *The Bahá'í Faith in America: Origins, 1892-1900*. Willmette, IL: Bahá'í Publishing Trust, 1985.

NATION OF ISLAM

Founded: 1920s
Membership: est. 20,000-40,000 (2000)

The Nation of Islam is an expression of the African pride movement of Marcus Garvey (1887–1940) and others in the first decades of the twentieth century (see AFRICAN ORTHODOX CHURCH). Timothy Drew (1886–1920) became convinced that Islam was the true religion of black people and founded Moorish Science Temple in Newark, New Jersey, and took the name Noble Drew Ali. According to Drew, African Americans were Moors whose forebears had lived in Morocco. Only by leaving the distorted white religion of Christianity could African Americans be free. His followers divided into several groups when he died in 1920.

Wallace D. Fard (1877-1933) led a group in Detroit, Michigan. He called himself the reincarnation of Noble Drew Ali and taught "The Religion of the Black Men of Asia and Africa," based at first on the Bible and the Quran. Fard's ideas eventually became more radical, attacking the Bible as a book of lies and claiming that African Americans were gods while the white race was the serpent devil that would ultimately be destroyed. Fard announced that he was a tool in the hands of Allah, called to tell the truth about the races and prepare for the final judgment. After his mysterious disappearance in 1933, his followers claimed that he had been Allah personified.

Fard was succeeded by Elijah Poole (1897–1975), known as Elijah Muhammad. Elijah Muhammad continued to preach Fard's gospel of black revolution by which African Americans would end white domination. He called for the creation of an independent Black Nation of Islam within the U.S. Building on the desperate conditions of poverty in the inner-city ghettos, the movement spread across the country and became increasingly militant after World War II.

Elijah Muhammad encouraged his members to spread his teachings among the millions of African American males imprisoned in the U.S. Among his prison converts was Malcolm X (1925–1965), one of the towering figures of the Black

Power movement of the 1960s. Malcolm used the symbol X to reject the name acquired during slavery. He urged African Americans to take charge of their own destiny rather than relying on the charity of white liberals. He also rejected the pacifist Christian approach of Martin Luther King, Jr., during the civil rights movement. Rather than calling for integration of African Americans into white society, Malcolm X and the Nation of Islam promoted a separate culture. His preaching helped to build membership in the Nation of Islam, but disagreements developed between Malcolm X and Elijah Muhammad after Malcolm discovered orthodox Islam. Malcolm was murdered in New York City in 1965, but his ideas have remained influential.

After his death in 1975, Elijah Muhammad was succeeded by his son, Warith Deen Mohammed, who reoriented and decentralized the movement. He also moved the organization closer to the normative Islamic tradition. Meanwhile, a splinter group led by Louis Farrakhan, based in Chicago, Illinois, continued to emphasize the more radical aspects of the Nation of Islam, especially black nationalism and the racial theories of Fard. Farrakhan's statements and actions have evoked both admiration and condemnation. Warith Deen Mohammed, meanwhile, joined with other Muslim leaders in 1992 to form the Muslim American Society, which is basically orthodox Sunni Islam* and claims a membership of two hundred thousand.

Although subject to controversy and occasional violence, the Nation of Islam has achieved some definite accomplishments. It established a chain of industries, such as barbershops, supermarkets, bakeries, restaurants, cleaning establishments, and farms, to relieve poverty among African Americans. Black Muslims do not gamble, smoke, drink alcohol, overeat, or buy on credit. They arrange parole for convicts and offer guidance for those released. They claim to give blacks self-respect and a sense of identity, and they have connected with many persons whom the mainstream Christian churches have been unable to reach.

For more information: www.noi.org

Headquarters: 7351 South Stoney Island Ave., Chicago, IL 60649

Suggestions for further reading:

Clegg, Claude Andrew III. *An Original Man: The Life and Times of Elijah Muhammed.* New York: St. Martin's Press, 1997.

Lee, Martha F. *The Nation of Islam: An American Millenerian Movement.* Studies in Religion and Society, Vol. 21. Lewiston, NY: Edwin Mellen Press, 1988.

Lincoln, C. Eric. *The Black Muslims in America.* Boston: The Beacon Press, 1961.

UNIFICATION CHURCH

Founded: 1954
Membership: statistics not available

One of the most controversial churches born in modern times is the Unification Church of the Rev. Sun Myung Moon (1920–). This church originated in Korea and burst upon the American scene in the 1970s. Its teaching is a blend of Eastern traditional philosophy and evangelical Christianity. Members hold that Satan distorted the original harmony of creation, but through the sacrifice of Jesus and revelations given to the Rev. Moon, that harmony is being restored. Central to Moon's teaching is that God is a balance of masculine and feminine traits (basically the yin and yang of Taoism) and that humans can restore this harmony of polarities through spiritual marriage. Humans can also connect with the spiritual world and experience spiritual growth through proper actions, attitudes, and devotions that blend Eastern and Western elements.

Sun Myung Moon was born in 1920 in Korea and studied at a Confucian school. Around 1930, his parents became fervent Presbyterians, and the young Moon became a Sunday school teacher. At Easter 1935, as he was praying in the Korean mountains, Moon had a vision of Jesus who asked him to continue the work Jesus had begun on earth nearly two thousand years before. Sun Myung Moon studied the Bible and many other religious teachings in order to unravel the mysteries of life and human history. Embracing asceticism, he came to an understanding of God's own suffering and longing to be reunited with God's children.

By 1945, Moon had organized the teachings that came to be known as the Divine Principle, and he began his public ministry. On May 1, 1954, in Seoul, Moon founded the Holy Spirit Association for the Unification of World Christianity, popularly called the Unification Church. Despite opposition from other churches and the government, including imprisonment of Moon and other leaders, the church quickly spread throughout South Korea. In 1959, the first missionaries arrived in the U.S.

347

Marriage is central to the teachings of the church, and the wedding of Moon to Hak Ja Han in 1960 was seen by his followers as the marriage of the Lamb foretold in the book of Revelation, marking the beginning of the restoration of human-kind back into God's lineage. Sun Myung Moon and Hak Ja Han established the position of True Parents and are considered the first couple to have the complete blessing of God and to be able to bring forth children with no original sin. The church teaches that all people, whether previously married or single, can receive the blessing of God upon their marriages through the Moons' standing as the True Parents. The number of couples who have received this blessing in large wedding ceremonies was 360,000 by 1995.

In 1971, Moon expanded his ministry by coming to the United States. He con-ducted a "Day of Hope" speaking tour throughout the U.S. in the early 1970s with the purpose of reviving traditional Judeo-Christian values. He was invited to the White House, where he met with President Richard Nixon. On two occasions, Moon addressed members of the U.S. Congress from both the House and the Senate. In 1975, Reverend Moon sent missionaries to 120 countries, making the Unification Church a worldwide faith. Controversy followed Moon and his fol-lowers, however, and in the 1980s he was convicted of tax evasion and imprisoned in the U.S. for thirteen months.

In 1992 Reverend Moon declared that he and his wife are the Messiah and True Parents of all humanity. For adherents, this marks the beginning of the Completed Testament Age. Since then, Mrs. Moon has taken a more active role in the world-wide work of the church. In a speech at a U.S. Congressional reception in 2004, Rev. Moon was officially crowned, and he then declared that he "is none other than humanity's Savior, Messiah, Returning Lord, and True Parent." Rev. Moon's organization owns the *Washington Times* newspaper in the nation's capital.

For more information: www.unification.net, www.ffwpui.org

Suggestions for further reading:

Barker, Eileen. *The Making of a Moonie*. Oxford, UK: Basil Blackwell, 1984.

Bromley, David G., and Anson Shupe. *"Moonies" in America*. Bervely Hills, CA: Sage Publications, 1979.

Chryssides, George D. *The Advent of Sun Myung Moon: The Origins, Beliefs, and Practices of the Unification Church*. New York: Saint Martin's Press, 1991.

INTERDENOMINATIONAL AGENCIES: WORKING TOGETHER IN COMMON CAUSE

Jerod Patterson

In America, religious belief is a matter of individual conscience—a private decision—as typified by the free exercise and establishment clauses of the Constitution. But this does not mean that American religion is a private matter. In fact, religion holds a conspicuous place in American public life. Because of this embrace of religious freedom, American religion exists at the intersection of private decision and public life. On one street, religious freedom enables Americans to make private decisions about their participation (or nonparticipation) in the faith community that best expresses their religious beliefs. This has given rise to the flourishing panoply of denominations that populate American religion. On the other street, religious freedom invites these diverse expressions of faith into American public life, producing a rich tradition of missions, social movements, and political activism. Where they meet, private decision and public life have produced a colorful, vibrant, and sometimes discordant intersection as a diversity of religious groups navigate life together in American society.

Since the nation's founding, this intersection has showcased a lively engagement of religious, social, and political issues by America's many ecclesiastical bodies. In the process, it has also proven an opportunity for different denominations to find common cause with one another. Many religious groups, for example, worked together to support the temperance movement in the late nineteenth and early twentieth century. In fact, almost every major social movement in American history—from abolition to the culture wars—has been accompanied by some form of denominational cooperation in the form of interdenominational agencies.

Interdenominational agencies form when different denominations, or persons of different denominational affiliation, band together in common cause. Because the convergent effect of religious freedom fosters an environment conducive to common causes, American religion has given birth to numerous interdenominational agencies that are important means for cross-denominational cooperation. Some are partnerships between denominations, but more often they are extra-ecclesial organizations initiated by laypersons or clergy. This section of the *Handbook* highlights thirteen groups that represent a broad spectrum of interdenominational agencies in America. Each agency included in this section exemplifies a larger constellation of organizations that share a similar heritage and orientation. Because these groups form and operate amidst the confluence of faith commitment and social engagement, they represent a kind of living religious history. This introduction offers a brief overview of the agencies and their particular context.

The American Bible Society is the most prominent of at least twelve Bible societies that operate in America. Largely begun by Protestants of various denominations in the early 1800s, these societies formed as part of a much larger missionary movement in America and Europe that emphasized the spread of the Christian religion at home and abroad. Later that century, students began to take a large part in the missionary movement, giving rise to interdenominational student missionary groups. InterVarsity Christian Fellowship/USA (founded 1941), whose British forbearer organization was founded in 1877, is a direct descendant of the student movement.

During the first part of the twentieth century, the rise of ecumenism and the social gospel produced a number of interdenominational agencies concerned with progressive social causes and greater Protestant unity. The National Council of Churches (founded 1950, predecessor founded 1908) and Church Women United (founded 1941) exemplify these groups. But at the same time these progressive organizations sought greater Protestant unity, internal wars were raging within historic mainline denominations. The progressive theology and social causes embraced by some roused fear among traditionalists that mainline denominations were abandoning the fundamentals of their faith. The so-called Scopes Monkey Trial (1925) is often regarded as the symbolic defeat of the traditionalists. The famous Tennessee court case involving the teaching of evolution in public schools led to public ridicule of outspoken traditionalists. In its wake, traditionalists largely withdrew from their denominational battles to establish traditional alternatives and even abandoned public life more generally.

By the 1940s a new generation of traditionalists, known as evangelicals, were eager to reenter public life. Many of these traditionalists had left their historic denominations in favor of new, more conservative ones. Still others remained in mainline denominations but identified more with evangelicals than with their denomination. Because evangelicalism is a trans-denominational identity, evangelicals began to form interdenominational agencies to help cultivate their shared identity and reengage public life. The National Association of Evangelicals (founded 1942) is one of many such agencies.

In addition to theological controversy, the dawn of the twentieth century signaled a time of great change in American society. During the late nineteenth and early twentieth centuries, an influx of immigrants from Ireland, Italy, Germany, and Eastern Europe brought large numbers of Catholics and Jews to the United States. For Catholics, the strength of Catholic identity and teachings on church authority have mitigated participation in interdenominational agencies. However, the reforms of the Second Vatican Council (1962-1965) helped to integrate Catholicism into the mainstream of American religion. As a result, Catholic presence in public life increased, as did ecumenical relationships and participation in interdenominational agencies. While official church participation in interdenominational agencies has been infrequent, numerous agencies claim lay Catholics and individual clergy among their members.

American Judaism, with its different expressions, has similarly evolved extraecclesial organizations. But in spite of these different expressions, the strength of Jewish identity has precluded the emergence of a notion of denominationalism as in Protestant Christianity. Judaism is a cultural identity as well as a religious one, and Jewish identity is seldom denominationally qualified. As a minority religion in a predominantly Christian society, Jewish agencies evolved as a way to nurture a sense of shared Jewish identity and community. B'nai B'rith (founded 1843), for instance, began in New York City as a means to serve and advocate for the Jewish community. In addition to senior and community services, the group founded the Anti-Defamation League in 1913 to help combat anti-Semitism and advocate for greater tolerance in American society.

Social and political challenges led to the emergence of numerous agencies in the latter half of the twentieth century. Following the advent of the New Deal, the federal government took a more active role in addressing social problems. In response to attempts by Roman Catholic parochial schools to participate in federally funded social welfare programs, the Americans United for Separation of Church and State (founded 1947) formed in order to oppose government partnership with religious organizations. Today, the organization is a preeminent voice for strict separation of church and state, often finding itself at odds with the government and religious groups alike.

In the aftermath of two world wars, Americans were also becoming acutely aware of the horrors of war and their nation's newfound role as a leader in the community of nations. Protestant missionaries organized World Vision (founded 1950), an international relief and development organization, to serve war torn and impoverished peoples throughout the world. As organizations such as World Vision worked for relief abroad, a tragic history of racial discrimination was erupting into the civil rights movement at home. African American clergy from various Protestant denominations formed the Southern Christian Leadership Conference (SCLC, founded 1957) to work for racial equality in America. Other interdenominational groups, including the National Council of Churches and the

Anti-Defamation League, stood alongside the SCLC in the fight for liberty and justice for Americans of every color and creed.

On the heels of the civil rights movement, religious and political fault lines began to converge as evangelical Protestants and conservative Catholics and Jews grew increasingly wary of progressive social causes such as the legalization of abortion, gay rights, and the Equal Rights Amendment. Beginning in the late 1970s, conservative religious leaders formed various interdenominational agencies that organized the so-called Religious Right into a significant political force. The Family Research Council (founded 1983) is one such agency. Sojourners (founded 1975), an organization of progressive evangelicals, Catholics, and other Protestants, represents a more liberal counterpart to groups of the Religious Right.

In more recent years, interdenominational agencies have continued to emerge, reflecting America's ever-changing religious landscape. While still less than one percent of the nation's population, the Islamic Society of North America (founded 1983) formed to serve America's growing Muslim population. Muslim college students played a major role in the group's formation. While providing a representative Muslim voice, the group affirms the diversity of Muslim schools of theology.

Following the 2000 presidential election, renewed interest in harnessing the power of faith communities as a force for positive social action led to the formation of an office of faith-based initiatives (founded 2001) in the White House. Began by Republican President George W. Bush and continued by his Democratic successor, Barack Obama, the office brings together religious groups and leaders from across American's religious spectrum to help deliver social services in local communities throughout the nation.

The vast number of denominations in America might falsely convey that American religion is beset with division and discord. Certainly American religion is not immune to infighting. But its embrace of religious freedom has enabled a remarkably amicable relationship between many different religious groups. Just as the breadth of this *Handbook* demonstrates the diversity of denominations in America, this section bespeaks their willingness to work together.

In this, interdenominational agencies represent the novelty of religious freedom, as they enable differently minded persons to maintain their personal faith commitments while working together in common cause.

AMERICAN BIBLE SOCIETY

Founded: 1816
Protestant, Catholic, Orthodox

The American Bible Society (ABS) is a para-church organization that translates, publishes, and distributes Bibles in America and internationally, and provides churches and other religious organizations with Bibles and Bible re-sources. Protestants have run the society since its founding in 1816, but the or-ganization is now intentionally ecumenical and provides Bibles and resources to American Catholics and Orthodox. The ABS aims to make the Bible readily accessible, affordable, and understandable in America and throughout the world. To accomplish this, the society translates, publishes, and distributes Bibles and resources independently and through partner agencies. The ABS is also a found-ing member of United Bible Societies, an international network of national Bible societies. Individual donors support the society, which is run by a board of trust-ees and president.

The first modern Bible society in England was founded in 1804 in order to make the Bible more affordable and accessible in parts of England, Wales, and other countries. Shortly thereafter, regional societies with a similar purpose were founded in America. In 1816 many of these regional societies helped to establish the American Bible Society and to print and distribute Bibles in the rapidly growing nation and abroad. Many prominent members of society pro-moted the ABS in its early years, including a former New York Governor and the first Chief Justice of the Supreme Court, John Jay, who served as ABS's second president.

The ABS first began to support Bible translation in 1818, when the society funded a partial translation of the Gospel of John into the language of the Dela-ware Indians. The ABS has translated all or part of the Bible into American lan-guages as diverse as Navajo, Gullah, Braille, and American Sign Language. The society's English translations include the *Today's English Version* (now the *Good News Translation*) and the *Contemporary English Version*. The ABS published the *African American Jubilee Bible*, which emphasizes themes relevant to the Afri-can American experience, and illustrated and children's Bibles. It also revised the *Good News Translation* in 1992 to reflect inclusive (gender neutral) language. The society produced a Catholic Edition of the *Good News Translation* and commem-orative publications to honor Papal visits to America. The ABS also worked with the Greek Orthodox Church and Greek Bible Society to produce a Greek version of *The Children's Bible*.

In addition to Bibles, the ABS also produces audiovisual and online resources. The society distributes its Bibles and resources independently and through part-ner agencies including churches and missionary and relief organizations.

Leadership: R. Lamar Vest (President and CEO)

For more information: www.americanbible.org

Contact: 1865 Broadway, New York, NY 10023. (212) 408-1200.

B'NAI B'RITH INTERNATIONAL

Founded: 1843
Jewish

B'nai B'rith, which means "children of the covenant," is an international Jewish community, service, and advocacy organization. Founded in New York City and now headquartered in Washington, D.C., B'nai B'rith operates chapters in more than fifty countries. In addition to humanitarian and service initiatives, the organization advocates for the Jewish community in domestic and international affairs. The group's advocacy focuses on ensuring the security of Israel, raising awareness of the Holocaust, opposing anti-Semitism, and promoting tolerance in society. B'nai B'rith has officially been recognized as a nongovernmental organization (NGO) by the United Nations since the UN's founding. The group also advocates for senior citizens and is the single largest sponsor of Jewish residence facilities for seniors. The organization carries out its work through five permanent centers. An executive staff headed by an elected president leads the group. The current president, Dennis W. Glick, has been active in B'nai B'rith for more than 40 years.

Founded in 1843 in New York City, B'nai B'rith was envisaged by its founders as a means to ameliorate the welfare of widowed and underprivileged Jews in New York City and the United States. The creation of an insurance policy for the widows and children of its members was the group's first initiative. In line with its focus on the needs of the Jewish community, the organization expanded throughout America and abroad via a system of local chapters. In recent years, this community focus became manifest in an organizational commitment to youth and seniors. The group runs a number of leadership development programs and camps for youth and young adults. In 1971, B'nai B'rith opened its first senior residence. Today the group supports senior residences in twenty-five communities and advocates on political issues pertinent to seniors.

B'nai B'rith is a vocal advocate for Jews in international and domestic affairs. As a UN-recognized nongovernmental organization, B'nai B'rith testifies at the UN on behalf of issues important to the Jewish community. These advocacy efforts are supported by the Center for Human Rights and Public Policy, one of five permanent centers run by B'nai B'rith. The other four centers similarly reflect the organization's commitment to enriching and defending Jewish community. The Center for Senior Services is responsible for the group's senior advocacy and housing services. The Center for Community Action spearheads the group's disaster relief efforts. The Center for Jewish Culture promotes Jewish identity and cultural art. The World Center in Jerusalem fosters relationships between Israeli Jews and Jews around the world, as well as providing aid and relief to Israelis.

Leadership: Dennis W. Glick (President)

354

For more information: www.bnaibrith.org

Contact: 2020 K Street NW, 7th Floor, Washington, DC 20006. (202) 857-6600.

NATIONAL COUNCIL OF CHURCHES IN CHRIST IN THE USA

Founded: 1950 (predecessor founded in 1908)
Mainline Protestant, historically black churches, Orthodox

The National Council of Churches in Christ in the USA, commonly known as the National Council of Churches (NCC), is an association of thirty-five denominations including Protestants, Anglicans, American branches of Eastern Orthodoxy, and historically black denominations. The organization's major foci are facilitating dialogue and cooperation among its member groups, advancing various social and political initiatives, and promoting theological and biblical scholarship, including the translation of the *Revised Standard Version* and *New Revised Standard Version* of the Bible. The NCC maintains five commissions to carry out its mission and offices in New York City and Washington, D.C. The organization is led by an annual General Assembly and a Governing Board composed of elected officers and other representatives from the organization.

The NCC is the successor organization to the Federal Council of Churches, founded in 1908 as an expression of the trans-denominational ecumenical movement of the early twentieth century. The thrust of the ecumenical movement was to stress the commonality of different Christian denominations rather than their differences. Since the mid-1800s, trans-denominational organizations had formed in both Europe and America to promote missionary, social, and political causes. By focusing on causes shared across denominations, the organizations of the ecumenical movement fostered a sense of common cause and shared identity among its members despite their denominational differences. The Federal Council of Churches focused largely on missionary activities and activism in line with the Social Gospel, such as Prohibition.

In 1950, twenty-five Protestant and four Orthodox bodies inaugurated the NCC as a larger and more robust version of its predecessor. Organized like the United Nations, the NCC would focus on missions and social activism by providing a locus of trans-denominational cooperation and offering denominations a means to influence public policy. It would also represent the United States in the World Council of Churches. Often viewed as politically progressive, the NCC was active in the civil rights movement, taking part in the 1963 March on Washington and supporting the 1964 Civil Rights Act and 1965 Voting Rights Act.

The NCC went through a difficult period of budget cuts and restructuring during the 1990s due in large part to the decline in mainline Protestant denominations. Today, the NCC remains a leading progressive religious voice, most known for its social and political advocacy for the environment, social welfare causes, and international justice. Some of this advocacy has created controversy within its member churches. The NCC also promotes interfaith dialogue through the Faith and Order Commission, which includes participants that are not member churches of the NCC, most notably Roman Catholics and evangelicals. One of the most successful endeavors of the NCC is the annual Crop Walk to raise money for hunger relief.

Leadership: Michael Kinnamon (General Secretary)

Information: www.nccusa.org

Contact: 475 Riverside Drive, 8th floor, New York, NY 10115. (202) 555-2350.

INTERVARSITY CHRISTIAN FELLOWSHIP/USA

Founded: 1941
Protestant, especially evangelical

InterVarsity Christian Fellowship/USA (InterVarsity/USA) is a large interdenominational ministry to college students and faculty. The organization engages its members in Bible study, evangelism, missions, and service. With more than a thousand paid staff, InterVarsity/USA maintains a presence on college campuses throughout the United States. It also hosts national conferences, runs four retreat centers, and operates InterVarsity Press, a major religious press. InterVarsity/USA has sister organizations in other countries, including Canada and the United Kingdom, both of which are older than the American organization. Together, these organizations helped to found the International Fellowship of Evangelical Students in 1947, an association of more than one hundred student missions organizations. The organization adheres to an evangelical Protestant doctrinal statement and its membership consists of evangelicals from numerous Protestant denominations.

InterVarsity originated in Cambridge, England, in 1877, during the student missionary movement of the late nineteenth century. During this time, students in Europe and North America became increasingly involved in service, evangelism, and international missions, which gave rise to numerous student oriented missions groups. InterVarsity began as a group of college students who met together for Bible study, prayer, and evangelism. It evolved into a larger organization and facilitated emerging student groups on other campuses in the UK. The group helped to found a sister organization in Canada in 1928, and an American group was founded in 1941. By 1950, InterVarsity/USA operated nearly five hundred chapters. It currently operates 855 chapters on 556 college campuses. The group's college presence includes specific ministries to undergraduates, graduate students, nursing students, fraternities and sororities, ethnic minorities, international students, and faculty members.

InterVarsity/USA's campus ministries consist of Bible study and prayer groups, and engaging students in local and international missions. InterVarsity/USA students participate in weekend and weeklong mission and service projects in several urban areas throughout the United States. Student members also participate in short- and long-term international mission projects. Every three years, InterVarsity/USA hosts a major convention called Urbana that highlights the organization's mission opportunities. Recent Urbana conferences have drawn more than twenty thousand student participants. In addition to its college campus and missions activities, InterVarsity/USA runs a major religious press, InterVarsity Press, which publishes religious books and Bible study resources. InterVarsity/USA operates four major retreat centers in Colorado, Michigan, California, and New Hampshire.

Leadership: Alec Hill (President)

For more information: www.intervarsity.org

Contact Information: P.O. Box 7895, Madison, WI 53707. (608) 274-9001.

CHURCH WOMEN UNITED

Founded: 1941
Protestant, Catholic, Orthodox

Church Women United (CWU) is an interdenominational association of Christian women that promotes progressive social causes through education and social activism. CWU is most known for sponsoring three annual celebrations: May Friendship Day, World Community Day, and Human Rights Celebration. The organization also raises awareness on various social problems through educational resources, publications, and activism. CWU is organized into over 1,200 state and local units and associated denominational women's groups. These subunits each manage the organization's regular activities and celebrations. The national structure is headed by an elected "Common Council" of representatives from each subunit and four national officers including an organization president. Every four years the Common Council meets to approve a budget and set the organization's priorities.

Founded in 1941, the CWU is one of the largest Christian women's groups, with a broadly ecumenical membership. The organization's current president, Margurite Carter, is a member of the non-denominational Dominion Power Christian Church in Los Angeles. The organization has long pursued a global agenda that advocates social and political causes particular to the welfare of women and families. CWU was an early supporter of the United

Nations, circulating petitions to encourage full participation in the UN by the United States. A recognized non-governmental organization (NGO) by the UN, CWU still continues its longstanding involvement with the UN and commitment to international human rights and women's issues.

Every four years, CWU's Common Council sets a "quadrennial priority" that outlines key advocacy priorities. The organization's current priorities include the promotion of diversity, universal healthcare, quality education, living wages, non-violence, responsibility on behalf of the media, and environmentalism. CWU considers these priorities important ways to strengthen the family and better society.

CWU promotes three annual celebrations. May Friendship Day (the first Friday in May) is a celebration of relationships within the local community. World Community Day (the first Friday in November) is a celebration that focuses on global justice and peace. The Human Rights Celebration (on or around December 10) is a celebration of the cause of human rights. Each of these celebrations, along with CWU's quadrennial priority, is promoted through educational materials, resources, and local activities including Bible studies and political activism.

Leadership: Margurite Carter (President)

For more information: www.churchwomen.org

Contact: 475 Riverside Drive, Suite 1626A, New York, NY 10115. (800) 298-5551.

NATIONAL ASSOCIATION OF EVANGELICALS

Founded: 1942
Evangelical Protestant

The National Association of Evangelicals (NAE) is an association of fifty-two evangelical Protestant denominations and more than one hundred other organizations, including para-church ministries and academic institutions. NAE members adhere to a basic statement of faith that contains commonly held evangelical theological commitments. The NAE's mission is to foster cooperation among its member groups in missions, ministry, and political action, and to provide a representative voice for evangelicals in matters of public importance. The association maintains a government affairs office in Washington, D.C., is the largest endorsing body for chaplains in the U.S. armed forces, and provides its member bodies with a variety of services, including human resources consulting and medical insurance for long and short-term missionaries.

The NAE is one of the largest and most prominent representative voices for evangelical Protestantism in the Unites States. Founded in 1942, the NAE represents one of the earliest and most enduring attempts by evangelical Protestants to reengage society following Protestant fundamentalism's retreat from the public square in the early twentieth century. After a number of losing battles over denominational leadership and subsequent denominational splits, by the 1940s evangelical Protestants were searching for a source of religious identity beyond their denominational affiliation. The NAE purposed to fill this void, offering an institutional expression of evangelical identity and a conservative alternative to the more liberal National Council of Churches (NCC) and its predecessor, the Federal Council of Churches.

The NAE has long struggled with its identity. In an attempt to distance itself from its fundamentalist predecessors, the NAE intended to present a positive vision for evangelical Protestantism. But the NAE spent much of its early existence countering the activities of the NCC. In response to the NCC's representation of America in the World Council of Churches, the NAE worked to resurrect the World Evangelical Alliance in 1951. When the NCC released the *Revised Standard Version* of the Bible, the NAE helped to organize a translation more agreeable to conservatives, the International Bible Society's *New International Version*. Not until the rise of the Religious Right in the late 1970s did the NAE develop a vision for the organization distinct from its progressive counterpart.

During the 1980s, NAE membership and influence increased significantly, but the association never fully freed itself from its identity crisis. In the late 1990s and 2000s the NAE attempted to expand evangelical political concerns beyond the Religious Right's traditional focus on abortion and gay rights by emphasizing environmental concerns, social justice, and human rights, which incited a backlash from certain evangelical leaders in the Religious Right. Its new president, Minnesota mega-church pastor Leith Anderson, has helped to refocus the NAE on its founding mission to present a positive vision for evangelical Protestantism.

Leadership: Leith Anderson (President)

For more information: www.nae.org

Contact: P.O. Box 23269, Washington, DC 20026. (210) 789-1011.

AMERICANS UNITED FOR SEPARATION
OF CHURCH AND STATE

Founded: 1947
Membership: Interreligious

Americans United for Separation of Church and State (AU) is an organization that engages in legal and political action to promote a strict separation between American government and religious organizations and activities. AU directs its affairs from a Washington, D.C., headquarters. It actively files and supports legal challenges to state and federal programs that the organization considers to infringe on the Establishment Clause of the First Amendment. The organization also monitors and advocates legislation that affects church-state relations. While it began as a Protestant organization, AU's supporters hail from a variety of denominations and faiths, including atheism. Individual donors support the organization. It is run by a board of trustees and Executive Director Barry Lynn, an ordained minister in the United Church of Christ.

Originally founded as Protestant and Other Americans United for the Separation of Church and State, AU was formed in 1947 as the initiative of Protestant clergy in response to attempts by Roman Catholic parochial schools to participate in federally funded social welfare programs. Differing views on church-state separation and the role of religion in public life have also led the AU to challenge the Roman Catholic Church's tax-exempt status and ask the IRS to investigate its clergy for electioneering. However, AU has consistently denied an anti-Catholic agenda. The organization has also challenged the activities of certain Protestant groups, especially those identified with the Religious Right, and interdenominational agencies involved in government supported social programs such as prison ministries.

Since its original concern with tax aid to religious schools, AU's agenda has evolved along with the American church-state debate. AU now lists eight causes among its primary concerns. In addition to opposing government funds for religious schools, such as school voucher programs, AU actively opposes prayer in public schools and the teaching of creationism and intelligent design. The influence of religious beliefs on government policy also concerns the organization, which opposes traditional marriage standards as religious constructs. AU takes action on these issues through public advocacy and filing or assisting likeminded groups in legal challenges.

AU's concerns extend beyond government action. The organization also opposes political activity on the part of churches and religious organizations as a violation of their non-profit tax status. AU solicits reports of churches and religious organizations that participate in political activity so the organization can file an official complaint with the IRS. The Alliance Defense Fund (www.alliancedefensefund.org) is a frequent opponent of the AU and its belief in strict separation of church and state.

Leadership: Barry Lynn (Executive Director)

For more information: www.au.org

Contact: 518 C Street NE, Washington, DC 20002. (202) 466-3234.

WORLD VISION

Founded: 1951
Protestant, Catholic, Orthodox

World Vision is an international relief and development organization that focuses particularly on meeting the needs of orphaned and underprivileged children.

In recent years, the group has spearheaded relief initiatives for communities affected by the HIV/AIDS epidemic, regions afflicted by civil war and international conflict, and places beset with natural disasters. A recognized nongovernmental agency by the United Nations, World Vision also advocates on behalf of children. The organization's relief and development programs are run through a network of interdependent national offices. World Vision employs more than thirty thousand staff members in almost one hundred countries, with ninety-seven percent of staff living and working in their native cultures. Its annual revenues exceed one billion dollars. In 2008, forty-two percent of the group's revenues were provided by private donations, with in-kind contributions and government grants making up the balance. World Vision is run by an executive staff.

Founded in 1951 by Bob Pierce, an evangelical Protestant missionary, World Vision began as an effort to help children orphaned in the Korean War. The organization launched its first child sponsorship program in 1953 to provide long-term aid to the children affected by the war. While maintaining an attention to the needs of children, during the 1960s the organization broadened its focus to encompass entire impoverished communities. Recognizing the need to help these communities break a cycle of poverty, World Vision began vocational and agricultural training programs alongside its aid and relief efforts.

During the 1980s, World Vision continued its expansion to include full-scale community development. The organization helps to drill wells to provide communities with clean drinking water, as well as assisting with local public health promotion. It also trains local residents in irrigation and farming techniques to help curb the effects of famine. In the 1990s, World Vision introduced a soon-popular "30-Hour Famine" program to raise awareness and funds to combat famine and global poverty. In recent years, the group has taken a more active role in advocating on behalf of children. World Vision urges nations and the UN to fight child exploitation and the sex trade, ban the use of land mines, disallow children from military service, and offer the same educational and advancement opportunities to female and male children alike.

Since its inception, World Vision has administered its programs through local partnerships. Originally using local churches to run the programs, as projects expanded in scope they proved too taxing on local churches to administer. Now, World Vision uses national offices staffed almost entirely by native residents to administer programs. World Vision employs and partners with all types of churches.

Leadership: Executive staff, Richard Stearns (President)

For more information: www.worldvision.org

Contact: 34834 Weyerhaeuser Way So., Federal Way, WA 98001. (253) 815-1000.

SOUTHERN CHRISTIAN LEADERSHIP CONFERENCE

Founded: 1957
Mostly Protestant, especially historically black churches

The Southern Christian Leadership Conference (SCLC) is a national interdenominational, faith-based organization that advances civil rights and community action. One the most prominent organizations to lead the 1960s civil rights movement in the American South, the SCLC has been headed by luminaries such as Martin Luther King, Jr., and Ralph Abernathy. In addition to its historic focus on civil rights, the organization's current activities also include advocacy to end poverty, violence, and classism, and support for economic advancement within historically marginalized communities. The SCLC is organized by local chapters and affiliates, which carry out the organization's activities. The organization is ecumenical but its membership predominantly hails from historically black Protestant churches and denominations. The SCLC is run by a board of directors and currently headed by interim President and CEO Byron Clay.

Black clergymen from the American South, including Martin Luther King, Jr., founded the SCLC in 1957 to better organize the movement to end systematic discrimination against African Americans. King served as the organization's first president until his assassination in 1968, at which time Ralph Abernathy assumed the presidency. With likeminded organizations, such as the Student Nonviolent Coordinating Committee, the SCLC took a leading role in organizing large-scale nonviolent protests, boycotts, and civil disobedience. Among the more prominent of the group's activities were major campaigns in Albany, Georgia, and Birmingham, Alabama, in which King and other protesters were assaulted and arrested by local police. The organization also helped organize the 1963 March on Washington, in which King delivered his famous "I Have a Dream" speech.

After the passage of the Civil Rights Act and Voting Rights Act legislation in 1964 and 1965, the SCLC increasingly turned its attention to ending poverty and violence, and providing educational and economic opportunity for African Americans. The organization's influence was weakened during the 1970s with the departure of prominent leaders and rise to prominence of other civil rights organizations. During the late 1990s and early 2000s, the SCLC grew increasingly inactive and financially troubled. But since the mid 2000s the organization began to regain its activity and financial stability. The SCLC currently advocates for economic and technological development in historically marginalized communities, improving public education and access to college, and empowering underrepresented communities in the political process.

Leadership: Byron Clay (Interim President and CEO)

For more information: www.sclcnational.org

Contact: P.O. Box 89128, Atlanta, GA 30312. (404) 522-1420.

SOJOURNERS

Founded: 1975
Evangelical Protestant, Mainline Protestant, Catholic

Best known for its monthly magazine, blogs, and outspoken leader, Sojourners is an interdenominational Christian organization dedicated to social justice issues and community action. Since its inception, Sojourners has published *Sojourners* magazine, which focuses on Christianity and social engagement. Founded by progressive evangelical Protestants, the organization is predominantly Protestant but intentionally ecumenical. Organized largely around its magazine publication, Sojourners is run by a board of directors and staff. Author and speaker Jim Wallis serves as the organization's president, executive director, and editor-in-chief of its magazine. Sojourners promotes an eclectic political agenda that is generally progressive but also expresses opposition to abortion and qualified support for school vouchers. Beginning in 1995, Sojourners has increasingly sponsored service initiatives designed to foster faith-based community action.

Sojourners was founded in 1975 by a group of progressive evangelical Protestants from suburban Chicago, Illinois. The group began as a small residential community at Trinity Evangelical Divinity School in 1971 before moving to inner city Washington and taking the name Sojourners. With common households and finances, Sojourners members lived and worshipped together, published their magazine, and took part in community service and political activism. The group also founded community ministries, including after-school and summer programs for local children. While the organization later discontinued its residential community, it continued to publish *Sojourners* magazine, serve the community, and advocate on political issues. Sojourners founded Call to Renewal in 1995, which broadened the organization's scope to promote faith-based community service on a large scale. The new organization focused specifically on alleviating poverty. In 2006 the organizations merged as Sojourners/Call to Renewal, and in 2007 the organization's name returned to Sojourners.

Today, Sojourners is primarily known for its magazine publication and political activism. The organization advocates a political agenda that includes a number of issues, including opposition to war and discrimination, and support for social welfare programs and immigrant rights. It readily offers Bible citations and theological explanations for each of its advocacy points. Sojourners frequently sponsors national conferences, workshops, and rallies to promote its political agenda. The group sends political action alerts to its members that encourage them to contact government officials, and publishes Bible study and sermon preparation resources for use in churches. Sojourners is led by Jim Wallis, an outspoken progressive evangelical Protestant and author of several books on Christianity and politics.

Leadership: Jim Wallis (President and Executive Director)
For more information: www.sojo.net
Contact: 3333 14th Street NW, Suite 200, Washington, DC 20010. (202) 328-8842.

FAMILY RESEARCH COUNCIL

Founded: 1983
Evangelical Protestant, Catholic, Orthodox

The Family Research Council (FRC) is a Washington, D.C., based political organization that promotes a conservative Christian political agenda in national politics. Now one of the leading voices of the Religious Right, the FRC pursues its agenda through church outreach, grassroots activism, the national media, and resource publication. The organization is a major proponent of traditional moral standards, an avid opponent of gay marriage and abortion, and frequently speaks out on bioethics issues. A board of directors and executive leadership team run the FRC, headed by its president, Tony Perkins, a former Louisiana state representative and candidate for the U.S. Senate. The FRC consists of offices of administration, development, academic affairs, communication, church outreach, government affairs, and policy. An ecumenical organization, the FRC is supported by individual donors. Evangelical Protestants and Roman Catholics comprise the majority of its membership.

The FRC was founded in 1983 as an initiative of a small group of Christian conservatives including Focus on the Family (Focus) founder Dr. James Dobson and former Reagan administration official Gerald Regier, who served as the organization's first president. The FRC worked closely with Focus until merging with it in 1988. In 1992, FRC reemerged from Focus as an independent organization but continues to share three members of its board of directors with its former parent organization, including Dobson. The FRC's founding purpose was to support public policies that encourage stronger marriages and families by fostering communication between likeminded researchers and policymakers. Under its second president, former Reagan policy advisor Gary Bauer, the FRC distinguished itself from most political groups associated with the Religious Right by focusing on policy research and refraining from political endorsements. In later years, however, the FRC redirected its primary focus from policy research to political activism.

Under its current president, Tony Perkins, the FRC has become increasingly involved in election politics and grassroots organizing. Enlisting local churches to advance the organization's political agenda is a priority for the FRC. The FRC created an office for church ministries, such as a "Pastor's Portal," which offers pastors regular political updates, sermon outlines that reiterate the organization's political agenda, and church bulletin inserts. The FRC also broadcasts a weekly radio program on Christian radio stations, publishes resources for voter registration and mobilization, and runs voter summits and straw polls. The organization is also known for its support of President George W. Bush's judicial nominees. In 2005, the FRC telecasted three church services—known as "Justice Sunday"—in which conservative politicians and church leaders spoke out against judicial activism and encouraged Christians to lobby the Senate to confirm Bush's nominees.

Leadership: Tony Perkins (President)

For more information: www.frc.org

Contact: 801 G Street NW, Washington, DC 20001. (202) 393-2100.

ISLAMIC SOCIETY OF NORTH AMERICA

Founded: 1983
Muslim

The Islamic Society of North America (ISNA) is the largest organization of Muslims in North America. The group represents Muslims of different theological schools and serves as an umbrella organization for other Muslim organizations, including student and professional groups. ISNA is committed to the peaceful and pluralistic participation of Muslims in society and provides important services that assist North American Muslims in their religious devotion. It also provides chaplaincy services, leadership development workshops, youth programs, and serves as a representative Muslim voice in interfaith dialogue. One of the group's most notable activities is its large annual convention, which hosts a number of influential Muslim and non-Muslim speakers. ISNA also publishes *Islamic Horizons*, a bimonthly magazine. A board of directors leads the group. Its current president is Ingrid Mattson, a Muslim convert and university professor.

ISNA's roots date back to the 1950s and 1960s as an increasing number of Muslim students came to the United States for college and graduate school. During this time, these students began to form independent Muslim student associations to help foster Muslim community in America. In 1963, representatives from these groups came together to form the Muslim Students Association (MSA), a national organization for Muslim students. As these students graduated, many chose to stay in the United States rather than returning to their native countries. The increasing number of Muslims in America highlighted the need for an organization similar to the MSA that could serve Muslims in many different walks of life, leading to the founding of ISNA in 1983.

ISNA exists to serve the spiritual, social, and educational needs of North American Muslims. Six priorities guide the organization's activities: leadership development, promoting youth involvement, improving the public image of

Islam, interfaith and coalition building, community development, and developing a solid financial foundation. Based on these priorities, ISNA offers a number of services to its members aimed at better enabling them to live their Muslim faith in a non-Muslim society. The organization runs a matrimonial service that provides opportunities for Muslims seeking a spouse, and an employment service where ISNA and its members can posts jobs online. The group also runs a food certification program that informs Muslims whether a product conforms to the standards of Islamic Law, and a service that helps to explain Muslim funeral rules. ISNA also provides addiction prevention assistance and a domestic violence forum to raise awareness of domestic violence in Muslim communities and work for prevention and solutions. In addition to these services, ISNA provides educational resources and workshops for members, advocates for Muslim interests, and engages in interfaith dialogue.

Leadership: Ingrid Mattson (President)

For more information: www.isna.net

Contact: 6555 South 750 East, P.O. Box 38 Plainfield, IN 46168. (317) 839-8157

WHITE HOUSE OFFICE OF FAITH-BASED AND NEIGHBORHOOD PARTNERSHIPS

Founded: 2001
Interreligious

The White House Office of Faith-based and Community Initiatives was created by President George W. Bush in January 2001, nine days after assuming the office of President. Under President Bush, the office's mission was to assist faith-based organizations in receiving government funds for participation in social service programs. Bush also created faith-based initiative centers in five federal agencies to coordinate with the White House office. In February 2009, President Barack Obama established a similar office in his White House, changing its name to the White House Office of Faith-based and Neighborhood Partnerships. Obama's name change reflects a shift in emphasis from government partnership with faith-based organizations to community-based social services regardless of religious affiliation. The office is currently under the direction of Joshua DuBois, a former associate minister at a Pentecostal church and Director of Religious Affairs for Obama's presidential campaign.

The First Amendment of the U.S. Constitution identifies a principle of separation between the government and religious establishment. However, the "wall of separation" between church and state referred to by President Thomas Jefferson has never precluded religious groups from participating in government-supported social services. Many hospitals, orphanages, colleges, and charities run by religious groups have received government funding throughout the nation's history. The Supreme Court has long affirmed this relationship, noting that religiously affiliated groups serve a secular purpose when they provide social services. As government social service programs expanded in America, especially during the twentieth century, religious groups became an important part of the growing system of public-private partnerships that deliver social services. The White House office builds on this tradition of inclusion of religious groups in public-private social service partnerships.

The White House office's immediate precursor was the "charitable choice" provisions during the Clinton administration, due in large part to the work of Senator John Ashcroft. Charitable choice codified the participation of religious groups in government social service programs in federal law. In the late 1990s, Texas Governor George W. Bush capitalized on charitable choice by actively partnering with faith-based organizations to administer state social services. He touted the success of these faith-based initiatives during his 2000 presidential campaign and pledged to replicate the initiatives if elected president. Shortly after assuming the presidency, Bush followed through on his pledge.

During his 2008 presidential campaign, Barack Obama expressed his desire to maintain a White House office for faith-based initiatives but shifted the focus from faith-based partnerships to community-based social services regardless of religious affiliation. In February 2009, Obama created his own White House office for faith-based initiatives and established a rotating advisory council with twenty-five members that includes religious and secular community service leaders.

Leadership: Joshua DuBois (Director)

For more information: www.whitehouse.gov

Contact: 1600 Pennsylvania Avenue NW, Washington, DC 20500.

APPENDICES

Appendix 1: Relationships of Church Bodies to One Another

The Early Church

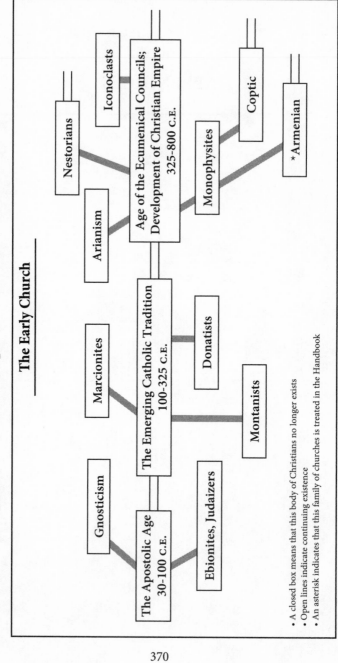

- A closed box means that this body of Christians no longer exists
- Open lines indicate continuing existence
- An asterisk indicates that this family of churches is treated in the Handbook

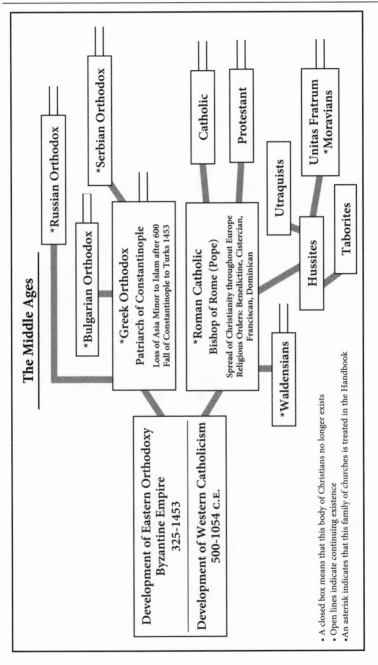

The Middle Ages

Development of Eastern Orthodoxy
Byzantine Empire
325–1453

Development of Western Catholicism
500–1054 C.E.

*Greek Orthodox
Patriarch of Constantinople

Loss of Asia Minor to Islam after 600
Fall of Constantinople to Turks 1453

*Russian Orthodox

*Serbian Orthodox

*Bulgarian Orthodox

*Roman Catholic
Bishop of Rome (Pope)

Spread of Christianity throughout Europe
Religious Orders: Benedictine, Cistercian,
Franciscan, Dominican

*Waldensians

Catholic

Protestant

Utraquists

Hussites

Taborites

Unitas Fratrum
*Moravians

• A closed box means that this body of Christians no longer exists
• Open lines indicate continuing existence
• An asterisk indicates that this family of churches is treated in the Handbook

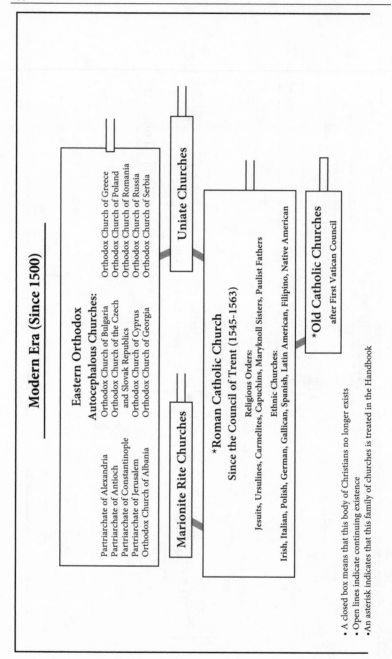

Modern Era (Since 1500)

Eastern Orthodox

Autocephalous Churches:

Orthodox Church of Bulgaria
Orthodox Church of the Czech and Slovak Republics
Orthodox Church of Cyprus
Orthodox Church of Georgia

Orthodox Church of Greece
Orthodox Church of Poland
Orthodox Church of Romania
Orthodox Church of Russia
Orthodox Church of Serbia

Partriarchate of Alexandria
Partriarchate of Antioch
Partriarchate of Constantinople
Partriarchate of Jerusalem
Orthodox Church of Albania

Uniate Churches

Marionite Rite Churches

*Roman Catholic Church
Since the Council of Trent (1545–1563)

Religious Orders:
Jesuits, Ursulines, Carmelites, Capuchins, Maryknoll Sisters, Paulist Fathers

Ethnic Churches:
Irish, Italian, Polish, German, Gallican, Spanish, Latin American, Filipino, Native American

*Old Catholic Churches
after First Vatican Council

• A closed box means that this body of Christians no longer exists
• Open lines indicate continuing existence
• An asterisk indicates that this family of churches is treated in the Handbook

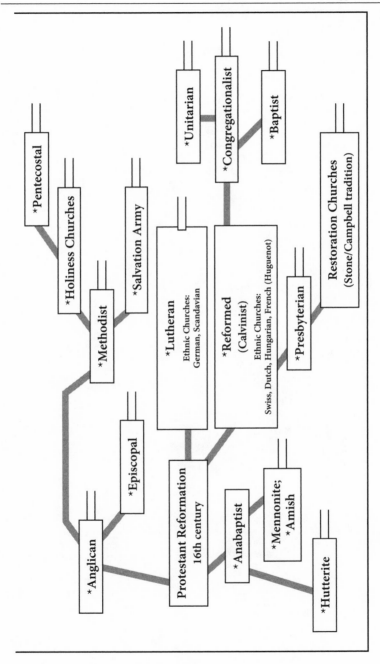

Appendix 2
Members of the National Association of Evangelicals (and date they joined)

Advent Christian General Conference (1986)
Assemblies of God (1943)
Baptist General Conference (1966)
The Brethren Church (1968)
Brethren in Christ Church (1949)
Christian Catholic Church (Evangelical Protestant) (1975)
The Christian and Missionary Alliance (1966)
Christian Church of North America (1953)
Christian Reformed Church in North America (1943-51; 1988)
Christian Union (1954)
Church of God (1944)
Church of God, Mountain Assembly, Inc. (1981)
Church of the Nazarene (1984)
Church of the United Brethren in Christ (1953)
Churches of Christ in Christian Union (1945)
Congregational Holiness Church (1990-92, 1994)
Conservative Baptist Association of America (1990)
Conservative Congregational Christian Conference (1951)
Conservative Lutheran Association (1984)
Elim Fellowship (1947)
Evangelical Church of North America (1969)
Evangelical Congregational Church (1962)
Evangelical Free Church of America (1943)
Evangelical Friends International of North America (1971)
Evangelical Mennonite Church (1944)
Evangelical Methodist Church (1952)
Evangelical Presbyterian Church (1982)
Evangelistic Missionary Fellowship (1982)
Fellowship of Evangelical Bible Churches (1948)
Fire Baptized Holiness Church of God of the Americas (1978)
Free Methodist Church of North America (1944)

General Association of General Baptists (1988)
Grace Communion International (1997)
International Church of the Foursquare Gospel (1952)
International Pentecostal Church of Christ (1946)
International Pentecostal Holiness Church (1943)
Mennonite Brethren Churches, USA (1946)
Midwest Congregational Christian Fellowship (1964)
Missionary Church, Inc. (1944)
Open Bible Standard Churches (1943)
Pentecostal Church of God (1954)
Pentecostal Free Will Baptist Church, Inc. (1988)
Presbyterian Church in America (1986)
Primitive Methodist Church USA (1946)
Reformed Episcopal Church (1990)
Reformed Presbyterian Church of North America (1946)
Regional Synod of Mid-America (Reformed Church in America) (1989)
The Salvation Army (1990)
The Wesleyan Church (1948)

Appendix 3
Member Communions of the National Council of the Churches of Christ in the U.S.A.

African Methodist Episcopal Church
African Methodist Episcopal Zion Church
The Alliance of Baptist Churches in the USA
American Baptist Churches in the USA
The Antiochian Orthodox Christian Archdiocese of North America
Diocese of the Armenian Church of America
Christian Church (Disciples of Christ)
Christian Methodist Episcopal Church
Church of the Brethren
The Coptic Orthodox Church in North America
The Episcopal Church
Evangelical Lutheran Church in America
Friends United Meeting
Greek Orthodox Archdiocese of North and South America
Hungarian Reformed Church in America
International Council of Community Churches
Korean Presbyterian Church in America
Malankara Orthodox Syrian Church
Mar Thoma Church
Moravian Church in America Northern Province and Southern Province
National Baptist Convention of America
National Baptist Convention, U.S.A., Inc.
National Missionary Baptist Convention of America
Orthodox Church in America
Patriarchal Parishes of the Russian Orthodox Church in the USA
Philadelphia Yearly Meeting of the Religious Society of Friends
Polish National Catholic Church of America
Presbyterian Church (U.S.A.)
Progressive National Baptist Convention, Inc.
Reformed Church in America
Serbian Orthodox Church in the U.S.A. and Canada

The Swedenborgian Church
Syrian Orthodox Church of Antioch
Ukrainian Orthodox Church of America
United Church of Christ
The United Methodist Church

Appendix 4
Members of Christian Churches Together
in the USA (formed in 2001)

AMEN (Alianza Nacional de Ministerios Evangelicos)
American Baptist Churches, USA
American Bible Society
Antiochian Orthodox Christian Archdiocese
Archdiocese of the Syrian Orthodox Church of Antioch
Armenian Orthodox Church in America
Bread for the World
Call to Renewal/Sojourners
Christian Church (Disciples of Christ)
Christian Reformed Church in NA
Church of God Ministries (Anderson, IN)
Church of God of Prophecy
Church of the Brethren
Cooperative Baptist Fellowship
Coptic Orthodox Church
Elim Fellowship
Episcopal Church
Evangelical Covenant Church
Evangelical Lutheran Church in America
Evangelicals for Social Action
Free Methodist Church
Friends United Meeting
Greek Orthodox Archdiocese of America
Habitat for Humanity International
International Council of Community Churches
International Pentecostal Holiness Church
Korean Presbyterian Church in America
Mennonite Church USA
Moravian Church
National Association of Congregational Christian Churches
National Baptist Convention of America
National Baptist Convention, USA
Open Bible Churches
Orthodox Church in America
Polish National Catholic Church
Reformed Church in America

Presbyterian Church USA
Salvation Army
The Vineyard USA
United Methodist Church
United Church of Christ
US Conference of Catholic Bishops
World Vision

Appendix 5: Directory of Denominational Headquarters and Web Sites

Acts 29 Network	1411 NW 50th St., Seattle, WA 98107	www.acts29network.org
Advent Christian Church General Conference	P.O. Box 23152, Charlotte, NC 28227	www.adventchristian.org
African Methodist Episcopal Church	1134 11th St. NW, Washington, D.C. 20001	www.ame-church.com
African Methodist Episcopal Zion Church	3225 Sugar Creek Road, Charlotte, NC 2826	www.amez.org
African Orthodox Church	122 West 129th Street, New York City, New York 1002	netministries.org/see/churches.exe/ch26904
Albanian Orthodox Archdiocese in America	523 East Broadway, South Boston, MA 02127	www.orthodoxalbania.org
Alliance of Baptist Churches	1328 16th NW, Washington, D.C. 20036	www.allianceofbaptists.org
American Association of Lutheran Churches	The Evangeli, 801 West 106th Street, Suite 203, Minneapolis, MN 55420-5603.	www.taalc.org
American Baptist Association	4605 N. State Line Ave., Texarkana, TX 75503	www.abaptist.org
American Baptist Churches in the U.S.A.	P.O. Box 851, Valley Forge, PA 19482-0851	www.abc-usa.org
American Bible Society	1865 Broadway, New York, NY 10023.	www.americanbible.org
American Carpatho-Russian Orthodox Church	312 Garfield St., Johnstown, PA 15906	www.acrod.org
American Catholic Church in the United States	5595 Rivendell Place Frederick, MD 21703-8673	www.accus.us
American Evangelical Christian Churches	P.O. Box 47312, Indianapolis, IN 46277	www.aeccministries.com
American Unitarian Conference	6806 Springfield Dr., Mason Neck, VA 22079	www.americanunitarian.org
American Waldensian Society	P.O. Box 398 Valdese, NC 28690	www.waldensian.org
Americans United for Separation of Church and State	518 C Street NE, Washington, DC 20002	www.au.org
Anglican Communion of North America	1001 Merchant St., Ambridge, PA 15003	www.theacna.org
Antiochian Orthodox Christian Archdiocese of North America	P.O. Box 5238, Englewood, NJ 07631-5258	www.antiochian.org
Apostolic Catholic Assyrian Church Of The East, North American Diocese	7201 N. Ashland, Chicago, IL 60626	www.cired.org

Apostolic Catholic Orthodox Church	1900 St. James Place, Suite 880, Houston, TX 77056-4129	www.apostoliccatholic.org
Apostolic Christian Churches of America	3420 North Sheridan Rd., Peoria, IL 61604	www.apostolicchristian.org
Apostolic Episcopal Church	8046 234th St., Queens, NY 11427	http://bertilpersson.com/
Apostolic Faith Mission Church of God	806 Muscogee Rd., Cantonment, FL 32533	
Apostolic Lutheran Church of America	124 Binney Hill Rd., New Ipswich, NH 03071	www.apostoliclutheran.org
Apostolic Overcoming Holy Church of God, Inc.	2257 St. Stephens Road, Mobile, Alabama 36617	www.aohchurch.com
Apostolic World Christian Fellowship	11 West Iowa St., Evansville, IN 47710	www.awcf.org
Armenian Apostolic Church of America	138 E. 39th St., New York, NY 10016-4885	www.armenianprelacy.org
Assemblies of God International	1445 Boonville Ave., Springfield, MO 65802	www.ag.org
Assemblies of the Lord Jesus Christ	875 N. White Station Rd., Memphis, TN 38122	www.aljc.org
Associate Reformed Presbyterian Church	One Cleveland St. Suite 110, Greenville S.C. 29601	www.arpsynod.org
Association of Free Lutheran Congregations	3110 E. Medicine Lake Blvd., Minneapolis, MN 55441	www.aflc.org
Association of Reformed Baptist Churches of America	P.O. Box 289, Carlisle, PA 17013	www.arbca.org
Association of Unity Churches	P.O. Box 610, Lee's Summit, MO 64063	www.unity.org
B'nai B'rith International	2020 K St. NW, 7th Floor, Washington, DC 20006	www.bnaibrith.org
Bahá'í Faith	Bahá'í National Center, 1233 Central Sts., Evanston, IL 60091	www.bahai.us
Baptist Bible Fellowship International	P.O. Box 191, Springfield, MO 65801	www.bbfi.org
Baptist General Convention of Texas	333 N. Washington, Dallas, TX 75246-1798	www.bgct.org
Baptist Missionary Association of America	P.O. Box 30910, Little Rock, AR 72260	www.bmaam.org
Beachy Amish Mennonite Churches	3015 Partridge Rd., P.O. Box 73, Partridge, KS 67566	www.beachyam.org
Berean Fundamental Church	P.O. Box 1264, Kearney, NE 68848	www.bereanchurchfellowship.org
Bible Fellowship Church	3000 Fellowship Dr., Whitehall, PA 18052	www.mybfc.org
Bible Presbyterian Church	P.O. Box 26164, Charlotte, NC 28221-6164	www.bpc.org
Bible Way Church of Our Lord Jesus Christ World Wide, Inc.	4949 Two-Notch Rd., Columbia, SC 29204	www.biblewaychurch.org
Bob Jones University	Greenville, SC 29614	www.bju.edu
Branch Davidians, General Association	The Branch, P.O. Box 1004, Kingsland, Texas 78639	www.the-branch.org/

Brethren Church (Ashland)	524 College Ave., Ashland, OH 44805	www.brethrenchurch.org
Brethren in Christ Church	P.O. Box A, 431 Grantham Rd., Grantham, PA 17207-0901	www.bic-church.org
Bulgarian Eastern Orthodox Church	550-A West 50th St., New York, NY 10019	http://www.bulgariandiocese.org/
Calvary Chapels	3800 S Fairview St. Santa Ana, CA 92704	www.chapelchapel.com
Christadelphians	1000 Mohawk Dr., Elgin, IL 60120-3148	www.christadelphia.org
Christian and Missionary Alliance	P.O. Box 35000, Colorado Springs, CO 80935-3500	www.cmalliance.org
Christian Church (Disciples of Christ)	P.O. Box 1986, Indianapolis, IN 46206	www.disciples.org
Christian Churches and Churches of Christ	P.O. Box 1232 Rapid City, SD 57709-1232	www.christian-church.org
Christian Congregation, Inc.	812 West Hemlock St., LaFollette, TN 37766	
Christian Methodist Episcopal Church	4466 Elvis Presley Blvd, Memphis, TN 38116	www.c-m-e.org
Christian Reformed Church in North America	2850 Kalamazoo Ave. SE, Grand Rapids, MI 49560	www.crcna.org
Church Communities International	Woodcrest, 2032 Rte 213, Rifton, NY 12471	www.Churchcommunities.org
Church of Christ (Holiness) U.S.A.	P.O. Box 3622, Jackson, MS 39207	www.cochusa.com
Church of Christ (Temple Lot)	P.O. Box 472, Independence, MO 64501-0472	www.churchofchrist-tl.org
Church of Christ, Scientist	175 Huntington Ave., Boston, MA 02115	www.tfccs.com
Church of God (Anderson, IN)	P.O. Box 2420, Anderson, IN 46018-2420	www.chog.org
Church of God (Cleveland, TN)	P.O. Box 2430, Cleveland, TN 37320-2430	www.churchofgod.org
Church of God General Conference	P.O. Box 100, Morrow, GA 30260	www.abc-coggc.org
Church of God (Holiness)	7407 - 7415 Metcalf Ave, Overland Park, KS 66204	www.cogh.net
Church of God (Seventh Day)	P.O. Box 33677, Denver, CO 80233	www.cog7.org
Church of God and Saints of Christ	100 South Mulberry Street, Hagerstown, MD 21740	www.cogasoc.net
Church of God in Christ	P.O. Box 320, Memphis, TN 38101	www.cogic.org
Church of God in Christ, Mennonite	Information and Gospel Publishers, CGIC, Mennonite, P.O. Box 230, Moundridge, KS 67107	www.cogicm.org
Church of God of Prophecy	P.O. Box 2910, Cleveland, TN 37320-2910	www.cogop.org
Church of Jesus Christ of Latter-day Saints	Joseph Smith Memorial Building 15 East South Temple St., Salt Lake City, UT 84150	www.lds.org

383

Church of Our Lord Jesus Christ of the Apostolic Faith	444 W. Penn St., Philadelphia, PA 19144	www.apostolic-faith.org
Church of the Brethren	1451 Dundee Ave., Elgin, IL 60120	www.brethren.org
Church of the Living God (Christian Workers for Fellowship)	430 Forest Ave., Cincinnati, OH 45229	
Church of the Lutheran Brethren of America	P.O. Box 655, Fergus Falls, MN 56538	www.clba.org
Church of the Lutheran Confession	501 Grover Rd., Eau Claire, WI 54701	www.clclutheran.org
Church of the Nazarene	17001 Prairie Star Pkwy., Lenexa, KS 66220	www.nazarene.org
Church of the United Brethren in Christ	302 Lake St., Huntington, IN 46750	www.ub.org
Church Women United	475 Riverside Dr., Suite 1626A, New York, NY 10115	www.churchwomen.org
Churches of Christ	P.O. Box 726, Kosciusko, MS 39090	www.church-of-christ.org
Churches of Christ in Christian Union	1426 Lancaster Pike, Box 30, Circleville, OH 43113	http://cccuhq.org
Churches of God, General Conference	700 Melrose Ave.,P.O. Box 926, Findlay, OH 45839	www.cggc.org
Communion of Evangelical Episcopal Churches	124 Broadwell Circle, Franklin, TN 37067	www.theceec.org
Community of Christ	1001 W. Walnut, Independence, MO 64050-3562	http://cofchrist.org
Congregational Holiness Church	3888 Fayetteville Hwy., Griffin, GA 30223	www.ch.church.com
Congregational Methodist Church	P.O. Box 9, Florence, MS 39073	congregationalmethodist.org
Conservative Baptist Association of America	3686 Stagecoach Rd., Suite F, Longmont, CO 80504-56601501	www.cbamerica.org
Conservative Congregational Christian Conference	8941 Highway 5, Lake Elmo, MN 55042	www.ccccusa.org
Conservative Mennonite Conference	9910 Rosedale-Milford Center Rd., Irwin, OH 43029	www.cmcrosedale.org
Converge Worldwide	2002 South Arlington Heights Rd., Arlington Heights, IL 60005	www.convergeww.org
Cooperative Baptist Fellowship	P.O. Box 450329, Atlanta, GA 31145-0329	www.thefellowship.info/
Coptic Orthodox Church	P.O. Box 384, Cedar Grove, NJ 07009	www.coptic.net
Cowboy Church Network of North America	11014 Sam Black Rd. Midland, NC 28107	www.cowboycn.org
Cumberland Presbyterian Church	1978 Union Ave., Memphis, TN 38104	www.cumberland.org
Cumberland Presbyterian Church in America	226 Church St., Huntsville, AL 35801	www.cumberland.org/cpca
Duck River and Kindred Association	P .O. Box 820, Tullahoma, TN 37388	www.duckriverbaptistassociation.org
Ecumenical Catholic Church USA	Vilatte Institute, 1100 Whispering Pines Dr., Dardenne Prairie, MO 63368-6958	www.ecc-usa.org

Ecumenical Catholic Communion	16738 E. Iliff Ave., Aurora, CO 80013	www.ecumenical-catholic-communion.org/
Elim Fellowship	College St., Lima, NY 14485	www.elim.edu
Emergent Village	P.O. Box 390104, Minneapolis MN 55439	www.emergentvillage.org
Episcopal Church	815 Second Ave., New York, NY 10017	www.episcopalchurch.org
Evangelical Anglican Church in America	1805 Las Lomas NE, Albuquerque, NM 87106	www.eaca.org
Evangelical Association of Reformed and Congregational Churches	P.O. Box 307, Lacey Spring, VA 22833	www.evangelicalassociation.org
Evangelical Church of North America	7733 9421 West River Rd., Minneapolis, MN 55444	www.theevangelicalchurch.com
Evangelical Congregational Church	100 West Park Ave., Myerstown, PA 17067	www.eccenter.com
Evangelical Covenant Church	5101 North Francisco Ave., Chicago, IL 60625	www.covchurch.org
Evangelical Free Church of America	901 East 78th St., Minneapolis, MN 55420-1300	www.efca.org
Evangelical Friends International	5350 Broadmoor Circle NW, Canton, OH 44709-1975	www.evangelicalfriends.org
Evangelical Lutheran Church in America	8765 West Higgins Rd., Chicago, IL 60631	www.elca.org
Evangelical Lutheran Synod	6 Browns Court, Mankato, MN 56001	www.evangelicallutheransynod.orgwww.evluthsyn.org
Evangelical Methodist Church	P.O. Box 17070, Indianapolis, IN 46217	www.emchurch.org
Evangelical Presbyterian Church	17197 N. Laurel Park Dr., Suite 567, Livonia, MI 48152-7912	www.epc.org
Family Research Council	801 G St. NW, Washington, DC 20001	www.frc.org
Fellowship of Evangelical Churches	1420 Kerrway Court, Fort Wayne, IN 46805	www.fecministries.org
Fellowship of Grace Brethren Churches	P.O. Box 386, Winona Lake, IN 46590	www.fgbc.org
Fire Baptized Holiness Church of God	901 Bishop William Edward Fuller, Sr. Highway, Greenville, S.C.	www.fbhchurch.org
Free Methodist Church of North America	P.O. Box 535002, Indianapolis, IN 46253	www.freemethodistchurch.org
Friends General Conference	1216 Arch St, #2B, Philadelphia, PA 19107	http://www.fgcquaker.org
Friends United Meeting	101 Quaker Hill Dr., Richmond, IN 47374-1980	www.fum.org
Full Gospel Fellowship of Churches and Ministries, International	4325 W. Ledbetter Dr., Dallas, TX 75233	www.fgfcmi.org

Fundamentalist Church of Jesus Christ of Latter Day Saints	Yearning for Zion Ranch, Eldorado, TX 76936	www.fldstruth.org
General Association of General Baptists	100 Stinson Dr., Poplar Bluff, MO 63901	www.generalbaptist.com
General Association of Regular Baptist Churches	1300 North Meacham Rd., Schaumburg, IL 60173	www.garbc.org
General Church of the New Jerusalem	P.O. Box 74311, Bryn Athyn, PA 19009	www.newchurch.org
Grace Communion International	300 West Green Street, Pasadena, CA 91123	www.graceci.org
Grace Gospel Fellowship	P.O. Box 9432 Grand Rapids, MI 49509	www.ggfusa.org
Great Commission Churches	P.O. Box 29154, Columbus, OH 43229	www.gccweb.org
Greek Orthodox Archdiocese of America	8-10 East 79th St., New York, NY 10021	www.goarch.org
Holy Eastern Orthodox Catholic and Apostolic Church	722 Cedar Point Blvd. #1, Cedar Point, N.C. 28584	www.theocacna.org
Hutterian Brethren	Crystal Spring Colony, Box 10, Ste Agathe, MB R0G 1Y0 Canada	www.hutterites.org
IFCA International	P.O. Box 810, Grandville, MI 49468	www.ifca.org
Independent Assemblies Of God, International	P. O. Box 2130, Laguna Hills, CA 92645-2130	www.iaogi.org
Independent Baptist Fellowship International	724 North Jim Wright Frwy., Ft. Worth, TX 76108	www.ibfi-nbbi.org
International Church of the Foursquare Gospel	P.O. Box 26902, Los Angeles, CA 90026-0176	www.foursquare.org
International Churches of Christ	530 Wilshire Blvd., Ste. 1750, Los Angeles, CA 90010	www.icoc.org
International Communion of the Charismatic Episcopal Church	122 Broadway, Malverne, NY 11565	www.iccec.org
International Council of Community Churches	21116 Washington Pkwy., Frankfort, IL 60423-3112	www.iccusa.com
International Fellowship of Christian Assemblies	1294 Rutledge Road, Transfer, PA 16154-9005	www.ccna.org
International Pentecostal Holiness Church	P.O. Box 12609, Oklahoma City, OK 73157	www.iphc.org
InterVarsity Christian Fellowship/USA	PO Box 7895, Madison, WI 53707	www.intervarsity.org
Islamic Center of Washington	2551 Massachusetts Ave. NW, Washington, D.C. 20008	http://www.theislamiccenter.com
Islamic Society of North America	P.O. Box 38, Plainfield, IN 46168	www.isna.net
Jehovah's Witnesses	25 Columbia Heights, Brooklyn, NY 11201-2483	www.jw.org
Jewish Reconstructionist Federation	101 Greenwood Ave. Suite 430 Jenkintown, PA 19046	www.jrf.org
Korean Methodist Church and Institute	633 W. 115th St. New York, NY 10025	www.rainbowlens.com
Korean Presbyterian Church in America	125 S. Vermont Ave., Los Angeles, CA 90004	www.kapc.org

Lakewood Church	P.O. Box 4600, Houston, TX 77210	www.lakewood.cc.org
Latvian Evangelical Lutheran Church in America	7225 Oak Highlands Dr., Kalamazoo, MI 49009	www.dcdraudze.org
Liberal Catholic Church International	741 Cerro Gordo Ave., San Diego, CA 92102	www.liberalcatholic.org
Liberal Catholic Church, Province of America	1206 Ayers Ave., Ojai, CA 93023	www.thelcc.org
Lubavitch World Headquarters	770 Eastern Pkwy., Brooklyn, NY 11213	www.lubavitch.com
Lutheran Church—Missouri Synod	1333 South Kirkwood Rd., St. Louis, MO 63122-7295	www.lcms.org
Malankara Orthodox Syrian Church	80-34 Commonwealth Blvd., Bellerose, NY 11426	http://malankaraorthodoxchurch.in/
Mar Thoma Orthodox Syrian Church of India	2320 S. Merrick Ave., Merrick, NY 11566	http://marthomachurch.org
Mariavite Old Catholic Church, Province Of North America	2803 10th St, Wyandotte, MI 48192-4907	www.mariavite.org
Mennonite Church USA	421 South Second St., Suite 600, Elkhart, IN 46516	www.mennonites.org
Messianic Jewish Alliance of America	P.O. Box 274, Springfield PA 19064	www.mjaa.org
Missionary Church	P.O. Box 9127, Fort Wayne, IN 46899-9127	www.mcusa.org
Moravian Church (Unitas Fratrum)	P.O. Box 1245, Bethlehem, PA 18016-1245	www.moravian.org
National Association of Congregational Christian Churches	P.O. Box 1620, Oak Creek, WI 53154	www.naccc.org
National Association of Evangelicals	P.O. Box 23269, Washington, DC 20026	www.nae.org
National Association Of Free Will Baptists	P.O. Box 5002, Antioch, TN 37011-5002	www.nafwb.org
National Baptist Convention of America	1320 Pierre Ave., Shreveport, LA 71103	www.nbcamerica.net
National Baptist Convention U.S.A., Inc.	1700 Baptist World Center Dr., Nashville, TN 37207	www.nationalbaptist.com
National Council of Churches in Christ in the USA	475 Riverside Dr., 8th floor, New York, NY 10115	www.nccusa.org
National Missionary Baptist Convention of America	2018 South Marsalis Avenue, Dallas, Texas 75216	www.nmbca.com
Nation of Islam	7351 South Stoney Island Ave., Chicago, IL 60649	www.noi.org
National Primitive Baptist Convention U.S.A.	P. O. Box 7451 Tallahassee, FL 32314	www.natlprimbaptconv.org
National Spiritualist Association of Churches	P.O. Box, 217 Lily Dale, NY 14752	www.nsac.org
Netherlands Reformed Congregations in North America	Netherlands Reformed Book and Publishing, 1233 Leffingwell NE, Grand Rapids, MI 49505	www.nrcrws.org
New Apostolic Church of North America	3753 North Troy St., Chicago, IL 60618	www.nak.org
North American Baptist Conference	1 South 210 Summit Ave, Oakbrook Terrace, IL 60181	www.nabconference.org

Church	Address	Website
Old Catholic Church	409 N. Lexington Pkwy., DeForest, WI 53532	www.oldcatholic.org
Old German Baptist Brethren	6952 N. Montgomery County Line Rd, Englewood, OH 45322-9748	www.cob-net.org
Old Order (Wisler) Mennonite Churches	376 N. Muddy Creek Rd., Denver, PA 17517	www.mhsc.ca
Old Regular Baptist Churches	No headquarters	http://pages.suddenlink.net/orb/orb/index.htm
Open Bible Standard Churches	2020 Bell Ave., Des Moines, IA 50315	www.openbible.org
Original Freewill Baptist Convention	P.O. Box 159, Ayden, NC 28513-0159	www.ofwb.org
Orthodox Church in America	P.O. Box , Syosset, NY 11791-0675	www.oca.org
Orthodox Presbyterian Church	607 North Easton Rd., Bldg. E, Box P, Willow Grove, PA 19090-0920	www.opc.org
Orthodox Union	11 Broadway, New York, NY 10004-1003	www.ou.org
Pentecostal Assemblies of the World, Inc	3939 Meadows Dr., Indianapolis, IN 46205	www.pawinc.org
Pentecostal Church of God	P.O. Box 850, Joplin, MO 64802	www.pcg.org
Pentecostal Free Will Baptist Church, Inc	P.O. Box 1568, Dunn, NC 28355	www.pfwb.org
Philadelphia Church of God	P.O. Box 37000, Edmond, OK 73083	www.pcog.org
Plymouth Brethren	John H. Rush, 2872 Illinois Ave., Dubuque, IA 52001	
Polish National Catholic Church of America	1006 Pittston Ave., Scranton, PA 18505	www.pncc.org
Presbyterian Church (U.S.A.)	100 Witherspoon St., Louisville, KY 40202	www.pcusa.org
Presbyterian Church in America	1700 North Brown Rd., Suite 105 Lawrenceville, GA 30043	www.pcanet.org
Progressive National Baptist Convention, Inc.	601 50th Street, NE, Washington, DC 20019	www.pnbc.org
Protestant Reformed Churches in America	4949 Ivanrest Ave., Grandville, MI 49418	www.prca.org (unofficial)
Reformed Catholic Church	P.O. Box 28710, Columbus OH 43228	www.reformedcatholicchurch.org
Reformed Church in America	475 Riverside Dr., 18th Floor, New York, NY 10115	www.rca.org
Reformed Episcopal Church	826 Second Ave. Blue Bell, PA 19422-1257	www.rechurch.org
Reformed Presbyterian Church of North America	7408 Penn Ave., Pittsburgh, PA 15208	www.reformedpresbyterian.org
Roman Catholic Church Council	3211 Fourth St., Washington, DC 20017	www.vatican.va
Romanian Orthodox Episcopate of America	2535 Grey Tower Rd., Jackson, MI 49201-9120	www.roea.org
Saddleback Church	1 Saddleback Pkwy., Lake Forest, CA 92630	www.saddleback.com

Schwenkfelder Church	105 Seminary St., Pennsburg, PA 18073	www.schwenkfelder.org
Separate Baptists in Christ	787 Kitchen Rd., Mooresville, IN 46158	www.separatebaptist.org
Serbian Orthodox Church in the U.S.A.	2311 M St, NW (Suite 402), Washington, DC 20037	www.serbianorthodoxchurch.org
Seventh Day Baptist General Conference	P.O. Box 1678, Janesville, WI 53547-16788	www.seventhdaybaptist.org
Seventh-day Adventist Church	12501 Old Columbia Pike, Silver Spring, MD 20904-6600	www.adventist.org
Society of St. Pius X	Regina Coeli House, 11485 N. Farley Road, Platte City, MO 64079	www.sspx.org
Sojourners	3333 14th St. NW, Suite 200, Washington, DC 20010	www.sojo.net
Southeast Christian Church	920 Blankenbaker Pkwy., Louisville, KY 40243-1845	www.southeastchristian.org
Southern Baptist Convention	901 Commerce St., Suite 750, Nashville, TN 37203	www.sbc.net
Southern Christian Leadership Conference	P.O. Box 89128, Atlanta, GA 30312	www.sclnational.org
Southern Methodist Church	P.O. Box 39, Orangeburg, SC 29116-0039	www.southernmethodistchurch.org
Southwide Baptist Fellowship	6205 North "W" St., Pensacola, FL 32505	www.wayoflife.org
Sufi Order International	P.O. Box 480, New Lebanon, NY 12125	www.sufiorder.org
Swedenborgian Church	11 Highland Ave., Newtonville, MA 02460	www.swedenborg.org
Syrian (Syriac) Orthodox Church of Antioch (Archdiocese of the Eastern United States)	260 Elm Avenue, Teaneck, NJ 07666	www.syrianorthodoxchurch.org
Potter's House	6777 W. Kiest Blvd, Dallas, Texas 75236	www.thepottershouse.org
Primitive Baptists	No headquarters	www.primitivebaptist.org
Salvation Army	615 Slaters Lane, Alexandria, VA 22313	www.salvationarmy.org
Sovereign Grace Baptists	No headquarters	www.sovgrace.net
Thomas Road Baptist Church	1 Mountainview Rd., Lynchburg, VA 24502	www.trbc.org
Trinity United Church Of Christ	400 West 95th St. Chicago, IL 60628	www.tucc.org
U.S. Mennonite Brethren	315 South Lincoln, P.O. Box 220, Hillsboro, KS - 67063-0220	www.usmb.org
Ukrainian Orthodox Church of the USA	135 Davidson Ave., Somerset, NJ 08873	www.uocofusa.org
Unification Church	4 West 43rd St., New York, NY 10036	www.unification.org
Union for Reform Judaism	633 Third Ave., New York, NY 10017-6778	www.urj.org
Unitarian Universalist Association	25 Beacon St., Boston, MA 02108	www.uua.org

389

United American Free Will Baptist Church	207 West Bella Vista St., Lakeland, FL 33805	www.uafwbc.org
United Church of Christ	700 Prospect Ave., Cleveland, OH 44115	www.ucc.org
United Church of God	P. O. Box 541027, Cincinatti, OH 45245-1027	www.ucg.org
United Holy Church of America, Inc.	312 Umstead St., Durham, NC 27702	http://www.uhcoa.org
United Methodist Church	P.O. Box 320, Nashville, TN 37202-0320	www.umc.org
United Pentecostal Church International	8855 Dunn Road, Hazelwood, MO 63042	www.upci.org
United Synagogue of Conservative Judaism	155 Fifth Ave, New York, NY 10010	www.uscj.org
Universal Fellowship of Metropolitan Community Churches	P.O. Box 1374 Abilene, TX 79604	www.mccchurch.org
Vineyard Churches International	5340 E. LaPalma Ave., Anaheim, CA 92807	www.vineyard.org
Volunteers of America	1660 Duke St., Alexandria, VA 22314-3421	www.voa.org
Wesleyan Church	P.O. Box 50434, Indianapolis, IN 46250	www.wesleyan.org
White House Office of Faith-based and Neighborhood Partnerships	1600 Pennsylvania Ave. NW, Washington, DC 20500	www.whitehouse.gov
Willow Creek Community Church	67 East Algonquin Rd. in South Barrington, IL 60010	www.willowcreek.org
Wisconsin Evangelical Lutheran Synod	2929 N Mayfair Rd. , Milwaukee, WI 53222	www.wels.net
World Baptist Fellowship	P. O. Box 13459, Arlington, TX 76094-0459	www.wbfi.net
World Changers Ministries	P.O. Box 490124, College Park, GA 30349	www.worldchangers.org
World Vision	34834 34834 Weyerhaeuser Way So., Federal Way, WA 98001	www.worldvision.org

INDEX

392

Evangelical Presbyterian Church, 123–
124, 375, 385
Evangelicals for Social Action, 379
Evangelical Synod of North America, 115,
131–132
Evangelical United Brethren (EUB), 149
Evangelical United Brethren Church, 193,
194, 204–205
Evangelistic Missionary Fellowship, 375
Ewing, Finis, 121
exclusive assemblies, Plymouth Brethren
(Christian Brethren) and, 284–285
Ezra, 34

Faith and Order Commission, 356
The Faith Club, 16
Falwell, Jerry, 273, 275, 280, 285–286
Falwell, Jonathan, 286, 292
Family Research Council, 352, 364–365,
385
Fard, Wallace D., 345
Farrakhan, Louis, 346
Federal Council of Churches, 355, 358
Federated churches, 290
Federation of Latvian Evangelical Luther-
an Churches, 108
Fellowship Grace Brethren Churches, 158
Fellowship of Evangelical Bible Churches,
375
Fellowship of Evangelical Churches, 138–
139, 385
Fellowship of Grace Brethren Churches,
152, 385
Fellowship of the Woodlands, 292
Festivals of Religious Freedom, 246
Fillmore, Charles, 329
Fillmore, Myrtle, 329
Finnish Apostolic Lutheran Church in
America, 104
Fire Baptized Holiness Church of God,
263, 266, 375, 385
First Baptist Church (Hammond, Indi-
ana), 292
First Great Awakening, 116, 149, 163, 187
First Vatican Council, 71, 76
Fisher, Mary, 144
Fitzsimmons, Thomas, 76
Fletcher, Francis, 91
Flores, Patricio F., 89
Flurry, George, 243, 246

Focus on the Family (Focus), 364
Foreign Mission Baptist Convention, 179
Foursquare Gospel Church. *See* Inter-
national Church of the Foursquare
Gospel
Fourth Lateran Council, 72
Fox, George, 144
Fox, Kate, 335
Fox, Margeretta, 335
Francescon, Luigi, 256
Francis I (France), 209
Francis of Assisi, Saint, 74, 81
Frederick the Great, 142
Free Baptists, 170
Free Church tradition, 153
Freemasonry, 261, 327
Free Methodist Church of North Ameri-
ca, 220–221, 375, 379, 385
Free Will Baptists, 178, 184, 190–191,
269–270
French Huguenots, 19
Friends (Quaker), 19, 45, 143–147; Con-
gregationalism and, 113; Evangelical
Friends International, 147, 375, 385;
Friends General Conference, 148,
385; Friends United Meeting, 148–
149, 377, 379, 385
Friends General Conference, 148, 385
Friends United Meeting, 148–149, 377,
379, 385
Friends World Committee for Consulta-
tion (F.W.C.C.), 146
Froehlich, S.H., 213–214
Fuller, William Edward, Sr., 263
Full Gospel Fellowship of Churches and
Ministers, International, 263–264,
385
fundamentalism: American Baptist As-
sociation and, 168; Congregational
Methodist Church and, 199; Evangeli-
cal (Independent) Methodist Church,
200; Holiness movement and, 213;
Independent Christian Churches and
Churches of Christ and, 226; Islamic
fundamentalism, 316–317; Jewish
Fundamentalism, 41; millennialism
and, 232; Pentecostalism and, 252;
See also Fundamentalist and Bible
churches

Hermes Trismegistus, 327
Herzl, Theodor, 31, 41
Hicksites, 145
Hindmarsh, Robert, 333
Hines, John, 97
Hitler, Adolf, 31
Hodur, Francis, 84
Hoeksema, Herman, 129
Holdeman, John, 137
Holiness Church, 257
Holiness churches, 212–213, 374; Apostolic Christian Churches of America, 213–214, 382; Apostolic Overcoming Holy Church of God, Inc., 214, 382; Christian and Missionary Alliance, 215, 375, 383; Churches of Christ in Christian Union, 219, 375, 384; Churches of God, General Conference, 220, 384; Church of Christ (Holiness) U.S.A., 215–216, 258, 383; Church of God (Anderson, Indiana), 216–217, 379, 383; Church of God (Holiness), 216–217, 383; Church of the Nazarene, 218–219, 375, 384; Free Methodist Church of North America, 220–221, 375, 379, 385; New Apostolic Church of North America, 221–222, 387; Wesleyan Church, 222–223, 376, 390
Holiness Church of Christ, 218
Holiness Methodist Church, 199
Holiness movement, 194, 199, 274
Holmes, Oliver Wendell, 248
Holy Catholic Church (Anglican Rite), 83
Holy Church of North Carolina, 270
Holy Eastern Orthodox Catholic and Apostolic Church in North America, 61, 386
Holyfield, Evander, 303
Holy Spirit Association for the Unification of World Christianity, 347
Holy Ukrainian Autocephalic Orthodox Church, 95
Hooker, Richard, 91
Hornshuh, Fred, 267
Houteff, Victor T., 234
Humanist Manifesto, 248
Hungarian Church, 79
Hungarian Reformed Church in America, 132, 377

Hus, John, 71, 158
Husain ibn Ali, 313
Hussites, 44, 71, 158, 372
Hutter, Jacob, 139
Hutterian Brethren, 139, 386
Hutterites, 374
Hybels, Bill, 292, 302

IFCA International, 282, 386
Ignatius, Bishop, 61
Ignatius of Antioch, 70
Independent Assemblies of God, International, 264, 386
Independent Baptist Fellowship International, 283, 386
Independent Christian Churches and Churches of Christ, 226–227
Independent Christian Church of Gloucester, 248
Independent Fundamental Churches of America, 282
Independent Fundamentalist Baptist Churches, 283
Independent Pentecostal Churches, 264
Indian Orthodox Churches. *See* Malankara Orthodox Syrian Church; Mar Thoma Orthodox Syrian Church
interdenominational agencies, 349–352; American Bible Society, 350, 352–353, 379, 381; Americans United for Separation of Church and State, 351, 359–360, 381; B'nai B'rith International, 351, 354–355, 382; Church Women United, 350, 357–358, 384; Family Research Council, 352, 364–365, 385; InterVarsity Christian Fellowship/USA, 350, 356–357, 386; Islamic Society of North America (ISNA), 312, 352, 365–366, 386; National Association of Evangelicals, 239, 282, 358–359, 375–376, 387; National Council of Churches of Christ in the USA, 350, 351, 355–356, 377–378, 387; Sojourners, 352, 363–364, 379, 389; Southern Christian Leadership Conference (SCLC), 351, 362, 389; White House Office of Faith-based and Neighborhood Partnerships, 352, 366–367, 390; World Vision, 351, 360–361, 380, 390

United Synagogue of Conservative Judaism, 39–40, 390
Judaizers, 371
Ju-Sam Yang, 200
Kabala, 37
Kahane, Meir, 41
Kahn, Hazrat Inayat, 314
Kahn, Pir Zia Inayat, 315
Kaplan, Clemis Eugene, 67
Kaplan, Mordecai M., 40
Karim, Cyril Aphrem, 67
Kehukee Association, 184
Keller, Helen, 333
Kelly, William, 284
Kennedy, John F., 89
Kerry, John, 89
Khadijah (wife of Mohammad), 306
Kim Young-Sam, 124
King, Martin Luther, Jr., 185, 346, 362
King, Samuel, 121
Kino, Eusebio, 209
Kivuva, John, 295
Knox, John, 112
Kook, Abraham Yitzak, 41
Kook, Zvi Yehuda, 41
Koorie, Hanna, 67
Korean Methodist Church, 200–201, 386
Korean Presbyterian Church in America, 20, 124–125, 377, 379, 386
Koresh, David, 234
Kowalski, Jan, 81
Kozlowska, Maria Felicia, 81
Krimmer Mennonite Brethren, 142
Kwok Pui-lan, 201

Laestadius, Lars Levi, 104
Lakewood Church, 292, 298, 387
Landmark Baptists, 163–164, 177–178, 183, 277
Las Casas, Bartolome de, 208
The Late Great Planet Earth (Lindsey), 274
Latter-Day Saints (Mormons), 19, 26, 319–321; Church of Christ (Temple Lot), 321–322, 383; The Church of Jesus Christ of Latter-Day Saints, 322–324, 383; Community of Christ, 324–325, 357, 384; Fundamentalist Church of Jesus Christ of Latter-Day Saints, 325–326, 386

Latvian Evangelical Lutheran Church in America, 108–109, 387
Laval, Bishop, 75
Law, William, 191
Lawson, Robert C., 260
Lee, F. J., 257
Lefebvre, Marcel, 90
Left Behind series (LaHaye and Jenkins), 275
Lewis, Samuel L., 314
Liberal Catholic Church, Province of the United States, 334–335, 387
Liberal Catholic Church International, 334, 387
Liberal Christian churches, 247
liberation theology, 302
Lieberman, Joseph, 32
Life and Advent Union, 233
Life Church, 292
Lindsay, Gordon, 263
Lindsey, Hal, 274
Living Church (Russian Orthodox), 63–64
Locke, John, 247
Long, Eddie, 292
Lord's New Church, 333
Louis XIV (France), 17
Loyola, Ignatius, 74
Lubavitcher Community (Hasidic Judaism), 37–38, 315
Lubavitch World Headquarters, 387
Lucas, Charles, 229
Luther, Martin, 44; Caspar Schwenckfeld von Ossig and, 161; Catholic churches and, 71; Lutheran churches and, 100, 101; Mennonites and, 133; Roman Catholic Church and, 77
Lutheran churches, 19, 45, 100–104, 374; American Association of Lutheran Churches, 104, 381; Apostolic Lutheran Church of America, 104–105, 382; Association of Free Lutheran Congregations, 105, 382; Church of the Lutheran Brethren of America, 105–106, 384; Church of the Lutheran Confession, 106, 384; Evangelical Lutheran Church in America, 97, 102, 106–108, 131, 377, 379, 385; Evangelical Lutheran Synod, 108, 385; Latvian Evangelical Lutheran Church

405

United American Free Will Baptist Church, 190–191, 390
United Bible Societies, 353
United Brethren Church, 149, 154–155
United Brethren in Christ, 193
United churches, 290
United Church of Christ, 21, 131–133, 378, 390; Christian Churches Together in the USA, 380; Evangelical Association of Reformed and Congregational Churches and, 123; Evangelical Lutheran Church in America and, 108; National Association of Congregational Christian Churches and, 125; Reformed Church in America and, 131; Trinity United Church of Christ and, 300–301
United Church of God, 244, 246–247, 390
United Episcopal Church, 95
United Holy Church of America, Inc., 270, 390
United Methodist Church, 21, 194, 204–206, 378, 390; Christian Churches Together in the USA, 380; Evangelical Church of North America and, 199; Evangelical United Brethren (EUB) and, 149; Korean Methodist Church and, 201
United Missionary Church, 141
United Pentecostal Church International, 271, 390
United Presbyterian Church in the U.S.A., 127, 128
United Presbyterian Church of North America, 128
United Synagogue of Conservative Judaism, 39–40, 390
United Synod of the Presbyterian Church, 116
Unity Churches, 329–330
Universal Episcopal Church, 98
Universal Fellowship of Metropolitan Community Churches, 301–302, 390
Universalist Primitive Baptists (No-Hellers), 185
Universalists, 248–249
See also Unitarians and Universalists
Universal Negro Improvement Association, 51
Urban VIII, Pope, 335

US Conference of Catholic Bishops, 380
Uskokovich, Archmandrite Mardary, 66
U.S. Mennonite Brethren Churches, 142–143, 389
Utraquists, 372

Valdes (Peter Waldo) 117–118
Varick, James, 197
Vilatte, Joseph René, 51, 82
Vineyard Churches International, 272, 295, 390
The Vineyard USA, 380
Vladimir of Kiev, 63
Vladimir the Great, Saint, 68
Volunteers of America, Inc., 206–207, 390

Waggoner, Bert, 272
Wahhab, Muhammad Ibn 'Abd al-, 315
Wahhabism, 315–316
Waldensians, 44, 117–118, 372
Wallis, Jim, 363
Walters, Alexander, 197
Walther, C.F.W., 109
Ware, Henry, 247
Warith Deen Mohammad, 346
Warner, Daniel S., 216
Warren, Rick, 292, 299
Washington, Booker T., 180
Washington, George, 32, 91
Watch Tower Bible and Tract Society of Pennsylvania, 241
Watts, Isaac, 192
Webb, Alexander Russell, 310
Webb, Thomas, 192
Webber, Robert, 99, 295
Wedgewood, J. I., 334
Weir, Moses T., 122
Wellspring Retreat and Resource Center, 282
Wesley, Charles, 191, 192
Wesley, John; Churches of Christ in Christian Union and, 219; Continuing Anglican Churches and, 95; Holiness movement and, 212; Methodism and, 191, 192; Moravian Church (Unitas Fratum) and, 159; Pietist movement and, 149; United Methodist Church and, 204; Wesleyan Church and, 222
Wesleyan Church, 222–223, 376, 390
Wesleyan Methodist Church, 222